Get the eBook FREE!
(PDF, ePub, Kindle, and liveBook all included)

We believe that once you buy a book from us, you should be able to read it in any format we have available. To get electronic versions of this book at no additional cost to you, purchase and then register this book at the Manning website.

Go to https://www.manning.com/freebook and follow the instructions to complete your pBook registration.

That's it!
Thanks from Manning!

Essential TypeScript 5, Third Edition

Essential TypeScript 5

THIRD EDITION

ADAM FREEMAN

MANNING
SHELTER ISLAND

Manning Publications Co.
20 Baldwin Road
PO Box 761
Shelter Island, NY 11964

Development editor:	Ian Hough
Technical editor:	Fabio Ferracchiati
Production Editor:	Aleksandar Dragosavljević
Copy Editor:	Katie Petito
Typesetter:	Bojan Stojanović
Cover Designer:	Marija Tudor

ISBN: 9781633437319
Printed in the United States of America

Dedicated to my lovely wife, Jacqui Griffyth.
(And also to Peanut.)

brief contents

vi

contents

1 Understanding TypeScript   1

preface

This is the 50th book I have written and the third edition of *Essential TypeScript*. TypeScript was new when I wrote the first edition, and my editor was reluctant to commission the book. I am glad I persisted because digging deep into a technology in its early days provides an excellent foundation for seeing it mature. Over the years, Microsoft has shaped TypeScript into a powerful and robust language that has been widely adopted and which makes JavaScript easer to use for countless developers. Originally associated with Angular, TypeScript is now supported by every major development framework and its approach to enhancing JavaScript has become the gold standard.

But TypeScript isn't a conventional stand-alone programming language: it is a set of enhancements that are applied to JavaScript. JavaScript is an elegant and expressive language, but it behaves like few other languages, and its unusual approach to data types causes endless confusion. TypeScript doesn't change the JavaScript type system, it just helps prevent unexpected results, and effective TypeScript development requires a good understanding of JavaScript. This book contains a primer that explains the most confusing JavaScript features so that you have the knowledge you will need to use and appreciate TypeScript.

I hope you find TypeScript as useful as I do, and that this book provides you with everything you need to use TypeScript to create reliable and predictable JavaScript applications. And, of course, I hope to greet you again in the preface of a future edition of *Essential TypeScript*.

about this book

Essential TypeScript 5, Third Edition was written to help you build applications using the latest version of TypeScript. It begins with setting up the development environment and creating a simple TypeScript application, followed by a primer for important JavaScript features, before diving into the detail of how TypeScript build on and transforms JavaScript. The final part of the book demonstrates three web applications created with TypeScript: a stand-alone application, an Angular application, and a React application.

Who should read this book

This book is for experienced developers who are new to TypeScript, or who have embarked on web application development only to find JavaScript confusing and unpredictable.

How this book is organized: a roadmap

The book has three parts. The first part covers setting up the development environment, creating a simple web application, and using the development tools.

The second part of the book focuses on the TypeScript features you will use every day, including basic type annotations, typed functions, arrays, objects and classes. This part of the book also describes the TypeScript support for generic types, which allow type-safe code to be written without needing to know exactly which types will be used at runtime, and decorators, which are a new feature in TypeScript 5.

The third part of this book shows TypeScript in context and creates a web application in three different ways: entirely stand-alone, using the Angular framework, and using the React framework. These chapters demonstrate how the features described in part 2 of this book are used together.

About the code

This book contains many examples of source code both in numbered listings and in line with normal text. In both cases, the source code is formatted in a fixed-width font to separate it from ordinary text. Code is also in bold to highlight statements that have changed from previous listings.

The source code for every chapter in this book is available at https://github .com/manningbooks/essential-typescript-5.

liveBook discussion forum

Purchase of *Essential TypeScript 5, Third Edition* includes free access to liveBook, Manning's online reading platform. Using liveBook's exclusive discussion features, you can attach comments to the book globally or to specific sections or paragraphs. It's a snap to make notes for yourself, ask and answer technical questions, and receive help from the author and other users. To access the forum, go to https://livebook.manning.com/book/essential-typescript-5-third-edition/ discussion.

You can also learn more about Manning's forums and the rules of conduct at https://livebook.manning.com/discussion.

Manning's commitment to our readers is to provide a venue where a meaningful dialogue between individual readers and between readers and the author can take place. It is not a commitment to any specific amount of participation on the part of the author, whose contribution to the forum remains voluntary (and unpaid). We suggest you try asking the author some challenging questions lest his interest stray! The forum and the archives of previous discussions will be accessible from the publisher's website as long as the book is in print.

about the author

ADAM FREEMAN is an experienced IT professional who started his career as a programmer. He has held senior positions in a range of companies, most recently serving as Chief Technology Officer and Chief Operating Officer of a global bank. He has written 50 programming books, focusing mostly on web application development. Now retired, he spends his time writing and trying to make furniture.

ABOUT THE TECHNICAL EDITOR

Fabio Claudio Ferracchiati is a senior consultant and a senior analyst/developer using Microsoft technologies. He works for TIM (www.telecomitalia.it). He is a Microsoft Certified Solution Developer for .NET, a Microsoft Certified Application Developer for .NET, a Microsoft Certified Professional, and a prolific author and technical reviewer. Over the past ten years, he's written articles for Italian and international magazines and coauthored more than ten books on a variety of computer topics.

about the cover illustration

The figure on the cover of *Essential TypeScript 5, Third Edition*, titled "Arabe," or "Arab," is taken from a book by Louis Curmer published in 1841. Each illustration is finely drawn and colored by hand.

In those days, it was easy to identify where people lived and what their trade or station in life was just by their dress. Manning celebrates the inventiveness and initiative of the computer business with book covers based on the rich diversity of regional culture centuries ago, brought back to life by pictures from collections such as this one.

Understanding TypeScript

This chapter covers

- Understanding the TypeScript developer features
- Deciding when to use TypeScript in a project
- Recognizing the limitations of TypeScript
- Understanding the contents of this book
- Reporting errors in this book
- Contacting the author

TypeScript is a superset of the JavaScript language that focuses on producing safe and predictable code that can be executed by any JavaScript runtime. Its headline feature is static typing, which makes working with JavaScript more predictable for programmers familiar with languages such as C# and Java. In this book, I explain what TypeScript does and describe the different features it provides.

1.1 Should you use TypeScript?

TypeScript isn't the solution to every problem, and it is important to know when you should use TypeScript and when it will simply get in the way. In the sections that follow, I describe the high-level features that TypeScript provides and the situations in which they can be helpful.

1

1.1.1   *Understanding the TypeScript developer productivity features*

TypeScript's headline features are focused on developer productivity, especially through the use of static types, which help make the JavaScript type system easier to work with. Other productivity features, such as access control keywords and a concise class constructor syntax, help prevent common coding errors.

The TypeScript productivity features are applied to JavaScript code. The TypeScript package includes a compiler that processes TypeScript files and produces pure JavaScript that can be executed by a JavaScript runtime, such as Node.js or a browser, as shown in figure 1.1.

Figure 1.1   The TypeScript transformation to JavaScript code

The combination of JavaScript and TypeScript features retains much of the flexible and dynamic nature of JavaScript while constraining the use of data types so they are familiar and more predictable for most developers. It also means that projects that use TypeScript can still make use of the wide range of third-party JavaScript packages that are available, including support for using TypeScript in complete frameworks for app development, such as those described in part 3.

TypeScript features can be applied selectively, which means you can use only those features useful for a specific project. If you are new to TypeScript and JavaScript, you are likely to start by using all of the TypeScript features. As you become more experienced and your depth of knowledge increases, you will find yourself using TypeScript with more focus and applying its features just to the parts of your code that are especially complex or that you expect to cause problems.

Some TypeScript features are implemented entirely by the compiler and leave no trace in the JavaScript code that is executed when the application runs. Other features are implemented by building on standard JavaScript and performing additional checks during compilation. This means you often have to understand how a feature works and how it is implemented to get the best results, which can make TypeScript features seem inconsistent and arcane.

More broadly, TypeScript enhances JavaScript, but the result is still JavaScript, and development in a TypeScript project is largely a process of writing JavaScript code. Some developers adopt TypeScript because they want to write web applications without learning how JavaScript works. They see that TypeScript is produced by Microsoft and assume that TypeScript is C# or Java for web development, which is an assumption that leads to confusion and frustration.

Effective TypeScript requires a good knowledge of JavaScript and the reasons it behaves as it does. Chapters 3 and 4 describe the JavaScript features you need to understand to get the best out of TypeScript and provide a solid foundation for understanding why TypeScript is such a powerful tool.

If you are willing to understand the JavaScript type system, then you will find TypeScript a pleasure to use. But if you are not willing to invest the time to become competent in JavaScript, then you should not use TypeScript. Adding TypeScript to a project when you don't have any JavaScript knowledge makes development more difficult because you will have two sets of language features to wrangle, neither of which will behave exactly as you expect.

1.1.2 Understanding the JavaScript version features

JavaScript has had a turbulent history but has recently become the focus of a concerted standardization and modernization effort, introducing new features that make JavaScript easier to use. The problem is that there are still lots of JavaScript runtimes that don't support these modern features, especially older browsers, which constrains JavaScript development to the small set of language features that are universally supported. JavaScript can be a challenging language to master, and this is made worse when the features intended to make development easier cannot be used.

The TypeScript compiler can transform JavaScript code written using modern features into code that conforms to older versions of the JavaScript language. This allows recent JavaScript features to be used with TypeScript during development while allowing older JavaScript runtimes to execute the code that the project produces.

The TypeScript compiler does a good job of dealing with most language features, but some features can't be translated effectively for older runtimes. If the earliest versions of JavaScript are your target, you will find that not all modern JavaScript features can be used during development because the TypeScript compiler doesn't have the means to represent them in legacy JavaScript.

That said, the need to generate legacy JavaScript code isn't important in all projects because the TypeScript compiler is just one part of an extended toolchain. The TypeScript compiler is responsible for applying the TypeScript features, but the result is modern JavaScript code that is further processed by other tools. This approach is commonly used in web application development, and you will see examples in part 3.

1.2 What do you need to know?

If you decide that TypeScript is the right choice for your project, then you should be familiar with the basics of JavaScript development. I provide a primer for the JavaScript features that are useful to understand TypeScript in chapters 3 and 4, but this isn't a complete JavaScript tutorial. In part 3 of this book, I demonstrate how TypeScript can be used with popular web application development frameworks, and knowledge of HTML and CSS is required for these examples.

1.3   How do you set up your development environment?

The development tools needed for TypeScript development are set up in chapter 2, where you will create your first TypeScript application. Some later chapters require additional packages, but full instructions are provided.

1.4   What Is the structure of this book?

This book is split into three parts, each of which covers a set of related topics.

Part 1, "Getting Started with TypeScript": Part 1 of this book provides the information you need to get started with TypeScript development. It includes a quick dive into building a TypeScript application, and a primer chapter on important features provided by JavaScript. Chapters 5 and 6 introduce the TypeScript development tools.

Part 2, "Understanding TypeScript": Part 2 of this book covers the TypeScript features for developer productivity, including static types. TypeScript provides a lot of different type features, which I describe in-depth and demonstrate with examples.

Part 3, "Creating Applications with TypeScript": TypeScript isn't used on its own, so part 3 of this book shows you how to use TypeScript to create web applications using the most popular web application frameworks. These chapters explain the TypeScript features that are useful for each framework and demonstrate how to achieve tasks commonly required during web application development. To provide the foundation for understanding what these frameworks do, I also show you how to create a stand-alone web application that doesn't rely on a web application framework.

1.5   Are there lots of examples?

There are loads of examples. The best way to learn TypeScript is by example, and I have packed as many of them into this book as I can. To maximize the number of examples in this book, I have adopted a simple convention to avoid listing the same code or content repeatedly. When I create a file, I will show its full contents, just as I have in listing 1.1. I include the name of the file and its folder in the listing's header, and I show the changes that I have made in bold.

> **Listing 1.1   Asserting an Unknown Value in the index.ts File in the src Folder**

```
function calculateTax(amount: number, format: boolean): string | number {
    const calcAmount = amount * 1.2;
    return format ? `$${calcAmount.toFixed(2)}` : calcAmount;
}

let taxValue = calculateTax(100, false);

switch (typeof taxValue) {
    case "number":
        console.log(`Number Value: ${taxValue.toFixed(2)}`);
        break;
    case "string":
        console.log(`String Value: ${taxValue.charAt(0)}`);
        break;
    default:
```

```
        let value: never = taxValue;
        console.log(`Unexpected type for value: ${value}`);
}

let newResult: unknown = calculateTax(200, false);
let myNumber: number = newResult as number;
console.log(`Number value: ${myNumber.toFixed(2)}`);
```

This is a listing from chapter 7, which shows the contents of a file called `index.ts` that can be found in the `src` folder. Don't worry about the content of the listing or the purpose of the file; just be aware that this type of listing contains the complete contents of a file and that the changes you need to make to follow the example are shown in bold.

Some code files become long, and the feature I am describing requires only a small change. Rather than list the complete file, I use an ellipsis (three periods in series) to indicate a partial listing, which shows just a portion of the file, as shown in listing 1.2.

Listing 1.2   Configuring Tools in the package.json File in the reactapp Folder

```
...
"scripts": {
  "json": "json-server data.js -p 4600",
  "serve": "react-scripts start",
  "start": "npm-run-all -p serve json",
  "build": "react-scripts build",
  "test": "react-scripts test",
  "eject": "react-scripts eject"
},
...
```

This is a listing from part 3, and it shows a set of changes applied to one part of a larger file. When you see a partial listing, you will know that the rest of the file does not have to change and that only the sections marked in bold are different.

In some cases, changes are required in different parts of a file, which makes it difficult to show as a partial listing. In this situation, I omit part of the file's contents, as shown in listing 1.3.

Listing 1.3   Applying a Decorator in the abstractDataSource.ts File in the src Folder

```
import { Product, Order } from "./entities";
import { minimumValue } from "../decorators";

export type ProductProp = keyof Product;

export abstract class AbstractDataSource {
    private _products: Product[];
    private _categories: Set<string>;
    public order: Order;
    public loading: Promise<void>;

    constructor() {
        this._products = [];
        this._categories = new Set<string>();
        this.order = new Order();
```

```
        this.loading = this.getData();
    }

    @minimumValue("price", 30)
    async getProducts(sortProp: ProductProp = "id",
            category? : string): Promise<Product[]> {
        await this.loading;
        return this.selectProducts(this._products, sortProp, category);
    }

    // ...other methods omitted for brevity...
}
```

In this listing, the changes are still marked in bold, and the parts of the file that are omitted from the listing are not affected by this example.

1.6   Where can you get the example code?

You can download the example projects for all the chapters in this book from https://github.com/manningbooks/essential-typescript-5. The download is available without charge and contains everything that you need to follow the examples without having to type in all of the code.

1.7   What if you have problems following the examples?

The first thing to do is to go back to the start of the chapter and begin over. Most problems are caused by skipping a step or not fully applying the changes shown in a listing. Pay close attention to the emphasis in code listings, which highlights the changes that are required.

Next, check the errata/corrections list, which is included in the book's GitHub repository. Technical books are complex, and mistakes are inevitable, despite my best efforts and those of my editors. Check the errata list for the list of known errors and instructions to resolve them.

If you still have problems, then download the project for the chapter you are reading from the book's GitHub repository, https://github.com/manningbooks/essential-typescript-5, and compare it to your project. I created the code for the GitHub repository by working through each chapter, so you should have the same files with the same contents in your project.

If you still can't get the examples working, then you can contact me at adam@adam-freeman.com for help. Please make it clear in your email which book you are reading, and which chapter/example is causing the problem. A page number or code listing is always helpful. Please remember that I get a lot of emails and that I may not respond immediately.

1.7.1   What if you find an error in the book?

You can report errors to me by email at adam@adam-freeman.com, although I ask that you first check the errata/corrections list for this book, which you can find

in the book's GitHub repository at https://github.com/manningbooks/essential
-typescript-5, in case it has already been reported.

I add errors that are likely to confuse readers, especially problems with example
code, to the errata/corrections file on the GitHub repository, with a grateful acknowl-
edgment to the first reader who reported it. I also publish a list of less serious issues,
which usually means errors in the text surrounding examples, and which are unlikely to
cause confusion.

> **Errata bounty**
>
> Manning has agreed to give a free ebook to readers who are the first to report errors that
> make it onto the GitHub errata list for this book. Readers can select any Manning ebook,
> not just my books.
>
> This is an entirely discretionary and experimental program. Discretionary means that
> only I decide which errors are listed in the errata and which reader is the first to make a
> report. Experimental means Manning may decide not to give away any more books at any
> time for any reason. There are no appeals, and this is not a promise or a contract or any
> kind of formal offer or competition. Or, put another way, this is a nice and informal way
> to say thank you and to encourage readers to report mistakes that I have missed when
> writing this book.

1.8　How do you contact the author?

You can email me at adam@adam-freeman.com. It has been a few years since I started
publishing an email address in my books. I wasn't entirely sure that it was a good idea,
but I am glad that I did it. I have received emails from around the world, from readers
working or studying in every industry, and—for the most part, anyway—the emails are
positive, polite, and a pleasure to receive.

I try to reply promptly, but I get many emails, and sometimes I get a backlog, especially when I have my head down trying to finish writing a book. I always try to help readers who are stuck with an example in the book, although I ask that you follow the steps
described earlier in this chapter before contacting me.

While I welcome reader emails, there are some common questions for which the
answers will always be "no." I am afraid that I won't write the code for your new startup,
help you with your college assignment, get involved in your development team's design
dispute, or teach you how to program.

1.9　What if you really enjoyed this book?

Please email me at adam@adam-freeman.com and let me know. It is always a delight
to hear from a happy reader, and I appreciate the time it takes to send those emails.
Writing these books can be difficult, and those emails provide essential motivation to
persist at an activity that can sometimes feel impossible.

1.10   *What if this book has made you angry?*

You can still email me at adam@adam-freeman.com, and I will still try to help you. Bear in mind that I can help only if you explain what the problem is and what you would like me to do about it. You should understand that sometimes the only outcome is to accept I am not the writer for you and that we will have closure only when you return this book and select another. I'll give careful thought to whatever has upset you, but after 25 years of writing books, I have come to accept that not everyone enjoys reading the books I like to write.

Summary

In this chapter, I explained when TypeScript is a good choice for projects. I also outlined the content and structure of this book, explained where to get the source code, and talked about how to contact me if you have problems with the examples in this book.

- TypeScript is a superset of JavaScript and requires an understanding of JavaScript for effective use.
- TypeScript is not a subset of C#, despite a similar code style.
- TypeScript's main feature is adding static types to JavaScript.
- The TypeScript compiler can target specific JavaScript versions, which allows recent language features to be used in applications that run on older runtimes.

In the next chapter, I give you a primer for the JavaScript type system, which provides the underpinnings for the features of TypeScript.

Part 1

Your first TypeScript application

This chapter covers

- Preparing the tools required for TypeScript development
- Creating and configuring a TypeScript project
- Using the TypeScript compiler to generate pure JavaScript code
- Executing pure JavaScript code using the Node.js runtime
- Preparing a TypeScript project for use with ECMAScript modules
- Installing and using a third-party JavaScript package
- Using type declarations for a third-party JavaScript package

The best way to get started with TypeScript is to dive in. In this chapter, I take you through a simple development process to create an application that keeps track of to-do items. Later chapters show how TypeScript features work in detail, but a simple example will be enough to demonstrate how the basic TypeScript features work. Don't worry if you don't understand everything in this chapter. The idea is just to get an overall sense of how TypeScript works and how it fits into an application.

2.1 Getting ready for this book

Four packages are required to get ready for this book. Perform each installation described in the following sections and run the test provided for each of them to ensure that the packages work as they should.

2.1.1 Step 1: Install Node.js

First, download and install Node.js, also known as Node, from https://nodejs.org/dist/v18.14.0. This URL provides the installers for all supported platforms for the 18.14.0 release, which is the version that I use in this book. During the installation, ensure that Node Package Manager (NPM) is selected for installation. Once the installation is complete, open a new command prompt and run the commands shown in listing 2.1 to check that Node and NPM are working.

Listing 2.1   Checking Node and NPM

```
node --version
npm --version
```

The output from the first command should be `v18.14.0`, indicating that Node is working and the correct version has been installed. The output from the second command should be `8.1.4`, which indicates that NPM is working, but the specific version isn't important.

2.1.2 Step 2: Install Git

The second task is to download and install the Git version management tool from https://git-scm.com/downloads. Git isn't required directly for TypeScript development, but some of the most commonly used packages depend on it. Once you have completed the installation, use a command prompt to run the command shown in listing 2.2 to check that Git is working. You may have to manually configure the executable paths.

Listing 2.2   Checking Git

```
git --version
```

At the time of writing, the latest version of Git for Windows and Linux is 2.39.1.

2.1.3 Step 3: Install TypeScript

The third step is to install the TypeScript package. Use a command prompt to run the command shown in listing 2.3.

Listing 2.3   Installing the TypeScript package

```
npm install --global typescript@5.0.2
```

Once the package has been installed, run the command shown in listing 2.4 to ensure that the compiler was installed correctly.

> **Listing 2.4   Testing the TypeScript compiler**

```
tsc --version
```

The TypeScript compiler is called `tsc`, and the output from the command in listing 2.4 should be `Version 5.0.2`.

2.1.4   *Install a programmer's editor*

The final step is to install a programmer's editor that supports TypeScript. Most popular editors can be used for TypeScript development, but if you don't have a preferred editor, then download and install Visual Studio Code from https://code.visualstudio .com. Visual Studio Code is an open-source, cross-platform code editor that is free to use and is the editor I used while writing the examples for this book.

If you are using Visual Studio Code, run the command `code` to start the editor or use the program icon created during installation, and you will see the welcome screen shown in figure 2.1. (You may need to add Visual Studio Code to your command prompt path before using the `code` command.)

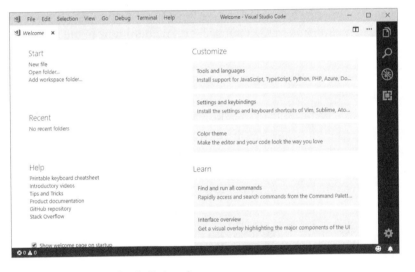

Figure 2.1   The Visual Studio Code welcome screen

> **TIP**   Some editors will let you specify a different version of TypeScript than the one contained in the project, which can cause errors to be displayed in the code editor even when the command-line tools show successful compilation. If you are using Visual Studio Code, for example, you will see the version of Type-Script that is used displayed at the bottom right of the editor window when you edit a TypeScript file. Click the version that is shown, click Select TypeScript Version, and select the version you require.

2.2 Creating the project

Now that the development tools are installed, it is time to start working with Type-Script, which I am going to do by building a simple to-do list application. The most common use for TypeScript is web application development, which I demonstrate for the popular frameworks in part 3 of this book. But for this chapter, I build a command-line application that will keep the focus on TypeScript and avoid the complexity of a web application framework.

The application will display a list of tasks, allow new tasks to be created, and allow existing tasks to be marked as complete. There will also be a filter to include already completed tasks in the list. Once the core features are in place, I will add support for storing data persistently so that changes are not lost when the application is terminated.

2.2.1 Initializing the project

To prepare a project folder for this chapter, open a command prompt, navigate to a convenient location, and create a folder named `todo`. Run the commands shown in listing 2.5 to navigate into the folder and initialize it for development.

> **Listing 2.5   Initializing the project folder**

```
cd todo
npm init --yes
```

The `npm init` command creates a `package.json` file, which is used to keep track of the packages required by the project and also to configure the development tools.

2.2.2 Creating the compiler configuration file

The TypeScript package installed in listing 2.3 includes a compiler, named `tsc`, which compiles TypeScript code to produce pure JavaScript. To define the configuration for the TypeScript compiler, create a file called `tsconfig.json` in the `todo` folder with the content shown in listing 2-6.

> **Listing 2.6   The contents of the tsconfig.json file in the todo folder**

```
{
    "compilerOptions": {
        "target": "ES2022",
        "outDir": "./dist",
        "rootDir": "./src",
        "module": "CommonJS"
    }
}
```

I describe the TypeScript compiler in chapter 5, but these settings tell the compiler that I want to use the latest version of JavaScript, that the project's TypeScript files will be found in the `src` folder, that the output it produces should be placed in the `dist` folder, and that the `CommonJS` setting should be used when loading code from separate files.

2.2.3   *Adding a TypeScript code file*

TypeScript code files have the `ts` file extension. To add the first code file to the project, create the `todo/src` folder and add to it a file called `index.ts` with the code shown in listing 2.7. This file follows the popular convention of calling the main file for an application `index`, followed by the `ts` file extension to indicate the file contains JavaScript code.

> **Listing 2.7   The contents of the index.ts file in the src folder**

```
console.clear();
console.log("Adam's Todo List");
```

The file contains regular JavaScript statements that use the `console` object to clear the command-line window and write out a simple message, which is just enough functionality to make sure that everything is working before starting on the application features.

2.2.4   *Compiling and executing the code*

TypeScript files must be compiled to produce pure JavaScript code that can be executed by browsers or the Node.js runtime installed at the start of this chapter. Use the command line to run the compiler in the `todo` folder using the command in listing 2.8.

> **Listing 2.8   Running the TypeScript compiler**

```
tsc
```

The compiler reads the configuration settings in the `tsconfig.json` file and locates the TypeScript files in the `src` folder. The compiler creates the `dist` folder and uses it to write out the JavaScript code. If you examine the `dist` folder, you will see that it contains an `index.js` file, where the `js` file extension indicates the file contains JavaScript code. If you examine the contents of the `index.js` file, you will see that it contains the following statements:

```
console.clear();
console.log("Adam's Todo List");
```

The TypeScript file and the JavaScript file contain the same statements because I have not yet used any TypeScript features. As the application starts to take shape, the contents of the TypeScript file will start to diverge from the JavaScript files that the compiler produces.

> **CAUTION**   Do not make changes to the files in the `dist` folder because they will be overwritten the next time the compiler runs. In TypeScript development, changes are made to files with the `ts` extension, which are compiled into JavaScript files with the `js` extension.

To execute the compiled code, use the command prompt to run the command shown in listing 2.9 in the `todo` folder.

Listing 2.9 Executing the compiled code

```
node dist/index.js
```

The `node` command starts the Node.js JavaScript runtime, and the argument specifies the file whose contents should be executed. If the development tools have been installed successfully, the command-prompt window should be cleared and display the following output:

```
Adam's Todo List
```

2.2.5 Defining the data model

The example application will manage a list of to-do items. The user will be able to see the list, add new items, mark items as complete, and filter the items. In this section, I start using TypeScript to define the data model that describes the application's data and the operations that can be performed on it. To start, add a file called `todoItem.ts` to the `src` folder with the code shown in listing 2.10.

Listing 2.10 The contents of the todoItem.ts file in the src folder

```
export class TodoItem {
    public id: number;
    public task: string;
    public complete: boolean = false;

    public constructor(id: number, task: string,
            complete: boolean = false) {
        this.id = id;
        this.task = task;
        this.complete = complete;
    }

    public printDetails() : void {
        console.log(`${this.id}\t${this.task} ${this.complete
            ? "\t(complete)": ""}`);
    }
}
```

Classes are templates that describe a data type. I describe classes in more detail in chapter 4, but the code in listing 2.10 will look familiar to any programmer with knowledge of languages such as C# or Java, even if not all of the details are obvious.

The class in listing 2.10 is named `TodoItem`, and it defines `id`, `task`, and `complete` properties and a `printDetails` method that writes a summary of the to-do item to the console. TypeScript is built on JavaScript, and the code in listing 2.10 is a mix of standard JavaScript features with enhancements that are specific to TypeScript. JavaScript supports classes with constructors, properties, and methods, for example, but features such as access control keywords (such as the `public` keyword) are provided by TypeScript. The headline TypeScript feature is static typing, which allows the type of each property and parameter in the `TodoItem` class to be specified, like this:

```
. . .
public id: number;
. . .
```

This is an example of a *type annotation*, and it tells the TypeScript compiler that the id property can only be assigned values of the number type. As I explain in chapter 3, JavaScript has a fluid approach to types, and the biggest benefit that TypeScript provides is making data types more consistent with other programming languages while still allowing access to the normal JavaScript approach when needed.

> **TIP**   Don't worry if you are not familiar with the way that JavaScript handles data types. chapters 3 and 4 provide details about the JavaScript features you need to understand to be effective with TypeScript.

I wrote the class in listing 2.10 to emphasize the similarity between TypeScript and languages such as C# and Java, but this isn't the way that TypeScript classes are usually defined. listing 2.11 revises the TodoItem class to use TypeScript features that allow classes to be defined concisely.

Listing 2.11   Using more concise code in the todoItem.ts file in the src folder

```
export class TodoItem {

    constructor(public id: number,
                public task: string,
                public complete: boolean = false) {
        // no statements required
    }

    printDetails() : void {
        console.log(`${this.id}\t${this.task} ${this.complete
            ? "\t(complete)": ""}`);
    }
}
```

Support for static data types is only part of the broader TypeScript objective of safer and more predictable JavaScript code. The concise syntax used for the constructor in listing 2.11 allows the TodoItem class to receive parameters and use them to create instance properties in a single step, avoiding the error-prone process of defining a property and explicitly assigning it the value received by a parameter.

The change to the printDetails method removes the public access control keyword, which isn't needed because TypeScript assumes that all methods and properties are public unless another access level is used. (The public keyword is still used in the constructor because that's how the TypeScript compiler recognizes that the concise constructor syntax is being used, as explained in chapter 11.)

CREATING THE TODO ITEM COLLECTION CLASS

The next step is to create a class that will collect together the to-do items so they can be managed more easily. Add a file named todoCollection.ts to the src folder with the code shown in listing 2.12.

Listing 2.12   The contents of the todoCollection.ts file in the src folder

```typescript
import { TodoItem } from "./todoItem";

export class TodoCollection {
    private nextId: number = 1;

    constructor(public userName: string,
                public todoItems: TodoItem[] = []) {
        // no statements required
    }

    addTodo(task: string): number {
        while (this.getTodoById(this.nextId)) {
            this.nextId++;
        }
        this.todoItems.push(new TodoItem(this.nextId, task));
        return this.nextId;
    }

    getTodoById(id: number) : TodoItem {
        return this.todoItems.find(item => item.id === id);
    }

    markComplete(id: number, complete: boolean) {
        const todoItem = this.getTodoById(id);
        if (todoItem) {
            todoItem.complete = complete;
        }
    }
}
```

CHECKING THE BASIC DATA MODEL FEATURES

Before going any further, I am going to make sure the initial features of the `Todo-Collection` class work as expected. I explain how to perform unit testing for Type-Script projects in chapter 6, but for this chapter, it will be enough to create some `TodoItem` objects and store them in a `TodoCollection` object. listing 2.13 replaces the code in the `index.ts` file, removing the placeholder statements added at the start of the chapter.

Listing 2.13   Testing the data model in the index.ts file in the src folder

```typescript
import { TodoItem } from "./todoItem";
import { TodoCollection } from "./todoCollection";

let todos = [
    new TodoItem(1, "Buy Flowers"), new TodoItem(2, "Get Shoes"),
    new TodoItem(3, "Collect Tickets"), new TodoItem(4, "Call Joe", true)];

let collection = new TodoCollection("Adam", todos);

console.clear();
console.log(`${collection.userName}'s Todo List`);

let newId = collection.addTodo("Go for run");
```

```
let todoItem = collection.getTodoById(newId);
todoItem.printDetails();
```

All the statements shown in listing 2.13 use pure JavaScript features. The `import` statements are used to declare dependencies on the `TodoItem` and `TodoCollection` classes, and they are part of the JavaScript modules feature, which allows code to be defined in multiple files (described in chapter 4). Defining an array and using the `new` keyword to instantiate classes are also standard features, along with the calls to the `console` object.

> **NOTE**   The code in listing 2.13 uses features that are recent additions to the JavaScript language. As I explain in chapter 5, the TypeScript compiler makes it easy to use modern JavaScript features, such as the `let` keyword, even when they are not supported by the JavaScript runtime that will execute the code, such as older browsers. The JavaScript features that are essential to understand for effective TypeScript development are described in chapters 3 and 4.

The TypeScript compiler tries to help developers without getting in the way. During compilation, the compiler looks at the data types that are used and the type information I applied in the `TodoItem` and `TodoCollection` classes and can infer the data types used in listing 2.13. The result is code that doesn't contain any explicit static type information but that the compiler can check for type safety anyway. To see how this works, listing 2.14 adds a statement to the `index.ts` file.

Listing 2.14   Adding a statement in the index.ts file in the src folder

```
import { TodoItem } from "./todoItem";
import { TodoCollection } from "./todoCollection";

let todos = [
    new TodoItem(1, "Buy Flowers"), new TodoItem(2, "Get Shoes"),
    new TodoItem(3, "Collect Tickets"), new TodoItem(4, "Call Joe", true)];

let collection = new TodoCollection("Adam", todos);

console.clear();
console.log(`${collection.userName}'s Todo List`);

let newId = collection.addTodo("Go for run");
let todoItem = collection.getTodoById(newId);
todoItem.printDetails();
collection.addTodo(todoItem);
```

The new statement calls the `TodoCollection.addTodo` method using a `TodoItem` object as the argument. The compiler looks at the definition of the `addTodo` method in the `todoItem.ts` file and can see that the method expects to receive a different type of data.

```
...
addTodo(task: string): number {
    while (this.getTodoById(this.nextId)) {
        this.nextId++;
    }
    this.todoItems.push(new TodoItem(this.nextId, task));
```

```
        return this.nextId;
}
...
```

The type information for the `addTodo` method tells the TypeScript compiler that the `task` parameter must be a `string` and that the result will be a `number`. (The `string` and `number` types are built-in JavaScript features and are described in chapter 3.) Run the command shown in listing 2.15 in the `todo` folder to compile the code.

Listing 2.15   Running the compiler

```
tsc
```

The TypeScript compiler processes the code in the project, detects that the parameter value used to call the `addTodo` method isn't the correct data type, and produces the following error:

```
src/index.ts:16:20 - error TS2345: Argument of type 'TodoItem' is not
    assignable to parameter of type 'string'.
16 collection.addTodo(todoItem);
                      ~~~~~~~~~
Found 1 error in src/index.ts:16
```

TypeScript does a good job of figuring out what is going on and identifying problems, allowing you to add as much or as little type information as you like in a project. In this book, I tend to add type information to make the listings easier to follow, since many of the examples in this book are related to how the TypeScript compiler handles data types. Listing 2.16 adds types to the code in the `index.ts` file and disables the statement that causes the compiler error.

Listing 2.16   Adding type information in the index.ts file in the src folder

```
import { TodoItem } from "./todoItem";
import { TodoCollection } from "./todoCollection";

let todos: TodoItem[] = [
    new TodoItem(1, "Buy Flowers"), new TodoItem(2, "Get Shoes"),
    new TodoItem(3, "Collect Tickets"), new TodoItem(4, "Call Joe", true)];

let collection: TodoCollection = new TodoCollection("Adam", todos);

console.clear();
console.log(`${collection.userName}'s Todo List`);

let newId: number = collection.addTodo("Go for run");
let todoItem: TodoItem = collection.getTodoById(newId);
todoItem.printDetails();
//collection.addTodo(todoItem);
```

The type information added to the statements in listing 2.16 doesn't change the way the code works, but it does make the data types being used explicit, which can make the purpose of the code easier to understand and doesn't require the compiler to infer the data types being used. Run the commands shown in listing 2.17 in the `todo` folder to compile and execute the code.

Listing 2.17   Compiling and executing

```
tsc
node dist/index.js
```

When the code is executed, the following output will be produced:

```
Adam's Todo List
5        Go for run
```

2.2.6   Adding features to the collection class

The next step is to add new capabilities to the `TodoCollection` class. First, I am going to change the way that `TodoItem` objects are stored so that a JavaScript `Map` is used, as shown in listing 2.18.

Listing 2.18   Using a map in the todoCollection.ts file in the src folder

```typescript
import { TodoItem } from "./todoItem";

export class TodoCollection {
    private nextId: number = 1;
    private itemMap = new Map<number, TodoItem>();

    constructor(public userName: string, todoItems: TodoItem[] = []) {
        todoItems.forEach(item => this.itemMap.set(item.id, item));
    }

    addTodo(task: string): number {
        while (this.getTodoById(this.nextId)) {
            this.nextId++;
        }
        this.itemMap.set(this.nextId, new TodoItem(this.nextId, task));
        return this.nextId;
    }

    getTodoById(id: number) : TodoItem {
        return this.itemMap.get(id);
    }

    markComplete(id: number, complete: boolean) {
        const todoItem = this.getTodoById(id);
        if (todoItem) {
            todoItem.complete = complete;
        }
    }
}
```

TypeScript supports generic types, which are placeholders for types that are resolved when an object is created. The JavaScript `Map`, for example, is a general-purpose collection that stores key/value pairs. Because JavaScript has such a dynamic type system, a `Map` can be used to store any mix of data types using any mix of keys. To restrict the types that can be used with the `Map` in listing 2.18, I provided generic type arguments that tell the TypeScript compiler which types are allowed for the keys and values.

```
...
private itemMap = new Map<number, TodoItem>();
...
```

The generic type arguments are enclosed in angle brackets (the < and > characters), and the Map in listing 2.18 is given generic type arguments that tell the compiler that the Map will store TodoItem objects using number values as keys. The compiler will produce an error if a statement attempts to store a different data type in the Map or use a key that isn't a number value. Generic types are an important TypeScript feature and are described in detail in chapter 12.

PROVIDING ACCESS TO TO-DO ITEMS

The TodoCollection class defines a getTodoById method, but the application will need to display a list of items, optionally filtered to exclude completed tasks. Listing 2.19 adds a method that provides access to the TodoItem objects that the TodoCollection is managing.

Listing 2.19 Providing access to items in the todoCollection.ts file in the src folder

```
import { TodoItem } from "./todoItem";

export class TodoCollection {
    private nextId: number = 1;
    private itemMap = new Map<number, TodoItem>();

    constructor(public userName: string, todoItems: TodoItem[] = []) {
        todoItems.forEach(item => this.itemMap.set(item.id, item));
    }

    addTodo(task: string): number {
        while (this.getTodoById(this.nextId)) {
            this.nextId++;
        }
        this.itemMap.set(this.nextId, new TodoItem(this.nextId, task));
        return this.nextId;
    }

    getTodoById(id: number) : TodoItem {
        return this.itemMap.get(id);
    }

    getTodoItems(includeComplete: boolean): TodoItem[] {
        return [...this.itemMap.values()]
            .filter(item => includeComplete || !item.complete);
    }

    markComplete(id: number, complete: boolean) {
        const todoItem = this.getTodoById(id);
        if (todoItem) {
            todoItem.complete = complete;
        }
    }
}
```

The getTodoItems method gets the objects from the Map using its values method and uses them to create an array using the JavaScript spread operator, which is three periods. The objects are processed using the filter method to select the objects that are required, using the includeComplete parameter to decide which objects are needed.

The TypeScript compiler uses the information it has been given to follow the types through each step. The generic type arguments used to create the Map tell the compiler that it contains TodoItem objects, so the compiler knows that the values method will return TodoItem objects and that this will also be the type of the objects in the array. Following this through, the compiler knows that the function passed to the filter method will be processing TodoItem objects and knows that each object will define a complete property. If I try to read a property or method not defined by the TodoItem class, the TypeScript compiler will report an error. Similarly, the compiler will report an error if the result of the return statement doesn't match the result type declared by the method.

In listing 2.20, I have updated the code in the index.ts file to use the new Todo-Collection class feature and display a simple list of to-do items to the user.

Listing 2.20   Getting the collection items in the index.ts file in the src folder

```
import { TodoItem } from "./todoItem";
import { TodoCollection } from "./todoCollection";

let todos: TodoItem[] = [
    new TodoItem(1, "Buy Flowers"), new TodoItem(2, "Get Shoes"),
    new TodoItem(3, "Collect Tickets"), new TodoItem(4, "Call Joe", true)];

let collection: TodoCollection = new TodoCollection("Adam", todos);

console.clear();
console.log(`${collection.userName}'s Todo List`);

//let newId: number = collection.addTodo("Go for run");
//let todoItem: TodoItem = collection.getTodoById(newId);
//todoItem.printDetails();
//collection.addTodo(todoItem);
collection.getTodoItems(true).forEach(item => item.printDetails());
```

The new statement calls the getTodoItems method defined in listing 2.19 and uses the standard JavaScript forEach method to write a description of each TodoItem object using the console object.

Run the commands shown in listing 2.21 in the todo folder to compile and execute the code.

Listing 2.21   Compiling and executing

```
tsc
node dist/index.js
```

When the code is executed, the following output will be produced:

```
Adam's Todo List
1        Buy Flowers
2        Get Shoes
3        Collect Tickets
4        Call Joe            (complete)
```

REMOVING COMPLETED TASKS

As tasks are added and then marked complete, the number of items in the collection will grow and eventually become difficult for the user to manage. Listing 2.22 adds a method that removes the completed items from the collection.

Listing 2.22 Removing completed items from the todoCollection.ts file in the src folder

```typescript
import { TodoItem } from "./todoItem";

export class TodoCollection {
    private nextId: number = 1;
    private itemMap = new Map<number, TodoItem>();

    constructor(public userName: string, todoItems: TodoItem[] = []) {
        todoItems.forEach(item => this.itemMap.set(item.id, item));
    }

    addTodo(task: string): number {
        while (this.getTodoById(this.nextId)) {
            this.nextId++;
        }
        this.itemMap.set(this.nextId, new TodoItem(this.nextId, task));
        return this.nextId;
    }

    getTodoById(id: number) : TodoItem {
        return this.itemMap.get(id);
    }

    getTodoItems(includeComplete: boolean): TodoItem[] {
        return [...this.itemMap.values()]
            .filter(item => includeComplete || !item.complete);
    }

    markComplete(id: number, complete: boolean) {
        const todoItem = this.getTodoById(id);
        if (todoItem) {
            todoItem.complete = complete;
        }
    }

    removeComplete() {
        this.itemMap.forEach(item => {
            if (item.complete) {
                this.itemMap.delete(item.id);
            }
        })
    }
}
```

The `removeComplete` method uses the `Map.forEach` method to inspect each `TodoItem` stored in the `Map` and calls the `delete` method for those whose `complete` property is `true`. Listing 2.23 updates the code in the `index.ts` file to invoke the new method.

Listing 2.23 Testing item removal in the index.ts file in the src folder

```
import { TodoItem } from "./todoItem";
import { TodoCollection } from "./todoCollection";

let todos: TodoItem[] = [
    new TodoItem(1, "Buy Flowers"), new TodoItem(2, "Get Shoes"),
    new TodoItem(3, "Collect Tickets"), new TodoItem(4, "Call Joe", true)];

let collection: TodoCollection = new TodoCollection("Adam", todos);

console.clear();
console.log(`${collection.userName}'s Todo List`);

//let newId: number = collection.addTodo("Go for run");
//let todoItem: TodoItem = collection.getTodoById(newId);
//todoItem.printDetails();
//collection.addTodo(todoItem);
collection.removeComplete();
collection.getTodoItems(true).forEach(item => item.printDetails());
```

Run the commands shown in listing 2.24 in the `todo` folder to compile and execute the code.

Listing 2.24 Compiling and executing

```
tsc
node dist/index.js
```

When the code is executed, the following output will be produced, showing that the completed task has been removed from the collection:

```
Adam's Todo List
1       Buy Flowers
2       Get Shoes
3       Collect Tickets
```

PROVIDING ITEM COUNTS

The final feature I need for the `TodoCollection` class is to provide counts of the total number of `TodoItem` objects, the number that are complete, and the number still outstanding.

I have focused on classes in earlier listings because this is the way that most programmers are used to creating data types. JavaScript objects can also be defined using literal syntax, for which TypeScript can check and enforce static types in the same way as for objects created from classes. When dealing with object literals, the TypeScript compiler focuses on the combination of property names and the types of their values, which is known as an object's *shape*. A specific combination of names and types is known as a *shape type*. Listing 2.25 adds a method to the `TodoCollection` class that returns an object that describes the items in the collection.

```
import { TodoItem } from "./todoItem";

type ItemCounts = {
    total: number,
    incomplete: number
}

export class TodoCollection {
    private nextId: number = 1;
    private itemMap = new Map<number, TodoItem>();

    constructor(public userName: string, todoItems: TodoItem[] = []) {
        todoItems.forEach(item => this.itemMap.set(item.id, item));
    }

    addTodo(task: string): number {
        while (this.getTodoById(this.nextId)) {
            this.nextId++;
        }
        this.itemMap.set(this.nextId, new TodoItem(this.nextId, task));
        return this.nextId;
    }

    getTodoById(id: number) : TodoItem {
        return this.itemMap.get(id);
    }

    getTodoItems(includeComplete: boolean): TodoItem[] {
        return [...this.itemMap.values()]
            .filter(item => includeComplete || !item.complete);
    }

    markComplete(id: number, complete: boolean) {
        const todoItem = this.getTodoById(id);
        if (todoItem) {
            todoItem.complete = complete;
        }
    }

    removeComplete() {
        this.itemMap.forEach(item => {
            if (item.complete) {
                this.itemMap.delete(item.id);
            }
        })
    }

    getItemCounts(): ItemCounts {
        return {
```

```
            total: this.itemMap.size,
            incomplete: this.getTodoItems(false).length
        };
    }
}
```

The `type` keyword is used to create a *type alias*, which is a convenient way to assign a name to a shape type. The type alias in listing 2.25 describes objects that have two number properties, named `total` and `incomplete`. The type alias is used as the result of the `getItemCounts` method, which uses the JavaScript object literal syntax to create an object whose shape matches the type alias. Listing 2.26 updates the `index.ts` file so that the number of incomplete items is displayed to the user.

Listing 2.26   Displaying item counts in the index.ts file in the src folder

```
import { TodoItem } from "./todoItem";
import { TodoCollection } from "./todoCollection";

let todos: TodoItem[] = [
    new TodoItem(1, "Buy Flowers"), new TodoItem(2, "Get Shoes"),
    new TodoItem(3, "Collect Tickets"), new TodoItem(4, "Call Joe", true)];

let collection: TodoCollection = new TodoCollection("Adam", todos);

console.clear();
//console.log(`${collection.userName}'s Todo List`);
console.log(`${collection.userName}'s Todo List `
    + `(${ collection.getItemCounts().incomplete } items to do)`);

//collection.removeComplete();
collection.getTodoItems(true).forEach(item => item.printDetails());
```

Run the commands shown in listing 2.27 in the `todo` folder to compile and execute the code.

Listing 2.27   Compiling and executing

```
tsc
node dist/index.js
```

When the code is executed, the following output will be produced:

```
Adam's Todo List (3 items to do)
1       Buy Flowers
2       Get Shoes
3       Collect Tickets
4       Call Joe         (complete)
```

2.3   *Using a third-party package*

The basic features are in place, but there is room for improvement. One of the joys of writing JavaScript code is the ecosystem of packages that can be incorporated into projects. TypeScript allows any JavaScript package to be used but with the addition of static type support. I am going to use the excellent Inquirer.js package (https://github.com/SBoudrias/Inquirer.js) to deal with prompting the user for commands and processing responses.

2.3.1 Preparing for the third-party package

One of the drawbacks of writing JavaScript code is the number of competing standards for distributing and using packages. There was no standard package format when JavaScript was first released, and several competing standards arose. The JavaScript language specification now includes a common standard for modules, referred to as *ECMAScript modules*. Most JavaScript runtimes, including Node.js, are implementing support for ECMAScript modules, and most popular JavaScript packages are being updated so they are published in this format.

TypeScript supports ECMAScript modules but requires some changes to the project to enable this feature. Listing 2.28 adds a configuration property to the `package.json` file that denotes that this project requires ECMAScript module support.

Listing 2.28   Adding a configuration property in the package.json file in the todo folder

```json
{
  "name": "todo",
  "version": "1.0.0",
  "description": "",
  "main": "index.js",
  "scripts": {
    "test": "echo \"Error: no test specified\" && exit 1"
  },
  "keywords": [],
  "author": "",
  "license": "ISC",
  "type": "module"
}
```

Listing 2.29 changes the TypeScript compiler configuration so that it looks for the `type` property in the `package.json` file to determine which type of modules are being used.

Listing 2.29   Configuring the compiler in the tsconfig.json file in the todo folder

```json
{
    "compilerOptions": {
        "target": "ES2022",
        "outDir": "./dist",
        "rootDir": "./src",
        "module": "Node16"
    }
}
```

So far, I have been able to declare dependencies between code files without specifying a file extension, such as with this statement from the `todoCollection.ts` file:

```
...
import { TodoItem } from "./todoItem";
...
```

I describe `import` statements in more detail in chapter 4, but what's important for this chapter is that I specified the file name without an extension. But the way that Node.js has implemented ECMAScript modules requires the file extension to be included, as shown in listing 2.30.

Listing 2.30   Adding a file extension in the todoCollection.ts file in the src folder

```
import { TodoItem } from "./todoItem.js";

type ItemCounts = {
    total: number,
    incomplete: number
}
...
```

The oddity here is that the `import` statement must specify the JavaScript file that will be generated from the TypeScript file. There are reasons for this, which I explain in later chapters, and the same change is required to the `import` statements in the `index.ts` file, as shown in listing 2.31.

Listing 2.31   Adding file extensions in the index.ts file in the src folder

```
import { TodoItem } from "./todoItem.js";
import { TodoCollection } from "./todoCollection.js";

let todos: TodoItem[] = [
    new TodoItem(1, "Buy Flowers"), new TodoItem(2, "Get Shoes"),
    new TodoItem(3, "Collect Tickets"), new TodoItem(4, "Call Joe", true)];
...
```

2.3.2   Installing and using the third-party package

To add Inquirer.js to the project, run the command shown in listing 2.32 in the `todo` folder.

Listing 2.32   Adding a package to the project

```
npm install inquirer@9.1.4
```

Packages are added to TypeScript projects just as they are for pure JavaScript projects, using the `npm install` command. To get started with the new package, I added the statements shown in listing 2.33 to the `index.ts` file.

Listing 2.33   Using a new package in the index.ts file in the src folder

```
import { TodoItem } from "./todoItem.js";
import { TodoCollection } from "./todoCollection.js";
import inquirer from "inquirer";

let todos: TodoItem[] = [
    new TodoItem(1, "Buy Flowers"), new TodoItem(2, "Get Shoes"),
    new TodoItem(3, "Collect Tickets"), new TodoItem(4, "Call Joe", true)];
```

```
let collection: TodoCollection = new TodoCollection("Adam", todos);

function displayTodoList(): void {
    console.log(`${collection.userName}'s Todo List `
        + `(${ collection.getItemCounts().incomplete } items to do)`);
    collection.getTodoItems(true).forEach(item => item.printDetails());
}

enum Commands {
    Quit = "Quit"
}

function promptUser(): void {
    console.clear();
    displayTodoList();
    inquirer.prompt({
        type: "list",
        name: "command",
        message: "Choose option",
        choices: Object.values(Commands)
    }).then(answers => {
        if (answers["command"] !== Commands.Quit) {
            promptUser();
        }
    })
}

promptUser();
```

TypeScript doesn't get in the way of using JavaScript code, and the changes in listing 2.33 make use of the Inquirer.js package to prompt the user and offer a choice of commands. There is only one command available currently, which is `Quit`, but I'll add more useful features shortly.

> **TIP** I don't describe the Inquirer.js API in detail in this book because it is not directly related to TypeScript. See https://github.com/SBoudrias/Inquirer.js for details if you want to use Inquirer.js in your own projects.

The `inquirer.prompt` method is used to prompt the user for a response and is configured using a JavaScript object. The configuration options I have chosen present the user with a list that can be navigated using the arrow keys, and a selection can be made by pressing Return. When the user makes a selection, the function passed to the `then` method is invoked, and the selection is available through the `answers.command` property.

Listing 2.33 shows how TypeScript code and the JavaScript code from the Inquirer.js package can be used seamlessly together. The `enum` keyword is a TypeScript feature that allows values to be given names, as described in chapter 9, and will allow me to define and refer to commands without needing to duplicate string values through the application. Values from the enum are used alongside the Inquirer.js features, like this:

```
...
if (answers["command"] !== Commands.Quit) {
...
```

Run the commands shown in listing 2.34 in the `todo` folder to compile and execute the code.

```
tsc
node dist/index.js
```

When the code is executed, the list of to-do items will be displayed, along with a prompt to select a command, as shown in figure 2.2, although there is only one command available, which is Quit.

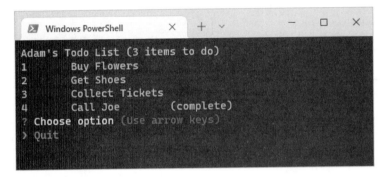

Figure 2.2   Prompting the user for a command

If you press the Return key, the Quit command will be selected, and the application will terminate.

2.3.3   Adding type declarations for the JavaScript package

TypeScript doesn't prevent JavaScript code from being used, but it isn't able to provide any assistance for its use. The compiler doesn't have any insight into the data types that are being used by Inquirer.js and has to trust that I am using the right types of arguments to prompt the user and that I am processing the response objects safely.

There are two ways to provide TypeScript with the information that it requires for static typing. The first approach is to describe the types yourself. I cover the features that TypeScript provides for describing JavaScript code in chapter 14. Manually describing JavaScript code isn't difficult, but it does take some time and requires good knowledge of the code you are describing.

The second approach is to use type declarations provided by someone else. The Definitely Typed project is a repository of TypeScript type declarations for thousands of JavaScript packages, including the Inquirer.js package. To install the type declarations, run the command shown in listing 2.35 in the `todo` folder.

Listing 2.35 Installing type definitions

```
npm install --save-dev @types/inquirer@9.0.3
```

Type declarations are installed using the `npm install` command, just like JavaScript packages. The `save-dev` argument is used for packages that are used in development but that are not part of the application. The package name is `@types/` followed by the name of the package for which type descriptions are required. For the Inquirer.js package, the type declarations package is `@types/inquirer` because `inquirer` is the name used to install the JavaScript package.

> **NOTE** See https://github.com/DefinitelyTyped/DefinitelyTyped for the details of the Definitely Typed project and the packages for which type declarations are available.

The TypeScript compiler detects type declarations automatically, and the package installed by the command in listing 2.35 allows the compiler to check the data types used by the Inquirer.js API. To demonstrate the effect of the type declarations, listing 2.36 uses a configuration property that isn't supported by Inquirer.js.

Listing 2.36 Adding a property in the index.ts file in the src folder

```
...
function promptUser(): void {
    console.clear();
    inquirer.prompt({
            type: "list",
            name: "command",
            message: "Choose option",
            choices: Object.values(Commands),
            badProperty: true
    }).then(answers => {
        // no action required
        if (answers["command"] !== Commands.Quit) {
            promptUser();
        }
    })
}
...
```

There is no configuration property named `badProperty` in the Inquirer.js API. Run the command shown in listing 2.37 in the `todo` folder to compile the code in the project.

Listing 2.37 Running the compiler

```
tsc
```

The compiler uses the type information installed in listing 2.35 and reports the following error:

```
src/index.ts:25:9 - error TS2769: No overload matches this call.
  Overload 1 of 2, '(questions: QuestionCollection<any>, initialAnswers?:
    Partial<any>): Promise<any> & { ui: Prompt<any>; }',
```

```
       gave the following error.
    Type '"list"' is not assignable to type '"number"'.
  Overload 2 of 2, '(questions: QuestionCollection<any>, initialAnswers?:
    Partial<any>): Promise<any>', gave the following error.
    Type '"list"' is not assignable to type '"number"'.

25        type: "list",
          ~~~~
Found 1 error in src/index.ts:25
```

The type declaration allows TypeScript to provide the same set of features throughout the application, even though the Inquirer.js package is pure JavaScript. However, as this example shows, there can be limitations to this feature, and the addition of a property that isn't supported has produced an error about the value assigned to the `type` property. This happens because it can be difficult to describe the types that pure JavaScript expects, and sometimes the error messages can be more of a general indication that something is wrong.

2.4 Adding commands

The example application doesn't do a great deal at the moment and requires additional commands. In the sections that follow, I add a series of new commands and provide the implementation for each of them.

2.4.1 Filtering items

The first command I will add allows the user to toggle the filter to include or exclude completed items, as shown in listing 2.38.

> **Listing 2.38   Filtering items in the index.ts file in the src folder**

```typescript
import { TodoItem } from "./todoItem.js";
import { TodoCollection } from "./todoCollection.js";
import inquirer from "inquirer";

let todos: TodoItem[] = [
    new TodoItem(1, "Buy Flowers"), new TodoItem(2, "Get Shoes"),
    new TodoItem(3, "Collect Tickets"), new TodoItem(4, "Call Joe", true)];

let collection: TodoCollection = new TodoCollection("Adam", todos);
let showCompleted = true;

function displayTodoList(): void {
    console.log(`${collection.userName}'s Todo List `
        + `(${ collection.getItemCounts().incomplete } items to do)`);
    //collection.getTodoItems(true).forEach(item => item.printDetails());
    collection.getTodoItems(showCompleted)
        .forEach(item => item.printDetails());


}

enum Commands {
```

```
    Toggle = "Show/Hide Completed",

    Quit = "Quit"
}

function promptUser(): void {
    console.clear();
    displayTodoList();
    inquirer.prompt({
        type: "list",
        name: "command",
        message: "Choose option",
        choices: Object.values(Commands),
        //badProperty: true

    }).then(answers => {
        switch (answers["command"]) {
            case Commands.Toggle:
                showCompleted = !showCompleted;
                promptUser();
                break;
        }

    })
}

promptUser();
```

The process for adding commands is to define a new value for the `Commands` enum and the statements that respond when the command is selected. In this case, the new value is `Toggle`, and when it is selected, the value of the `showCompleted` variable is changed so that the `displayTodoList` function includes or excludes completed items. Run the commands shown in listing 2.39 in the `todo` folder to compile and execute the code.

Listing 2.39 Compiling and executing

```
tsc
node dist/index.js
```

Select the `Show/Hide Completed` option and press Return to toggle the completed tasks in the list, as shown in figure 2.3.

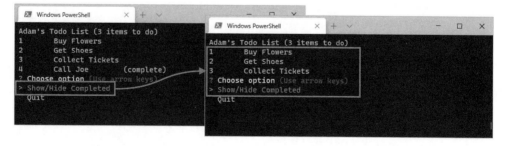

Figure 2.3 Toggling completed items

2.4.2   *Adding tasks*

The example application isn't much use unless the user can create new tasks. Listing 2.40 adds support for creating new TodoItem objects.

Listing 2.40   Adding tasks in the index.ts file in the src folder

```typescript
import { TodoItem } from "./todoItem.js";
import { TodoCollection } from "./todoCollection.js";
import inquirer from "inquirer";

let todos: TodoItem[] = [
    new TodoItem(1, "Buy Flowers"), new TodoItem(2, "Get Shoes"),
    new TodoItem(3, "Collect Tickets"), new TodoItem(4, "Call Joe", true)];

let collection: TodoCollection = new TodoCollection("Adam", todos);
let showCompleted = true;

function displayTodoList(): void {
    console.log(`${collection.userName}'s Todo List `
        + `(${ collection.getItemCounts().incomplete } items to do)`);
    collection.getTodoItems(showCompleted)
        .forEach(item => item.printDetails());
}

enum Commands {
    Add = "Add New Task",

    Toggle = "Show/Hide Completed",
    Quit = "Quit"
}

function promptAdd(): void {
    console.clear();
    inquirer.prompt({ type: "input", name: "add", message: "Enter task:"})
        .then(answers => {if (answers["add"] !== "") {
            collection.addTodo(answers["add"]);
        }
        promptUser();
    })
}

function promptUser(): void {
    console.clear();
    displayTodoList();
    inquirer.prompt({
        type: "list",
        name: "command",
        message: "Choose option",
        choices: Object.values(Commands),
    }).then(answers => {
        switch (answers["command"]) {
            case Commands.Toggle:
                showCompleted = !showCompleted;
```

```
                    promptUser();
                    break;
                case Commands.Add:
                    promptAdd();
                    break;

            }
        })
}

promptUser();
```

The Inquirer.js package can present different types of questions to the user. When the user selects the `Add` command, the `input` question type is used to get the task from the user, which is used as the argument to the `TodoCollection.addTodo` method. Run the commands shown in listing 2.41 in the `todo` folder to compile and execute the code.

Listing 2.41   Compiling and executing

```
tsc
node dist/index.js
```

Select the `Add New Task` option, enter some text, and press Return to create a new task, as shown in figure 2.4.

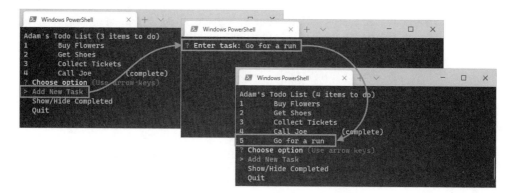

Figure 2.4   Adding a new task

2.4.3   *Marking tasks complete*

Completing a task is a two-stage process that requires the user to select the item they want to complete. Listing 2.42 adds the commands and an additional prompt that will allow the user to mark tasks complete and remove the completed items.

Listing 2.42   Completing items in the index.ts file in the src folder

```
import { TodoItem } from "./todoItem.js";
import { TodoCollection } from "./todoCollection.js";
```

```typescript
import inquirer from "inquirer";

let todos: TodoItem[] = [
    new TodoItem(1, "Buy Flowers"), new TodoItem(2, "Get Shoes"),
    new TodoItem(3, "Collect Tickets"), new TodoItem(4, "Call Joe", true)];

let collection: TodoCollection = new TodoCollection("Adam", todos);
let showCompleted = true;

function displayTodoList(): void {
    console.log(`${collection.userName}'s Todo List `
        + `(${ collection.getItemCounts().incomplete } items to do)`);
    collection.getTodoItems(showCompleted)
        .forEach(item => item.printDetails());
}

enum Commands {
    Add = "Add New Task",
    Complete = "Complete Task",

    Toggle = "Show/Hide Completed",
    Purge = "Remove Completed Tasks",

    Quit = "Quit"
}

function promptAdd(): void {
    console.clear();
    inquirer.prompt({ type: "input", name: "add", message: "Enter task:"})
        .then(answers => {if (answers["add"] !== "") {
            collection.addTodo(answers["add"]);
        }
        promptUser();
    })
}

function promptComplete(): void {
    console.clear();
    inquirer.prompt({ type: "checkbox", name: "complete",
        message: "Mark Tasks Complete",
        choices: collection.getTodoItems(showCompleted).map(item =>
            ({name: item.task, value: item.id, checked: item.complete}))
    }).then(answers => {
        let completedTasks = answers["complete"] as number[];
        collection.getTodoItems(true).forEach(item =>
            collection.markComplete(item.id,
                completedTasks.find(id => id === item.id) != undefined));
        promptUser();
    })
}

function promptUser(): void {
    console.clear();
    displayTodoList();
    inquirer.prompt({
        type: "list",
```

```
        name: "command",
        message: "Choose option",
        choices: Object.values(Commands),
    }).then(answers => {
        switch (answers["command"]) {
            case Commands.Toggle:
                showCompleted = !showCompleted;
                promptUser();
                break;
            case Commands.Add:
                promptAdd();
                break;
            case Commands.Complete:
                if (collection.getItemCounts().incomplete > 0) {
                    promptComplete();
                } else {
                    promptUser();
                }
                break;
            case Commands.Purge:
                collection.removeComplete();
                promptUser();
                break;
        }
    })
}

promptUser();
```

The changes add a new prompt to the application that presents the user with the list of tasks and allows their state to be changed. The `showCompleted` variable is used to determine whether completed items are shown, creating a link between the `Toggle` and `Complete` commands.

The only new TypeScript feature of note is found in this statement:

```
...
let completedTasks = answers["complete"] as number[];
...
```

Even with type definitions, there are times when TypeScript isn't able to correctly assess the types that are being used. In this case, the Inquirer.js package allows any data type to be used in the prompts shown to the user, and the compiler isn't able to determine that I have used only `number` values, which means that only `number` values can be received as answers. I used a *type assertion* to address this problem, which allows me to tell the compiler to use the type that I specify, even if it has identified a different data type (or no data type at all). When a type assertion is used, it overrides the compiler, which means that I am responsible for ensuring that the type I assert is correct. Run the commands shown in listing 2.43 in the `todo` folder to compile and execute the code.

> **Listing 2.43   Compiling and executing**

```
tsc
node dist/index.js
```

Select the `Complete Task` option, select one or more tasks to change using the space-bar, and then press Return. The state of the tasks you selected will be changed, which will be reflected in the revised list, as shown in figure 2.5.

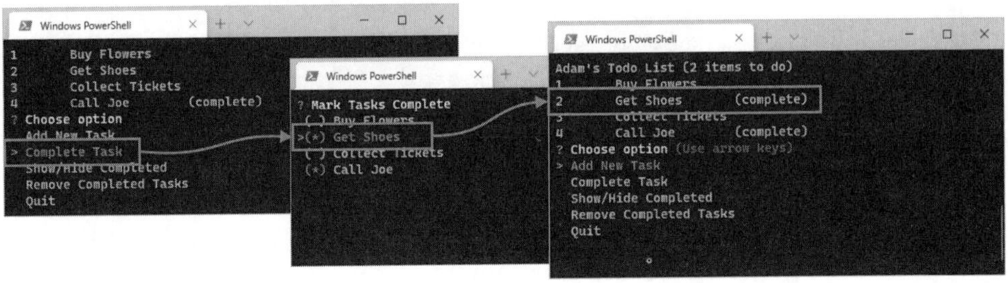

Figure 2.5   Completing items

2.5 *Persistently storing data*

To store the to-do items persistently, I am going to use another open-source package because there is no advantage in creating functionality when there are well-written and well-tested alternatives available. Run the commands shown in listing 2.44 in the `todo` folder to install the Lowdb package and the type definitions that describe its API to TypeScript.

Listing 2.44   Adding a package

```
npm install lowdb@5.1.0
```

Lowdb is an excellent database package that stores data in a JSON file and that is used as the data storage component for the `json-server` package, which I use to create HTTP web services in part 3 of this book.

Notice that I didn't install any type declarations for this package. TypeScript has become so popular that many packages, including Lowdb, ship with type declarations as part of the JavaScript package.

> **TIP**   I don't describe the Lowdb API in detail in this book because it is not directly related to TypeScript. See https://github.com/typicode/lowdb for details if you want to use Lowdb in your projects.

I am going to implement persistent storage by deriving from the `TodoCollection` class. In preparation, I changed the access control keyword used by the `TodoCollection` class so that subclasses can access the `Map` that contains the `TodoItem` objects, as shown in listing 2.45.

Listing 2.45 Changing access control in the todoCollection.ts file in the src folder

```typescript
import { TodoItem } from "./todoItem.js";

type ItemCounts = {
    total: number,
    incomplete: number
}

export class TodoCollection {
    private nextId: number = 1;
    protected itemMap = new Map<number, TodoItem>();

    constructor(public userName: string, todoItems: TodoItem[] = []) {
        todoItems.forEach(item => this.itemMap.set(item.id, item));
    }

    // ...methods omitted for brevity...
}
```

The `protected` keyword tells the TypeScript compiler that a property can be accessed only by a class or its subclasses. To create the subclass, I added a file called `jsonTodo-Collection.ts` to the `src` folder with the code shown in listing 2.46.

Listing 2.46 The contents of the jsonTodoCollection.ts file in the src folder

```typescript
import { TodoItem } from "./todoItem.js";
import { TodoCollection } from "./todoCollection.js";
import { LowSync } from "lowdb";
import { JSONFileSync } from "lowdb/node";

type schemaType = {
    tasks: { id: number; task: string; complete: boolean; }[]
};

export class JsonTodoCollection extends TodoCollection {
    private database: LowSync<schemaType>;

    constructor(public userName: string, todoItems: TodoItem[] = []) {
        super(userName, []);
        this.database = new LowSync(new JSONFileSync("Todos.json"));
        this.database.read();

        if (this.database.data == null) {
            this.database.data = { tasks : todoItems};
            this.database.write();
            todoItems.forEach(item => this.itemMap.set(item.id, item));
        } else {
            this.database.data.tasks.forEach(item =>
                this.itemMap.set(item.id,
                    new TodoItem(item.id, item.task, item.complete)));
        }
    }

    addTodo(task: string): number {
        let result = super.addTodo(task);
```

```
        this.storeTasks();
        return result;
    }

    markComplete(id: number, complete: boolean): void {
        super.markComplete(id, complete);
        this.storeTasks();
    }

    removeComplete(): void {
        super.removeComplete();
        this.storeTasks();
    }

    private storeTasks() {
        this.database.data.tasks = [...this.itemMap.values()];
        this.database.write();
    }
}
```

The type definition for Lowdb uses a schema to describe the structure of the data that will be stored, which is then applied using generic type arguments so that the TypeScript compiler can check the data types being used. For the example application, I need to store only one data type, which I describe using a type alias.

```
...
type schemaType = {
    tasks: { id: number; task: string; complete: boolean; }[]
};
...
```

The schema type is used when the Lowdb database is created, and the compiler can check the way that data is used when it is read from the database as in this statement, for example:

```
...
this.database.data.tasks.forEach(item => this.itemMap.set(item.id,
    new TodoItem(item.id, item.task, item.complete)));
...
```

The compiler knows that the `tasks` property presented by the data corresponds to the `tasks` property in the schema type and will return an array of objects with `id`, `task`, and `complete` properties.

Listing 2.47 uses the `JsonTodoCollection` class in the `index.ts` file so that data will be stored persistently by the example application.

> **Listing 2.47   Using the persistent collection in the index.ts file in the src folder**

```
import { TodoItem } from "./todoItem.js";
import { TodoCollection } from "./todoCollection.js";
import inquirer from "inquirer";
import { JsonTodoCollection } from "./jsonTodoCollection.js";


let todos: TodoItem[] = [
    new TodoItem(1, "Buy Flowers"), new TodoItem(2, "Get Shoes"),
    new TodoItem(3, "Collect Tickets"), new TodoItem(4, "Call Joe", true)];
```

```
let collection: TodoCollection = new JsonTodoCollection("Adam", todos);
let showCompleted = true;
```

`...`

Run the commands shown in listing 2.48 in the `todo` folder to compile and execute the code for the final time in this chapter.

> **Listing 2.48 Compiling and executing**

```
tsc
node dist/index.js
```

When the application starts, a file called `Todos.json` will be created in the `todo` folder and used to store a JSON representation of the `TodoItem` objects, ensuring that changes are not lost when the application is terminated.

Summary

In this chapter, I created a simple example application to introduce you to TypeScript development and demonstrate some important TypeScript concepts. You saw that TypeScript provides features that supplement JavaScript, focus on type safety, and help avoid common patterns that trip up developers, especially those coming to JavaScript from languages such as C# or Java.

You saw that TypeScript isn't used in isolation and that a JavaScript runtime is required to execute the JavaScript code that the TypeScript compiler produces. The advantage of this approach is that projects written with TypeScript have full access to the broad spectrum of JavaScript packages that are available, many of which have type definitions available for easy use.

- TypeScript development can be done with freely available tools.
- TypeScript builds on the JavaScript language, with the main feature being static types.
- The output from the TypeScript compiler is pure JavaScript, which can be executed by a suitable JavaScript runtime.
- TypeScript applications can use standard JavaScript packages, although a basic understanding of JavaScript modules can be required to prepare a TypeScript project before installing a package.
- Some JavaScript packages include type information for use with TypeScript.
- Separate type declaration packages are available for popular packages that don't include type declarations.

The application I created in this chapter uses some of the most essential TypeScript features, but there are many more available, as you can tell from the size of this book. In the next chapter, I put TypeScript in context and describe the structure and content of this book.

JavaScript primer, part 1

This chapter covers

- Using the JavaScript types
- Coercing JavaScript types
- Defining and using JavaScript functions and arrays
- Creating and implementing JavaScript objects
- Understanding the `this` keyword

Effective TypeScript development requires an understanding of how JavaScript deals with data types. This can be a disappointment to developers who adopt TypeScript because they found JavaScript confusing, but understanding JavaScript makes understanding TypeScript easier and provides valuable insights into what TypeScript offers and how its features work. In this chapter, I introduce the basic JavaScript type features, continuing with more advanced features in chapter 4.

3.1 Preparing for this chapter

To prepare for this chapter, create a folder called `primer` in a convenient location. Open a command prompt, navigate to the `primer` folder, and run the command shown in listing 3.1.

> **TIP** You can download the example project for this chapter—and for all the other chapters in this book—from https://github.com/manningbooks/essential-typescript-5.

Listing 3.1 Preparing the project folder

```
npm init --yes
```

To install a package that will automatically execute the JavaScript file when its contents change, run the command shown in listing 3.2 in the primer folder.

Listing 3.2 Installing a package

```
npm install nodemon@2.0.20
```

The package, called nodemon, will be downloaded and installed. Once the installation is complete, create a file called index.js in the primer folder with the contents shown in listing 3.3.

Listing 3.3 The contents of the index.js file in the primer folder

```
let hatPrice = 100;
console.log(`Hat price: ${hatPrice}`);
```

Run the command shown in listing 3.4 to execute the contents of the JavaScript file and monitor it for changes.

Listing 3.4 Starting the JavaScript file monitor

```
npx nodemon index.js
```

The nodemon package will execute the contents of the index.js file and produce the following output:

```
[nodemon] 2.0.20
[nodemon] to restart at any time, enter `rs`
[nodemon] watching path(s): *.*
[nodemon] watching extensions: js,mjs,json
[nodemon] starting `node index.js`
Hat price: 100
[nodemon] clean exit - waiting for changes before restart
```

I have highlighted the part of the output that comes from the index.js file. To ensure that changes are detected correctly, alter the contents of the index.js file as shown in listing 3.5.

Listing 3.5 Making a change in the index.js file in the primer folder

```
let hatPrice = 100;
console.log(`Hat price: ${hatPrice}`);
let bootsPrice = "100";
console.log(`Boots price: ${bootsPrice}`);
```

When you save the changes, the nodemon package should detect that the index.js file has been modified and execute the code it contains. The code in listing 3.5 produces the following output, which is shown without the information provided by the nodemon package:

```
Hat price: 100
Boots price: 100
```

3.2   *Getting confused by JavaScript*

JavaScript has many features that are similar to other programming languages, and developers tend to start with code that looks like the statements in listing 3.5. Even if you are new to JavaScript, the statements in listing 3.5 will be familiar.

The building blocks for JavaScript code are statements, which are executed in the order they are defined. The `let` keyword is used to define variables (as opposed to the `const` keyword, which defines constant values) followed by a name. The value of a variable is set using the assignment operator (the equal sign) followed by a value.

JavaScript provides some built-in objects to perform common tasks, such as writing strings to the command prompt with the `console.log` method. Strings can be defined as literal values, using single or double quotes, or as template strings, using backtick characters and inserting expressions into the template using the dollar sign and braces.

But at some point, unexpected results appear. The cause of the confusion is the way that JavaScript deals with types. Listing 3.6 shows a typical problem.

> **Listing 3.6   Adding statements in the index.ts file in the primer folder**

```
let hatPrice = 100;
console.log(`Hat price: ${hatPrice}`);
let bootsPrice = "100";
console.log(`Boots price: ${bootsPrice}`);

if (hatPrice == bootsPrice) {
    console.log("Prices are the same");
} else {
    console.log("Prices are different");
}

let totalPrice = hatPrice + bootsPrice;
console.log(`Total Price: ${totalPrice}`);
```

The new statements compare the values of the `hatPrice` and `bootsPrice` variables and assign their total to a new variable named `totalPrice`. The `console.log` method is used to write messages to the command prompt and produces the following output when the code is executed:

```
Hat price: 100
Boots price: 100
Prices are the same
Total Price: 100100
```

Most developers will notice that the value for `hatPrice` has been expressed as a number, while the `bootsPrice` value is a string of characters, enclosed in double quotes. But in most languages, performing operations on different types would be an error. JavaScript is different; comparing a string and a number succeeds, but trying to total the values actually concatenates them. Understanding the results from listing 3.6—and the reasons behind them—reveals the details of how JavaScript approaches data types and why TypeScript can be so helpful.

3.3 Understanding JavaScript types

It can seem that JavaScript doesn't have data types or that types are used inconsistently, but that's not true. JavaScript just works differently than most popular programming languages, and it only seems to behave inconsistently until you know what to expect. The foundation for the JavaScript language is a set of built-in types, which are described in table 3.1.

Table 3.1 The JavaScript built-in types

Name	Description
number	This type is used to represent numeric values. Unlike other programming languages, JavaScript doesn't differentiate between integer and floating-point values, both of which can be represented using this type.
string	This type is used to represent text data.
boolean	This type can have `true` and `false` values.
symbol	This type is used to represent unique constant values, such as keys in collections.
null	This type can be assigned only the value `null` and is used to indicate a nonexistent or invalid reference.
undefined	This type is used when a variable has been defined but has not been assigned a value.
object	This type is used to represent compound values, formed from individual properties and values.

The first six types in the table are the JavaScript primitive data types. The primitive types are always available, and every value in a JavaScript application either is a primitive type itself or is composed from primitive types. The sixth type is `object` and is used to represent objects.

3.3.1 Working with primitive data types

If you look back at listing 3.6, you will see that there are no types declared in the code. In other languages, you are required to declare the data type of a variable before it can be used, like this fragment of code from one of my C# books:

```
...
string name = "Adam";
...
```

This statement specifies that the type of the `name` variable is a `string` and assigns it the value `Adam`. In JavaScript, *values* have types, not variables. To define a variable that holds a string, you assign a string value, as shown in listing 3.7.

Listing 3.7 Creating a string variable in the index.js file in the primer folder

```
let hatPrice = 100;
console.log(`Hat price: ${hatPrice}`);
let bootsPrice = "100";
console.log(`Boots price: ${bootsPrice}`);
```

```
if (hatPrice == bootsPrice) {
    console.log("Prices are the same");
} else {
    console.log("Prices are different");
}

let totalPrice = hatPrice + bootsPrice;
console.log(`Total Price: ${totalPrice}`);
```

let myVariable = "Adam";

The JavaScript runtime only has to figure out which of the types from table 3.1 it should use for the value assigned to `myVariable`. The small set of types supported by JavaScript makes the process simpler, and the runtime knows that any value enclosed in double quotes must be a `string`. You can confirm the type of a value using the `typeof` keyword, as shown in listing 3.8.

Listing 3.8   Getting a value type in the index.js file in the primer folder

```
let hatPrice = 100;
console.log(`Hat price: ${hatPrice}`);
let bootsPrice = "100";
console.log(`Boots price: ${bootsPrice}`);

if (hatPrice == bootsPrice) {
    console.log("Prices are the same");
} else {
    console.log("Prices are different");
}

let totalPrice = hatPrice + bootsPrice;
console.log(`Total Price: ${totalPrice}`);

let myVariable = "Adam";
console.log(`Type: ${typeof myVariable}`);
```

The `typeof` keyword identifies a value's type and produces the following output when the code is executed:

```
Hat price: 100
Boots price: 100
Prices are the same
Total Price: 100100
Type: string
```

Listing 3.9 assigns a new value to `myVariable` and displays the type again.

Listing 3.9   Assigning a new value in the index.js file in the primer folder

```
let hatPrice = 100;
console.log(`Hat price: ${hatPrice}`);
let bootsPrice = "100";
console.log(`Boots price: ${bootsPrice}`);

if (hatPrice == bootsPrice) {
    console.log("Prices are the same");
```

```
    } else {
        console.log("Prices are different");
    }

    let totalPrice = hatPrice + bootsPrice;
    console.log(`Total Price: ${totalPrice}`);

    let myVariable = "Adam";
    console.log(`Type: ${typeof myVariable}`);
    myVariable = 100;
    console.log(`Type: ${typeof myVariable}`);
```

When the changes are saved, the code will produce the following output:

```
Hat price: 100
Boots price: 100
Prices are the same
Total Price: 100100
Type: string
Type: number
```

Changing the value assigned to a variable changes the type reported by the `typeof` keyword because values have types. The type of the value initially assigned to `myVariable` was `string`, and then the variable was assigned a `number` value. This dynamic approach to types is made easier by the limited range of types that JavaScript supports, which makes it easier to determine which of the built-in types is being used. For example, all numbers are represented by the `number` type, which means that integers and floating-point values are all handled using `number`, which would not be possible with a more complex set of types.

Understanding the typeof null oddity

When the `typeof` keyword is used on `null` values, the result is `object`. This is a long-standing behavior that dates back to the earliest days of JavaScript and that hasn't been changed because so much code has been written that expects this behavior.

3.3.2 Understanding type coercion

When an operator is applied to values of different types, the JavaScript runtime converts one value into an equivalent value in the other type, a process known as *type coercion*. It is the type coercion feature—also known as *type conversion*—that causes the inconsistent results from listing 3.6, although, as you will learn, the results are not inconsistent once you understand how this feature works. There are two points in the code in listing 3.6 where types are coerced.

```
...
let hatPrice = 100;
console.log(`Hat price: ${hatPrice}`);
let bootsPrice = "100";
console.log(`Boots price: ${bootsPrice}`);

if (hatPrice == bootsPrice) {
...
```

The double equal sign performs a comparison using type coercion so that JavaScript will try to convert the values it is working with to produce a useful result. This is known as the JavaScript *abstract equality comparison,* and when a `number` is compared to a `string`, the `string` value is converted to a `number` value, and then the comparison is performed. This means when the `number` value `100` is compared with the `string` value `100`, the `string` is converted to the `number` value `100`, and this is the reason why the `if` expression evaluates to `true`.

> **TIP** You can read the sequence of steps that JavaScript follows in an abstract equality comparison in the JavaScript specification, https://262.ecma-international.org/13.0/#sec-islooselyequal. The specification is well-written and surprisingly interesting. But before you spend a day getting lost in the implementation details, you should bear in mind that TypeScript constrains the use of some of the most unusual and exotic features.

The second time coercion is used in listing 3.6 is when the prices are totaled.

```
...
let totalPrice = hatPrice + bootsPrice;
...
```

When you use the + operator on a `number` and a `string`, one of the values is converted. The confusing part is that the conversion isn't the same as for comparisons. If either of the values is a `string`, the other value is converted to a `string`, and both `string` values are concatenated. This means that when the `number` value `100` is added to the `string` value `100`, the `number` is converted to a `string` and concatenated to produce the `string` result `100100`.

Avoiding Unintentional Type Coercion

Type coercion can be a useful feature, and it has gained a poor reputation only because it is applied unintentionally, which is easy to do when the types being processed are changed with new values. As you will learn in later chapters, TypeScript provides features that help manage unwanted coercion. But JavaScript also provides features to prevent coercion, as shown in listing 3.10.

> **Listing 3.10   Preventing coercion in the index.js file in the primer folder**

```
let hatPrice = 100;
console.log(`Hat price: ${hatPrice}`);
let bootsPrice = "100";
console.log(`Boots price: ${bootsPrice}`);

if (hatPrice === bootsPrice) {
    console.log("Prices are the same");
} else {
    console.log("Prices are different");
}

let totalPrice = Number(hatPrice) + Number(bootsPrice);
console.log(`Total Price: ${totalPrice}`);
```

```
let myVariable = "Adam";
console.log(`Type: ${typeof myVariable}`);
myVariable = 100;
console.log(`Type: ${typeof myVariable}`);
```

The double equal sign (==) performs a comparison that applies type coercion. The triple equal sign (===) applies a strict comparison that will return `true` only if the values have the same type and are equal.

To prevent string concatenation, values can be explicitly converted to numbers before the + operator is applied using the built-in `Number` function, with the effect that numeric addition is performed. The code in listing 3.10 produces the following output:

```
Hat price: 100
Boots price: 100
Prices are different
Total Price: 200
Type: string
Type: number
```

APPRECIATING THE VALUE OF EXPLICITLY APPLIED TYPE COERCION

Type coercion can be a useful feature when it is explicitly applied. One useful feature is the way that values are coerced into the `boolean` type by the logical OR operator (| |). Values that are `null` or `undefined` are converted into the `false` value, and this makes an effective tool for providing fallback values, as shown in listing 3.11.

> Listing 3.11 Handling null values in the index.js file in the primer folder

```
let hatPrice = 100;
console.log(`Hat price: ${hatPrice}`);
let bootsPrice = "100";
console.log(`Boots price: ${bootsPrice}`);

if (hatPrice === bootsPrice) {
    console.log("Prices are the same");
} else {
    console.log("Prices are different");
}

let totalPrice = Number(hatPrice) + Number(bootsPrice);
console.log(`Total Price: ${totalPrice}`);

let myVariable = "Adam";
console.log(`Type: ${typeof myVariable}`);
myVariable = 100;
console.log(`Type: ${typeof myVariable}`);

let firstCity;
let secondCity = firstCity || "London";
console.log(`City: ${ secondCity }`);
```

The value of the variable named `secondCity` is set with an expression that checks the `firstCity` value: if `firstCity` is converted to the `boolean` value `true`, then the value of `secondCity` will be the value of `firstCity`.

The `undefined` type is used when variables are defined but have not been assigned a value, which is the case for the variable named `firstCity`, and the use of the `||` operator ensures that the fallback value for `secondCity` will be used when `firstCity` is `undefined` or `null`.

UNDERSTANDING NULLISH COALESCING

One problem with the logical OR operator is that it isn't just `null` or `undefined` that is converted into a `false` value, which can cause unexpected results, as shown in listing 3.12.

Listing 3.12   The effect of type coercion in the index.js file in the primer folder

```
let hatPrice = 100;
console.log(`Hat price: ${hatPrice}`);
let bootsPrice = "100";
console.log(`Boots price: ${bootsPrice}`);

let taxRate; // no tax rate has been defined
console.log(`Tax rate: ${taxRate || 10}%`);
taxRate = 0; // zero-rated for tax
console.log(`Tax rate: ${taxRate || 10}%`);
```

In addition to `null` and `undefined`, the logical OR operator will also coerce the number value `0` (zero), the empty string value (`""`), and the special `NaN` number value to `false`. These values, in addition to the `false` value, are collectively known as the JavaScript "falsy" values and cause a lot of confusion. In listing 3.12, the logical OR operator uses the fallback value when the `taxRate` variable is assigned zero and produces the following output:

```
Hat price: 100
Boots price: 100
Tax rate: 10%
Tax rate: 10%
```

The code doesn't differentiate between an unassigned value and the zero value, which can be a problem when zero is a required value. In this example, it is impossible to set a tax rate of zero, even though this is a legitimate rate. To address this problem, JavaScript supports the nullish coalescing operator, `??`, which only coerces `undefined` and `null` values and not the other falsy values, as shown in listing 3.13.

Listing 3.13   Using the nullish operator in the index.js file in the primer folder

```
let hatPrice = 100;
console.log(`Hat price: ${hatPrice}`);
let bootsPrice = "100";
console.log(`Boots price: ${bootsPrice}`);

let taxRate; // no tax rate has been defined
console.log(`Tax rate: ${taxRate ?? 10}%`);
taxRate = 0; // zero-rated for tax
console.log(`Tax rate: ${taxRate ?? 10}%`);
```

In the first statement, the fallback value will be used because `taxRate` is `undefined`. In the second statement, the fallback value will not be used because zero is not coerced by the `??` operator, producing the following output:

```
Hat price: 100
Boots price: 100
Tax rate: 10%
Tax rate: 0%
```

3.3.3 Working with functions

The fluid approach that JavaScript takes to types is followed through in other parts of the language, including functions. Listing 3.14 adds a function to the example Java-Script file and removes some of the statements from previous examples for brevity.

> Listing 3.14 Defining a function in the index.js file in the primer folder

```
let hatPrice = 100;
console.log(`Hat price: ${hatPrice}`);
let bootsPrice = "100";
console.log(`Boots price: ${bootsPrice}`);

function sumPrices(first, second, third) {
    return first + second + third;
}

let totalPrice = sumPrices(hatPrice, bootsPrice);
console.log(`Total Price: ${totalPrice}`);
```

A function's parameter types are determined by the values used to invoke the function. A function may assume that it will receive `number` values, for example, but there is nothing to prevent the function from being invoked with `string`, `boolean`, or `object` arguments. Unexpected results can be produced if the function doesn't take care to validate its assumptions, either because the JavaScript runtime coerces values or because features specific to a single type are used.

The `sumPrices` function in listing 3.14 uses the + operator, intended to sum a set of `number` parameters, but one of the values used to invoke the function is a string, and as explained earlier in the chapter, the + operator applied to a `string` value performs concatenation. The code in listing 3.14 produces the following output:

```
Hat price: 100
Boots price: 100
Total Price: 100100undefined
```

JavaScript doesn't enforce a match between the number of parameters defined by a function and the number of arguments used to invoke it. Any parameter for which a value is not provided will be `undefined`. In the listing, no value is provided for the parameter named `third`, and the `undefined` value is converted to the `string` value undefined and included in the concatenation output.

```
Total Price: 100100undefined
```

WORKING WITH FUNCTION RESULTS

The differences between JavaScript types and those of other languages are magnified by functions. A consequence of the JavaScript type features is that the arguments used to invoke a function can determine the type of the function's result, as shown in listing 3.15.

> **Listing 3.15   Invoking a function in the index.js file in the primer folder**

```
let hatPrice = 100;
console.log(`Hat price: ${hatPrice}`);
let bootsPrice = "100";
console.log(`Boots price: ${bootsPrice}`);

function sumPrices(first, second, third) {
    return first + second + third;
}

let totalPrice = sumPrices(hatPrice, bootsPrice);
console.log(`Total: ${totalPrice} ${typeof totalPrice}`);

totalPrice = sumPrices(100, 200, 300);
console.log(`Total: ${totalPrice} ${typeof totalPrice}`);

totalPrice = sumPrices(100, 200);
console.log(`Total: ${totalPrice} ${typeof totalPrice}`);
```

The value of the `totalPrice` variable is set three times by invoking the `sumPrices` function. After each function call, the `typeof` keyword is used to determine the type of the value returned by the function. The code in listing 3.15 produces the following output:

```
Hat price: 100
Boots price: 100
Total: 100100undefined string
Total: 600 number
Total: NaN number
```

The first function call includes a `string` argument, which causes all of the function's parameters to be converted to `string` values and concatenated, meaning that the function returns the `string` value `100100undefined`.

The second function call uses three `number` values, which are added together and produce the `number` result `600`. The final function call uses number arguments but doesn't provide a third value, which causes an `undefined` parameter. JavaScript coalesces `undefined` to the special `number` value `NaN` (meaning not a number). The result of addition that includes `NaN` is `NaN`, which means that the type of the result is `number` but the value isn't useful and is unlikely to be what was intended.

AVOIDING ARGUMENT MISMATCH PROBLEMS

Although the results in the previous section can confuse, they are the outcomes described in the JavaScript specification. The problem isn't that JavaScript is unpredictable but that its approach is different from other popular programming languages.

JavaScript provides features that can be used to avoid these issues. The first is default parameter values that are used if the function is invoked without a corresponding argument, as shown in listing 3.16.

Listing 3.16 Using a default parameter value in the index.js file in the primer folder

```
let hatPrice = 100;
console.log(`Hat price: ${hatPrice}`);
let bootsPrice = "100";
console.log(`Boots price: ${bootsPrice}`);

function sumPrices(first, second, third = 0) {
    return first + second + third;
}

let totalPrice = sumPrices(hatPrice, bootsPrice);
console.log(`Total: ${totalPrice} ${typeof totalPrice}`);

totalPrice = sumPrices(100, 200, 300);
console.log(`Total: ${totalPrice} ${typeof totalPrice}`);

totalPrice = sumPrices(100, 200);
console.log(`Total: ${totalPrice} ${typeof totalPrice}`);
```

The name of the `third` parameter is followed by the equal sign and the value that should be used if the function is invoked without a corresponding value. The result is that the statement that invokes the `sumPrices` function with two `number` values will no longer produce the `NaN` result, as shown in the output:

```
Hat price: 100
Boots price: 100
Total: 1001000 string
Total: 600 number
Total: 300 number
```

A more flexible approach is a rest parameter, which is prefixed with three periods (. . .) and must be the last parameter defined by the function, as shown in listing 3.17.

Listing 3.17 Using a rest parameter in the index.js file in the primer folder

```
let hatPrice = 100;
console.log(`Hat price: ${hatPrice}`);
let bootsPrice = "100";
console.log(`Boots price: ${bootsPrice}`);

function sumPrices(...numbers) {
    return numbers.reduce(function(total, val) {
        return total + val
    }, 0);
}

let totalPrice = sumPrices(hatPrice, bootsPrice);
console.log(`Total: ${totalPrice} ${typeof totalPrice}`);
```

```
totalPrice = sumPrices(100, 200, 300);
console.log(`Total: ${totalPrice} ${typeof totalPrice}`);

totalPrice = sumPrices(100, 200);
console.log(`Total: ${totalPrice} ${typeof totalPrice}`);
```

A rest parameter is an array containing all the arguments for which parameters are not defined. The function in listing 3.17 defines only a rest parameter, which means that its value will be an array containing all of the arguments used to invoke the function. The contents of the array are summed using the built-in array `reduce` method. JavaScript arrays are described in the "Working with Arrays" section, and the `reduce` method is used to invoke a function for each object in the array to produce a single result value. This approach ensures that the number of arguments doesn't affect the result, but the function invoked by the `reduce` method uses the addition operator, which means that `string` values will still be concatenated. The listing produces the following output:

```
Hat price: 100
Boots price: 100
Total: 100100 string
Total: 600 number
Total: 300 number
```

To ensure the function produces a useful sum of its parameter values however they are received, they can be converted to numbers and filtered to remove any that are NaN, as shown in listing 3.18.

Listing 3.18   Converting and filtering parameters in the index.js file in the primer folder

```
let hatPrice = 100;
console.log(`Hat price: ${hatPrice}`);
let bootsPrice = "100";
console.log(`Boots price: ${bootsPrice}`);

function sumPrices(...numbers) {
    return numbers.reduce(function(total, val) {
        return total + (Number.isNaN(Number(val)) ? 0 : Number(val));
    }, 0);
}

let totalPrice = sumPrices(hatPrice, bootsPrice);
console.log(`Total: ${totalPrice} ${typeof totalPrice}`);

totalPrice = sumPrices(100, 200, 300);
console.log(`Total: ${totalPrice} ${typeof totalPrice}`);

totalPrice = sumPrices(100, 200, undefined, false, "hello");
console.log(`Total: ${totalPrice} ${typeof totalPrice}`);
```

The `Number.isNaN` method is used to check whether a `number` value is NaN, and the code in listing 3.18 explicitly converts each parameter to a `number` and substitutes zero for those that are NaN. Only parameter values that can be treated as numbers are processed, and the `undefined`, `boolean`, and `string` arguments added to the final function call do not affect the result:

```
Hat price: 100
Boots price: 100
Total: 200 number
Total: 600 number
Total: 300 number
```

USING ARROW FUNCTIONS

Arrow functions—also known as *fat arrow functions* or *lambda expressions*—are an alternative way of concisely defining functions and are often used to define functions that are arguments to other functions. Listing 3.19 replaces the standard function used with the array `reduce` method with an arrow function.

> **Listing 3.19   Using an arrow function in the index.js file in the primer folder**

```javascript
let hatPrice = 100;
console.log(`Hat price: ${hatPrice}`);
let bootsPrice = "100";
console.log(`Boots price: ${bootsPrice}`);

function sumPrices(...numbers) {
    return numbers.reduce((total, val) =>
        total + (Number.isNaN(Number(val)) ? 0 : Number(val)));
}

let totalPrice = sumPrices(hatPrice, bootsPrice);
console.log(`Total: ${totalPrice} ${typeof totalPrice}`);

totalPrice = sumPrices(100, 200, 300);
console.log(`Total: ${totalPrice} ${typeof totalPrice}`);

totalPrice = sumPrices(100, 200, undefined, false, "hello");
console.log(`Total: ${totalPrice} ${typeof totalPrice}`);
```

There are three parts to an arrow function: the input parameters, then an equal sign with a greater-than sign (the "arrow"), and finally the result value. The `return` keyword and curly braces are required only if the arrow function needs to execute more than one statement. This listing produces the same output as listing 3.18.

Arrow functions can be used anywhere that a function is required, and their use is a matter of personal preference, except for the issue described in the "Understanding the this Keyword" section. Listing 3.20 redefines the `sumPrices` function in the arrow syntax. This listing produces the same output as listing 3.18.

> **Listing 3.20   Replacing a function in the index.js file in the primer folder**

```javascript
let hatPrice = 100;
console.log(`Hat price: ${hatPrice}`);
let bootsPrice = "100";
console.log(`Boots price: ${bootsPrice}`);

let sumPrices = (...numbers) => numbers.reduce((total, val) =>
    total + (Number.isNaN(Number(val)) ? 0 : Number(val)));

let totalPrice = sumPrices(hatPrice, bootsPrice);
console.log(`Total: ${totalPrice} ${typeof totalPrice}`);
```

```
totalPrice = sumPrices(100, 200, 300);
console.log(`Total: ${totalPrice} ${typeof totalPrice}`);

totalPrice = sumPrices(100, 200, undefined, false, "hello");
console.log(`Total: ${totalPrice} ${typeof totalPrice}`);
```

Functions—regardless of which syntax is used—are values, too. They are a special category of the `object` type, described in the "Working with Objects" section, and functions can be assigned to variables passed as arguments to other functions and used like any other value.

In listing 3.20, the arrow syntax is used to define a function that is assigned a variable called `sumPrices`. Functions are special because they can be invoked, but being able to treat functions as values allows complex functionality to be expressed concisely, although it is easy to create code that can be difficult to read. There are more examples of arrow functions and using functions as values throughout the book.

3.4   *Working with arrays*

JavaScript arrays follow the approach taken by most programming languages, except they are dynamically resized and can contain any combination of values and, therefore, any combination of types. Listing 3.21 shows how an array is defined and used.

> Listing 3.21   Defining and using an array in the index.js file in the primer folder

```
let names = ["Hat", "Boots", "Gloves"];
let prices = [];

prices.push(100);
prices.push("100");
prices.push(50.25);

console.log(`First Item: ${names[0]}: ${prices[0]}`);

let sumPrices = (...numbers) => numbers.reduce((total, val) =>
    total + (Number.isNaN(Number(val)) ? 0 : Number(val)));

let totalPrice = sumPrices(...prices);
console.log(`Total: ${totalPrice} ${typeof totalPrice}`);
```

The size of an array is not specified when it is created, and capacity will be allocated automatically as items are added or removed. JavaScript arrays are zero-based and are defined using square brackets, optionally with the initial contents separated by commas. The `names` array in the example is created with three `string` values. The `prices` array is created empty, and the `push` method is used to append items to the end of the array. The listing produces the following output:

```
First Item: Hat: 100
Total: 250.25 number
```

Elements in the array can be read or set using square brackets or processed using the methods described in table 3.2.

Table 3.2 Useful array methods

Method	Description
`concat(otherArray)`	This method returns a new array that concatenates the array on which it has been called with the array specified as the argument. Multiple arrays can be specified.
`join(separator)`	This method joins all the elements in the array to form a string. The argument specifies the character used to delimit the items.
`pop()`	This method removes and returns the last item in the array.
`shift()`	This method removes and returns the first element in the array.
`push(item)`	This method appends the specified item to the end of the array.
`unshift(item)`	This method inserts a new item at the start of the array.
`reverse()`	This method returns a new array that contains the items in reverse order.
`slice(start,end)`	This method returns a section of the array.
`sort()`	This method sorts the array. An optional comparison function can be used to perform custom comparisons. Alphabetic sorting is performed if no comparison function is defined.
`splice(index, count)`	This method removes `count` items from the array, starting at the specified `index`. The removed items are returned as the result of the method.
`every(test)`	This method calls the `test` function for each item in the array and returns `true` if the function returns `true` for all of them and `false` otherwise.
`some(test)`	This method returns `true` if calling the `test` function for each item in the array returns `true` at least once.
`filter(test)`	This method returns a new array containing the items for which the `test` function returns `true`.
`find(test)`	This method returns the first item in the array for which the `test` function returns `true`.
`findIndex(test)`	This method returns the index of the first item in the array for which the `test` function returns `true`.
`forEach(callback)`	This method invokes the `callback` function for each item in the array, as described in the previous section.
`includes(value)`	This method returns `true` if the array contains the specified value.
`map(callback)`	This method returns a new array containing the result of invoking the `callback` function for every item in the array.
`reduce(callback)`	This method returns the accumulated value produced by invoking the callback function for every item in the array.

3.4.1 *Using the spread operator on arrays*

The spread operator can be used to expand the contents of an array so that its elements can be used as arguments to a function. The spread operator is three periods (`...`) and is used in listing 3.21 to pass the contents of an array to the `sumPrices` function.

```
...
let totalPrice = sumPrices(...prices);
...
```

The operator is used before the array name. The spread operator can also be used to expand the contents of an array for easy concatenation, as shown in listing 3.22.

Listing 3.22   Using the spread operator in the index.js file in the primer folder

```
let names = ["Hat", "Boots", "Gloves"];
let prices = [];

prices.push(100);
prices.push("100");
prices.push(50.25);

console.log(`First Item: ${names[0]}: ${prices[0]}`);

let sumPrices = (...numbers) => numbers.reduce((total, val) =>
    total + (Number.isNaN(Number(val)) ? 0 : Number(val)));

let totalPrice = sumPrices(...prices);
console.log(`Total: ${totalPrice} ${typeof totalPrice}`);

let combinedArray = [...names, ...prices];
combinedArray.forEach(element =>
    console.log(`Combined Array Element: ${element}`));
```

The spread operator is used to create an array that contains the elements from the names and prices arrays. The code in listing 3.22 produces the following output:

```
First Item: Hat: 100
Total: 250.25 number
Combined Array Element: Hat
Combined Array Element: Boots
Combined Array Element: Gloves
Combined Array Element: 100
Combined Array Element: 100
Combined Array Element: 50.25
```

3.4.2   *Destructuring arrays*

Values from arrays can be unpacked using a destructuring assignment, which assigns selected values to variables, as shown in listing 3.23.

Listing 3.23   Destructuring an array in the index.js file in the primer folder

```
let names = ["Hat", "Boots", "Gloves"];

let [one, two] = names;
console.log(`One: ${one}, Two: ${two}`);
```

The left side of the expression is used to specify the variables to which values will be assigned. In this example, the first value in the names array will be assigned to a variable named one, and the second value will be assigned to a variable named two. The number of variables doesn't have to match the number of elements in the array: any elements for which there are no variables in the destructuring assignment are ignored, and any variables in the destructuring assignment for which there is no corresponding array element will be `undefined`. The code in listing 3.23 produces the following output:

```
One: Hat, Two: Boots
```

IGNORING ELEMENTS WHEN DESTRUCTURING AN ARRAY

You can ignore elements by not specifying a name in the assignment, as shown in listing 3.24.

> **Listing 3.24 Ignoring elements in the index.js file in the primer folder**

```
let names = ["Hat", "Boots", "Gloves"];

let [, , three] = names;
console.log(`Three: ${three}`);
```

No name is specified in the first two positions in the assignment, which means the first two elements in the array are ignored. The third element is assigned to the variable named `three`, and the code produces the following output:

```
Three: Gloves
```

ASSIGNING REMAINING ELEMENTS TO AN ARRAY

The last variable name in a destructuring assignment can be prefixed with three periods (. . .), known as the *rest expression* or *rest pattern*, which assigns any remaining elements to an array, as shown in listing 3.25. (The rest expression is often referred to as the *spread operator* for consistency since both are three periods and behave in similar ways.)

> **Listing 3.25 Assigning remaining elements in the index.js file in the primer folder**

```
let names = ["Hat", "Boots", "Gloves"];

let [, , three] = names;
console.log(`Three: ${three}`);

let prices = [100, 120, 50.25];
let [, ...highest] = prices.sort((a, b) => a - b);
highest.forEach(price => console.log(`High price: ${price}`));
```

The `prices` array is sorted, the first element is discarded, and the remaining elements are assigned to an array named `highest`, which is enumerated so that the values can be written to the console, producing the following output:

```
Three: Gloves
High price: 100
High price: 120
```

3.5   *Working with objects*

JavaScript objects are collections of properties, each of which has a name and a value. The simplest way to define an object is to use the literal syntax, as shown in listing 3.26.

Listing 3.26   Creating an object in the index.js file in the primer folder

```
let hat = {
    name: "Hat",
    price: 100
};

let boots = {
    name: "Boots",
    price: "100"
}

let sumPrices = (...numbers) => numbers.reduce((total, val) =>
    total + (Number.isNaN(Number(val)) ? 0 : Number(val)));

let totalPrice = sumPrices(hat.price, boots.price);
console.log(`Total: ${totalPrice} ${typeof totalPrice}`);
```

The literal syntax uses braces to contain a list of property names and values. Names are separated from their values with colons and from other properties with commas. Objects can be assigned to variables, used as arguments to functions, and stored in arrays. Two objects are defined in listing 3.26 and assigned to variables named `hat` and `boots`. The properties defined by the object can be accessed through the variable name, as shown in this statement, which gets the values of the `price` properties defined by both objects:

```
...
let totalPrice = sumPrices(hat.price, boots.price);
...
```

The code in listing 3.26 produces the following output:

```
Total: 200 number
```

3.5.1   *Adding, changing, and deleting object properties*

Like the rest of JavaScript, objects are dynamic. Properties can be added and removed, and values of any type can be assigned to properties, as shown in listing 3.27.

Listing 3.27   Manipulating an object in the index.js file in the primer folder

```
let hat = {
    name: "Hat",
    price: 100
};

let boots = {
    name: "Boots",
    price: "100"
}
```

```
let gloves = {
    productName: "Gloves",
    price: "40"
}

gloves.name = gloves.productName;
delete gloves.productName;
gloves.price = 20;

let sumPrices = (...numbers) => numbers.reduce((total, val) =>
    total + (Number.isNaN(Number(val)) ? 0 : Number(val)));

let totalPrice = sumPrices(hat.price, boots.price, gloves.price);
console.log(`Total: ${totalPrice} ${typeof totalPrice}`);
```

The `gloves` object is created with `productName` and `price` properties. The statements that follow create a `name` property, use the `delete` keyword to remove a property, and assign a `number` value to the `price` property, replacing the previous `string` value. The code in listing 3.27 produces the following output:

```
Total: 220 number
```

GUARDING AGAINST UNDEFINED OBJECTS AND PROPERTIES

Care is required when using objects because they may not have the shape (the term used for the combination of properties and values) that you expect or that was originally used when the object was created.

Because the shape of an object can change, setting or getting the value of a property that has not been defined is not an error. If you set a nonexistent property, then it will be added to the object and assigned the specified value. If you read a nonexistent property, then you will receive `undefined`. One useful way to ensure that code always has values to work with is to rely on the type coercion feature and the nullish or logical OR operators, as shown in listing 3.28.

Listing 3.28 Guarding against undefined values in the index.js file in the primer folder

```
let hat = {
    name: "Hat",
    price: 100
};

let boots = {
    name: "Boots",
    price: "100"
}

let gloves = {
    productName: "Gloves",
    price: "40"
}

gloves.name = gloves.productName;
delete gloves.productName;
gloves.price = 20;
```

```
let propertyCheck = hat.price ?? 0;
let objectAndPropertyCheck = (hat ?? {}).price ?? 0;
console.log(`Checks: ${propertyCheck}, ${objectAndPropertyCheck}`);
```

The code can be difficult to read, but the `??` operator will coerce `undefined` and `null` values to `false` and other values to `true`. The checks can be used to provide a fallback for an individual property, for an object, or a combination of both.

The first check in listing 3.28 assumes the `hat` variable has been assigned a value but checks to make sure `hat.price` is defined and has been assigned a value. The second statement is more cautious—but harder to read—and checks that a value has been assigned to `hat` before also checking the `price` property. The code in listing 3.28 produces the following output:

```
Checks: 100, 100
```

The second check in listing 3.28 can be simplified using optional chaining, as shown in listing 3.29.

Listing 3.29   Using optional chaining in the index.js file in the primer folder

```
let hat = {
    name: "Hat",
    price: 100
};

let boots = {
    name: "Boots",
    price: "100"
}

let gloves = {
    productName: "Gloves",
    price: "40"
}

gloves.name = gloves.productName;
delete gloves.productName;
gloves.price = 20;

let propertyCheck = hat.price ?? 0;
let objectAndPropertyCheck = hat?.price ?? 0;
console.log(`Checks: ${propertyCheck}, ${objectAndPropertyCheck}`);
```

The optional changing operator (the `?` character) will stop evaluating an expression if the value it is applied to is `null` or `undefined`. In the listing, I have applied the operator to `hat`, which means that the expression won't try to read the value of the price property if `hat` is `undefined` or `null`. The result is that the fallback value will be used if `hat` or `hat.price` is `undefined` or `null`.

3.5.2   *Using the spread and rest operators on objects*

The spread operator can be used to expand the properties and values defined by an object, which makes it easy to create one object based on the properties defined by another, as shown in listing 3.30.

```
let hat = {
    name: "Hat",
    price: 100
};

let boots = {
    name: "Boots",
    price: "100"
}

let otherHat = { ...hat };
console.log(`Spread: ${otherHat.name}, ${otherHat.price}`);
```

The spread operator is used to include the properties of the `hat` object as part of the object literal syntax. The use of the spread operator in listing 3.30 has the effect of copying the properties from the `hat` object to the new `otherHat` object. The code in listing 3.30 produces the following output:

```
Spread: Hat, 100
```

The spread operator can also be combined with other properties to add, replace, or absorb properties from the source object, as shown in listing 3.31.

```
let hat = {
    name: "Hat",
    price: 100
};

let boots = {
    name: "Boots",
    price: "100"
}

let additionalProperties = { ...hat, discounted: true};
console.log(`Additional: ${JSON.stringify(additionalProperties)}`);

let replacedProperties = { ...hat, price: 10};
console.log(`Replaced: ${JSON.stringify(replacedProperties)}`);

let { price , ...someProperties } = hat;
console.log(`Selected: ${JSON.stringify(someProperties)}`);
```

The property names and values expanded by the spread operator are treated as though they had been expressed individually in the object literal syntax, which means the shape of an object can be altered by mixing the spread operator with other properties. This statement, for example:

```
...
let additionalProperties = { ...hat, discounted: true};
...
```

will be expanded so that the properties defined by the `hat` object will be combined with the `discounted` property, equivalent to this statement:

```
let additionalProperties = { name: "Hat", price: 100, discounted: true};
```

If a property name is used twice in the object literal syntax, then the second value is the one that will be used. This feature can be used to change the value of a property that is obtained through the spread operator and means that this statement:

```
...
let replacedProperties = { ...hat, price: 10};
...
```

will be expanded so that it is equivalent to this statement:

```
let replacedProperties = { name: "Hat", price: 100, price: 10};
```

The effect is an object that has the `name` property and value from the `hat` object but with a `price` property whose value is 10. The rest operator (which is the same three periods as the spread operator) can be used to select properties or to exclude them when used with the object literal syntax. This statement defines variables named `price` and `someProperties`:

```
...
let { price , ...someProperties } = hat;
...
```

The properties defined by the `hat` object are decomposed. The `hat.price` property is assigned to the new price property, and all the other properties are assigned to the `someProperties` object.

The built-in `JSON.stringify` method creates a string representation of an object using the JSON data format. It is useful only for representing simple objects; it doesn't usefully deal with functions, for example, but it helps understand how objects are composed, and the code in listing 3.31 produces the following output:

```
Additional: {"name":"Hat","price":100,"discounted":true}
Replaced: {"name":"Hat","price":10}
Selected: {"name":"Hat"}
```

3.5.3   Defining getters and setters

Getters and setters are functions that are invoked when a property value is read or assigned, as shown in listing 3.32.

> **Listing 3.32   Using getters and setters in the index.js file in the primer folder**

```
let hat = {
    name: "Hat",
    _price: 100,
    priceIncTax: 100 * 1.2,

    set price(newPrice) {
        this._price = newPrice;
        this.priceIncTax = this._price * 1.2;
    },

    get price() {
        return this._price;
    }
```

```
};

let boots = {
    name: "Boots",
    price: "100",

    get priceIncTax() {
        return Number(this.price) * 1.2;
    }
}

console.log(`Hat: ${hat.price}, ${hat.priceIncTax}`);
hat.price = 120;
console.log(`Hat: ${hat.price}, ${hat.priceIncTax}`);

console.log(`Boots: ${boots.price}, ${boots.priceIncTax}`);
boots.price = "120";
console.log(`Boots: ${boots.price}, ${boots.priceIncTax}`);
```

The example introduces a `priceIncTax` property whose value is updated automatically when the `price` property is set. The `hat` object does this by using a getter and setter for the `price` property to update a backing property named `_price`. When a new value is assigned to the `price` property, the setter updates the backing property and the `priceIncTax` property. When the value of the `price` property is read, the getter responds with the value of the `_price` property. (A backing property is required because getters and setters are treated as properties and cannot have the same name as any of the conventional properties defined by the object.)

> ## Understanding JavaScript private properties
>
> JavaScript doesn't have any built-in support for private properties, except in classes (which I describe in chapter 4). By private, I mean a property that can be accessed only by an object's methods, getters, and setters. There are techniques to achieve a similar effect outside of classes, but they are complex, and so the most common approach is to use a naming convention to denote properties not intended for public use. This doesn't prevent access to these properties, but it does at least make it obvious that doing so is undesirable. A widely used naming convention is to prefix the property name with an underscore, as demonstrated with the `_price` property in listing 3.32. This technique isn't required in TypeScript development, which has its own approach to private properties, as described in chapter 11.

The `boots` object defines the same behavior as the `hat` object but does so by creating a getter that has no corresponding setter, which has the effect of allowing the value to be read but not modified and demonstrates that getters and setters don't have to be used together. The code in listing 3.32 produces the following output:

```
Hat: 100, 120
Hat: 120, 144
Boots: 100, 120
Boots: 120, 144
```

3.5.4 Defining methods

JavaScript can be confusing at first, but digging into the details reveals a consistency that isn't always apparent from casual use. One example is methods, which build on the features described in earlier sections, as shown in listing 3.33.

Listing 3.33   Defining methods in the index.js file in the primer folder

```
let hat = {
    name: "Hat",
    _price: 100,
    priceIncTax: 100 * 1.2,

    set price(newPrice) {
        this._price = newPrice;
        this.priceIncTax = this._price * 1.2;
    },

    get price() {
        return this._price;
    },

    writeDetails: function() {
        console.log(`${this.name}: ${this.price}, ${this.priceIncTax}`);
    }
};

let boots = {
    name: "Boots",
    price: "100",

    get priceIncTax() {
        return Number(this.price) * 1.2;
    }
}

hat.writeDetails();
hat.price = 120;
hat.writeDetails();

console.log(`Boots: ${boots.price}, ${boots.priceIncTax}`);
boots.price = "120";
console.log(`Boots: ${boots.price}, ${boots.priceIncTax}`);
```

A method is a property whose value is a function, which means that all the features and behaviors that functions provide, such as default and rest parameters, can be used for methods. The method in listing 3.33 is defined using the `function` keyword, but there is a more concise syntax available, as shown in listing 3.34.

Listing 3.34   Using the concise methods syntax in the index.js file in the primer folder

```
...
writeDetails() {
    console.log(`${this.name}: ${this.price}, ${this.priceIncTax}`);
}
...
```

The `function` keyword and colon that separates a property name from its value are omitted, allowing methods to be defined in a style that many developers find natural. The following output is produced by the listings in this section:

```
Hat: 100, 120
Hat: 120, 144
Boots: 100, 120
Boots: 120, 144
```

3.6 Understanding the this keyword

The `this` keyword can be confusing to even experienced JavaScript programmers. In other programming languages, `this` is used to refer to the current instance of an object created from a class. In JavaScript, the `this` keyword can often appear to work the same way—right up until the moment a change breaks the application and `undefined` values start to appear.

To demonstrate, I used the fat arrow syntax to redefine the method on the `hat` object, as shown in listing 3.35.

Listing 3.35   Using the fat arrow syntax in the index.js file in the primer folder

```javascript
let hat = {
    name: "Hat",
    _price: 100,
    priceIncTax: 100 * 1.2,

    set price(newPrice) {
        this._price = newPrice;
        this.priceIncTax = this._price * 1.2;
    },

    get price() {
        return this._price;
    },

    writeDetails: () =>
        console.log(`${this.name}: ${this.price}, ${this.priceIncTax}`)
};

let boots = {
    name: "Boots",
    price: "100",

    get priceIncTax() {
        return Number(this.price) * 1.2;
    }
}

hat.writeDetails();
hat.price = 120;
hat.writeDetails();

console.log(`Boots: ${boots.price}, ${boots.priceIncTax}`);
```

```
boots.price = "120";
console.log(`Boots: ${boots.price}, ${boots.priceIncTax}`);
```

The method uses the same `console.log` statement as listing 3.34, but when the change is saved and the code is executed, the output shows `undefined` values, like this:

undefined: undefined, undefined
undefined: undefined, undefined
```
Boots: 100, 120
Boots: 120, 144
```

Understanding why this happens and being able to fix the problem requires taking a step back and examining what the `this` keyword really does in JavaScript.

3.6.1   *Understanding the this keyword in stand-alone functions*

The `this` keyword can be used in any function, even when that function isn't used as a method, as shown in listing 3.36.

> **Listing 3.36   Invoking a function in the index.js file in the primer folder**

```
function writeMessage(message) {
    console.log(`${this.greeting}, ${message}`);
}

greeting = "Hello";

writeMessage("It is sunny today");
```

The `writeMessage` function reads a property named `greeting` from `this` in one of the expressions in the template string passed to the `console.log` method. The `this` keyword doesn't appear again in the listing, but when the code is saved and executed, the following output is produced:

```
Hello, It is sunny today
```

JavaScript defines a global object, which can be assigned values that are available throughout an application. The global object is used to provide access to the essential features in the execution environment, such as the `document` object in browsers that allows interaction with the Document Object Model API.

Values assigned names without using the `let`, `const`, or `var` keyword are assigned to the global object. The statement that assigns the string value `Hello` creates a variable in the global scope. When the function is executed, `this` is assigned the global object, so reading `this.greeting` returns the `string` value `Hello`, explaining the output produced by the application.

The standard way to invoke a function is to use parentheses that contain arguments, but in JavaScript, this is a convenience syntax that is translated into the statement shown in listing 3.37.

> **Listing 3.37   Invoking a function in the index.js file in the primer folder**

```
function writeMessage(message) {
    console.log(`${this.greeting}, ${message}`);
}
```

```
greeting = "Hello";

writeMessage("It is sunny today");
writeMessage.call(global, "It is sunny today");
```

As explained earlier, functions are objects, which means they define methods, including the `call` method. It is this method that is used to invoke a function behind the scenes. The first argument to the `call` method is the value for `this`, which is set to the global object. This is the reason that `this` can be used in any function and why it returns the global object by default.

The new statement in listing 3.37 uses the `call` method directly and sets the `this` value to the global object, with the same result as the conventional function call before it, which can be seen in the following output produced by the code when executed:

```
Hello, It is sunny today
Hello, It is sunny today
```

The name of the global object changes based on the execution environment. In code executed by Node.js, `global` is used, but `window` or `self` may be required in browsers. At the time of writing, there is a proposal to standardize the name `global`, but it has yet to be adopted universally.

> ### Understanding the effect of strict mode
>
> JavaScript supports strict mode, which disables or restricts features that have historically caused poor-quality software or that prevent the runtime from executing code efficiently. When strict mode is enabled, the default value for `this` is `undefined` to prevent accidental use of the global object, and values with global scope must be explicitly defined as properties on the global object. See https://developer.mozilla.org/en-US/docs/Web/JavaScript/Reference/Strict_mode for details. The TypeScript compiler provides a feature for automatically enabling strict mode in the JavaScript code it generates, as described in chapter 5.

3.6.2 Understanding this in methods

When a function is invoked as an object's method, `this` is set to the object, as shown in listing 3.38.

Listing 3.38   **Invoking a function as a method in the index.js file in the primer folder**

```javascript
let myObject = {
    greeting: "Hi, there",

    writeMessage(message) {
        console.log(`${this.greeting}, ${message}`);
    }
}

greeting = "Hello";

myObject.writeMessage("It is sunny today");
```

When the function is invoked via the object, the statement that invokes the function is equivalent to using the `call` method with the object as the first argument, like this:

```
...
myObject.writeMessage.call(myObject, "It is sunny today");
...
```

Care is required because `this` is set differently if the function is accessed outside of its object, which can happen if the function is assigned to a variable, as shown in listing 3.39.

Listing 3.39   Invoking a function in the index.js file in the primer folder

```
let myObject = {
    greeting: "Hi, there",

    writeMessage(message) {
        console.log(`${this.greeting}, ${message}`);
    }
}

greeting = "Hello";

myObject.writeMessage("It is sunny today");

let myFunction = myObject.writeMessage;
myFunction("It is sunny today");
```

Functions can be used like any other value, including assigning them to variables outside of the object in which they were defined, as shown in the listing. If the function is invoked through the variable, then `this` will be set to the global object. This often causes problems when functions are used as arguments to other methods or as callbacks to handle events, and the effect is that the same function will behave differently based on how it is invoked, as shown in the output produced by the code in listing 3.39:

```
Hi, there, It is sunny today
Hello, It is sunny today
```

3.6.3   Changing the behavior of the this keyword

One way to control the `this` value is to invoke functions using the `call` method, but this is awkward and must be done every time the function is invoked. A more reliable method is to use the function's `bind` method, which is used to set the value for `this` regardless of how the function is invoked, as shown in listing 3.40.

Listing 3.40   Setting the this value in the index.js file in the primer folder

```
let myObject = {
    greeting: "Hi, there",

    writeMessage(message) {
        console.log(`${this.greeting}, ${message}`);
    }
}
```

```
myObject.writeMessage = myObject.writeMessage.bind(myObject);

greeting = "Hello";

myObject.writeMessage("It is sunny today");

let myFunction = myObject.writeMessage;
myFunction("It is sunny today");
```

The `bind` method returns a new function that will have a persistent value for `this` when it is invoked. The function returned by the `bind` method is used to replace the original method, ensuring consistency when the `writeMessage` method is invoked. Using `bind` is awkward because the reference to the object isn't available until after it has been created, which leads to a two-step process of creating the object and then calling `bind` to replace each of the methods for which a consistent `this` value is required. The code in listing 3.40 produces the following output:

```
Hi, there, It is sunny today
Hi, there, It is sunny today
```

The value of `this` is always set to `myObject`, even when the `writeMessage` function is invoked as a stand-alone function.

3.6.4 *Understanding this in arrow functions*

To add to the complexity of `this`, arrow functions don't work in the same way as regular functions. Arrow functions don't have their own `this` value and inherit the closest value of `this` they can find when they are executed. To demonstrate how this works, listing 3.41 adds an arrow function to the example.

> Listing 3.41   Using an arrow function in the index.js file in the primer folder

```
let myObject = {
    greeting: "Hi, there",

    getWriter() {
        return (message) => console.log(`${this.greeting}, ${message}`);
    }
}

greeting = "Hello";

let writer = myObject.getWriter();
writer("It is raining today");

let standAlone = myObject.getWriter;
let standAloneWriter = standAlone();
standAloneWriter("It is sunny today");
```

In listing 3.41, the `getWriter` function is a regular function that returns an arrow function as its result. When the arrow function returned by `getWriter` is invoked, it works its way up its scope until it locates a value for `this`. As a consequence, the way that the `getWriter` function is invoked determines the value of `this` for the arrow function. Here are the first two statements that invoke the functions:

```
...
let writer = myObject.getWriter();
writer("It is raining today");
...
```

These two statements can be combined as follows:

```
...
myObject.getWriter()("It is raining today");
...
```

The combined statement is a little harder to read, but it helps emphasize that the value of `this` is based on how a function is invoked. The `getWriter` method is invoked through `myObject` and means that the value of `this` will be set to `myObject`. When the arrow function is invoked, it finds a value of `this` from the `getWriter` function. The result is that when the `getWriter` method is invoked through `myObject`, the value of `this` in the arrow function will be `myObject`, and the `this.greeting` expression in the template string will be `Hi, there`.

The statements in the second set treat `getWriter` as a stand-alone function, so `this` will be set to the global object. When the arrow function is invoked, the `this.greeting` expression will be `Hello`. The code in listing 3.41 produces the following output, confirming the `this` value in each case:

```
Hi, there, It is raining today
Hello, It is sunny today
```

3.6.5   *Returning to the original problem*

I started this section by redefining a function in the arrow syntax and showing that it behaved differently, producing `undefined` in its output. Here is the object and its function:

```
...
let hat = {
    name: "Hat",
    _price: 100,
    priceIncTax: 100 * 1.2,

    set price(newPrice) {
        this._price = newPrice;
        this.priceIncTax = this._price * 1.2;
    },

    get price() {
        return this._price;
    },

    writeDetails: () =>
        console.log(`${this.name}: ${this.price}, ${this.priceIncTax}`)
};
...
```

The behavior changed because arrow functions don't have their own `this` value, and the arrow function isn't enclosed by a regular function that can provide one. To resolve the issue and be sure that the results will be consistent, I must return to a regular function and use the `bind` method to fix the `this` value, as shown in listing 3.42.

Listing 3.42 Resolving the function problem in the index.js file in the primer folder

```javascript
let hat = {
    name: "Hat",
    _price: 100,
    priceIncTax: 100 * 1.2,

    set price(newPrice) {
        this._price = newPrice;
        this.priceIncTax = this._price * 1.2;
    },

    get price() {
        return this._price;
    },

    writeDetails() {
        console.log(`${this.name}: ${this.price}, ${this.priceIncTax}`);
    }
};

let boots = {
    name: "Boots",
    price: "100",

    get priceIncTax() {
        return Number(this.price) * 1.2;
    }
}

hat.writeDetails = hat.writeDetails.bind(hat);
hat.writeDetails();
hat.price = 120;
hat.writeDetails();

console.log(`Boots: ${boots.price}, ${boots.priceIncTax}`);
boots.price = "120";
console.log(`Boots: ${boots.price}, ${boots.priceIncTax}`);
```

With these changes, the value of `this` for the `writeDetails` method will be its enclosing object, regardless of how it is invoked, producing the following output:

```
Hat: 100, 120
Hat: 120, 144
Boots: 100, 120
Boots: 120, 144
```

Summary

In this chapter, I introduced the basic features of the JavaScript type system. These are features that often confuse because they work differently from those in other programming languages. Understanding these features make working with TypeScript easier because they provide insight into the problems that TypeScript solves. JavaScript has a set of built-in data types that are used to represent all values.

- JavaScript will attempt to convert data types when they are combined with an operator.
- JavaScript functions can be defined with a literal syntax that declares parameters and a function body or using the fat arrow/lambda function syntax.
- JavaScript functions can accept a variable number of arguments, which can be captured using a rest parameter.
- JavaScript functions do not formally declare results and can return any result type.
- JavaScript arrays are variable-length and can accept values of any type.
- JavaScript objects are a collection of properties and values and can be defined using a literal syntax.
- JavaScript objects can be altered to add, change, or remove properties.
- JavaScript objects can be defined with methods, which are functions assigned to a property.
- The `this` keyword refers to different objects depending on how functions are invoked.

In the next chapter, I describe more of the JavaScript type features that are useful for understanding TypeScript.

JavaScript primer, part 2

This chapter covers

- Working with JavaScript object prototypes
- Defining JavaScript classes
- Generating and consuming sequences
- Using JavaScript collections
- Creating and using JavaScript modules

In this chapter, I continue describing the JavaScript features that are important to TypeScript development. I focus on the JavaScript support for objects, the different ways they can be defined, and how they relate to JavaScript classes. I also demonstrate the features for handling sequences of values, the JavaScript collections, and the modules feature, which allows a project to be split up into multiple JavaScript files.

4.1 Preparing for this chapter

In this chapter, I continue to use the `primer` project created in chapter 3. To prepare for this chapter, replace the contents of the `index.js` file in the `primer` folder with the code shown in listing 4.1.

> **TIP** You can download the example project for this chapter—and for all the other chapters in this book—from https://github.com/manningbooks/essential-typescript-5.

Listing 4.1   Replacing the code in the index.js file in the primer folder

```
let hat = {
    name: "Hat",
    price: 100,
    getPriceIncTax() {
        return Number(this.price) * 1.2;
    }
};

console.log(`Hat: ${hat.price}, ${hat.getPriceIncTax() }`);
```

Open a new command prompt, navigate to the `primer` folder, and run the command shown in listing 4.2 to start monitoring and executing the JavaScript file.

Listing 4.2   Starting the development tools

```
npx nodemon index.js
```

The `nodemon` package will execute the contents of the `index.js` file and produce the following output:

```
[nodemon] 2.0.20
[nodemon] to restart at any time, enter `rs`
[nodemon] watching: *.*
[nodemon] starting `node index.js`
Hat: 100, 120
[nodemon] clean exit - waiting for changes before restart
```

4.2   *Understanding JavaScript object inheritance*

JavaScript objects have a link to another object, known as the *prototype*, from which they inherit properties and methods. Since prototypes are objects and have a prototype, objects form an inheritance chain that allows complex features to be defined once and used consistently.

When an object is created using the literal syntax, such as the `hat` object in listing 4.1, its prototype is `Object`, which is a built-in object provided by JavaScript. `Object` provides basic features that all objects inherit, including a method named `toString` that returns a string representation of an object, as shown in listing 4.3.

Listing 4.3   Using an object in the index.js file in the primer folder

```
let hat = {
    name: "Hat",
    price: 100,
    getPriceIncTax() {
        return Number(this.price) * 1.2;
    }
};

console.log(`Hat: ${hat.price}, ${hat.getPriceIncTax() }`);
console.log(`toString: ${hat.toString()}`);
```

The first `console.log` statement receives a template string that includes the `price` property, which is one of the `hat` object's properties. The new statement invokes the `toString` method. None of the `hat` object's properties is named `toString`, so the JavaScript runtime turns to the `hat` object's prototype, which is `Object` and which does provide a property named `toString`, producing the following output:

```
Hat: 100, 120
toString: [object Object]
```

The result produced by the `toString` method isn't especially useful, but it does illustrate the relationship between the `hat` object and its prototype, as shown in figure 4.1.

Figure 4.1   An object and its prototype

4.2.1   Inspecting and modifying an object's prototype

`Object` is the prototype for most objects, but it also provides methods that are used directly, rather than through inheritance, and that can be used to get information about prototypes. Table 4.1 describes the most useful of these methods.

Table 4.1   Useful object methods

Name	Description
`getPrototypeOf`	This method returns an object's prototype.
`setPrototypeOf`	This method changes the prototype of an object.
`getOwnPropertyNames`	This method returns the names of an object's properties.

Listing 4.4 uses the `getPrototypeOf` method to confirm that two objects created using the literal syntax share the same prototype.

Listing 4.4   Comparing prototypes in the index.js file in the primer folder

```javascript
let hat = {
    name: "Hat",
    price: 100,
    getPriceIncTax() {
        return Number(this.price) * 1.2;
    }
};

let boots = {
    name: "Boots",
    price: 100,
    getPriceIncTax() {
        return Number(this.price) * 1.2;
```

```
        }
    }

let hatPrototype = Object.getPrototypeOf(hat);
console.log(`Hat Prototype: ${hatPrototype}`);

let bootsPrototype = Object.getPrototypeOf(boots);
console.log(`Boots Prototype: ${bootsPrototype}`);

console.log(`Common prototype: ${ hatPrototype === bootsPrototype}`);

console.log(`Hat: ${hat.price}, ${hat.getPriceIncTax() }`);
console.log(`toString: ${hat.toString()}`);
```

The listing introduces another object and compares its prototype, producing the following output:

```
Hat Prototype: [object Object]
Boots Prototype: [object Object]
Common prototype: true
Hat: 100, 120
toString: [object Object]
```

The output shows that the hat and boots objects have the same prototype, as illustrated by figure 4.2.

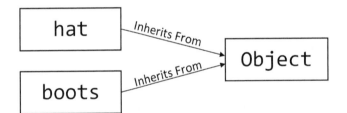

Figure 4.2   Objects and a common prototype

Because prototypes are regular JavaScript objects, new properties can be defined on prototypes, and new values can be assigned to existing properties, as shown in listing 4.5.

Listing 4.5   Changing a prototype property in the index.js file in the primer folder

```
let hat = {
    name: "Hat",
    price: 100,
    getPriceIncTax() {
        return Number(this.price) * 1.2;
    }
};

let boots = {
    name: "Boots",
```

```
        price: 100,
        getPriceIncTax() {
            return Number(this.price) * 1.2;
        }
}

let hatPrototype = Object.getPrototypeOf(hat);
hatPrototype.toString = function() {
    return `toString: Name: ${this.name}, Price: ${this.price}`;
}

console.log(hat.toString());
console.log(boots.toString());
```

Listing 4.5 assigns a new function to the `toString` method through the `hat` object's prototype. Because objects maintain a link to their prototype, the new `toString` method will be used for the `boots` object, too, as shown by the following output:

```
toString: Name: Hat, Price: 100
toString: Name: Boots, Price: 100
```

4.2.2 Creating custom prototypes

Changes to `Object` should be made cautiously because they affect all the other objects in the application. The new `toString` function in listing 4.5 produces more useful output for the `hat` and `boots` objects but assumes that there will be `name` and `price` properties, which won't be the case when `toString` is called on other objects.

A better approach is to create a prototype specifically for those objects that are known to have `name` and `price` properties, which can be done using the `Object` `.setPrototypeOf` method, as shown in listing 4.6.

> Listing 4.6 Using a custom prototype in the index.js file in the primer folder

```
let ProductProto = {
    toString: function() {
        return `toString: Name: ${this.name}, Price: ${this.price}`;
    }
}

let hat = {
    name: "Hat",
    price: 100,
    getPriceIncTax() {
        return Number(this.price) * 1.2;
    }
};

let boots = {
    name: "Boots",
    price: 100,
    getPriceIncTax() {
        return Number(this.price) * 1.2;
    }
}

Object.setPrototypeOf(hat, ProductProto);
```

```
Object.setPrototypeOf(boots, ProductProto);
```

```
console.log(hat.toString());
console.log(boots.toString());
```

Prototypes can be defined just like any other object. In the listing, an object named `ProductProto` that defines a `toString` method is used as the prototype for the `hat` and `boots` objects. The `ProductProto` object is just like any other object, and that means it also has a prototype, which is `Object`, as shown in figure 4.3.

Figure 4.3   A chain of prototypes

The effect is a chain of prototypes that the JavaScript works its way along until it locates a property or method or reaches the end of the chain. The code in listing 4.6 produces the following output:

```
toString: Name: Hat, Price: 100
toString: Name: Boots, Price: 100
```

4.2.3   Using constructor functions

A constructor function is used to create a new object, configure its properties, and assign its prototype, all of which is done in a single step with the `new` keyword. Constructor functions can be used to ensure that objects are created consistently and that the correct prototype is applied, as shown in listing 4.7.

> **Listing 4.7   Using a constructor function in the index.js file in the primer folder**

```
let Product = function(name, price) {
    this.name = name;
    this.price = price;
}

Product.prototype.toString = function() {
    return `toString: Name: ${this.name}, Price: ${this.price}`;
}

let hat = new Product("Hat", 100);
let boots = new Product("Boots", 100);

console.log(hat.toString());
console.log(boots.toString());
```

Constructor functions are invoked with the `new` keyword, followed by the function or its variable name and the arguments that will be used to configure the object, like this:

```
...
let hat = new Product("Hat", 100);
```

...

The JavaScript runtime creates a new object and uses it as the `this` value to invoke the constructor function, providing the argument values as parameters. The constructor function can configure the object's properties using `this`, which is set to the new object.

```
...
let Product = function(name, price) {
    this.name = name;
    this.price = price;
}
...
```

The prototype for the new object is set to the object returned by the `prototype` property of the constructor function. This leads to constructors being defined in two parts—the function itself is used to configure the object's properties, while the object returned by the `prototype` property is used for the properties and methods that should be shared by all the objects the constructor creates. In the listing, a `toString` property is added to the `Product` constructor function prototype and used to define a method:

```
...
Product.prototype.toString = function() {
    return `toString: Name: ${this.name}, Price: ${this.price}`;
}
...
```

The result is the same as the previous example, but using a constructor function can help ensure that objects are created consistently and have their prototypes set correctly.

4.2.4 Chaining constructor functions

Using the `setPrototypeOf` method to create a chain of custom prototypes is easy, but doing the same thing with constructor functions requires a little more work to ensure that objects are configured correctly by the functions and get the right prototypes in the chain. Listing 4.8 introduces a new constructor function and uses it to create a chain with the `Product` constructor.

Listing 4.8 Chaining constructor functions in the index.js file in the primer folder

```
let Product = function(name, price) {
    this.name = name;
    this.price = price;
}

Product.prototype.toString = function() {
    return `toString: Name: ${this.name}, Price: ${this.price}`;
}

let TaxedProduct = function(name, price, taxRate) {
    Product.call(this, name, price);
    this.taxRate = taxRate;
}
Object.setPrototypeOf(TaxedProduct.prototype, Product.prototype);
```

```
TaxedProduct.prototype.getPriceIncTax = function() {
    return Number(this.price) * this.taxRate;
}

TaxedProduct.prototype.toTaxString = function() {
    return `${this.toString()}, Tax: ${this.getPriceIncTax()}`;
}

let hat = new TaxedProduct("Hat", 100, 1.2);
let boots = new Product("Boots", 100);

console.log(hat.toTaxString());
console.log(boots.toString());
```

Two steps must be taken to arrange the constructors and their prototypes in a chain. The first step is to use the `call` method to invoke the next constructor so that new objects are created correctly. In the listing, I want the `TaxedProduct` constructor to build on the `Product` constructor, so I have to use `call` on the `Product` function so that it adds its properties to new objects:

```
...
Product.call(this, name, price);
...
```

The `call` method allows the new object to be passed to the next constructor through the `this` value.

The second step is to link the prototypes together:

```
...
Object.setPrototypeOf(TaxedProduct.prototype, Product.prototype);
...
```

Notice that the arguments to the `setPrototypeOf` method are the objects returned by the constructor function's `prototype` properties and not the functions themselves. Linking the prototypes ensures that the JavaScript runtime will follow the chain when it looks for properties that are not an object's own. Figure 4.4 shows the new set of prototypes.

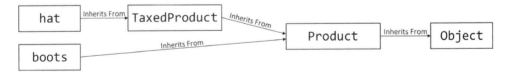

Figure 4.4   A more complex prototype chain

The `TaxedProduct` prototype defines a `toTaxString` method that invokes `toString`, which will be found by the JavaScript runtime on the `Product` prototype, and the code in listing 4.8 produces the following output:

```
toString: Name: Hat, Price: 100, Tax: 120
toString: Name: Boots, Price: 100
```

Accessing overridden prototype methods

A prototype can override a property or method by using the same name as one defined further along the chain. This is also known as *shadowing* in JavaScript, and it takes advantage of the way that the JavaScript runtime follows the chain.

Care is required when building on an overridden method, which must be accessed through the prototype that defines it. The `TaxedProduct` prototype can define a `toString` method that overrides the one defined by the `Product` prototype and can invoke the overridden method by accessing the method directly through the prototype and using `call` to set the `this` value.

```
...
TaxedProduct.prototype.toString = function() {
    let chainResult = Product.prototype.toString.call(this);
    return `${chainResult}, Tax: ${this.getPriceIncTax()}`;
}
...
```

This method gets a result from the `Product` prototype's `toString` method and combines it with additional data in a template string.

4.2.5   Checking prototype types

The `instanceof` operator is used to determine whether a constructor's prototype is part of the chain for a specific object, as shown in listing 4.9.

Listing 4.9   Checking prototypes in the index.js file in the primer folder

```
let Product = function(name, price) {
    this.name = name;
    this.price = price;
}

Product.prototype.toString = function() {
    return `toString: Name: ${this.name}, Price: ${this.price}`;
}

let TaxedProduct = function(name, price, taxRate) {
    Product.call(this, name, price);
    this.taxRate = taxRate;
}
Object.setPrototypeOf(TaxedProduct.prototype, Product.prototype);

TaxedProduct.prototype.getPriceIncTax = function() {
    return Number(this.price) * this.taxRate;
}

TaxedProduct.prototype.toTaxString = function() {
    return `${this.toString()}, Tax: ${this.getPriceIncTax()}`;
}

let hat = new TaxedProduct("Hat", 100, 1.2);
let boots = new Product("Boots", 100);
```

```
console.log(hat.toTaxString());
console.log(boots.toString());
console.log(`hat and TaxedProduct: ${ hat instanceof TaxedProduct}`);
console.log(`hat and Product: ${ hat instanceof Product}`);
console.log(`boots and TaxedProduct: ${ boots instanceof TaxedProduct}`);
console.log(`boots and Product: ${ boots instanceof Product}`);
```

The new statements use `instanceof` to determine whether the prototypes of the `TaxedProduct` and `Product` constructor functions are in the chains of the `hat` and `boots` objects. The code in listing 4.9 produces the following output:

```
toString: Name: Hat, Price: 100, Tax: 120
toString: Name: Boots, Price: 100
hat and TaxedProduct: true
hat and Product: true
boots and TaxedProduct: false
boots and Product: true
```

> **TIP**   Notice that the `instanceof` operator is used with the constructor function. The `Object.isPrototypeOf` method is used directly with prototypes, which can be useful if you are not using constructors.

4.2.6   *Defining static properties and methods*

Properties and methods that are defined on the constructor function are often referred to as *static*, meaning they are accessed through the constructor and not individual objects created by that constructor (as opposed to *instance properties*, which are accessed through an object). The `Object.setPrototypeOf` and `Object.get` `PrototypeOf` methods are good examples of `static` methods. Listing 4.10 simplifies the example for brevity and introduces a static method.

> **Listing 4.10   Defining a static method index.js file in the primer folder**

```
let Product = function(name, price) {
    this.name = name;
    this.price = price;
}

Product.prototype.toString = function() {
    return `toString: Name: ${this.name}, Price: ${this.price}`;
}

Product.process = (...products) =>
    products.forEach(p => console.log(p.toString()));

Product.process(new Product("Hat", 100, 1.2), new Product("Boots", 100));
```

The static `process` method is defined by adding a new property to the `Product` function object and assigning it a function. Remember that JavaScript functions are objects, and properties can be freely added and removed from objects. The `process` method defines a rest parameter and uses the `forEach` method to invoke the `toString` method for each object it receives and writes the result to the console. The code in listing 4.10 produces the following output:

```
toString: Name: Hat, Price: 100
toString: Name: Boots, Price: 100
```

4.2.7 Using JavaScript classes

JavaScript classes were added to the language to ease the transition from other popular programming languages. Behind the scenes, JavaScript classes are implemented using prototypes, which means that JavaScript classes have some differences from those in languages such as C# and Java. In listing 4.11, I removed the constructors and prototypes and introduced a `Product` class.

> **Listing 4.11 Defining a class in the index.js file in the primer folder**

```javascript
class Product {
    constructor(name, price) {
        this.name = name;
        this.price = price;
    }

    toString() {
        return `toString: Name: ${this.name}, Price: ${this.price}`;
    }
}

let hat = new Product("Hat", 100);
let boots = new Product("Boots", 100);

console.log(hat.toString());
console.log(boots.toString());
```

Classes are defined with the `class` keyword, followed by a name for the class. The class syntax may appear more familiar, but classes are translated into the underlying JavaScript prototype system described in the previous section.

Objects are created from classes using the `new` keyword. The JavaScript runtime creates a new object and invokes the class `constructor` function, which receives the new object through the `this` value and which is responsible for defining the object's properties. Methods defined by classes are added to the prototype assigned to objects created using the class. The code in listing 4.11 produces the following output:

```
toString: Name: Hat, Price: 100
toString: Name: Boots, Price: 100
```

USING INHERITANCE IN CLASSES

Classes can inherit features using the `extends` keyword and invoke the superclass constructor and methods using the `super` keyword, as shown in listing 4.12.

> **Listing 4.12 Extending a class in the index.js file in the primer folder**

```javascript
class Product {
    constructor(name, price) {
        this.name = name;
        this.price = price;
    }
}
```

```
    toString() {
        return `toString: Name: ${this.name}, Price: ${this.price}`;
    }
}

class TaxedProduct extends Product {

    constructor(name, price, taxRate = 1.2) {
        super(name, price);
        this.taxRate = taxRate;
    }

    getPriceIncTax() {
        return Number(this.price) * this.taxRate;
    }

    toString() {
        let chainResult = super.toString();
        return `${chainResult}, Tax: ${this.getPriceIncTax()}`;
    }
}

let hat = new TaxedProduct("Hat", 100);
let boots = new TaxedProduct("Boots", 100, 1.3);

console.log(hat.toString());
console.log(boots.toString());
```

A class declares its superclass using the `extends` keyword. In the listing, the `Taxed-Product` class uses the `extend` keyword to inherit from the `Product` class. The `super` keyword is used in the constructor to invoke the superclass constructor, which is equivalent to chaining constructor functions.

```
...
constructor(name, price, taxRate = 1.2) {
    super(name, price);
    this.taxRate = taxRate;
}
...
```

The `super` keyword must be used before the `this` keyword and is generally used in the first statement in the constructor. The `super` keyword can also be used to access superclass properties and methods, like this:

```
...
toString() {
    let chainResult = super.toString();
    return `${chainResult}, Tax: ${this.getPriceIncTax()}`;
}
...
```

The `toString` method defined by the `TaxedProduct` class invoked the superclass's `toString` method, which is equivalent to overriding prototype methods. The code in listing 4.12 produces the following output:

```
toString: Name: Hat, Price: 100, Tax: 120
toString: Name: Boots, Price: 100, Tax: 130
```

DEFINING STATIC METHODS

The `static` keyword is applied to create static methods that are accessed through the class, rather than the object it creates, as shown in listing 4.13.

> **Listing 4.13 Defining a static method in the index.js file in the primer folder**

```
class Product {
    constructor(name, price) {
        this.name = name;
        this.price = price;
    }

    toString() {
        return `toString: Name: ${this.name}, Price: ${this.price}`;
    }
}

class TaxedProduct extends Product {

    constructor(name, price, taxRate = 1.2) {
        super(name, price);
        this.taxRate = taxRate;
    }

    getPriceIncTax() {
        return Number(this.price) * this.taxRate;
    }

    toString() {
        let chainResult = super.toString();
        return `${chainResult}, Tax: ${this.getPriceIncTax()}`;
    }

    static process(...products) {
        products.forEach(p => console.log(p.toString()));
    }
}

TaxedProduct.process(new TaxedProduct("Hat", 100, 1.2),
    new TaxedProduct("Boots", 100));
```

The `static` keyword is used on the `process` method defined by the `TaxedProduct` class and is accessed as `TaxedProduct.process`. The code in listing 4.13 produces the following output:

```
toString: Name: Hat, Price: 100, Tax: 120
toString: Name: Boots, Price: 100, Tax: 120
```

CREATING PRIVATE FIELDS, PROPERTIES, AND METHODS

The most recent version of JavaScript introduced support for private members in classes, which prevents them from being used outside of the class that defines them. Listing 4.14 demonstrates the use of a private method.

Listing 4.14   A private method in the index.js file in the primer folder

```javascript
class Product {
    constructor(name, price) {
        this.name = name;
        this.price = price;
    }

    toString() {
        return `toString: Name: ${this.name}, Price: ${this.price}`;
    }
}

class TaxedProduct extends Product {

    constructor(name, price, taxRate = 1.2) {
        super(name, price);
        this.taxRate = taxRate;
    }

    getPriceIncTax() {
        return Number(this.price) * this.taxRate;
    }

    toString() {
        let chainResult = super.toString();
        return `${chainResult}, ${this.#getDetail()}`;
    }

    #getDetail() {
        return `Tax: ${this.getPriceIncTax()}`;
    }
}

let hat = new TaxedProduct("Hat", 100);
let boots = new TaxedProduct("Boots", 100, 1.3);

console.log(hat.toString());

console.log(boots.toString());
```

The # character is put in front of the method name to create a *hash name*, which indicates that the class member can only be accessed within the class. The # character is used when using the private class member, like this:

```
...
return `${chainResult}, ${this.#getDetail()}`;
...
```

The listing produces the same output as the previous example. The #getTaxString method can only be accessed from within the TaxedProduct class and it is an error to use it elsewhere, as shown in listing 4.15.

> **Listing 4.15 Using a private method in the index.js file in the primer folder**

```
...
console.log(hat.toString());
console.log(boots.toString());

console.log(boots.#getDetail());
...
```

When this example is executed, the following error will be produced:

```
...
SyntaxError: Private field '#getDetail' must be declared in an
enclosing class
...
```

4.3 *Using iterators and generators*

Iterators are objects that return a sequence of values. Iterators are used with the collections described later in this chapter, but they can also be useful in their own right. An iterator defines a function named `next` that returns an object with `value` and `done` properties: the `value` property returns the next value in the sequence, and the `done` property is set to `true` when the sequence is complete. Listing 4.16 shows the definition and use of an iterator.

> **Listing 4.16 Using an iterator in the index.js file in the primer folder**

```
class Product {
    constructor(name, price) {
        this.name = name;
        this.price = price;
    }

    toString() {
        return `toString: Name: ${this.name}, Price: ${this.price}`;
    }
}

function createProductIterator() {
    const hat = new Product("Hat", 100);
    const boots = new Product("Boots", 100);
    const umbrella = new Product("Umbrella", 23);

    let lastVal;

    return {
        next() {
            switch (lastVal) {
                case undefined:
                    lastVal = hat;
                    return { value: hat, done: false };
                case hat:
                    lastVal = boots;
                    return { value: boots, done: false };
                case boots:
                    lastVal = umbrella;
```

```
                    return { value: umbrella, done: false };
                case umbrella:
                    return { value: undefined, done: true };
            }
        }
    }
}

let iterator = createProductIterator();
let result = iterator.next();
while (!result.done) {
    console.log(result.value.toString());
    result = iterator.next();
}
```

The `createProductIterator` function returns an object that defines a `next` function. Each time the `next` method is called, a different `Product` object is returned, and then, once the set of objects has been exhausted, an object whose `done` property is `true` is returned to indicate the end of the data. A `while` loop is used to process the iterator data, calling `next` after each object has been processed. The code in listing 4.16 produces the following output:

```
toString: Name: Hat, Price: 100
toString: Name: Boots, Price: 100
toString: Name: Umbrella, Price: 23
```

4.3.1   Using a generator

Writing iterators can be awkward because the code has to maintain state data to keep track of the current position in the sequence each time the next function is invoked. A simpler approach is to use a generator, which is a function that is invoked once and uses the `yield` keyword to produce the values in the sequence, as shown in listing 4.17.

Listing 4.17   Using a generator in the index.js file in the primer folder

```
class Product {
    constructor(name, price) {
        this.name = name;
        this.price = price;
    }

    toString() {
        return `toString: Name: ${this.name}, Price: ${this.price}`;
    }
}

function* createProductIterator() {
    yield new Product("Hat", 100);
    yield new Product("Boots", 100);
    yield new Product("Umbrella", 23);
}

let iterator = createProductIterator();
let result = iterator.next();
```

```
while (!result.done) {
    console.log(result.value.toString());
    result = iterator.next();
}
```

Generator functions are denoted with an asterisk, like this:

```
...
function* createProductIterator() {
...
```

Generators are consumed in the same way as iterators. The JavaScript runtime creates the `next` function and executes the generator function until it reaches the `yield` keyword, which provides a value in the sequence. Execution of the generator function continues gradually each time the `next` function is invoked. When there are no more `yield` statements to execute, an object whose `done` property is `true` is created automatically.

Generators can be used with the spread operator, allowing the sequence to be used as a set of function parameters or to populate an array, as shown in listing 4.18.

> **Listing 4.18   Using the spread operator in the index.js file in the primer folder**

```
class Product {
    constructor(name, price) {
        this.name = name;
        this.price = price;
    }

    toString() {
        return `toString: Name: ${this.name}, Price: ${this.price}`;
    }
}

function* createProductIterator() {
    yield new Product("Hat", 100);
    yield new Product("Boots", 100);
    yield new Product("Umbrella", 23);
}

[...createProductIterator()].forEach(p => console.log(p.toString()));
```

The `new` statement in listing 4.18 uses the sequence of values from the generator to populate an array, which is enumerated using the `forEach` method. The code in listing 4.18 produces the following output:

```
toString: Name: Hat, Price: 100
toString: Name: Boots, Price: 100
toString: Name: Umbrella, Price: 23
```

4.3.2   *Defining iterable objects*

Stand-alone functions for iterators and generators can be useful, but the most common requirement is for an object to provide a sequence as part of some broader functionality. Listing 4.19 defines an object that groups related data items and provides a generator to allow the items to be sequenced.

Listing 4.19   Defining an object with a sequence in the index.js file in the primer folder

```
class Product {
    constructor(name, price) {
        this.name = name;
        this.price = price;
    }

    toString() {
        return `toString: Name: ${this.name}, Price: ${this.price}`;
    }
}

class GiftPack {
    constructor(name, prod1, prod2, prod3) {
        this.name = name;
        this.prod1 = prod1;
        this.prod2 = prod2;
        this.prod3 = prod3;
    }

    getTotalPrice() {
        return [this.prod1, this.prod2, this.prod3]
            .reduce((total, p) => total + p.price, 0);
    }

    *getGenerator() {
        yield this.prod1;
        yield this.prod2;
        yield this.prod3;
    }
}

let winter = new GiftPack("winter", new Product("Hat", 100),
    new Product("Boots", 80), new Product("Gloves", 23));

console.log(`Total price: ${ winter.getTotalPrice() }`);

[...winter.getGenerator()].forEach(p => console.log(`Product: ${ p }`));
```

The `GiftPack` class keeps track of a set of related products. One of the methods defined by `GiftPack` is named `getGenerator` and is a generator that yields the products.

> **TIP**   The asterisk appears before generator method names.

This approach works, but the syntax for using the iterator is a little awkward because the `getGenerator` method has to be explicitly called, like this:

```
...
[...winter.getGenerator()].forEach(p => console.log(`Product: ${ p }`));
...
```

A more elegant approach is to use the special method name for the generator, which tells the JavaScript runtime that the method provides the default iteration support for an object, as shown in listing 4.20.

```
class Product {
    constructor(name, price) {
        this.name = name;
        this.price = price;
    }

    toString() {
        return `toString: Name: ${this.name}, Price: ${this.price}`;
    }
}

class GiftPack {
    constructor(name, prod1, prod2, prod3) {
        this.name = name;
        this.prod1 = prod1;
        this.prod2 = prod2;
        this.prod3 = prod3;
    }

    getTotalPrice() {
        return [this.prod1, this.prod2, this.prod3]
            .reduce((total, p) => total + p.price, 0);
    }

    *[Symbol.iterator]() {
        yield this.prod1;
        yield this.prod2;
        yield this.prod3;
    }
}

let winter = new GiftPack("winter", new Product("Hat", 100),
    new Product("Boots", 80), new Product("Gloves", 23));

console.log(`Total price: ${ winter.getTotalPrice() }`);

[...winter].forEach(p => console.log(`Product: ${ p }`));
```

The `Symbol.iterator` property is used to denote the default iterator for an object. (Don't worry about `Symbol` at the moment—it is the least used of the JavaScript primitives, and its purpose is described in the next section.) Using the `Symbol.iterator` value as the name for a generator allows the object to be iterated directly, like this:

```
...
[...winter].forEach(p => console.log(`Product: ${ p }`));
...
```

I no longer have to invoke a method to get a generator, which produces clearer and more elegant code.

4.4   *Using JavaScript collections*

Traditionally, collections of data in JavaScript have been managed using objects and arrays, where objects are used to store data by key, and arrays are used to store data by index. JavaScript also provides dedicated collection objects that provide more structure, although they can also be less flexible, as explained in the sections that follow.

4.4.1   *Storing data by key using an object*

Objects can be used as collections, where each property is a key/value pair, with the property name being the key, as shown in listing 4.21.

Listing 4.21   Using an object as a Collection in the index.js file in the primer folder

```
class Product {
    constructor(name, price) {
        this.name = name;
        this.price = price;
    }

    toString() {
        return `toString: Name: ${this.name}, Price: ${this.price}`;
    }
}

let data = {
    hat: new Product("Hat", 100)
}

data.boots = new Product("Boots", 100);

Object.keys(data).forEach(key => console.log(data[key].toString()));
```

This example uses an object named `data` to collect `Product` objects. New values can be added to the collection by defining new properties, like this:

```
...
data.boots = new Product("Boots", 100);
...
```

`Object` provides useful methods for getting the set of keys or values from an object, which table 4.2 summarizes for quick reference.

Table 4.2   The object methods for keys and values

Name	Description
`Object.keys(object)`	This method returns an array containing the property names defined by the object.
`Object.values(object)`	This method returns an array containing the property values defined by the object.

Listing 4.21 uses the `Object.keys` method to get an array containing the property names defined by the `data` object and uses the array `forEach` method to get the corresponding value. When a property name is assigned to a variable, the corresponding value can be obtained using square brackets, like this:

```
...
Object.keys(data).forEach(key => console.log(data[key].toString()));
...
```

The contents of the square brackets are evaluated as an expression, and specifying a variable name, such as `key`, returns its value. The code in listing 4.21 produces the following output:

```
toString: Name: Hat, Price: 100
toString: Name: Boots, Price: 100
```

4.4.2 Storing data by key using a map

Objects are easy to use as basic collections, but there are some limitations, such as being able to use only string values as keys. JavaScript also provides `Map`, which is purpose-built for storing data using keys of any type, as shown in listing 4.22.

> **Listing 4.22 Using a map in the index.js file in the primer folder**

```
class Product {
    constructor(name, price) {
        this.name = name;
        this.price = price;
    }

    toString() {
        return `toString: Name: ${this.name}, Price: ${this.price}`;
    }
}

let data = new Map();
data.set("hat", new Product("Hat", 100));
data.set("boots", new Product("Boots", 100));

[...data.keys()].forEach(key => console.log(data.get(key).toString()));
```

The API provided by `Map` allows items to be stored and retrieved, and iterators are available for the keys and values. The code in listing 4.22 produces the same output as the previous example. Table 4.3 describes the most commonly used methods.

Table 4.3   Useful Map methods

Name	Description
`set(key, value)`	This method stores a value with the specified key.
`get(key)`	This method retrieves the value stored with the specified key.
`keys()`	This method returns an iterator for the keys in the `Map`.
`values()`	This method returns an iterator for the values in the `Map`.
`entries()`	This method returns an iterator for the key/value pairs in the Map, each of which is presented as an array containing the key and value. This is the default iterator for `Map` objects.

4.4.3   *Using symbols for map keys*

The main advantage of using a `Map` is that any value can be used as a key, including `Symbol` values. Each `Symbol` value is unique and immutable and ideally suited as an identifier for objects. Listing 4.23 defines a new `Map` that uses `Symbol` values as keys.

NOTE   `Symbol` values can be useful, but they can be difficult to work with because they are not human-readable and have to be created and handled carefully. See https://developer.mozilla.org/en-US/docs/Web/JavaScript/ Reference/Global_Objects/Symbol for more details.

Listing 4.23   Using symbol values as keys in the index.js file in the primer folder

```
class Product {
    constructor(name, price) {
        this.id = Symbol();
        this.name = name;
        this.price = price;
    }
}

class Supplier {
    constructor(name, productids) {
        this.name = name;
        this.productids = productids;
    }
}

let acmeProducts = [new Product("Hat", 100), new Product("Boots", 100)];
let zoomProducts = [new Product("Hat", 100), new Product("Boots", 100)];

let products = new Map();
```

```
[...acmeProducts, ...zoomProducts].forEach(p => products.set(p.id, p));
let suppliers = new Map();
suppliers.set("acme", new Supplier("Acme Co", acmeProducts.map(p => p.id)));
suppliers.set("zoom",
    new Supplier("Zoom Shoes", zoomProducts.map(p => p.id)));

suppliers.get("acme").productids.forEach(id =>
        console.log(`Name: ${products.get(id).name}`));
```

The benefit of using `Symbol` values as keys is that there is no possibility of two keys colliding, which can happen if keys are derived from the value's characteristics. The previous example used the `Product.name` value as the key, which is subject to two objects being stored with the same key, such that one replaces the other. In this example, each `Product` object has an `id` property that is assigned a `Symbol` value in the constructor and that is used to store the object in the `Map`. Using a `Symbol` allows me to store objects that have identical `name` and `price` properties and retrieve them without difficulty. The code in listing 4.23 produces the following output:

```
Name: Hat
Name: Boots
```

4.4.4   Storing data by index

In chapter 3, you saw how data can be stored in an array. JavaScript also provides `Set`, which stores data by index but has performance optimizations and—most usefully—stores only unique values, as shown in listing 4.24.

> **Listing 4.24   Using a set in the index.js file in the primer folder**

```
class Product {
    constructor(name, price) {
        this.id = Symbol();
        this.name = name;
        this.price = price;
    }
}

let product = new Product("Hat", 100);

let productArray = [];
let productSet = new Set();

for (let i = 0; i < 5; i++) {
    productArray.push(product);
    productSet.add(product);
}

console.log(`Array length: ${productArray.length}`);
console.log(`Set size: ${productSet.size}`);
```

This example adds the same `Product` object five times to an array and a `Set` and then prints out how many items each contains, producing the following output:

```
Array length: 5
Set size: 1
```

For my projects, the need to allow or prevent duplicate values is the reason to choose between an array and a `Set`. The API provided by `Set` provides comparable features to working with an array; table 4.4 describes the most useful methods.

Table 4.4   Useful Set methods

Name	Description
add(value)	This method adds the value to the Set.
entries()	This value returns an iterator for the items in the Set, in the order in which they were added.
has(value)	This value returns true if the Set contains the specified value.
forEach(callback)	This method invokes a function for each value in the Set.

4.5   *Using modules*

Most applications are too complex to have all the code in a single file. To break up an application into manageable chunks, JavaScript supports *modules*. There have been many different approaches to modules since JavaScript was introduced, but there has been consolidation recently and you need to know about only two types of module for most JavaScript projects:

1 ECMAScript modules.
2 CommonJS modules.

ECMAScript is the official name of JavaScript, and the term *ECMAScript module* refers to the recent additions to the JavaScript language specification that describe modules. This is the "official" module specification, and most JavaScript runtimes and popular third-party packages support this type of module, including the Node.js runtime used in this book.

CommonJS is an older specification that became a de facto standard because it was supported by Node.js, prior to the adoption of the actual standard ECMAScript modules. The examples used in earlier editions of this book used the CommonJS module format.

> **TIP**   You should use ECMAScript modules for most projects, just as long as they are supported by your JavaScript runtime, such as Node.js or your browser. Not only are ECMAScript modules the "real" standard, but an ECMAScript module can import from a CommonJS module, which means that you can mix and match module formats.

4.5.1 Declaring the module type

Before using modules, you must choose between the ECMAScript and CommonJS formats, so that the Node.js runtime knows how to handle files. This can be done by creating code files with the `.mjs` extension (for ECMAScript) or the `.csj` extension (for CommonJS). My preference is to configure the project using the `package.json` file, as shown in listing 4.25.

Listing 4.25 Setting the module type in the package.json file in the primer folder

```
{
  "name": "primer",
  "version": "1.0.0",
  "description": "",
  "main": "index.js",
  "scripts": {
    "test": "echo \"Error: no test specified\" && exit 1"
  },
  "keywords": [],
  "author": "",
  "license": "ISC",
  "dependencies": {
    "nodemon": "^2.0.20"
  },
  "type": "module"
}
```

Adding the `type` property to the `package.json` file sets the module type without needing to use special file extensions. The values for this property are `module`, for ECMAScript modules, and `commonjs` for CommonJS modules.

4.5.2 Creating a JavaScript module

Each JavaScript module is contained in a JavaScript file. To create a module, I added a file called `tax.js` to the `primer` folder and added the code shown in listing 4.26.

Listing 4.26 The contents of the tax.js file in the primer folder

```
export default function(price) {
    return Number(price) * 1.2;
}
```

The function defined in the `tax.js` file receives a `price` value and applies a 20 percent tax rate. The function itself is simple, and it is the `export` and `default` keywords that are important. The `export` keyword is used to denote the features that will be available outside the module. By default, the contents of the JavaScript file are private and must be explicitly shared using the `export` keyword before they can be used in the rest of the application. The `default` keyword is used when the module contains a single feature, such as the function defined in listing 4.26. Together, the `export` and `default` keywords are used to specify that the only function in the `tax.js` file is available for use in the rest of the application.

4.5.3   *Using a JavaScript module*

Another JavaScript keyword is required to use a module: the `import` keyword. In listing 4.27, I used the `import` keyword in the `index.js` file to use the function defined in the `tax.js` file.

> **Listing 4.27   Using a module in the index.js file in the primer folder**

```
import calcTax from "./tax.js";

class Product {
    constructor(name, price) {
        this.id = Symbol();
        this.name = name;
        this.price = price;
    }
}

let product = new Product("Hat", 100);
let taxedPrice = calcTax(product.price);
console.log(`Name: ${ product.name }, Taxed Price: ${taxedPrice}`);
```

The `import` keyword is used to declare a dependency on the module. The `import` keyword can be used in several different ways, but this is the format you will use most often when working with modules you have created within your project.

The `import` keyword is followed by an identifier, which is the name by which the function in the module will be known when it is used, and the identifier in this example is `calcTax`. The `from` keyword follows the identifier, which is then followed by the location of the module. It is important to pay close attention to the location because different behaviors are created by different location formats, as described in the "Understanding Module Locations" sidebar.

During the build process, the JavaScript runtime will detect the `import` statement and will load the contents of the `tax.js` file. The identifier used in the `import` statement can be used to access the function in the module, in just the same way that locally defined functions are used.

```
...
let taxedPrice = calcTax(product.price);
...
```

When the code is executed, the value assigned to the `taxedPrice` variable is calculated using the function defined in the `tax.js` file and produces the following output:

```
Name: Hat, Taxed Price: 120
```

> **Understanding module locations**
>
> The location of a module specifies where the JavaScript runtime will look for the code file that contains the module's code. For modules defined in the project, the location is specified as a relative path, starting with one or two periods, indicating that the path is relative to the current file or the current file's parent directory. In listing 4.27, the location starts with a period.

(continued)

```
. . .
import calcTax from "./tax.js";
. . .
```

This location tells the build tools that there is a dependency on the `tax` module, which can be found in the same folder as the file that contains the `import` statement.

If you omit the initial period or periods, then the `import` statement declares a dependency on a module that is not in the local project. The locations that are searched for the module will vary depending on the application framework and build tools you are using, but the most common location to search is the `node_modules` folder, which is where packages are installed during the project setup. This location is used to access features provided by third-party packages. You will see examples of using modules from third-party packages in part 3 of this book, but for quick reference, here is an `import` statement from the chapter that covers development with React:

```
. . .
import React, { Component } from "react";
. . .
```

The location for this `import` statement doesn't start with a period and will be interpreted as a dependency on the `react` module in the project's `node_modules` folder, which is the package that provides the core React application features.

4.5.4 Exporting named features from a module

A module can assign names to the features it exports. This is the approach that I prefer, and in listing 4.28, I have given a name to the function exported by the `tax` module.

Listing 4.28 Exporting a named feature in the tax.js file in the primer folder

```
export function calculateTax(price) {
    return Number(price) * 1.2;
}
```

The function provides the same feature but is exported using the name `calculateTax` and no longer uses the `default` keyword. In listing 4.29, I have imported the feature using its new name in the `index.js` file.

Listing 4.29 Importing a named feature in the index.js file in the primer folder

```
import { calculateTax } from "./tax.js";

class Product {
    constructor(name, price) {
        this.id = Symbol();
        this.name = name;
        this.price = price;
    }
}
```

```
let product = new Product("Hat", 100);
let taxedPrice = calculateTax(product.price);
console.log(`Name: ${ product.name }, Taxed Price: ${taxedPrice}`);
```

The name of the feature to be imported is specified in curly braces (the { and } char-acters) and is used by this name in the code. A module can export default and named features, as shown in listing 4.30.

Listing 4.30   Exporting named and default features in the tax.js file in the primer folder

```
export function calculateTax(price) {
    return Number(price) * 1.2;
}

export default function calcTaxandSum(...prices) {
    return prices.reduce((total, p) => total += calculateTax(p), 0);
}
```

The new feature is exported using the default keyword. In listing 4.31, I have imported the new feature as the default export from the module.

Listing 4.31   Importing a default feature in the index.js file in the primer folder

```
import calcTaxAndSum, { calculateTax } from "./tax.js";

class Product {
    constructor(name, price) {
        this.id = Symbol();
        this.name = name;
        this.price = price;
    }
}

let product = new Product("Hat", 100);
let taxedPrice = calculateTax(product.price);
console.log(`Name: ${ product.name }, Taxed Price: ${taxedPrice}`);

let products = [new Product("Gloves", 23), new Product("Boots", 100)];
let totalPrice = calcTaxAndSum(...products.map(p => p.price));
console.log(`Total Price: ${totalPrice.toFixed(2)}`);
```

This is a common pattern with web application frameworks such as React, where the core features are provided by the default export of a module and optional features are available as named exports. The code in listing 4.31 produces the following output:

```
Name: Hat, Taxed Price: 120
Total Price: 147.60
```

4.5.5   *Defining multiple named features in a module*

Modules can contain more than one named function or value, which is useful for grouping related features. To demonstrate, I added a file called utils.js to the primer folder with the code shown in listing 4.32.

Listing 4.32 The contents of the utils.js file in the primer folder
---

```
import { calculateTax } from "./tax.js";

export function printDetails(product) {
    let taxedPrice = calculateTax(product.price);
    console.log(`Name: ${product.name}, Taxed Price: ${taxedPrice}`);
}

export function applyDiscount(product, discount = 5) {
    product.price = product.price - discount;
}
```

This module defines two functions to which the `export` keyword has been applied. Unlike the previous example, the `default` keyword is not used, and each function has its own name. When importing from a module that contains multiple features, the names of the features that are used are specified as a comma-separated list between the braces, as shown in listing 4.33.

Listing 4.33 Importing named features in the index.js file in the primer folder
---

```
import calcTaxAndSum, { calculateTax } from "./tax.js";
import { printDetails, applyDiscount } from "./utils.js";

class Product {
    constructor(name, price) {
        this.id = Symbol();
        this.name = name;
        this.price = price;
    }
}

let product = new Product("Hat", 100);
applyDiscount(product, 10);
//let taxedPrice = calculateTax(product.price);
printDetails(product);

let products = [new Product("Gloves", 23), new Product("Boots", 100)];
let totalPrice = calcTaxAndSum(...products.map(p => p.price));
console.log(`Total Price: ${totalPrice.toFixed(2)}`);
```

The braces that follow the `import` keyword surround the functions I want to use. I only need to declare dependencies on the functions that I require, and there is no need to add functions that are not used to the `import` statement. The code in listing 4.33 produces the following output:

```
Name: Hat, Taxed Price: 112
Total Price: 147.60
```

Summary

In this chapter, I described the JavaScript features for dealing with objects, sequences of values, collections, and the use of modules. These are all JavaScript features, but, as you will learn, understanding them helps put TypeScript into context and sets the foundation for effective TypeScript development. JavaScript objects have a prototype from which they inherit properties and methods.

- Objects can be created in a literal form or using a constructor function.
- JavaScript classes create a consistent template for creating objects.
- JavaScript classes support private fields, properties, and methods.
- Iterators and generators produce sequences of values.
- JavaScript objects and arrays can be used as simple collections, but you can also use a built-in map collection.
- Modules are used to structure a project, using either the ECMAScript or CommonJS module formats.

In the next chapter, I introduce the TypeScript compiler, which is at the heart of the features that TypeScript provides to developers.

Using the TypeScript compiler

In this chapter, I show you how to use the TypeScript compiler, which is responsible for transforming TypeScript code into JavaScript that can be executed by browsers or the Node.js runtime. I also describe the compiler configuration options that are most useful for TypeScript development, including those that are used with the web application frameworks covered in part 3 of this book.

5.1 Preparing for this chapter

To prepare for this chapter, open a command prompt, navigate to a convenient location, and create a folder named `tools`. Run the commands shown in listing 5.1 to navigate to the `tools` folder and to tell the Node Package Manager (NPM) to create a file named `package.json`. This file will be used to keep track of the packages added to the project, as described in the "Using the Node Package Manager" section.

Listing 5.1   Creating the package.json file

```
cd tools
npm init --yes
```

Use the command prompt to run the commands shown in listing 5.2 in the `tools` folder to install the package required for this chapter.

Listing 5.2   Adding packages using the Node Package Manager

```
npm install --save-dev typescript@5.0.2
npm install --save-dev tsc-watch@6.0.0
```

The `install` argument tells NPM to download and add a package to the current folder. The `--save-dev` argument tells NPM that these are packages for use in development but not part of the application. The final argument is the name of the package, followed by the @ symbol, followed by the version that is required.

> **NOTE**   It is important to use the versions specified for the examples in this book. You may encounter unexpected behavior or errors if you use different versions.

To create a configuration file for the TypeScript compiler, add a file called `tsconfig` `.json` to the `tools` folder with the content shown in listing 5.3.

Listing 5.3   The contents of the tsconfig.json file in the tools folder

```
{
    "compilerOptions": {
        "target": "ES2022",
        "outDir": "./dist",
        "rootDir": "./src"
    }
}
```

To complete the setup, create the `tools/src` folder and add to it a file called `index` `.ts` that contains the code in listing 5.4.

Listing 5.4   The contents of the index.ts file in the src folder

```
function printMessage(msg: string): void {
    console.log(`Message: ${ msg }`);
}

printMessage("Hello, TypeScript");
```

To compile the TypeScript code, run the command shown in listing 5.5 in the `tools` folder.

Listing 5.5 Compiling the TypeScript code

```
tsc
```

To execute the compiled code, run the command shown in listing 5.6 in the `tools` folder.

Listing 5.6 Running the compiled code

```
node dist/index.js
```

If the project has been set up successfully, the following output will be displayed at the command prompt:

```
Message: Hello, TypeScript
```

5.2 Understanding the project structure

The structure of the example project is one that you will see in most JavaScript and TypeScript development, with some variations for the main framework used for the application, such as React or Angular. Figure 5.1 shows the contents of the `tools` folder.

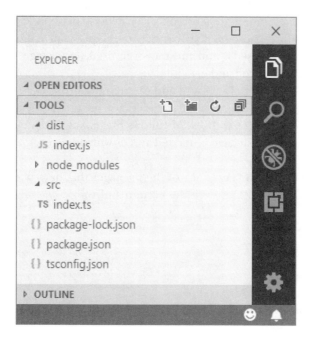

Figure 5.1 The contents of the example project folder

The figure shows how the project folder is displayed by Visual Studio Code, which is the editor I use throughout this book. Table 5.1 describes each of the items in the project, and I provide more details about the most important items in the sections that follow.

Table 5.1   The project files and folders

Name	Description
dist	This folder contains the output from the compiler.
node_modules	This folder contains the packages that the application and development tools require, as described in the "Using the Node Package Manager" section.
src	This folder contains the source code files that will be compiled by the TypeScript compiler.
package.json	This folder contains the set of top-level package dependencies for the project, as described in the "Using the Node Package Manager" section.
package-lock.json	This file contains a complete list of the package dependencies for the project.
tsconfig.json	This file contains the configuration settings for the TypeScript compiler.

5.3   *Using the Node Package Manager*

TypeScript and JavaScript development depends on a rich ecosystem of packages. Most TypeScript projects will require packages that contain the TypeScript compiler, the application framework (if one is used), and the tools required to package the compiled code so that it can be distributed and executed.

NPM is used to download these packages and add them to the project's node_modules folder. Each package declares a set of dependencies on other packages and specifies the versions that it can work with. NPM follows this chain of dependencies, working out which version of each package is needed and downloading everything that is required.

The package.json file is used to keep track of the packages that have been added using the npm install command. Here are the contents of the package.json file from the example project:

```
{
  "name": "tools",
  "version": "1.0.0",
  "description": "",
  "main": "index.js",
  "scripts": {
    "test": "echo \"Error: no test specified\" && exit 1"
  },
  "keywords": [],
  "author": "",
  "license": "ISC",
  "devDependencies": {
    "tsc-watch": "^6.0.0",
    "typescript": "^5.0.2"
  }
}
```

The basic content of the file was created by the `npm init` command in listing 5.1 and was then modified by each use of the `npm install` command in listing 5.2. Packages are separated into the tools used during the development process and those that form part of the application. Packages used during development are installed with the `save-dev` argument and are recorded in the `devDependencies` section of the `package.json` file. Packages that are included in the application are installed without the `--save-dev` argument and are stored in a section named `dependencies`. Only tool packages were installed in listing 5.2, which is why all of the packages are in the `devDependencies` section and why the `package.json` file doesn't contain a `dependencies` section at all. Examples later in the book add packages to the `dependencies` section, but the focus in this chapter is on the tools that are used for TypeScript development. Table 5.2 describes each of the packages that have been added to the example project.

Understanding global and local packages

Package managers can install packages so they are specific to a single project (known as a local install) or so they can be accessed from anywhere (known as a *global install*). In chapter 2, you installed the `typescript` package globally, which allows the `tsc` command to be used to compile code anywhere. In listing 5.2, the same package is installed locally, even though the functionality is already available. This is so that other packages in the same project can access the functionality provided by the TypeScript compiler.

Table 5.2   The packages added to the example project

Name	Description
`tsc-watch`	This package watches a source code folder, runs the TypeScript compiler when there is a change, and executes the compiled JavaScript code.
`typescript`	This is the package that contains the TypeScript compiler and its supporting tools.

For each package, the `package.json` file includes details of the version numbers that are acceptable, using the format described in table 5.3.

Table 5.3   The package version numbering system

Format	Description
`5.0.2`	Expressing a version number directly will accept only the package with the exact matching version number, e.g., 5.0.2.
`*`	Using an asterisk accepts any version of the package to be installed.
`>5.0.2 >=5.0.2`	Prefixing a version number with > or >= accepts any version of the package that is greater than or greater than or equal to a given version.
`<5.0.2 <=5.0.2`	Prefixing a version number with < or <= accepts any version of the package that is less than or less than or equal to a given version.

Table 5.3   The package version numbering system *(continued)*

Format	Description
~5.0.2	Prefixing a version number with a tilde (the ~ character) accepts versions to be installed even if the patch level number (the last of the three version numbers) doesn't match. For example, specifying ~5.0.2 will accept version 5.0.3 or 5.0.3 (which would contain patches to version 5.0.2) but not version 5.1.0 (which would be a new minor release).
^5.0.2	Prefixing a version number with a caret (the ^ character) will accept versions even if the minor release number (the second of the three version numbers) or the patch number doesn't match. For example, specifying ^5.0.2 will allow versions 5.0.3 and 5.1.0, but not version 6.0.0.

NPM is a sophisticated tool, and understanding its use is an important part of Java-Script and TypeScript development. Table 5.4 describes some NPM commands that you may find useful during development. All of these commands should be run inside the project folder, which is the one that contains the `package.json` file.

Table 5.4   Useful NPM commands

Command	Description
npm install	This command performs a local install of the packages specified in the `package.json` file.
npm install package@version	This command performs a local install of a specific version of a package and updates the `package.json` file to add the package to the `dependencies` section.
npm install --save-dev package@version	This command performs a local install of a specific version of a package and updates the `package.json` file to add the package to the `devDependencies` section, which is used to add packages to the project that are required for development but are not part of the application.
npm install --global package@version	This command will perform a global install of a specific version of a package.
npm list	This command will list all the local packages and their dependencies.
npm run	This command will execute one of the scripts defined in the `package.json` file.
npx package	This command runs the code contained in a package.

The `node_modules` folder is typically excluded from version control because it contains a large number of files and because packages can contain platform-specific components that don't work when a project is checked out on a new machine. Instead, the `npm install` command is used to create a new `node_modules` folder and install the required packages.

This approach can produce a different set of packages each time the `npm install` command is run because dependencies can be expressed as a range of versions, as described in table 5.4. To ensure consistency, NPM creates the `package-lock.json` file, which contains a complete list of the packages installed in the `node_module` folder, along with the versions that were used. The `package-lock.json` file is updated by NPM when changes are made to the packages in the project and the versions it contains are used by the `npm install` command.

> **NOTE** The `package.json` and `package-lock.json` files should be checked in for revision control to ensure everyone on the development team gets the same packages. When you pull updates from the repository, make sure you run the `npm install` command to receive any new packages that have been added by another developer.

5.4 Understanding the compiler configuration file

The TypeScript compiler, `tsc`, is responsible for compiling TypeScript files. It is the compiler that is responsible for implementing TypeScript features, such as static types, and the result is pure JavaScript from which the TypeScript keywords and expressions have been removed.

The TypeScript compiler has a lot of configuration options, as described later in this chapter. A configuration file is used to override the default settings and ensures a consistent configuration is always used. The name of the configuration file is `tsconfig.json`, which was created with this content in listing 5.3:

```
{
    "compilerOptions": {
        "target": "ES2022",
        "outDir": "./dist",
        "rootDir": "./src"
    }
}
```

The `tsconfig.json` file can contain several top-level configuration settings, as described in table 5.5, although the file used by the example project contains only `compilerOptions` settings, which are described in the "Useful Compiler Configuration Settings" section.

Table 5.5 The top-level configuration settings of the tsconfig.json file

Name	Description
`compilerOptions`	This section groups the settings that the compiler will use, as described in the "Useful Compiler Configuration Settings" section.
`files`	This setting specifies the files that will be compiled, which overrides the default behavior where the compiler searches for files to compile.

Table 5.5   The top-level configuration settings of the tsconfig.json file (continued)

Name	Description
include	This setting is used to select files for compilation by pattern. If unspecified, files with the `.ts`, `tsx`, and `.d.ts` extensions will be selected. (TSX files and files with the `.d.ts` extension are described in part 3.)
exclude	This setting is used to exclude files from the compilation by pattern.
compileOnSave	When set to `true`, this setting is a hint to the code editor that it should run the compiler each time a file is saved. This feature is not supported by all editors, and the watch feature, described in the next section, provides a more useful alternative.

The `files`, `include`, and `exclude` options are useful if you have an unusual project structure to accommodate, such as when integrating TypeScript into a project that contains another framework or toolkit that has a conflicting set of files. You can see the set of files that the compiler has found for compilation by using the `listFiles` setting, which can be defined in the `compilerOptions` section of the `tsconfig.json` file or specified on the command line. As an example, run the command shown in listing 5.7 in the `tools` folder to see the files that are selected by the compiler configuration.

Listing 5.7   Displaying the list of files for compilation

```
tsc --listFiles
```

The `listFiles` argument displays a long list of files that the compiler has located, as follows:

```
...
C:/npm/node_modules/typescript/lib/lib.es5.d.ts
C:/npm/node_modules/typescript/lib/lib.es2015.d.ts
C:/npm/node_modules/typescript/lib/lib.es2016.d.ts
C:/npm/node_modules/typescript/lib/lib.es2017.d.ts
C:/npm/node_modules/typescript/lib/lib.es2018.d.ts
C:/npm/node_modules/typescript/lib/lib.es2020.d.ts
C:/npm/node_modules/typescript/lib/lib.es2021.d.ts
C:/npm/node_modules/typescript/lib/lib.es2022.d.ts
...
```

The files displayed by the `listFiles` option include the type declarations that the compiler has located. As explained in chapter 2, type declarations describe the data types used by JavaScript code so that it can be safely used in a TypeScript application. The TypeScript package includes type declarations for different versions of the JavaScript language and for the APIs that are available in Node.js and browsers. Type declarations are described in more detail in part 3, and these specific files are described in the "Using the Version Targeting Feature" section of this chapter.

NOTE The paths for the type declaration files are outside of the project because the `tsc` command runs the TypeScript compiler from the package installed globally in chapter 2. The same package has been installed locally in the `node_modules` folder and is used when creating a development pipeline, as described in the next section. If you need to run the compiler from the package installed locally in the project, then you can use the `npx` command, such that `npx tsc --listFiles` has the same effect as the command in listing 5.7 but uses the local package.

This file appears at the end of the list produced by the `listFile` option:

```
...
C:/tools/src/index.ts
...
```

As part of the discovery process, the TypeScript compiler looks for TypeScript files in the location specified by the `rootDir` setting in the `tsconfig.json` file. The compiler examines the `src` folder and discovers the `index.ts` file.

5.5 *Compiling TypeScript code*

The compiler checks the TypeScript code to enforce features like static types and emits pure JavaScript code from which the TypeScript additions have been removed. The compiler can be run directly from the command line and will process all the files shown by the `listfile` option. Run the command shown in listing 5.8 in the `tools` folder to start the compiler.

Listing 5.8 Running the compiler

```
tsc
```

There is only one TypeScript file in the project—the `src/index.ts` file—and the configuration settings in the `tsconfig.json` file tell the compiler that it should place the JavaScript it emits into the `dist` folder. If you examine the contents of the `dist` folder, you will see it contains a file called `index.js`, with the following contents:

```
function printMessage(msg) {
    console.log(`Message: ${msg}`);
}
printMessage("Hello, TypeScript");
```

The `index.js` file contains the compiled code from the `index.ts` file in the `src` folder but without the additional type information for the `printMessage` function. The relationship between the TypeScript code and the JavaScript code the compiler produces won't always be as direct, especially when the compiler has been instructed to target a different version of JavaScript, as described in the "Using the Version Targeting Feature" section.

CAUTION Do not edit the JavaScript files in the `dist` folder because your changes will be overwritten the next time the TypeScript compiler runs. Changes must be made only to the TypeScript files.

5.5.1   *Understanding compiler errors*

The TypeScript compiler checks the code it compiles to make sure it conforms to the JavaScript language specification and to apply the TypeScript features, such as static types and access control keywords. To create a simple example of a compiler error, listing 5.9 adds a statement that uses the wrong data type to invoke the `printMessage` function.

> **Listing 5.9   Creating a type mismatch in the index.ts file in the src folder**

```
function printMessage(msg: string): void  {
    console.log(`Message: ${ msg }`);
}

printMessage("Hello, TypeScript");
printMessage(100);
```

Run the command shown in listing 5.10 in the `tools` folder to execute the compiler.

> **TIP**   The `printMessage` function specifies the data type it is willing to accept through its `msg` parameter using a type annotation, which is described in chapter 7. For this chapter, it is enough to know that invoking the `printMessage` function with a number value is a TypeScript error.

> **Listing 5.10   Running the compiler**

```
tsc
```

The compiler detects that the type of the argument in the new statement is `number` and not the `string` that is specified by the `printMessage` function, and it produces the following message:

```
src/index.ts:6:14 - error TS2345: Argument of type 'number' is not
    assignable to parameter of type 'string'.

6 printMessage(100);
               ~~~
Found 1 error in src/index.ts:6
```

In most respects, the TypeScript compiler works like any compiler. But there is one difference that can catch out the unwary: by default, the compiler continues to emit JavaScript code even when it encounters an error. If you examine the contents of the `index.js` file in the `dist` folder, you will see that it contains the following output:

```
function printMessage(msg) {
    console.log(`Message: ${msg}`);
}
printMessage("Hello, TypeScript");
printMessage(100);
```

This is an odd behavior that can cause problems with chains of tools that execute or further process the JavaScript emitted by the TypeScript compiler because they will operate on JavaScript files that contain potential problems. Fortunately, this behavior can be disabled by setting the `noEmitOnError` configuration setting to `true` in the `tsconfig.json` file, as shown in listing 5.11.

Listing 5.11 Changing the configuration in the tsconfig.json file in the tools folder

```
{
    "compilerOptions": {
        "target": "ES2022",
        "outDir": "./dist",
        "rootDir": "./src",
        "noEmitOnError": true
    }
}
```

When the compiler runs, output will be generated only when there are no errors detected in the JavaScript code.

5.5.2 *Using watch mode and executing the compiled code*

Manually running the compiler after every code change quickly becomes tiresome, so the TypeScript compiler supports watch mode, where it monitors the project and automatically compiles files when a change is detected. Run the command shown in listing 5.12 in the `tools` folder to start the compiler in watch mode.

Listing 5.12 Starting the compiler in watch mode

```
tsc --watch
```

The compiler will start, report the same error as shown in the previous section, and then start monitoring the project for code changes. To trigger a compile, comment out the problem statement added to the `index.ts` file, as shown in listing 5.13.

> **CAUTION** You may encounter a bug in Node.js when running the TypeScript compiler in watch mode. If you see a `Check failed: U_SUCCESS(status)` error, then may need to update to the latest version of Node.js. Alternatively, just jump ahead to the next section because the TypeScript compiler watch mode is used only in this part of the chapter and not relied on again in this book.

Listing 5.13 Commenting out a statement in the index.ts file in the src folder

```
function printMessage(msg: string): void {
    console.log(`Message: ${ msg }`);
}

printMessage("Hello, TypeScript");
//printMessage(100);
```

When the change is saved, the compiler will run automatically. There are no errors in the code, and the compiler produces the following output:

```
[6:37:35 AM] File change detected. Starting incremental compilation...
[6:37:35 AM] Found 0 errors. Watching for file changes.
```

To execute the compiled code, open a second command prompt, navigate to the `tools` folder, and run the command shown in listing 5.14.

Listing 5.14   Executing the compiled code

```
node dist/index.js
```

The Node.js runtime will execute the statements in the index.js file in the dist folder and produce the following output:

```
Message: Hello, TypeScript
```

AUTOMATICALLY EXECUTING CODE AFTER COMPILATION

The compiler's watch mode doesn't automatically execute compiled code. It can be tempting to combine the watch mode with a tool that executes a command when a file change is detected, but this can be difficult because the JavaScript files are not all written at the same time and there is no easy way to reliably determine when compilation has been completed.

If you are using a web development framework such as React or Angular, the TypeScript compiler is integrated into a larger toolchain that will automatically execute the compiled code, as demonstrated in part 3. For stand-alone projects, there are open-source packages available that build on the functionality provided by the compiler to offer additional features. One such package is ts-watch, which was installed in the example project in listing 5.2. The ts-watch package starts the compiler in watch mode, observes its output, and executes commands based on the compilation results. Run the command shown in listing 5.15 in the tools folder to start the ts-watch package.

Listing 5.15   Starting the package command

```
npx tsc-watch --onsuccess "node dist/index.js"
```

The onsuccess argument specifies a command that is executed when compilation succeeds without errors. Make the change shown in listing 5.16 to the index.ts file to trigger a compilation and execute the result.

> **TIP** See https://github.com/gilamran/tsc-watch for details of the other options provided by the ts-watch package.

Listing 5.16   Making a change in the index.ts file in the src folder

```
function printMessage(msg: string): void  {
    console.log(`Message: ${ msg }`);
}

printMessage("Hello, TypeScript");
printMessage("It is sunny today");
```

When the change is saved, the TypeScript compiler will detect the change and compile the TypeScript file. The ts-watch package will see that no errors are reported by the compiler and run the command that executes the compiled code, producing the following output:

```
7:20:25 AM - File change detected. Starting incremental compilation...
7:20:25 AM - Found 0 errors. Watching for file changes.
Message: Hello, TypeScript
Message: It is sunny today
```

> **NOTE** The TypeScript compiler also provides an API that can be used to create custom tools, which can be useful if you need to integrate the compiler into a complex workflow. Microsoft doesn't provide extensive documentation for the API, but there are some notes and examples at https://github.com/Microsoft/TypeScript/wiki/Using-the-Compiler-API.

STARTING THE COMPILER USING NPM

The TypeScript compiler doesn't respond to changes on all of its configuration properties, and there will be times when you will need to stop and then start the compiler. Instead of typing in the command in listing 5.16, a more reliable method is to use the `scripts` section of the `package.json` file, as shown in listing 5.17.

Listing 5.17 Adding to the scripts section of the package.json file in the tools folder

```
{
  "name": "tools",
  "version": "1.0.0",
  "description": "",
  "main": "index.js",
  "scripts": {
    "start": "tsc-watch --onsuccess \"node dist/index.js\""
  },
  "keywords": [],
  "author": "",
  "license": "ISC",
  "devDependencies": {
    "tsc-watch": "^6.0.0",
    "typescript": "^5.0.2"
  }
}
```

Care must be taken to escape the quote characters required for the `onsuccess` argument. Save the changes to the `package.json` file and then run the command shown in listing 5.18 in the `tools` folder.

Listing 5.18 Starting the compiler

```
npm start
```

The effect is the same, but the compiler can now be started without having to remember the combination of package and filenames, which can become complex in real projects.

5.6 *Using the version targeting feature*

TypeScript relies on the most recent versions of the JavaScript language, which introduced features such as classes. To make it easier to adopt TypeScript, the compiler can generate JavaScript code that targets older versions of the JavaScript language, which means that recent features can be used during development to create code that can be executed by older JavaScript runtimes, such as legacy browsers.

The version of the JavaScript language targeted by the compiler is specified by the `target` setting in the `tsconfig.json` file, as shown in listing 5.19.

Listing 5.19   Selecting a target version in the tsconfig.json file in the tools folder

```
{
    "compilerOptions": {
        "target": "ES5",
        "outDir": "./dist",
        "rootDir": "./src",
        "noEmitOnError": true
    }
}
```

The target setting selects a JavaScript version from the list described in table 5.6.

NOTE   The `ES` in these settings refers to ECMAScript, which is the standard that defines the features implemented by the JavaScript language. The history of JavaScript and ECMAScript is long, tortured, and not at all interesting. For TypeScript development, JavaScript and ECMAScript can be regarded as being the same, which is how I have approached them in the book. See https://en.wikipedia.org/wiki/ECMAScript if you want to get into the details.

Table 5.6   The values for the target setting

Name	Description
ES3	This value targets the third edition of the language specification that was defined in December 1999 and is considered to be the baseline for the language. This is the default value when the `target` setting is not defined.
ES5	This value targets the fifth edition of the language specification that was defined in December 2009 and focuses on consistency. (There was no fourth edition.)
ES6	This value targets the sixth edition of the language specification and added features required for creating complex applications, such as classes and modules, arrow functions, and promises.
ES2015	This value is equivalent to ES6.
ES2016	This value targets the seventh edition of the language specification, which introduced the `includes` method for arrays and an exponentiation operator.
ES2017	This value targets the eighth edition of the language specification, which introduced features for inspecting objects and new keywords for asynchronous operations.
ES2018	This value targets the ninth edition of the language specification, which introduced the spread and rest operators and improvements for string handling and asynchronous operations.
ES2019	This value targets the tenth edition of the language specification, which includes new array features, changes to error handling, and improvements to JSON formatting.

Table 5.6 **The values for the target setting** *(continued)*

Name	Description
ES2020	This value targets the 11th edition of the language specification, which includes support for the nullish operator, optional chaining, and loading modules dynamically.
ES2021	This value targets the 12th edition of the language specification, which includes support for new logical assignment operators, weak memory references, and separators for numeric literal values.
ES2022	This value targets the 13th edition of the language specification, which includes support for private class members.
esNext	This value refers to the features that are expected to be included in the next edition of the specification. The specific features supported by the TypeScript compiler can change between releases. This is an advanced setting that should be used with caution.

The earlier versions of the ECMAScript standard were given numbers, but recent versions are named for the year in which they were completed. This change happened partway through the definition of ES6, which is why it is known as both ES6 and ES2015. The biggest changes to the language were introduced in ES6/ES2015, which can be regarded as the start of "modern" JavaScript. The release of ES6 marked the switch to annual updates to the language specification, which is why the 2016–2022 editions contain only a small number of changes.

The setting in listing 5.19 specifies es5, which means that modern features such as the let keyword and fat-arrow functions will not be supported. To show how the compiler deals with these features, make the changes shown in listing 5.20 to the index.ts file.

Listing 5.20 Using modern features in the index.ts file in the src folder

```
let printMessage = (msg: string)
    : void =>  console.log(`Message: ${ msg }`);

let message = ("Hello, TypeScript");
printMessage(message);
```

When the changes to the file are saved, the code will be compiled and executed. The JavaScript generated by the compiler can be seen by examining the index.js file in the dist folder, which contains the following statements:

```
var printMessage = function (msg) {
    return console.log("Message: ".concat(msg));
};
var message = ("Hello, TypeScript");
printMessage(message);
```

The let keyword has been replaced with var, and the fat-arrow function has been replaced with a traditional function. The code achieves the same effect as when targeting a more recent version of JavaScript and produces the following output:

```
Message: Hello, TypeScript
```

5.7   *Setting the library files for compilation*

The output from the `listFiles` compiler option showed the files that the compiler discovers and included a series of type declaration files. These files provide the compiler with type information about the features available in different versions of JavaScript and the features provided for applications running in the browser, which are able to create and manage HTML content using the Document Object Model (DOM) API.

The compiler defaults to the type information it requires based on the `target` property, which means that errors will be generated when features from later versions of JavaScript are used, as shown in listing 5.21.

> **Listing 5.21   Using a later JavaScript feature in the index.ts file in the src folder**

```
let printMessage = (msg: string)
    : void =>  console.log(`Message: ${ msg }`);

let message = ("Hello, TypeScript");
printMessage(message);

let data = new Map();
data.set("Bob", "London");
data.set("Alice", "Paris");
data.forEach((val, key) => console.log(`${key} lives in ${val}`));
```

The `Map` was added to JavaScript as part of the ES2015 specification, and it is not part of the version selected by the `target` property in the `tsconfig.json` file. When the changes to the code file are saved, the compiler will generate the following warning:

```
src/index.ts(6,16): error TS2583: Cannot find name 'Map'. Do you need to
change your target library? Try changing the 'lib' compiler option to
'es2015' or later.
6:50:49 AM - FoundZ 1 error. Watching for file changes.
```

To resolve this problem, I can target a later version of the JavaScript language, or I can change the type definitions used by the compiler with the `lib` configuration property, which is set to an array of values from table 5.7.

Table 5.7   The values for the lib compiler option

Name	Description
ES5, ES2015, ES2016, ES2017, ES2018, ES2019, ES2020, ES2021	These values select type definition files that correspond to a specific version of the JavaScript specification. The old naming scheme can be used as well so that the value ES6 can be used in place of ES2015.
ESnext	This value selects features that are proposed additions to the JavaScript specification but have not yet been formally adopted. The set of features will change over time.
DOM	This value selects type information files for the Document Object Model (DOM) API that web applications use to manipulate the HTML content presented by browsers. This setting is also useful for Node.js applications.
WebWorker	This value selects type information for the web worker feature, which allows web applications to perform background tasks.

There are also values that can be used to select specific features from one version of the language specification. Table 5.8 describes the most useful single-feature settings.

Table 5.8   Useful per-feature values for the lib compiler option

Name	Description
es2015.Core	This setting includes type information for the main features introduced by ES2015.
es2015.Collection	This setting includes type information for the Map and Set collections, described in chapters 4 and 13.
es2015.Generator es2015.Iterable	These settings include type information for the generator and iterator features described in chapter 4 and 13.
es2015.Promise	This setting includes type information for promises, which describe asynchronous actions.
es2015.Reflect	This setting includes type information for the reflection features that provide access to properties and prototypes, as described in part 3.

It is important to think through the implications of using the `lib` configuration setting because it just tells the TypeScript compiler that the runtime for the application can be relied on to support a specific set of features, such as the Map in this case. The compiler can adapt the JavaScript it generates for different language features, but that doesn't extend to objects like collections. Changing the `lib` setting tells the compiler that there will be a nonstandard set of features available when the compiled JavaScript is executed, and it is your responsibility to ensure this is the case, either because you know more about the runtime than the compiler or because the application uses a polyfill such as `core-js` (https://github.com/zloirock/core-js).

The Node.js version installed in chapter 2 supports most of the recent JavaScript features and can be relied on to have Map, which means that I can safely change the `lib` setting in the `tsconfig.json` file, as shown in listing 5.22.

Listing 5.22   Changing the configuration in the tsconfig.json file in the tools folder

```
{
    "compilerOptions": {
        "target": "ES5",
        "outDir": "./dist",
        "rootDir": "./src",
        "noEmitOnError": true,
        "lib": ["es5", "dom", "es2015.collection"]
    }
}
```

The set of types I have selected includes the standard types for the version of JavaScript selected by the `target` property, the `dom` setting (which provides access to the `console` object), and the ES2015 collections feature from table 5.8.

The compiler will detect the change to the configuration file and recompile the code. The change to the `lib` setting tells the compiler that the `Map` will be available, and no error is reported. When the compiler code is executed, it produces the following output:

```
Message: Hello, TypeScript
Bob lives in London
Alice lives in Paris
```

This example runs because the Node.js version used in this book supports the `Map` feature. In this situation, I knew more about the runtime than the TypeScript compiler, and changing the `lib` setting produces an example that runs, although the same effect could have been achieved by changing the `target` setting to a more recent JavaScript version that the compiler knows includes collections. If I were targeting a runtime that supported only ES5, then I would have to provide a polyfill implementation of `Map`, such as the one included in the `core-js` package.

5.8   *Selecting a module format*

In chapter 4, I explained how modules can be used to break a JavaScript application into multiple files, making a project easier to manage. The TypeScript compiler can be configured to specify the module format that is used by the JavaScript it emits, ensuring that the output code can be executed by the target runtime.

As a demonstration, add a file called `calc.ts` to the `src` folder with the code shown in listing 5.23.

> **Listing 5.23   The contents of the calc.ts file in the src folder**

```
export function sum(...vals: number[]): number {
    return vals.reduce((total, val) => total += val);
}
```

The new file uses the `export` keyword to make a function named `sum` that reduces an array of `number` values to create a total. Listing 5.24 imports the function into the `index.ts` file and calls the function.

> **Listing 5.24   Using a module in the index.ts file in the src folder**

```
import { sum } from "./calc";

let printMessage = (msg: string): void =>
    console.log(`Message: ${ msg }`);

let message = ("Hello, TypeScript");
printMessage(message);

let total = sum(100, 200, 300);
console.log(`Total: ${total}`);
```

When the file is saved, the compiler will process the code files, and the resulting Java-Script produces the following output:

```
Message: Hello, TypeScript
Total: 600
```

Examine the contents of the `index.js` file in the `dist` folder, and you will see that the TypeScript compiler has introduced code to deal with the modules:

```
"use strict";
Object.defineProperty(exports, "__esModule", { value: true });
var calc_1 = require("./calc");
var printMessage = function (msg) { return console.log("Message:
    ".concat(msg)); };
var message = ("Hello, TypeScript");
printMessage(message);
var total = (0, calc_1.sum)(100, 200, 300);
console.log("Total: ".concat(total));
```

The TypeScript compiler uses the `target` configuration property to select the approach taken to deal with modules. When the target is `ES5`, it uses the CommonJS module style, which was the result of an earlier attempt to introduce a module standard before ECMAScript modules were widely adopted. The Node.js runtime supports the `commonjs` module system, which is why the code generated by the TypeScript compiler executes without problems.

When later versions of the JavaScript language are targeted, the TypeScript compiler switches to the ECMAScript module format, which means that the `import` and `export` keywords are passed on from the TypeScript code to the JavaScript code without being changed.

Listing 5.25 changes the compiler configuration to select the version of JavaScript and removes the `lib` setting so that the compiler will use the default type definitions.

> **Listing 5.25 Changing the configuration in the tsconfig.json file in the tools folder**

```
{
    "compilerOptions": {
        "target": "ES2022",
        "outDir": "./dist",
        "rootDir": "./src",
        "noEmitOnError": true,
        //"lib": ["es5", "dom", "es2015.collection"]
    }
}
```

When the change to the configuration file is saved, the compiler will regenerate the JavaScript using standard modules. Node.js doesn't support ECMAScript modules without some additional changes, and the code emitted by the compiler produces the following error when the JavaScript code is executed:

```
...
import { sum } from "./calc";
^^^^^^

SyntaxError: Cannot use import statement outside a module
...
```

The first required change is to configure the project to tell Node.js that it should use ECMAScript modules, which is done in the `package.json` file, as shown in listing 5.26.

Listing 5.26   Specifying a module format in the package.json file in the tools folder

```json
{
  "name": "tools",
  "version": "1.0.0",
  "description": "",
  "main": "index.js",
  "scripts": {
    "start": "tsc-watch --onsuccess \"node dist/index.js\""
  },
  "keywords": [],
  "author": "",
  "license": "ISC",
  "devDependencies": {
    "tsc-watch": "^6.0.0",
    "typescript": "^5.0.2"
  },
  "type": "module"
}
```

The `type` property can be set to `module`, for ECMAScript modules, or `commonjs`, for CommonJS modules. One further change is required, which is to include the file extension in file name in the `import` statement, as shown in listing 5.27

Listing 5.27   Adding a file extension in the index.ts file in the src folder

```typescript
import { sum } from "./calc.js";

let printMessage = (msg: string): void =>  console.log(`Message: ${ msg }`);

let message = ("Hello, TypeScript");
printMessage(message);

let total = sum(100, 200, 300);

console.log(`Total: ${total}`);
```

This requirement is an oddity because it requires the file extension of the JavaScript file that is produced by the compiler to be specified in the TypeScript file. The TypeScript development team has adopted the principle of not rewriting paths in `import` statements, which means that the path component of the `import` statement, which specifies the file name, must be written for the JavaScript runtime and not the TypeScript compiler.

Given the extent to which the TypeScript compiler rewrites code, this seems like an odd and awkward omission to me, but it is unlikely to change and so `import` statements must be written with the `js`, and not `ts`, file extension.

Using the module format-specific file extensions

An alternative to using the `package.json` file to specify a module format is to use file extensions. The `mjs` extension denotes an ECMAScript module and the `cjs` extension denotes a `CommonJS` module. The TypeScript compiler supports the `mts` and `cts` extensions for TypeScript files, which produce JavaScript files with the `mjs` and `cjs` extensions. If you use this feature, you will still need to include the JavaScript file extension in the `import` statement to use the features defined in the module. I use the file extension feature in chapter 15, in an example that requires matching the module format used by a third-party package.

5.8.1 Specifying a module format

The module system can be explicitly selected using the `module` setting in the `tsconfig.json` file, using the values described in table 5.9.

Table 5.9 The Module Formats

Name	Description
None	This value disables modules.
CommonJS	This value selects the CommonJS module format, which is supported by Node.js.
AMD	This value selects the Asynchronous Module Definition (AMD), which is supported by the `RequireJS` module loader.
System	This value selects the module format supported by the SystemJS module loader.
UMD	This value selects the Universal Module Definition (UMD) module format.
ES2015, ES6	This value selects the module format specified in the ES2016 language specification.
ES2020	This value selects the module format specified in the ES2020 language specification, which includes dynamic loading of modules.
ES2022	This value selects the module format specified in the ES2022 language specification, which supports initializing a module with asynchronous data.
ESNext	This value selects the module features that have been proposed for the next version of the JavaScript language.
Node16	This value targets Node.js, using ECMAScript modules or CommonJS modules based on file extensions and the configuration in the `package.json` file.
NodeNext	This value selects the module features that have been proposed for the next version of Node.js.

For web applications, especially those built using a framework like React or Angular, the module format will be dictated by the framework's toolchain, which will include either a bundler, which packages up all of the modules into a single JavaScript file during deployment, or a module loader, which sends HTTP requests to the webserver to get JavaScript files as they are required. You will see examples of using the Type-Script compiler with these frameworks in part 3.

The most useful setting for projects that target the Node.js runtime is `Node16`, as shown in listing 5.28, which ensures that the type of module produced by the Type-Script compiler is configured using the `type` property in the `package.json` file or the `mts` and `cts` file extensions. You don't have to set the module property at all, and the default behavior will work, but using the `Node16` setting ensures that a mismatch between the TypeScript compiler and Node.js won't arise. (You may see the module setting flagged with a warning by your code editor. You can ignore this warning, which is resolved in the next listing).

Listing 5.28   Selecting a module format in the tsconfig.json file in the tools folder

```
{
    "compilerOptions": {
        "target": "ES2022",
        "outDir": "./dist",
        "rootDir": "./src",
        "noEmitOnError": true,
        //"lib": ["es5", "dom", "es2015.collection"]
        "module": "Node16"
    }
}
```

If you look at the `index.js` file in the `dist` folder, you will see the generated JavaScript code deals with the `calc.js` file like this:

```
...
import { sum } from "./calc.js";
...
```

The `import` statement in the TypeScript file is the same statement used for ECMAScript modules, and so the TypeScript compiler includes the statement without modification in the JavaScript file. Listing 5.29 changes the `type` property in the `package.json` file to specify the `CommonJS` module format.

Listing 5.29   Changing the module format in the package.json file in the tools folder

```
{
  "name": "tools",
  "version": "1.0.0",
  "description": "",
  "main": "index.js",
  "scripts": {
```

```
    "start": "tsc-watch --onsuccess \"node dist/index.js\""
  },
  "keywords": [],
  "author": "",
  "license": "ISC",
  "devDependencies": {
    "tsc-watch": "^6.0.0",
    "typescript": "^5.0.2"
  },
  "type": "commonjs"
}
```

The TypeScript compiler will run when the `package.json` file is saved. If you examine the `index.js` file again, you will see that the change in the `package.json` file has led to a change in the module format:

```
...
Object.defineProperty(exports, "__esModule", { value: true });

const calc_js_1 = require("./calc.js");
...
```

The compiler has generated statements required for the CommonJS module format and the code produces the following output when it is executed:

```
Message: Hello, TypeScript
Total: 600
```

> **Understanding module resolution**
>
> The TypeScript compiler can use different approaches to resolving dependencies on modules, which it selects based on the module format that is being used. The two most commonly-used modes are *classic*, which searches for modules in the local project, and *Node*, which locates modules in the `node_modules` folder. The default settings are suitable for most projects but can be overridden using the `moduleResolution` configuration property in the `tsconfig.json` file using the `classic` or `node` value.

5.9 *Useful compiler configuration settings*

The TypeScript compiler supports a large number of configuration options. In part 2, I include a table at the start of each chapter that lists the compiler settings used by the features in the examples. For quick reference, table 5.10 lists the compiler options used in this book. Many of these options won't make sense at the moment, but each one is described when it is used, and all will make sense by the end of this book.

> **TIP** See https://www.typescriptlang.org/docs/handbook/compiler-options .html for the complete set of options the compiler supports.

Table 5.10   The TypeScript compiler options used in this book

Name	Description
allowJs	This option includes JavaScript files in the compilation process.
allowSyntheticDefaultImports	This option allows imports from modules that do not declare a default export. This option is used to increase code compatibility.
baseUrl	This option specifies the root location used to resolve module dependencies.
checkJs	This option tells the compiler to check JavaScript code for common errors.
declaration	This option produces type declaration files, which provide type information for JavaScript code.
downlevelIteration	This option enables support for iterators when targeting older versions of JavaScript.
emitDecoratorMetadata	This option includes decorator metadata in the JavaScript emitted by the compiler and is used with the `experimentalDecorators` option.
esModuleInterop	This option adds helper code for importing from modules that do not declare a default export and is used in conjunction with the `allowSyntheticDefault Imports` option.
experimentalDecorators	This option enables support for decorators.
forceConsistentCasingInFileNames	This option ensures that names in `import` statements match the case used by the imported file.
importHelpers	This option determines whether helper code is added to the JavaScript to reduce the amount of code that is produced overall.
isolatedModules	This option treats each file as a separate module, which increases compatibility with the Babel tool.
jsx	This option specifies how HTML elements in JSX/TSX files are processed.
jsxFactory	This option specifies the name of the factory function that is used to replace HTML elements in JSX/TSX files.
lib	This option selects the type declaration files the compiler uses.
module	This option specifies the format used for modules.
moduleResolution	This option specifies the style of module resolution that should be used to resolve dependencies.
noEmit	This option prevents the compiler from emitting JavaScript code, with the result that it only checks code for errors.
noImplicitAny	This option prevents the implicit use of the `any` type, which the compiler uses when it can't infer a more specific type.

Table 5.10 The TypeScript compiler options used in this book *(continued)*

Name	Description
noImplicitReturns	This option requires all paths in a function to return a result.
noUncheckedIndexedAccess	This option does not allow properties accessed via an index signature to be accessed until they have been guarded against undefined values.
noUnusedParameters	This option causes the compiler to produce a warning if a function defines parameters that are not used.
outDir	This option specifies the directory in which the Java-Script files will be placed.
paths	This option specifies the locations used to resolve module dependencies.
resolveJsonModule	This option allows JSON files to be imported as though they were modules.
rootDir	This option specifies the root directory that the compiler will use to locate TypeScript files.
skipLibCheck	This option speeds up compilation by skipping the normal checking of declaration files.
sourceMap	This option determines whether the compiler generates source maps for debugging.
strict	This option enables stricter checking of TypeScript code.
strictNullChecks	This option prevents null and undefined from being accepted as values for other types.
suppressExcessPropertyErrors	This option prevents the compiler from generating errors for objects that define properties not in a specified shape.
target	This option specifies the version of the JavaScript language that the compiler will target in its output.
typeRoots	This option specifies the root location that the compiler uses to look for declaration files.
types	This option specifies a list of declaration files to include in the compilation process.

Summary

In this chapter, I introduced the TypeScript compiler, which is responsible for transforming TypeScript code into pure JavaScript. I explained how the compiler is configured, demonstrated the different ways that it can be used, showed you how to change the version of the JavaScript language that is targeted, and explained how to change the way that modules are resolved. I finished this chapter by listing the configuration options used in this book, which may not make sense now but will become clearer as you progress through the examples.

- TypeScript projects have a structure that keeps the TypeScript code written by the developer separate from the JavaScript code executed by the runtime.
- The TypeScript tools are added to a project using the standard JavaScript package manager, NPM, or one of its competitors.
- The TypeScript compiler processes the TypeScript files in the project and generates pure JavaScript files.
- The tsconfig.json file is used to configure the way the compiler generates JavaScript files.
- The TypeScript compiler can be used in watch mode, where TypeScript files are compiled when change is detected, but a third-party package, such as `tsc-watch`, is required to automatically execute the generated JavaScript files.
- The TypeScript compiler can generate code that conforms to different versions of the JavaScript language specification.
- The TypeScript compiler can generate code that uses different JavaScript module formats and has support for using the same configuration settings as Node.js to determine which format is used.

In the next chapter, I continue with the theme of TypeScript developer tools and explain how to perform debugging and unit testing of TypeScript code.

Testing and debugging TypeScript

6

This chapter covers

- Debugging TypeScript code using Visual Studio Code and the Node.js debugger
- Using a linter to find problems in code the compiler won't detect
- Writing and executing unit tests on TypeScript code

In this chapter, I continue the theme of TypeScript development tools started in chapter 5, which introduced the TypeScript compiler. I show you the different ways that TypeScript code can be debugged, demonstrate the use of TypeScript and the linter, and explain how to set up unit testing for TypeScript code.

6.1 Preparing for this chapter

For this chapter, I continue using the `tools` project created in chapter 5. No changes are required for this chapter.

> **TIP** You can download the example project for this chapter—and for all the other chapters in this book—from https://github.com/manningbooks/essential-typescript-5.

Open a new command prompt and use it to run the command shown in listing 6.1 in the `tools` folder to start the compiler in watch mode using the `tsc-watch` package installed in chapter 5.

Listing 6.1   Starting the compiler

```
npm start
```

The compiler will start, the TypeScript files in the project will be compiled, and the following output will be displayed:

```
7:04:50 AM - Starting compilation in watch mode...
7:04:52 AM - Found 0 errors. Watching for file changes.
Message: Hello, TypeScript
Total: 600
```

6.2   Debugging TypeScript code

The TypeScript compiler does a good job of reporting syntax errors or problems with data types, but there will be times when you have code that compiles successfully but doesn't execute in the way you expected. Using a debugger allows you to inspect the state of the application as it is executing and can reveal why problems occur. In the sections that follow, I show you how to debug a TypeScript application that is executed by Node.js. In part 3, I show you how to debug TypeScript web applications.

6.2.1   Preparing for debugging

The difficulty with debugging a TypeScript application is that the code being executed is the product of the compiler, which transforms the TypeScript code into pure Java-Script. To help the debugger correlate the JavaScript code with the TypeScript code, the compiler can generate files known as *source maps*. Listing 6.2 enables source maps in the `tsconfig.json` file.

Listing 6.2   Enabling source maps in the tsconfig.json file in the tools folder

```
{
    "compilerOptions": {
        "target": "ES2022",
        "outDir": "./dist",
        "rootDir": "./src",
        "noEmitOnError": true,
        "module": "Node16",
        "sourceMap": true
    }
}
```

When the compiler next compiles the TypeScript files, it will also generate a map file, which has the `map` file extension, alongside the JavaScript files in the `dist` folder.

ADDING BREAKPOINTS

Code editors that have good TypeScript support, such as Visual Studio Code, allow breakpoints to be added to code files. My experience with this feature has been mixed, and I have found them unreliable, which is why I rely on the less elegant but more predictable `debugger` JavaScript keyword. When a JavaScript application is executed through a debugger, execution halts when the `debugger` keyword is encountered, and control is passed to the developer. The advantage of this approach is that it is reliable and universal, but you must remember to remove the `debugger` keyword before deployment. Most runtimes ignore the `debugger` keyword during normal execution, but it isn't a behavior that can be counted on. (Linting, described later in this chapter, can help avoid leaving the `debugger` keyword in code files.) In listing 6.3, I have added the `debugger` keyword to the `index.ts` file.

> **Listing 6.3 Adding the debugger keyword in the index.ts file in the src folder**

```
import { sum } from "./calc.js";

let printMessage = (msg: string): void => console.log(`Message: ${ msg }`);

let message = ("Hello, TypeScript");
printMessage(message);

debugger;

let total = sum(100, 200, 300);

console.log(`Total: ${total}`);
```

There will be no change in the output when the code is executed because Node.js ignores the `debugger` keyword by default.

6.2.2 Using Visual Studio Code for debugging

Most good code editors have some degree of support for debugging TypeScript and JavaScript code. In this section, I show you how to perform debugging with Visual Studio Code to give you an idea of the process. There may be different steps required if you use another editor, but the basic approach is likely to be similar.

To set up the configuration for debugging, select Add Configuration from the Run menu and select Node.js from the list of environments when prompted, as shown in figure 6.1.

> **NOTE** If selecting the Add Configuration menu doesn't work, try selecting Start Debugging instead.

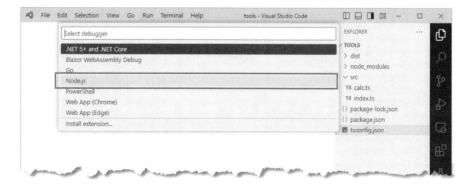

Figure 6.1 Selecting the debugger environment

The editor will create a .vscode folder in the project and add to it a file called launch .json, which is used to configure the debugger. Change the value of the program property so that the debugger executes the JavaScript code from the dist folder, as shown in listing 6.4.

Listing 6.4   Changing the code path in the launch.json file in the .vscode folder

```json
{
    "version": "0.2.0",
    "configurations": [
        {
            "type": "node",
            "request": "launch",
            "name": "Launch Program",
            "skipFiles": [
                "<node_internals>/**"
            ],
            "program": "${workspaceFolder}/dist/index.js",
            "outFiles": [
                "${workspaceFolder}/**/*.js"
            ]
        }
    ]
}
```

Save the changes to the launch.json file and select Start Debugging from the Run menu. Visual Studio Code will execute the index.js file in the dist folder under the control of the Node.js debugger. Execution will continue as normal until the debugger statement is reached, at which point execution halts and control is transferred to the debugging pop-up, as shown in figure 6.2.

Figure 6.2   Debugging an application using Visual Studio Code

The state of the application is displayed in the sidebar, showing the variables that are set at the point that execution was halted. A standard set of debugging features is available, including setting watches, stepping into and over statements, and resuming execution. The Debug Console window allows JavaScript statements to be executed in the context of the application so that entering a variable name and pressing Return, for example, will return the value assigned to that variable.

6.2.3 *Using the integrated Node.js debugger*

Node.js provides a basic integrated debugger. Open a new command prompt and use it to run the command shown in listing 6.5 in the `tools` folder.

> **NOTE** There are no hyphens before the `inspect` argument in listing 6.5. Using hyphens enables the remote debugger described in the following section.

Listing 6.5 Starting the Node.js debugger

```
node inspect dist/index.js
```

The debugger starts, loads the `index.js` file, and halts execution. Enter the command shown in listing 6.6 and press Return to continue execution.

Listing 6.6 Continuing execution

```
c
```

The debugger halts again when the `debugger` statement is reached. You can execute expressions to inspect the state of the applications using the `exec` command, although expressions have to be quoted as strings. Enter the command shown in listing 6.7 at the debug prompt.

Listing 6.7 Evaluating an expression in the Node.js debugger

```
exec("message")
```

Press Return, and the debugger will display the value of the `message` variable, producing the following output:

```
'Hello, TypeScript'
```

Type `help` and press Return to see a list of commands. Press `Control+C` twice to end the debugging session and return to the regular command prompt.

6.2.4 *Using the remote Node.js debugging feature*

The integrated Node.js debugger is useful but awkward to use. The same features can be used remotely using the Google Chrome developer tools feature. First, start Node.js by running the command shown in listing 6.8 in the `tools` folder.

Listing 6.8 Starting Node.js in remote debugger mode

```
node --inspect-brk dist/index.js
```

The `inspect-brk` argument starts the debugger and halts execution immediately. This is required for the example application because it runs and then exits. For applications that start and then enter an indefinite loop, such as a web server, the `inspect` argument can be used. When it starts, Node.js will produce a message like this:

```
Debugger listening on ws://127.0.0.1:9229/e3cf5393-23c8-4393-99a1
For help, see: https://nodejs.org/en/docs/inspector
```

The URL in the output is used to connect to the debugger and take control of execution. Open a new Chrome window and navigate to `chrome://inspect`. Click the Configure button and add the IP address and port from the URL from the previous message. For my machine, this is `127.0.0.1:9229`, as shown in figure 6.3.

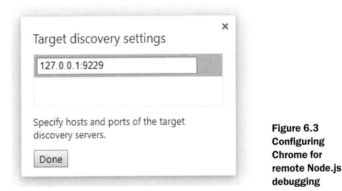

Figure 6.3
Configuring
Chrome for
remote Node.js
debugging

Click the Done button and wait a moment while Chrome locates the Node.js runtime. Once it has been located, it will appear in the Remote Target list, as shown in figure 6.4.

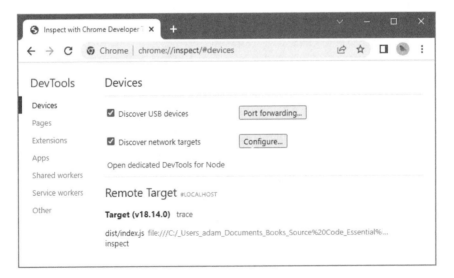

Figure 6.4   Discovering the Node.js runtime

Click the "inspect" link to open a new Chrome developer tools window that is connected to the Node.js runtime. Control of execution is handled by the standard developer tool buttons, and resuming execution will let the runtime proceed until the debugger statement is reached. The initial view of the code in the debugger window will be of the JavaScript code, but the source maps will be used once execution resumes, as shown in figure 6.5.

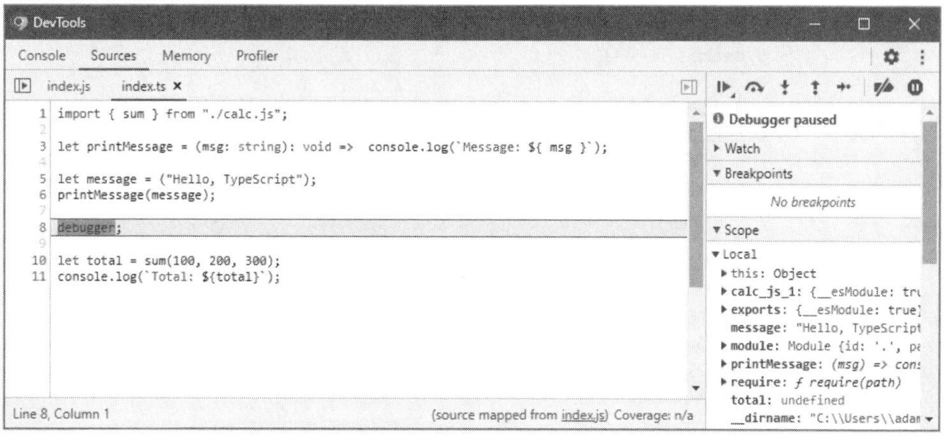

Figure 6.5   Debugging with the Chrome developer tools

6.3   *Using the TypeScript linter*

A linter is a tool that checks code files using a set of rules that describe problems that cause confusion, produce unexpected results, or reduce the readability of the code. The standard linter package for TypeScript is `typescript-eslint`, which adapts the popular JavaScript linter package `eslint` to work with TypeScript. To add the linter to the project, use a command prompt to run the commands shown in listing 6.9 in the `tools` folder.

> **NOTE**   The standard TypeScript linter used to be TSLint, but this has been deprecated in favor of the `typescript-eslint` package.

Listing 6.9   Adding packages to the example project

```
npm install --save-dev eslint@8.36.0
npm install --save-dev @typescript-eslint/parser@5.55.0
npm install --save-dev @typescript-eslint/eslint-plugin@5.55.0
```

To create the configuration required to use the linter, add a file called `.eslintrc` to the `tools` folder with the content shown in listing 6.10.

Listing 6.10   The contents of the .eslintrc file in the tools folder

```
{
    "root": true,
    "ignorePatterns": ["node_modules", "dist"],
    "parser": "@typescript-eslint/parser",
    "parserOptions": {
      "project": "./tsconfig.json"
    },
    "plugins": [
      "@typescript-eslint"
    ],
    "extends": [
      "eslint:recommended",
      "plugin:@typescript-eslint/eslint-recommended",
      "plugin:@typescript-eslint/recommended"
    ]
}
```

The linter comes with preconfigured sets of rules that are specified using the `extends` setting, as described in table 6.1.

Table 6.1   The TSLint preconfigured rule sets

Name	Description
`eslint:recommended`	This is the set of rules suggested by the ESLint development team and is intended for general JavaScript development.
`@typescript-eslint/ eslint-recommended`	This set overrides the `recommended` set to disable rules that are not required for linting TypeScript code.
`@typescript-eslint/ recommended`	This set contains additional rules that are specific to Type-Script code.

Stop the `node` process using `Control+C` and run the command shown in listing 6.11 in the `tools` folder to run the linter on the example project. (Don't omit the period at the end of the command.)

Listing 6.11   Running the TypeScript linter

```
npx eslint .
```

The `project` argument tells the linter to use the compiler settings file to locate the source files it will check, although there is only one TypeScript file in the example project. The linter will check the code and produce the following output:

```
C:\tools\src\index.ts

  3:5   error   'printMessage' is never reassigned.
     Use 'const' instead  prefer-const

  5:5   error   'message' is never reassigned.
     Use 'const' instead         prefer-const
  8:1   error   Unexpected 'debugger' statement no-debugger
```

```
10:5  error  'total' is never reassigned.
      Use 'const' instead         prefer-const

4 problems (4 errors, 0 warnings)
  3 errors and 0 warnings potentially fixable with the `--fix` option.
```

The linter locates the TypeScript code files and checks them for compliance with the rules specified in the configuration file. The code in the example project breaks two of the linter's rules: the `prefer-const` rule requires the `const` keyword to be used in place of `let` when the value assigned to a variable isn't changed, and the `no-debugger` rule prevents the `debugger` keyword from being used.

6.3.1 Disabling linting rules

The problem is that the value of a linting rule is often a matter of personal style and preference, and even when the rule is useful, it isn't always helpful in every situation. Linting works best when you only get warnings that you want to address. If you receive a list of warnings that you don't care about, then there is a good chance you won't pay attention when something important is reported.

The `prefer-const` rule highlights a deficiency in my coding style, but it is one that I have learned to accept. I know that I should use `const` instead of `let`, and that's what I try to do. But my coding habits are deeply ingrained, and my view is that some problems are not worth fixing, especially since doing so requires breaking my concentration on the larger flow of the code I write. I accept my imperfections and know that I will continue to use `let`, even when I know that `const` would be a better choice. I don't want the linter to highlight this problem, and the linter can be configured to disable rules, as shown in listing 6.12.

> **Listing 6.12 Disabling a linter rule in the .eslintrc file in the tools folder**

```
{
    "root": true,
    "ignorePatterns": ["node_modules", "dist"],
    "parser": "@typescript-eslint/parser",
    "parserOptions": {
      "project": "./tsconfig.json"
    },
    "plugins": [
      "@typescript-eslint"
    ],
    "extends": [
      "eslint:recommended",
      "plugin:@typescript-eslint/eslint-recommended",
      "plugin:@typescript-eslint/recommended"
    ],
    "rules": {
      "prefer-const": 0
    }
}
```

The `rules` configuration section is populated with the names of the rules and a value of `1` or `0` to enable or disable the rules. By setting a value of 0 for the `prefer-const` rule, I have told the linter to ignore my use of the `let` keyword when `const` would be a better choice.

Some rules are useful in a project but disabled for specific files or statements. This is the category into which the `no-debugger` rule falls. As a general principle, the `debugger` keyword should not be left in code files in case it causes problems during code execution. However, when investigating a problem, `debugger` is a useful way to reliably take control of the execution of the application, as demonstrated earlier in this chapter.

In these situations, it doesn't make sense to disable a rule in the linter's configuration file. Instead, a comment that starts with `eslint-disable-line` followed by one or more rule names disables rules for a single statement, as shown in listing 6.13.

> **Listing 6.13   Disabling a rule for a single statement in the index.ts file in the src folder**

```
import { sum } from "./calc.js";

let printMessage = (msg: string): void => console.log(`Message: ${ msg }`);

let message = ("Hello, TypeScript");
printMessage(message);

debugger; // eslint-disable-line no-debugger

let total = sum(100, 200, 300);
console.log(`Total: ${total}`);
```

The comment in listing 6.13 tells the linter not to apply the `no-debugger` rule to the highlighted statement. Run the command in listing 6.11 again, and you will see that the configuration change and the linter comment suppress the earlier warnings.

> **TIP** Rules can be disabled for all the statements that follow a block comment (one that starts with `/*` and ends with `*/`) that starts with `eslint-disable`. You can disable all linting rules by using the `eslint-disable` or `eslint -disable-line` comment without any rule names.

The joy and misery of linting

Linters can be a powerful tool for good, especially in a development team with mixed levels of skill and experience. Linters can detect common problems and subtle errors that lead to unexpected behavior or long-term maintenance issues. I like this kind of linting, and I like to run my code through the linting process after I have completed a major application feature or before I commit my code into version control.

But linters can also be a tool of division and strife. In addition to detecting coding errors, linters can be used to enforce rules about indentation, brace placement, the use of semicolons and spaces, and dozens of other style issues. Most developers have style preferences that they adhere to and believe that everyone else should, too. I certainly do:

(continued)

I like four spaces for indentation, and I like opening braces to be on the same line as the expression they relate to. I know that these are part of the "one true way" of writing code, and the fact that other programmers prefer two spaces, for example, has been a source of quiet amazement to me since I first started writing code.

Linters allow people with strong views about formatting to enforce them on others, generally under the banner of being "opinionated." The logic is that developers spend too much time arguing about different coding styles, and everyone is better off being forced to write in the same way. My experience is that developers will just find something else to argue about and that forcing a code style is often just an excuse to make one person's preferences mandatory for an entire development team.

I often help readers when they can't get book examples working (my email address is adam@adam-freeman.com if you need help), and I see all sorts of coding styles every week. I know, deep in my heart, that anyone who doesn't follow my personal coding preferences is just plain wrong. But rather than forcing them to code my way, I get my code editor to reformat the code, which is a feature that every capable editor provides.

My advice is to use linting sparingly and focus on the issues that will cause real problems. Leave formatting decisions to the individuals and rely on code editor reformatting when you need to read code written by a team member who has different preferences.

6.4 Unit testing TypeScript

Some unit test frameworks provide support for TypeScript, although that isn't as useful as it may sound. Supporting TypeScript for unit testing means allowing tests to be defined in TypeScript files and, sometimes, automatically compiling the TypeScript code before it is tested. Unit tests are performed by executing small parts of an application, and that can be done only with JavaScript since the JavaScript runtime environments have no knowledge of TypeScript features. The result is that unit testing cannot be used to test TypeScript features, which are solely enforced by the TypeScript compiler.

For this book, I have used the Jest test framework, which is easy to use and supports TypeScript tests. Also, with the addition of an extra package, it will ensure that the TypeScript files in the project are compiled into JavaScript before tests are executed. Run the commands shown in listing 6.14 in the `tools` folder to install the packages required for testing.

Listing 6.14 Adding packages to the project

```
npm install --save-dev jest@29.4.3
npm install --save-dev ts-jest@29.0.5
npm install --save-dev @types/jest@29.4.0
```

The `jest` package contains the testing framework. The `ts-jest` package is a plugin to the Jest framework and is responsible for compiling TypeScript files before tests are applied. The `@types/jest` package contains the TypeScript definitions for the Jest API.

Deciding whether to unit test

Unit testing is a contentious topic. This section assumes you do want to do unit testing and shows you how to set up the tools and apply them to TypeScript. It isn't an introduction to unit testing, and I make no effort to persuade skeptical readers that unit testing is worthwhile. If you would like an introduction to unit testing, then there is a good article here: https://en.wikipedia.org/wiki/Unit_testing.

I like unit testing, and I use it in my projects—but not all of them and not as consistently as you might expect. I tend to focus on writing unit tests for features and functions that I know will be hard to write and are likely to be the source of bugs in deployment. In these situations, unit testing helps structure my thoughts about how to best implement what I need. I find that just thinking about what I need to test helps produce ideas about potential problems, and that's before I start dealing with actual bugs and defects.

But unit testing is a tool and not a religion, and only you know how much testing you require. If you don't find unit testing useful or if you have a different methodology that suits you better, then don't feel you need to unit test just because it is fashionable. (However, if you don't have a better methodology and you are not testing at all, then you are probably letting users find your bugs, which is rarely ideal.)

6.4.1   Configuring the test framework

To configure Jest, add a file named `jest.config.js` to the `tools` folder with the content shown in listing 6.15.

Listing 6.15   The contents of the jest.config.js file in the tools folder

```
module.exports = {
    "roots": ["src"],
    "transform": {"^.+\\.tsx?$": "ts-jest"}
}
```

The `roots` setting is used to specify the location of the code files and unit tests. The `transform` property is used to tell Jest that files with the `ts` and `tsx` file extension should be processed with the `ts-jest` package, which ensures that changes to the code are reflected in tests without needing to explicitly start the compiler. (TSX files are described in chapter 15.)

6.4.2   Creating unit tests

Tests are defined in files that have the `test.ts` file extension and are conventionally created alongside the code files they relate to. To create a simple unit test for the example application, add a file called `calc.test.ts` to the `src` folder and add the code shown in listing 6.16.

Listing 6.16   The contents of the calc.test.ts file in the src folder

```
import { sum } from "./calc";

test("check result value", () => {
    let result = sum(10, 20, 30);
    expect(result).toBe(60);
});
```

Tests are defined using the `test` function, which is provided by Jest. The `test` arguments are the name of the test and a function that performs the testing. The unit test in listing 6.16 is given the name `check result value`, and the test invokes the `sum` function with three arguments and inspects the results. Jest provides the `expect` function that is passed the result and used with a matcher function that specifies the expected result. The matcher in listing 6.16 is `toBe`, which tells Jest that the expected result is a specific value. Table 6.2 describes the most useful matcher functions. (You can find the full list of matcher functions at https://jestjs.io/docs/en/expect.)

Notice that the `import` statement in listing 6.16 doesn't specify the file extension. This is because the Jest package is publishing using the `CommonJS` module format, and not the ECMAScript format that TypeScript is configured to use. As noted in earlier chapters, it will take some time before everyone converges on ECMAScript modules and, until then, attention must be paid to file names in `import` statements.

Table 6.2   Useful Jest matcher functions

Name	Description
toBe(value)	This method asserts that a result is the same as the specified value (but need not be the same object).
toEqual(object)	This method asserts that a result is the same object as the specified value.
toMatch(regexp)	This method asserts that a result matches the specified regular expression.
toBeDefined()	This method asserts that the result has been defined.
toBeUndefined()	This method asserts that the result has not been defined.
toBeNull()	This method asserts that the result is null.
toBeTruthy()	This method asserts that the result is truthy.
toBeFalsy()	This method asserts that the result is falsy.
toContain(substring)	This method asserts that the result contains the specified substring.
toBeLessThan(value)	This method asserts that the result is less than the specified value.
toBeGreaterThan(value)	This method asserts that the result is more than the specified value.

6.4.3 *Starting the test framework*

Unit tests can be run as a one-off task or by using a watch mode that runs the tests when changes are detected. I find the watch mode to be most useful so I have two command prompts open: one for the output from the compiler and one for the unit tests. To start the tests, open a new command prompt, navigate to the `tools` folder, and run the command shown in listing 6.17. You can ignore the warnings about version mismatches produced by the `ts-jest` package.

Listing 6.17 Starting the unit test framework in watch mode

```
npx jest --watchAll
```

Jest will start, locate the test files in the project, and execute them, producing the following output:

```
PASS  src/calc.test.ts
  check result value (3ms)
Test Suites: 1 passed, 1 total
Tests:       1 passed, 1 total
Snapshots:   0 total
Time:        3.214s
Ran all test suites.
Watch Usage
 ' Press f to run only failed tests.
 ' Press o to only run tests related to changed files.
 ' Press p to filter by a filename regex pattern.
 ' Press t to filter by a test name regex pattern.
 ' Press q to quit watch mode.
 ' Press Enter to trigger a test run.
```

The output shows that Jest discovered one test and ran it successfully. When additional tests are defined or when any of the source code in the application changes, Jest will run the tests again and issue a new report. To see what happens when a test fails, make the change shown in listing 6.18 to the `sum` function that is the subject of the test.

Listing 6.18 Making a test fail in the calc.ts file in the src folder

```
export function sum(...vals: number[]): number {
    return vals.reduce((total, val) => total += val) + 10;
}
```

The `sum` function no longer returns the value expected by the unit test, and Jest produces the following warning:

```
FAIL  src/calc.test.ts
  check result value (6ms)
  check result value
    expect(received).toBe(expected) // Object.is equality
    Expected: 60
    Received: 70
      3 | test("check result value", () => {
      4 |     let result = sum(10, 20, 30);
```

```
> 5 |        expect(result).toBe(60);
   |                         ^
  6 | });
     at Object.<anonymous> (src/calc.test.ts:5:20)
Test Suites: 1 failed, 1 total
Tests:       1 failed, 1 total
Snapshots:   0 total
Time:        4.726s
Ran all test suites.
Watch Usage: Press w to show more.
```

The output shows the result expected by the test and the result that was received. Failed tests can be resolved by fixing the source code to conform to the expectations of the test or, if the purpose of the source code has changed, updating the test to reflect the new behavior. Listing 6.19 modifies the unit test.

Listing 6.19 Changing a unit test in the calc.test.ts file in the src folder

```
import { sum } from "./calc";

test("check result value", () => {
    let result = sum(10, 20, 30);
    expect(result).toBe(70);
});
```

When the change to the test is saved, Jest runs the tests again and reports success.

```
PASS  src/calc.test.ts
  check result value (3ms)
Test Suites: 1 passed, 1 total
Tests:       1 passed, 1 total
Snapshots:   0 total
Time:        5s
Ran all test suites.
Watch Usage: Press w to show more.
```

Summary

In this chapter, I introduced three tools that are often used to support TypeScript development. The Node.js debugger is a useful way to inspect the state of applications as they are executed, the linter helps avoid common coding errors that are not detected by the compiler but that cause problems nonetheless, and the unit test framework is used to confirm that code behaves as expected. TypeScript can be debugged using the integrated debugger included in Visual Studio Code or using the debugger integrated into Node.js.

- Breakpoints can be created using the code editor or with the `debugger` keyword.
- The TypeScript linter checks TypeScript code for common problems.
- TypeScript relies on third-party frameworks, such as Jest, for unit testing.
- In the next chapter, I start describing TypeScript features in depth, starting with static type checking.

Part 2

Understanding
static types

In this chapter, I introduce the key TypeScript features for working with data types. The features I describe in this chapter are the foundations for working with TypeScript, and they are the building blocks for the advanced features described in later chapters.

I start by showing how TypeScript's types differ from pure JavaScript's types. I demonstrate that the TypeScript compiler can infer data types from code, and then I introduce features that provide precise control over data types, either by giving the TypeScript compiler information about how sections of code are expected to behave or by changing the way that the compiler is configured. Table 7.1 summarizes the chapter.

Table 7.1 Chapter summary

Problem	Solution	Listing
Specify a type	Use a type annotation or allow the compiler to infer a type	10–13
Inspect the types that the compiler infers	Enable the `declarations` compiler option and inspect the compiled code	14, 15
Allow any type to be used	Specify the `any` or `unknown` types	16–19, 29, 30
Prevent the compiler from inferring the `any` type	Enable the `noImplicitAny` compiler option	20
Combine types	Use a type union	21, 22
Override the type expected by the compiler	Use a type assertion	23–25
Test for a primitive value type	Use the `typeof` operator as a type guard	26–28
Prevent `null` or `undefined` from being accepted as values of other types	Enable the `strictNullChecks` compiler option	31–33
Override the compiler to remove `null` values from a union	Use a non-`null` assertion or use a type guard	34, 35
Allow a variable to be used when it has not been assigned a value	Use the definite assignment assertion	36, 37

For quick reference, table 7.2 lists the TypeScript compiler options used in this chapter.

Table 7.2 The TypeScript compiler options used in this chapter

Name	Description
`declaration`	This option produces type declaration files when enabled, which can be useful in understanding how types have been inferred. These files are described in more detail in chapter 15.
`noImplicitAny`	This option prevents the implicit use of the `any` type, which the compiler uses when it can't infer a more specific type.
`outDir`	This option specifies the directory in which the JavaScript files will be placed.
`rootDir`	This option specifies the root directory that the compiler will use to locate TypeScript files.
`strictNullChecks`	This option prevents `null` and `undefined` from being accepted as values for other types.
`target`	This option specifies the version of the JavaScript language that the compiler will target in its output.

7.1 *Preparing for this chapter*

To create the example project for this chapter, create a folder called `types` in a convenient location. Open a new command prompt, navigate to the `types` folder, and run the command shown in listing 7.1 to initialize the folder for use with NPM.

TIP You can download the example project for this chapter—and for all the other chapters in this book—from https://github.com\manningbooks/ essential-typescript-5.

Listing 7.1   Initializing the Node Package Manager

```
npm init --yes
```

Run the command shown in listing 7.2 in the types folder to add the packages required for this chapter.

Listing 7.2   Adding packages to the project

```
npm install --save-dev typescript@5.0.2
npm install --save-dev tsc-watch@6.0.0
```

To configure the TypeScript compiler, add a file called tsconfig.json to the types folder with the content shown in listing 7.3.

Listing 7.3   The contents of the tsconfig.json file in the types folder

```
{
    "compilerOptions": {
        "target": "ES2022",
        "outDir": "./dist",
        "rootDir": "./src"
    }
}
```

These configuration settings tell the TypeScript compiler to generate code for the most recent JavaScript implementations, using the src folder to look for TypeScript files and the dist folder for its outputs. To configure NPM so that it can start the compiler, add the configuration entry shown in listing 7.4 to the package.json file.

Listing 7.4   Configuring NPM in the package.json file in the types folder

```
{
  "name": "types",
  "version": "1.0.0",
  "description": "",
  "main": "index.js",
  "scripts": {
    "start": "tsc-watch --onsuccess \"node dist/index.js\""
  },
  "keywords": [],
  "author": "",
  "license": "ISC",
  "devDependencies": {
    "tsc-watch": "^6.0.0",
    "typescript": "^5.0.2"
  }
}
```

To create the entry point for the project, create the `types/src` folder and add to it a file called `index.ts` with the code shown in listing 7.5.

Listing 7.5 The contents of the index.ts file in the src folder

```
console.log("Hello, TypeScript");
```

Use the command prompt to run the command shown in listing 7.6 in the `types` folder to start the TypeScript compiler.

Listing 7.6 Starting the TypeScript compiler

```
npm start
```

The compiler will compile the code in the `index.ts` file, execute the output, and then enter watch mode, producing the following output:

```
6:43:06 AM - Starting compilation in watch mode...

6:43:08 AM - Found 0 errors. Watching for file changes.
Hello, TypeScript
```

7.2 Understanding static types

As I explained in chapter 4, JavaScript is dynamically typed. The biggest obstacle that JavaScript presents to programmers who are used to other languages is that *values* have types instead of variables. As a quick reminder of how this works, replace the code in the `index.ts` file with the statements shown in listing 7.7.

Listing 7.7 Replacing the contents of the index.ts file in the src folder

```
let myVar;

myVar = 12;
myVar = "Hello";
myVar = true;
```

The type of the variable named `myVar` changes based on the value assigned to it. The JavaScript `typeof` keyword can be used to determine a type, as shown in listing 7.8.

Listing 7.8 Displaying the variable type in the index.ts file in the src folder

```
let myVar;
console.log(`${myVar} = ${typeof myVar}`);
myVar = 12;
console.log(`${myVar} = ${typeof myVar}`);
myVar = "Hello";
console.log(`${myVar} = ${typeof myVar}`);
myVar = true;
console.log(`${myVar} = ${typeof myVar}`);
```

Save the changes to the file, and you will see the following output when the compiled code is executed:

```
undefined = undefined
12 = number
Hello = string
true = boolean
```

The first statement in listing 7.8 defines the variable without assigning a value, which means that its type is `undefined`. A variable whose type is `undefined` will always have a value of `undefined`, which can be seen in the output.

The value `12` is a `number`, and as soon as the value is assigned, the data type of the variable changes. The value `Hello` is a `string`, and the value `false` is a `boolean`; you can see the data type as each value is assigned to the variable. You don't need to tell JavaScript the data type, which it automatically infers from the value. For quick reference, table 7.3 describes the built-in types that JavaScript provides.

Table 7.3   The JavaScript built-in types

Name	Description
number	This type is used to represent numeric values.
string	This type is used to represent text data.
boolean	This type can have `true` and `false` values.
symbol	This type is used to represent unique constant values, such as keys in collections.
null	This type can be assigned only the value `null` and is used to indicate a nonexistent or invalid reference.
undefined	This type is used when a variable has been defined but has not been assigned a value.
object	This type is used to represent compound values, formed from individual properties and values.

Dynamic types offer flexibility, but they can also lead to problems, as shown in listing 7.9, which replaces the code in the `index.ts` file with a function and a set of statements that invoke it.

Listing 7.9   Defining a function in the index.ts file in the src folder

```
function calculateTax(amount) {
    return amount * 1.2;
}

console.log(`${12} = ${calculateTax(12)}`);
console.log(`${"Hello"} = ${calculateTax("Hello")}`);
console.log(`${true} = ${calculateTax(true)}`);
```

Function parameter types are also dynamic, which means that the `calculateTax` function may receive values of any type. The statements that follow the function invoke it with `number`, `string`, and `boolean` values, producing the following results when the code is executed:

```
12 = 14.399999999999999
Hello = NaN
true = 1.2
```

From a JavaScript perspective, there is nothing wrong with this example. Function parameters can receive values of any type, and JavaScript has handled each type exactly as it should. But the `calculateTax` function has been written with the assumption that it will only receive `number` values, which is why only the first result makes sense. (The second result, `NaN`, means not a number, and the third result is obtained by coercing `true` to the number value `1` and using that in the calculation—see chapter 4 for details of JavaScript type coercion.)

It is easy to understand the function's assumption about its parameter type when you can see the code next to the statements that use it, but it's much harder when the function has been written by another programmer and is deep inside a complex project or package.

7.2.1 Creating a static type with a type annotation

Most developers are used to static types. TypeScript's static type feature makes type assumptions explicit and allows the compiler to report an error when different data types are used. Static types are defined using *type annotations*, as shown in listing 7.10.

> **Listing 7.10   Using a type annotation in the index.ts file in the src folder**

```
function calculateTax(amount: number): number {
    return amount * 1.2;
}

console.log(`${12} = ${calculateTax(12)}`);
console.log(`${"Hello"} = ${calculateTax("Hello")}`);
console.log(`${true} = ${calculateTax(true)}`);
```

There are two annotations in listing 7.10, which are defined using a colon followed by the static type, as shown in figure 7.1.

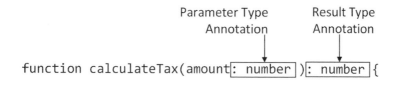

Figure 7.1   Applying type annotations

The type annotation on the function parameter tells the compiler that the function accepts only `number` values. The annotation that follows the function signature indicates the result type and tells the compiler that the function returns only `number` values.

When the code is compiled, the TypeScript compiler analyzes the data types of the values passed to the `calculateTax` function and detects that some of the values have the wrong type, producing the following error messages:

```
src/index.ts(6,42): error TS2345: Argument of type 'string' is not
assignable to parameter of type 'number'.
src/index.ts(7,39): error TS2345: Argument of type 'boolean' is not
assignable to parameter of type 'number'.
```

TIP You may also see warnings in your code editor if it has good support for TypeScript. I use Visual Studio Code for TypeScript development, and it highlights problems directly in the editor window.

Type annotations can also be applied to variables and constants, as shown in listing 7.11.

> **Listing 7.11 Applying annotations to variables in the index.ts file in the src folder**

```
function calculateTax(amount: number): number {
    return amount * 1.2;
}

let price: number = 100;
let taxAmount: number = calculateTax(price);
let halfShare: number = taxAmount / 2;

console.log(`Full amount in tax: ${taxAmount}`);
console.log(`Half share: ${halfShare}`);
```

Annotations are applied after the name, using a colon and a type, just as with the annotations applied to the function. The three variables in listing 7.11 are all annotated to tell the compiler they will be used for `number` values, producing the following output when the code is executed:

```
Full amount in tax: 120
Half share: 60
```

7.2.2 *Using implicitly defined static types*

The TypeScript compiler can infer types, meaning that you can benefit from static types without using annotations, as shown in listing 7.12.

> **Listing 7.12 Relying on implicit types in the index.ts file in the src folder**

```
function calculateTax(amount: number) {
    return amount * 1.2;
}

let price = 100;
let taxAmount = calculateTax(price);
let halfShare = taxAmount / 2;

console.log(`Full amount in tax: ${taxAmount}`);
console.log(`Half share: ${halfShare}`);
```

The TypeScript compiler can infer the type of the `price` variable based on the literal value that it is assigned when it is defined. The compiler knows that `100` is a `number` value and treats the `price` variable as though it has been defined with a `number` type annotation, which means that it is an acceptable value to use as an argument to the `calculateTax` function.

The compiler is also able to infer the result of the `calculateTax` function because it knows that only `number` parameters will be accepted, that `1.2` is a `number` value, and that the result of the multiplication operator on two `number` values is a `number`.

The result from the function is assigned to the `taxAmount` variable, which the compiler is also able to infer as a `number`. Finally, the compiler knows the type produced by the division operator on two `number` values and can infer the type of the `halfShare` variable, too.

The TypeScript compiler remains silent when types are used correctly, and it is easy to forget that the code is being checked. To see what happens when the inferred types don't match, change the function in the `index.ts` file as shown in listing 7.13.

> **Listing 7.13 Changing the result type in the index.ts file in the src folder**

```
function calculateTax(amount: number) {
    return (amount * 1.2).toFixed(2);
}

let price = 100;
let taxAmount = calculateTax(price);
let halfShare = taxAmount / 2;

console.log(`Full amount in tax: ${taxAmount}`);
console.log(`Half share: ${halfShare}`);
```

The `toFixed` method formats `number` values so they have a fixed number of digits after the decimal point. The result of the `toFixed` method is a `string`, which changes the result from the `calculateTax` function. When the TypeScript compiler works its way through the chain of types, it sees the division operator applied to a `string` and a `number`:

```
...
let halfShare = taxAmount / 2;
...
```

This is legal JavaScript and will be dealt with by type coercion, as described in chapter 3. In this case, the `string` value will be converted to a `number`, and the outcome will be either the division of two `number` values or `NaN` if the `string` value cannot be converted.

In TypeScript, automatic type coercion is restricted, and the compiler reports an error instead of trying to convert values:

```
src/index.ts(7,17): error TS2362: The left-hand side of an arithmetic
operation must be of type 'any', 'number', 'bigint' or an enum type.
```

The TypeScript compiler doesn't prevent the use of the JavaScript type features, but it does generate errors when it sees statements that can lead to problems.

There can be times, especially when you are first starting to use TypeScript, when you will receive errors because the compiler infers types in a way that you don't expect. In almost every instance, the compiler will be correct, but there is a useful compiler feature that can be enabled to reveal the types that are used in the code, as shown in listing 7.14.

Listing 7.14　Configuring the compiler in the tsconfig.json file in the types folder

```
{
    "compilerOptions": {
        "target": "ES2022",
        "outDir": "./dist",
        "rootDir": "./src",
        "declaration": true
    }
}
```

The `declaration` setting tells the compiler to generate files that contain type information alongside the JavaScript code it produces. I describe these files in detail in chapter 15, but for now, it is enough to know they help identify the types that the compiler has inferred, even though this is not their intended purpose. The configuration change will take effect when the compiler next runs. To trigger compilation, add the statement shown in listing 7.15 to the `index.ts` file and then save the changes.

Listing 7.15　Adding a statement to the index.ts file in the src folder

```
function calculateTax(amount: number) {
    return (amount * 1.2).toFixed(2);
}

let price = 100;
let taxAmount = calculateTax(price);
let halfShare = taxAmount / 2;

console.log(`Price: ${price}`);
console.log(`Full amount in tax: ${taxAmount}`);
console.log(`Half share: ${halfShare}`);
```

When the compiler runs, it will generate a file named `index.d.ts` in the `dist` folder, which contains the following content:

```
declare function calculateTax(amount: number): string;
declare let price: number;
declare let taxAmount: string;
declare let halfShare: number;
```

The purpose of the `declare` keyword—and the file itself—is explained in chapter 15, but this file reveals the types that the compiler has inferred for the statements in listing 7.15, showing that the return types for the `calculateTax` function and the `taxAmount` variable are `string`. When you get a compiler error, looking at the files generated when the `declaration` setting is `true` can be helpful, especially if you can't see any obvious cause.

7.2.3　*Using the any type*

TypeScript doesn't stop you from using the flexibility of the JavaScript type system, but it does try to prevent you from using it accidentally. To allow all types as function parameters and results or be able to assign all types to variables and constants, TypeScript provides the any type, as shown in listing 7.16.

Listing 7.16　Using the any type in the index.ts file in the src folder

```
function calculateTax(amount: any): any {
    return (amount * 1.2).toFixed(2);
}

let price = 100;
let taxAmount = calculateTax(price);
let halfShare = taxAmount / 2;

console.log(`Price: ${price}`);
console.log(`Full amount in tax: ${taxAmount}`);
console.log(`Half share: ${halfShare}`);
```

These annotations tell the compiler that the amount parameter can accept any value and that the function's result may be of any type. The use of the any type stops the compiler from reporting the error produced by listing 7.15 because it no longer validates that the result from the calculateTax function can be used with the division operator. The code will run successfully because JavaScript converts the division operands to number values automatically so that the string returned by calculateTax is parsed to a number, producing the following result when the code is executed:

```
Price: 100
Full amount in tax: 120.00
Half share: 60
```

When you use the any type, you take responsibility for ensuring that your code doesn't misuse types, just as you would if you were using pure JavaScript. In listing 7.17, I have changed the calculateTax function so that it prepends a currency symbol to its result.

Listing 7.17　Changing the function result in the index.ts file in the src folder

```
function calculateTax(amount: any): any {
    return `$${(amount * 1.2).toFixed(2)}`;
}

let price = 100;
let taxAmount = calculateTax(price);
let halfShare = taxAmount / 2;

console.log(`Price: ${price}`);
console.log(`Full amount in tax: ${taxAmount}`);
console.log(`Half share: ${halfShare}`);
```

The function's result cannot be parsed into a number value, so the code produces this output when it is executed:

```
Price: 100
Full amount in tax: $120.00
Half share: NaN
```

One consequence of using `any` is that it can be assigned to all other types without triggering a compiler warning, as shown in listing 7.18.

Listing 7.18   Assigning the any type in the index.ts file in the src folder

```
function calculateTax(amount: any): any {
    return `$${(amount * 1.2).toFixed(2)}`;
}

let price = 100;
let taxAmount = calculateTax(price);
let halfShare = taxAmount / 2;

console.log(`Price: ${price}`);
console.log(`Full amount in tax: ${taxAmount}`);
console.log(`Half share: ${halfShare}`);

let newResult: any = calculateTax(200);
let myNumber: number = newResult;
console.log(`Number value: ${myNumber.toFixed(2)}`);
```

The `any` value `newResult` is assigned to a `number` without causing a compiler warning. At runtime, the `calculateTax` method returns a `string` result, which doesn't define the `toFixed` method invoked in the last statement in listing 7.18 and produces the following error when the code is executed:

```
console.log(`Number value: ${myNumber.toFixed(2)}`);
                                        ^
TypeError: myNumber.toFixed is not a function
```

The compiler trusts that the `any` value can be treated as a `number`, which means a type mismatch occurs at runtime. The `any` type allows full use of the JavaScript type features, which can be useful but can lead to unexpected results when types are coerced automatically at runtime.

> **TIP** TypeScript also provides the `unknown` type to provide deliberate access to the dynamic type features while restricting accidental use, as described in the "Using the Unknown Type" section.

USING IMPLICITLY DEFINED ANY TYPES

The TypeScript compiler will use `any` when it is assigning types implicitly and cannot identify a more specific type to use. This makes it easier to selectively apply TypeScript in an existing JavaScript project and can simplify working with third-party JavaScript packages. In listing 7.19, I have removed the type annotation from the `calculateTax` parameter.

```
function calculateTax(amount): any {
    return `$$${(amount * 1.2).toFixed(2)}`;
}

let price = 100;
let taxAmount = calculateTax(price);
let halfShare = taxAmount / 2;

let personVal = calculateTax("Bob");

console.log(`Price: ${price}`);
console.log(`Full amount in tax: ${taxAmount}`);
console.log(`Half share: ${halfShare}`);
console.log(`Name: ${personVal}`);
```

The compiler will use an implicit `any` for the function parameter because it isn't able to determine a better type to use, which is why no compiler error will be reported when the function is invoked with a `string` argument, producing the following output:

```
Price: 100
Full amount in tax: $120.00
Half share: NaN
Name: $NaN
```

You can confirm the `implicit` use of `any` by inspecting the contents of the `index` `.d.ts` file in the `dist` folder, which will contain the following description of the `calculateTax` function:

```
...
declare function calculateTax(amount: any): any;
...
```

DISABLING IMPLICIT ANY TYPES

Explicitly using `any` provides an escape hatch from type checking, which can be useful when applied cautiously. Allowing the compiler to use `any` implicitly creates gaps in type checking that you may not even notice and that can undermine the benefit of using TypeScript.

It is good practice to disable the implicit use of `any` by setting the compiler's `noImplicityAny` setting, as shown in listing 7.20. (The implicit use of `any` is also disabled when you enable the `strict` compiler setting.)

```
{
    "compilerOptions": {
        "target": "ES2022",
        "outDir": "./dist",
        "rootDir": "./src",
        "declaration": true,
        "noImplicitAny": true
    }
}
```

Save the changes to the compiler configuration file, and the code will be recompiled with the following error:

```
src/index.ts(1,23): error TS7006: Parameter 'amount' implicitly has an
'any' type.
```

The compiler will display this warning when it cannot infer a more specific type, although this doesn't prevent the explicit use of `any`.

7.3   *Using type unions*

At one end of the type safety spectrum is the `any` feature, which allows complete freedom. At the other end of the spectrum are type annotations for a single type, which narrows the range of allowable values. Between these two extremes, TypeScript provides *type unions*, which specify a set of types. In listing 7.21, I have defined a function that returns different data types and used a type annotation with a union to describe the result to the compiler.

> **Listing 7.21   Using a type union in the index.ts file in the src folder**

```
function calculateTax(amount: number, format: boolean): string | number {
    const calcAmount = amount * 1.2;
    return format ? `$${calcAmount.toFixed(2)}` : calcAmount;
}

let taxNumber = calculateTax(100, false);
let taxString = calculateTax(100, true);
```

The type returned by the `calculateTax` function is the union of the `string` and `number` types, which is defined using the bar character between type names, as shown in figure 7.2. The union in listing 7.21 uses two types, but you can combine as many types as you need to create a union.

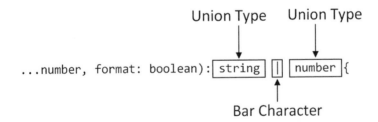

Figure 7.2   Defining a type union

It is important to understand that a type union is handled as a type in its own right, whose features are the intersection of the individual types. This means that the type of the `taxNumber` variable in listing 7.21, for example, is `string | number` and not `number`, even though the `calculateTax` function returns a number when the `boolean` argument is `false`. To emphasize the effect of the union type, listing 7.22 makes the variable types explicit.

Listing 7.22 Declaring union types explicitly in the index.ts file in the src folder

```
function calculateTax(amount: number, format: boolean): string | number {
    const calcAmount = amount * 1.2;
    return format ? `$$${calcAmount.toFixed(2)}` : calcAmount;
}

let taxNumber: string | number  = calculateTax(100, false);
let taxString: string | number  = calculateTax(100, true);

console.log(`Number Value: ${taxNumber.toFixed(2)}`);
console.log(`String Value: ${taxString.charAt(0)}`);
```

You can only use the properties and methods defined by all the types in the union, which can be useful for complex types (as described in chapter 10) but is limited by the small common API presented by primitive values. The only method shared by the number and string types that are used in the union in listing 7.22 is the toString method, as shown in figure 7.3.

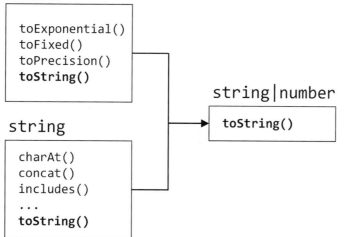

Figure 7.3   The effect of a type union

This means that the other methods defined by the number and string types cannot be used, and the use of the toFixed and charAt methods in listing 7.22 produces the following compiler messages:

```
src/index.ts(9,40): error TS2339: Property 'toFixed' does not exist on type
'string | number'.
  Property 'toFixed' does not exist on type 'string'.
src/index.ts(10,40): error TS2339: Property 'charAt' does not exist on type
'string | number'.
  Property 'charAt' does not exist on type 'number'.
```

7.4   Using Type Assertions

A *type assertion* tells the TypeScript compiler to treat a value as a specific type, known as *type narrowing*. A type assertion is one of the ways that you can narrow a type from a union, as shown in listing 7.23.

Listing 7.23   Using type assertions in the index.ts file in the src folder

```
function calculateTax(amount: number, format: boolean): string | number {
    const calcAmount = amount * 1.2;
    return format ? `$${calcAmount.toFixed(2)}` : calcAmount;
}

let taxNumber = calculateTax(100, false) as number;
let taxString = calculateTax(100, true) as string;

console.log(`Number Value: ${taxNumber.toFixed(2)}`);
console.log(`String Value: ${taxString.charAt(0)}`);
```

A type is asserted using the `as` keyword, followed by the required type, as illustrated in figure 7.4.

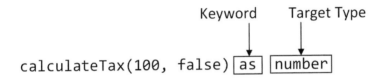

Figure 7.4   Asserting a type

In the listing, the `as` keyword is used to tell the compiler that the value assigned to the `taxNumber` variable is a `number` and that the value assigned to the `taxString` variable is a `string`:

```
...
let taxNumber = calculateTax(100, false) as number;
let taxString = calculateTax(100, true) as string;
...
```

> **CAUTION**   No type conversion is performed by a type assertion, which only tells the compiler what type it should apply to a value for type checking.

When a type is asserted in this way, TypeScript uses the asserted type as the type for the variable, which means that the highlighted statements in listing 7.23 are equivalent to these statements:

```
...
let taxNumber: number = calculateTax(100, false) as number;
let taxString: string = calculateTax(100, true) as string;
...
```

The type asserts select a specific type from the union, which means that the methods and properties available on that type can be used, preventing the errors reported for listing 7.22 and producing the following output:

```
Number Value: 120.00
String Value: $
```

7.4.1 Asserting to an unexpected type

The compiler checks that the type used in an assertion is expected. When using an assertion from a type union, for example, the assertion must be to one of the types in the union. To see what happens when asserting to a type that the compiler doesn't expect, add the statements shown in listing 7.24 to the index.ts file.

> **Listing 7.24 Asserting to an unexpected type in the index.ts file in the src folder**

```
function calculateTax(amount: number, format: boolean): string | number {
    const calcAmount = amount * 1.2;
    return format ? `$${calcAmount.toFixed(2)}` : calcAmount;
}

let taxNumber = calculateTax(100, false) as number;
let taxString = calculateTax(100, true) as string;
let taxBoolean = calculateTax(100, false) as boolean;

console.log(`Number Value: ${taxNumber.toFixed(2)}`);
console.log(`String Value: ${taxString.charAt(0)}`);
console.log(`Boolean Value: ${taxBoolean}`);
```

The type assertion tells the compiler to treat a string | number value as a boolean. The compiler knows that boolean is not one of the types in the union and produces the following error when the code is compiled:

```
src/index.ts(8,18): error TS2352: Conversion of type 'string | number' to
type 'boolean' may be a mistake because neither type sufficiently overlaps
with the other. If this was intentional, convert the expression to
'unknown' first.
  Type 'number' is not comparable to type 'boolean'.
```

In most situations, you should review the data types and the type assertion and correct the problem by expanding the type union or asserting to a different type. However, you can force the assertion and override the compiler's warning by first asserting to any and then to the type you require, as shown in listing 7.25. (The compiler error refers to the unknown type, which I explain in the "Using the Unknown Type" section.)

> **Listing 7.25 Asserting to an unexpected type in the index.ts file in the src folder**

```
function calculateTax(amount: number, format: boolean): string | number {
    const calcAmount = amount * 1.2;
    return format ? `$${calcAmount.toFixed(2)}` : calcAmount;
}

let taxNumber = calculateTax(100, false) as number;
let taxString = calculateTax(100, true) as string;
```

```
let taxBoolean = calculateTax(100, false) as any as boolean;

console.log(`Number Value: ${taxNumber.toFixed(2)}`);
console.log(`String Value: ${taxString.charAt(0)}`);
console.log(`Boolean Value: ${taxBoolean}`);
```

This additional step prevents the compiler from warning about the change and treats the result from the function as a `boolean` value. However, as noted earlier, assertions only affect the type-checking process and do not perform type coercion, which can be seen in the results produced when the code is compiled:

```
Number Value: 120.00
String Value: $
Boolean Value: 120
```

The result produced by the function has been described to the compiler as the `string | number` union and asserted as a `boolean`. But when the code is executed, the function produces a `number`, whose value is written to the console.

7.5   Using a type guard

For primitive values, the `typeof` keyword can be used to test for a specific type without needing a type assertion, as shown in listing 7.26.

> **Listing 7.26   Using a type guard in the index.ts file in the src folder**

```
function calculateTax(amount: number, format: boolean): string | number {
    const calcAmount = amount * 1.2;
    return format ? `$${calcAmount.toFixed(2)}` : calcAmount;
}

let taxValue = calculateTax(100, false);

if (typeof taxValue === "number") {
    console.log(`Number Value: ${taxValue.toFixed(2)}`);

} else if (typeof taxValue === "string") {
    console.log(`String Value: ${taxValue.charAt(0)}`);
}
```

To test a type, the `typeof` keyword is applied to a value, producing a `string` that can be compared to the names of the primitive JavaScript types, such as `number` and `boolean`.

> **NOTE** The `typeof` keyword can be used only with the JavaScript primitive types. A different approach is required to differentiate between objects, as described in chapter 3 and chapter 10.

The compiler doesn't implement the `typeof` keyword, which is part of the JavaScript specification. Instead, the compiler trusts that the statements in the conditional block will be executed at runtime only if the value being tested is of the specified type. This knowledge allows the compiler to treat the value as the type being tested. For example, the first test in listing 7.26 is for `number`:

```
...
if (typeof taxValue === "number") {
    console.log(`Number Value: ${taxValue.toFixed(2)}`);
}
...
```

The TypeScript compiler knows that the statements inside the `if` code block will be executed only if `taxValue` is a `number` and allows the `number` type's `toFixed` method to be used without the need for a type assertion, producing the following result when the code is compiled:

```
Number Value: 120.00
```

The compiler is adept at recognizing type guard statements, even when they are not in a conventional `if...else` block. The code in listing 7.27 produces the same result as listing 7.26 but uses a `switch` statement to differentiate between types. Within each block, the compiler treats `taxValue` as though it has been defined with only the type selected by the `case` statement.

> **Listing 7.27 Type guarding in a switch statement in the index.ts file in the src folder**

```
function calculateTax(amount: number, format: boolean): string | number {
    const calcAmount = amount * 1.2;
    return format ? `$${calcAmount.toFixed(2)}` : calcAmount;
}

let taxValue = calculateTax(100, false);

switch (typeof taxValue) {
    case "number":
        console.log(`Number Value: ${taxValue.toFixed(2)}`);
        break;
    case "string":
        console.log(`String Value: ${taxValue.charAt(0)}`);
        break;
}
```

7.5.1 Understanding the never type

TypeScript provides the `never` type for situations where a type guard has dealt with all of the possible types for a value. In listing 7.27, for example, the `switch` statement is a type guard for the `number` and `string` types, which are the only types that will be returned in the `string | number` union from the function. Once all the possible types have been handled, the compiler will only allow a value to be assigned to the `never` type, as shown in listing 7.28.

> **Listing 7.28 Using the never type in the index.ts file in the src folder**

```
function calculateTax(amount: number, format: boolean): string | number {
    const calcAmount = amount * 1.2;
    return format ? `$${calcAmount.toFixed(2)}` : calcAmount;
}
```

```
let taxValue = calculateTax(100, false);

switch (typeof taxValue) {
    case "number":
        console.log(`Number Value: ${taxValue.toFixed(2)}`);
        break;
    case "string":
        console.log(`String Value: ${taxValue.charAt(0)}`);
        break;
    default:
        let value: never = taxValue;
        console.log(`Unexpected type for value: ${value}`);
}
```

Something has gone wrong if execution reaches the `default` clause of the `switch` statement, and TypeScript provides the `never` type to ensure you can't accidentally use a value once type guards have been used to exhaustively narrow a value to all of its possible types.

7.6   *Using the unknown type*

In the "Using the any Type" section, I explained that an `any` value can be assigned to all other types, which creates a gap in the compiler's type checking. TypeScript also supports the `unknown` type, which is a safer alternative to `any`. An `unknown` value can be assigned only `any` or itself unless a type assertion or type guard is used. Listing 7.29 repeats the statements from the example that showed how the `any` type behaves but uses `unknown` instead.

> **Listing 7.29   Using any and unknown types in the index.ts file in the src folder**

```
function calculateTax(amount: number, format: boolean): string | number {
    const calcAmount = amount * 1.2;
    return format ? `$${calcAmount.toFixed(2)}` : calcAmount;
}

let taxValue = calculateTax(100, false);

switch (typeof taxValue) {
    case "number":
        console.log(`Number Value: ${taxValue.toFixed(2)}`);
        break;
    case "string":
        console.log(`String Value: ${taxValue.charAt(0)}`);
        break;
    default:
        let value: never = taxValue;
        console.log(`Unexpected type for value: ${value}`);
}

let newResult: unknown = calculateTax(200, false);
let myNumber: number = newResult;
console.log(`Number value: ${myNumber.toFixed(2)}`);
```

An unknown value can't be assigned to another type without a type assertion, so the compiler produces the following error when it compiles the code:

```
src/index.ts(18,5): error TS2322: Type 'unknown' is not assignable to type 'number'.
```

Listing 7.30 uses a type assertion to override the warning and tell the compiler to assign the unknown value as a number.

> **Listing 7.30 Asserting an unknown value in the index.ts file in the src folder**

```
function calculateTax(amount: number, format: boolean): string | number {
    const calcAmount = amount * 1.2;
    return format ? `$${calcAmount.toFixed(2)}` : calcAmount;
}

let taxValue = calculateTax(100, false);

switch (typeof taxValue) {
    case "number":
        console.log(`Number Value: ${taxValue.toFixed(2)}`);
        break;
    case "string":
        console.log(`String Value: ${taxValue.charAt(0)}`);
        break;
    default:
        let value: never = taxValue;
        console.log(`Unexpected type for value: ${value}`);
}

let newResult: unknown = calculateTax(200, false);
let myNumber: number = newResult as number;
console.log(`Number value: ${myNumber.toFixed(2)}`);
```

Unlike the earlier example, the unknown value is really a number, so the code doesn't generate a runtime error and produces the following output when executed:

```
Number Value: 120.00
Number value: 240.00
```

7.7   Using nullable types

There is a hole in the TypeScript static type system: the JavaScript null and undefined types. The null type can be assigned only the null value and is used to represent something that doesn't exist or is invalid. The undefined type can be assigned only the undefined value and is used when a variable has been defined but not yet assigned a value.

The problem is that, by default, TypeScript treats null and undefined as legal values for all types. The reason for this is convenience because a lot of existing JavaScript code that may be required for integration into an application uses these values as part of its normal operation, but it does lead to inconsistencies in type checking, as shown in listing 7.31.

Listing 7.31   Using nullable types in the index.ts file in the src folder

```
function calculateTax(amount: number, format: boolean): string | number {
    if (amount === 0) {
        return null;
    }
    const calcAmount = amount * 1.2;
    return format ? `$$${calcAmount.toFixed(2)}` : calcAmount;
}

let taxValue: string | number = calculateTax(0, false);

switch (typeof taxValue) {
    case "number":
        console.log(`Number Value: ${taxValue.toFixed(2)}`);
        break;
    case "string":
        console.log(`String Value: ${taxValue.charAt(0)}`);
        break;
    default:
        let value: never = taxValue;
        console.log(`Unexpected type for value: ${value}`);
}

let newResult: unknown = calculateTax(200, false);
let myNumber: number = newResult as number;
console.log(`Number value: ${myNumber.toFixed(2)}`);
```

The change to the calculateTax shows a typical use of null, where it is used as a
result if the value of the amount parameter is zero, indicating an invalid condition.
The result type for the function and the type of the taxValue variable are string |
number. But, in JavaScript, changing the value assigned to a variable can change its
type, and that is what happens in the example: the second call to the calculateTax
function returns null, which changes the taxValue type to null. When the type
guard statements inspect the type of the variable, they fail to narrow its type to one of
those in the string | number union and produce the following output:

```
Unexpected type for value: null
Number value: 240.00
```

Under normal circumstances, the compiler will report an error if a value of one type
is assigned to a variable of a different type, but the compiler remains silent because it
allows null and undefined to be treated as values for all types.

> **NOTE**   In addition to type inconsistencies, nullable values can lead to runtime
> errors that are difficult to detect during development and often encountered
> by users. In listing 7.31, for example, there is no easy way for consumers of the
> calculateTax function to know that a null value may be returned and to
> understand when that might happen. It is easy to see the null value and the
> reasons for its use in the example but much harder to do the same thing in a
> real project or a third-party package.

7.7.1 *Restricting nullable assignments*

The use of null and undefined can be restricted by enabling the strictNullChecks compiler setting, as shown in listing 7.32. (This setting is also enabled by the strict setting.)

Listing 7.32 Enabling strict null checks in the tsconfig.json file in the types folder

```json
{
    "compilerOptions": {
        "target": "ES2022",
        "outDir": "./dist",
        "rootDir": "./src",
        "declaration": true,
        "noImplicitAny": true,
        "strictNullChecks": true
    }
}
```

When true, this setting tells the compiler not to allow null or undefined values to be assigned to other types. Save the change to the configuration file, and the compiler will recompile the index.ts file and generate the following error:

```
src/index.ts(3,9): error TS2322: Type 'null' is not assignable to type
'string | number'.
```

The configuration change tells the compiler to produce an error when null or undefined values are assigned to another type. In this example, the error occurs because the null value returned by the calculateTax function isn't one of the types in the union that describes the function's result.

To resolve the error, the function can be rewritten not to use null, or the type union used to describe its result can be expanded to include null, which is the approach taken in listing 7.33.

Listing 7.33 Expanding a type union in the index.ts file in the src folder

```typescript
function calculateTax(amount: number, format: boolean)
        : string | number | null {
    if (amount === 0) {
        return null;
    }
    const calcAmount = amount * 1.2;
    return format ? `$${calcAmount.toFixed(2)}` : calcAmount;
}

let taxValue: string | number | null = calculateTax(0, false);

switch (typeof taxValue) {
    case "number":
        console.log(`Number Value: ${taxValue.toFixed(2)}`);
        break;
    case "string":
        console.log(`String Value: ${taxValue.charAt(0)}`);
```

```
        break;
    default:
        if (taxValue === null) {
            console.log("Value is null");
        } else {
            console.log(typeof taxValue);
            let value: never = taxValue;
            console.log(`Unexpected type for value: ${value}`);
        }
}
```

Expanding the type union makes it obvious that `null` values may be returned by the function, ensuring that code that uses the function knows that `string`, `number`, or `null` values have to be dealt with. As explained in chapter 3, using `typeof` on `null` values returns `object`, so guarding against `null` values is done using an explicit value check, which the TypeScript compiler understands as a type guard. The code in listing 7.33 produces the following result when it is executed:

```
Value is null
```

7.7.2 *Removing null from a union with an assertion*

Remember that unions present the intersection of the API of each type. The `null` and `undefined` values don't present any properties or methods, which means that values for nullable type unions can't be used directly, even if the non-null types have an intersection of useful properties or methods (of which there are examples in later chapters). A non-null assertion tells the compiler that a value isn't `null`, which removes `null` from the type union and allows the intersection of the other types to be used, as shown in listing 7.34.

> **CAUTION** A non-null assertion should be used only when you know that a `null` value cannot occur. A runtime error will be caused if you apply the assertion and a null value does occur. A safer approach is to use a type guard, as described in the next section.

Listing 7.34   Using a non-null assertion in the index.ts file in the src folder

```
function calculateTax(amount: number, format: boolean)
        : string | number | null {
    if (amount === 0) {
        return null;
    }
    const calcAmount = amount * 1.2;
    return format ? `$${calcAmount.toFixed(2)}` : calcAmount;
}

let taxValue: string | number = calculateTax(100, false)!;

switch (typeof taxValue) {
    case "number":
        console.log(`Number Value: ${taxValue.toFixed(2)}`);
```

```
        break;
    case "string":
        console.log(`String Value: ${taxValue.charAt(0)}`);
        break;
    default:
        if (taxValue === null) {
            console.log("Value is null");
        } else {
            console.log(typeof taxValue);
            let value: never = taxValue;
            console.log(`Unexpected type for value: ${value}`);
        }
    }
}
```

A non-null value is asserted by applying the ! character after the value, as illustrated in figure 7.5. The assertion in the listing tells the compiler that the result from the `calculateTax` function will not be `null`, which allows it to be assigned to the `taxValue` variable, whose type is `string | number`.

Non-Null Assertion

```
calculateTax(100, false) ! ;
```

Figure 7.5 Asserting a non-null value

The code in listing 7.34 produces this output when it is compiled and executed:

```
Number Value: 120.00
```

7.7.3 *Removing null from a union with a type guard*

An alternative approach is to filter out `null` or `undefined` values using a type guard, as shown in listing 7.35. This approach has the advantage of testing values at runtime.

Listing 7.35 Removing null values with a type guard in the index.ts file in the src folder

```
function calculateTax(amount: number, format: boolean)
        : string | number | null {
    if (amount === 0) {
        return null;
    }
    const calcAmount = amount * 1.2;
    return format ? `$${calcAmount.toFixed(2)}` : calcAmount;
}

let taxValue: string | number | null = calculateTax(100, false);
if (taxValue !== null) {
    let nonNullTaxValue: string | number = taxValue;
    switch (typeof taxValue) {
        case "number":
            console.log(`Number Value: ${taxValue.toFixed(2)}`);
```

```
                break;
            case "string":
                console.log(`String Value: ${taxValue.charAt(0)}`);
                break;
        }
    } else {
        console.log("Value is not a string or a number");
    }
```

The compiler knows that the test for `null` values means that the value can be treated as the non-nullable `string | number` union type with the `if` code block. (The compiler also knows that `taxValue` can be `null` only in the `else` code block.) The code in listing 7.35 produces this output when it is compiled and executed:

```
Number Value: 120.00
```

7.7.4 *Using the definite assignment assertion*

If the `strictNullChecks` option is enabled, the compiler will report an error if a variable is used before it is assigned a value. This is a helpful feature, but there can be times where a value is assigned in a way that isn't visible to the compiler, as shown in listing 7.36.

> **CAUTION** I use the built-in JavaScript `eval` function in listing 7.36 to execute a string as a code statement. The `eval` function is considered dangerous and should not be used in real projects.

Listing 7.36 **Using an unassigned variable in the index.ts file in the src folder**

```
function calculateTax(amount: number, format: boolean)
        : string | number | null {
    if (amount === 0) {
        return null;
    }
    const calcAmount = amount * 1.2;
    return format ? `$${calcAmount.toFixed(2)}` : calcAmount;
}

let taxValue: string | number | null;
eval("taxValue = calculateTax(100, false)");

if (taxValue !== null) {
    let nonNullTaxValue: string | number = taxValue;
    switch (typeof taxValue) {
        case "number":
            console.log(`Number Value: ${taxValue.toFixed(2)}`);
            break;
        case "string":
            console.log(`String Value: ${taxValue.charAt(0)}`);
            break;
    }
} else {
    console.log("Value is not a string or a number");
}
```

The `eval` function accepts a `string` and executes it as a code statement. The Type-Script compiler isn't able to determine the effect of the `eval` function and doesn't realize that it assigns a value to `taxValue`. When the code is compiled, the compiler reports the following errors:

```
src/index.ts(13,5): error TS2454: Variable 'taxValue' is used before being
assigned.
src/index.ts(14,9): error TS2322: Type 'string | number | null' is not
assignable to type 'string | number'.
  Type 'null' is not assignable to type 'string | number'.
src/index.ts(14,44): error TS2454: Variable 'taxValue' is used before being
assigned.
src/index.ts(15,20): error TS2454: Variable 'taxValue' is used before being
assigned.
```

The definitive assignment assertion tells TypeScript that a value will be assigned before the variable is used, as shown in listing 7.37.

> **Listing 7.37   Using definitive assignment assertion in the index.ts file in the src folder**

```
function calculateTax(amount: number, format: boolean)
        : string | number | null {
    if (amount === 0) {
        return null;
    }
    const calcAmount = amount * 1.2;
    return format ? `$${calcAmount.toFixed(2)}` : calcAmount;
}

let taxValue!: string | number | null;
eval("taxValue = calculateTax(100, false)");

if (taxValue !== null) {
    let nonNullTaxValue: string | number = taxValue;
    switch (typeof taxValue) {
        case "number":
            console.log(`Number Value: ${taxValue.toFixed(2)}`);
            break;
        case "string":
            console.log(`String Value: ${taxValue.charAt(0)}`);
            break;
    }
} else {
    console.log("Value is not a string or a number");
}
```

The definitive assignment assertion is a `!` character, but it is applied after the name when the variable is defined, unlike the non-null assertion that is applied in expressions. Just as with the other assertions, you are responsible for ensuring that a value is assigned. You may encounter a runtime error if you use an assertion but don't perform an assignment. The assertion in listing 7.37 allows the code to be compiled, which produces the following output when it is executed:

```
Number Value: 120.00
```

Summary

In this chapter, I explained how TypeScript can be used to restrict the JavaScript type system by performing type checking. I demonstrated how type annotations can be used to specify the types that can be used and how the compiler can infer types from code statements. I explained the use of the any, unknown, and never types; type unions; and guards that restrict the range of types.

- Static types are the headline TypeScript feature and make the JavaScript type system easier to use and more predictable for most programmers.
- Types can be defined explicitly with a type annotation or left to the compiler to infer implicitly from context.
- Type unions are combinations of types, which means that variables can be assigned values with any type that is contained in the union.
- Type assertions tell the compiler that a value has a specific type, which can specify a specific type from the set defined in a union or override the compiler's understanding of a given type.
- The JavaScript typeof keyword can be used as an alternative to a type assertion for the JavaScript primitive types.
- The any type is used to denote a variable that can be assigned values of any type.
- Values with the unknown type can only be assigned to a different type using a type assertion or by assignment via the any type.
- The never type is used to prevent values from accidentally being used when they don't have an expected type.
- By default, TypeScript allows null and undefined values to be assigned to any variable, but this behavior can be changed by setting the strictNullChecks compiler configuration property.

In the next chapter, I explain how TypeScript deals with functions in more depth.

Using functions

8

This chapter covers

- Defining functions with static data types for the parameters and results
- Working with optional function parameters
- Defining function parameters with default values
- Using rest parameters to capture multiple argument values
- Overloading function types
- Using assert functions as type guards

In this chapter, I explain how TypeScript is applied to functions, showing you how TypeScript helps prevent common problems when defining functions, dealing with parameters, and producing results. Table 8.1 summarizes the chapter.

Table 8.1 Chapter summary

Problem	Solution	Listing
Allow a function to be called with fewer arguments than parameters	Define optional parameters or define parameters with default values	7, 8
Allow a function to be called with more arguments than parameters	Use a rest parameter	9, 10
Restrict the types that can be used for parameter values and results	Apply type annotations to parameters or function signatures	11, 17, 18

Table 8.1   Chapter summary *(continued)*

Problem	Solution	Listing
Prevent null values from being used as function arguments	Enable the `strictNullChecks` compiler option	12–14
Ensure that all function code paths return a result	Enable the `noImplicitReturns` compiler option	15, 16
Describe the relationship between the types of a function's parameters and its result	Overload the function's types	19, 20
Describe the effect of an `assert` function	Use the `assert` keyword	21–23

For quick reference, table 8.2 lists the TypeScript compiler options used in this chapter.

Table 8.2   The TypeScript compiler options used in this chapter

Name	Description
`target`	This option specifies the version of the JavaScript language that the compiler will target in its output.
`outDir`	This option specifies the directory in which the JavaScript files will be placed.
`rootDir`	This option specifies the root directory that the compiler will use to locate TypeScript files.
`declaration`	This option produces type declaration files when enabled, which can be useful in understanding how types have been inferred. These files are described in more detail in chapter 15.
`strictNullChecks`	This option prevents `null` and `undefined` from being accepted as values for other types.
`noImplicitReturns`	This option requires all paths in a function to return a result.
`noUnusedParameters`	This option causes the compiler to produce a warning if a function defines parameters that are not used.

8.1   Preparing for this chapter

In this chapter, I continue to use the `types` project created in chapter 7. To prepare for this chapter, replace the contents of the `index.ts` file in the `src` folder with the code shown in listing 8.1.

TIP   You can download the example project for this chapter—and for all the other chapters in this book—from https://github.com/manningbooks/essential-typescript-5.

> **Listing 8.1   The contents of the index.ts file in the src folder**

```
function calculateTax(amount) {
    return amount * 1.2;
}

let taxValue = calculateTax(100);
console.log(`Total Amount: ${taxValue}`);
```

Comment out the compiler options that prevent the implicit use of the any type and the assignment of the null and undefined values to other types, as shown in listing 8.2.

> **Listing 8.2   Disabling compiler options in the tsconfig.json file in the types folder**

```
{
    "compilerOptions": {
        "target": "ES2022",
        "outDir": "./dist",
        "rootDir": "./src",
        "declaration": true,
        // "noImplicitAny": true,
        // "strictNullChecks": true
    }
}
```

Open a new command prompt, navigate to the types folder, and run the command shown in listing 8.3 to start the TypeScript compiler so it automatically executes code after it has been compiled.

> **Listing 8.3   Starting the TypeScript compiler**

```
npm start
```

The compiler will compile the code in the index.ts file, execute the output, and then enter watch mode, producing the following output:

```
6:52:41 AM - Starting compilation in watch mode...

6:52:43 AM - Found 0 errors. Watching for file changes.
Total Amount: 120
```

8.2   Defining functions

TypeScript transforms JavaScript functions to make them more predictable and to make the data type assumptions explicit so they can be checked by the compiler. The index.ts file contains this simple function:

```
...
function calculateTax(amount) {
    return amount * 1.2;
}
...
```

Chapter 7 demonstrated how TypeScript features like type annotations can be applied to functions. In the sections that follow, I revisit these features and describe the other ways that TypeScript enhances functions.

8.2.1   *Redefining functions*

One of the most important changes that TypeScript introduces is a warning when a function is redefined. In JavaScript, a function can be defined more than once, and the most recent implementation is used when the function is invoked. This leads to a common problem for developers who have moved to JavaScript from another language, as shown in listing 8.4.

> **Listing 8.4   Redefining a function in the index.ts file in the src folder**

```
function calculateTax(amount) {
    return amount * 1.2;
}

function calculateTax(amount, discount) {
    return calculateTax(amount) - discount;
}

let taxValue = calculateTax(100);
console.log(`Total Amount: ${taxValue}`);
```

Many languages support function overloading, which allows multiple functions to be defined with the same name as long as they have different numbers of parameters or if the parameters have different types. If you are used to this style of programming, the code in listing 8.4 looks perfectly normal, and you will assume the second calculateTax function builds on the first calculateTax function to apply a discount.

JavaScript doesn't support function overloading, and when you define two functions with the same name, the second function replaces the first, regardless of the function's parameters. The number of arguments used to call a function is not important in JavaScript—if there are more parameters than arguments, then the extra parameters are undefined. If there are more arguments than parameters, the function can either ignore them or use the special arguments value, which provides access to all the arguments used to invoke the function. If the code in listing 8.4 were executed, the first calculateTax function would be ignored, and the second function would be invoked, but without a value for the second parameter. When the function is executed, it would invoke itself repeatedly, until the call stack becomes exhausted and an error is produced.

To avoid this problem, the TypeScript compiler reports an error when more than one function is defined with the same name. Here are the error messages produced by the compiler for the code in listing 8.4:

```
src/index.ts(1,10): error TS2393: Duplicate function implementation.
src/index.ts(5,10): error TS2393: Duplicate function implementation.
```

The practical effect of not being able to overload functions is that different names must be used (such as calculateTax and calculateTaxWithDiscount, for example) or a single function adapts its behavior based on its parameters. I find the first approach works well for complex groups of features, and I prefer the second approach for simpler tasks. Listing 8.5 takes the second approach and consolidates the functionality into a single function.

Listing 8.5 Consolidating functions in the index.ts file in the src folder

```
function calculateTax(amount, discount) {
    return (amount * 1.2) - discount;
}

let taxValue = calculateTax(100, 0);
console.log(`Total Amount: ${taxValue}`);
```

The code in listing 8.6 produces the following output when compiled and executed:

```
Total Amount: 120
```

8.2.2 Understanding function parameters

I had to make two changes in listing 8.5 to get the code to compile. The first was to remove the duplicate `calculateTax` function and combine the functionality in a single function. The second change was to the statement that calls the function, to which I added a second argument:

```
...
let taxValue = calculateTax(100, 0);
...
```

TypeScript has a stricter approach than JavaScript and expects functions to be used with the same number of arguments as there are parameters. Add the statements shown in listing 8.6 to the `index.ts` file to see how the compiler responds to different numbers of arguments.

Listing 8.6 Calling a function in the index.ts file in the src folder

```
function calculateTax(amount, discount) {
    return (amount * 1.2) - discount;
}

let taxValue = calculateTax(100, 0);
console.log(`2 args: ${taxValue}`);
taxValue = calculateTax(100);
console.log(`1 arg: ${taxValue}`);
taxValue = calculateTax(100, 10, 20);
console.log(`3 args: ${taxValue}`);
```

The first new call to the function doesn't provide enough arguments, and the second provides too many. The compiler reports the following errors when the code is compiled:

```
src/index.ts(7,12): error TS2554: Expected 2 arguments, but got 1.
src/index.ts(9,34): error TS2554: Expected 2 arguments, but got 3.
```

The compiler insists on matching arguments to parameters to make the expectations in the code explicit, just as for the features described in chapter 7. When you examine a set of parameters, you can't easily determine how the function will behave if some of them don't receive values. And when a function is invoked with a different number of arguments, it is difficult to determine whether this is intentional or an error. TypeScript tackles both of these problems by requiring arguments that correspond to all parameters unless the function indicates that it can be more flexible using the features described in the following sections.

> **TIP**   If the `noUnusedParameters` option is enabled, the compiler will warn you if a function defines parameters that it doesn't use.

USING OPTIONAL PARAMETERS

Function parameters are mandatory by default, but this can be changed by using optional parameters, as shown in listing 8.7. (I have also commented out the statement that has too many arguments, which I return to in the following sections.)

Listing 8.7   Defining an optional parameter in the index.ts file in the src folder

```
function calculateTax(amount, discount?) {
    return (amount * 1.2) - (discount || 0);
}

let taxValue = calculateTax(100, 0);
console.log(`2 args: ${taxValue}`);
taxValue = calculateTax(100);
console.log(`1 arg: ${taxValue}`);
//taxValue = calculateTax(100, 10, 20);
//console.log(`3 args: ${taxValue}`);
```

Optional parameters are defined by placing a question mark after the parameter name, as illustrated in figure 8.1.

> **NOTE**   Optional parameters must be defined after the required parameters. This means that I cannot reverse the order of the `amount` and `discount` parameters in listing 8.7, for example, because `amount` is required and `discount` is optional.

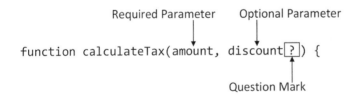

Figure 8.1   Defining an optional parameter

Callers of the `calculateTax` function can omit a value for the `discount` parameter, which will provide the function with an `undefined` value parameter. Functions that declare optional parameters must ensure they can operate when values are not supplied, and the function in listing 8.7 does this using the logical OR operator (||) to coalesce undefined values to zero if the `discount` parameter is undefined, like this:

```
...
return (amount * 1.2) - (discount || 0);
...
```

The `discount` parameter is used in the same way as the required parameter, and the only change is that the function must be able to deal with the possibility of an `undefined` value.

The user of the function doesn't have to take any special measures to deal with the optional parameter. In the case of the example, this means the `calculateTax` function can be used with one or two arguments. The code in listing 8.7 produces the following output when it is executed:

```
2 args: 120
1 arg: 120
```

USING A PARAMETER WITH A DEFAULT VALUE

If there is a fallback value that should be used for an optional parameter, then it can be applied when the parameter is defined, as shown in listing 8.8.

> **Listing 8.8   Using a default parameter value in the index.ts file in the src folder**

```
function calculateTax(amount, discount = 0) {
    return (amount * 1.2) - discount;
}

let taxValue = calculateTax(100, 0);
console.log(`2 args: ${taxValue}`);
taxValue = calculateTax(100);
console.log(`1 arg: ${taxValue}`);
//taxValue = calculateTax(100, 10, 20);
//console.log(`3 args: ${taxValue}`);
```

A parameter with a default value is known as a *default-initialized parameter*. The name of the parameter is followed by the assignment operator (a single = character) and the value, as shown in figure 8.2. Notice that no question mark is used when defining a parameter with a default value.

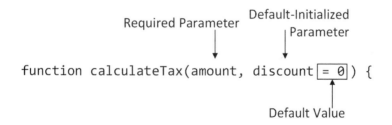

Figure 8.2   Defining a default parameter value

Using a default value means that the code in the function doesn't have to check for `undefined` values and means that the fallback value can be changed in a single location and take effect throughout the function.

TIP   Parameters with default values are still optional parameters, even though no question mark is used, and must be defined after the function's required parameters.

The code in listing 8.8 produces the following output when it compiled and executed:

```
2 args: 120
1 arg: 120
```

USING A REST PARAMETER

The counterpart to optional parameters is the *rest parameter*, which allows a function to accept a variable number of arguments, which are grouped and presented together. A function can have one rest parameter only, and it must be the last parameter, as shown in listing 8.9.

> **Listing 8.9   Defining a rest parameter in the index.ts file in the src folder**

```
function calculateTax(amount, discount = 0, ...extraFees) {
    return (amount * 1.2) - discount
        + extraFees.reduce((total, val) => total + val, 0);
}

let taxValue = calculateTax(100, 0);
console.log(`2 args: ${taxValue}`);
taxValue = calculateTax(100);
console.log(`1 arg: ${taxValue}`);
taxValue = calculateTax(100, 10, 20);
console.log(`3 args: ${taxValue}`);
```

A rest parameter is defined by prefixing the parameter name with an ellipsis (three periods), as shown in figure 8.3.

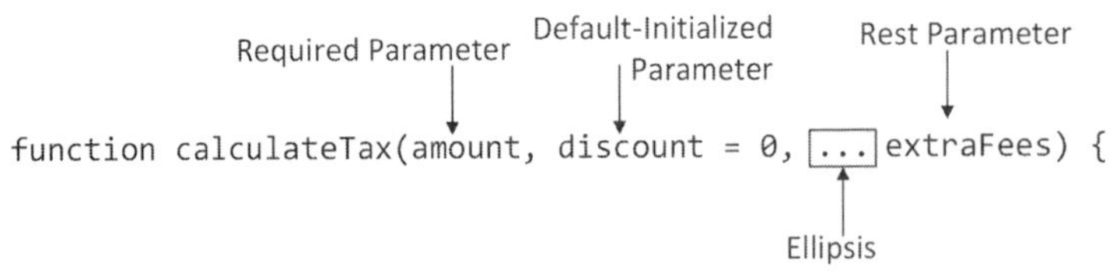

Required Parameter   Default-Initialized Parameter   Rest Parameter

```
function calculateTax(amount, discount = 0, [...]extraFees) {
```

Ellipsis

Figure 8.3   Defining a rest parameter

Any arguments for which there are no corresponding parameters are assigned to the rest parameter, which is an array. The array will always be initialized and will contain no items if there were no extra arguments. The addition of the rest parameter means that the `calculateTax` function can be called with one or more arguments: the first argument is assigned to the amount parameter, the section argument (if there is one) is assigned to the discount parameter, and any other arguments are added to the `extraFees` parameter array.

The process of grouping arguments into the rest parameter array is done automatically, and no special measures are required when calling the function. The user of the function can define additional arguments and separate them with commas, as shown in listing 8.10.

Listing 8.10 Using additional function arguments in the index.ts file in the src folder

```
function calculateTax(amount, discount = 0, ...extraFees) {
    return (amount * 1.2) - discount
        + extraFees.reduce((total, val) => total + val, 0);
}

let taxValue = calculateTax(100, 0);
console.log(`2 args: ${taxValue}`);
taxValue = calculateTax(100);
console.log(`1 arg: ${taxValue}`);
taxValue = calculateTax(100, 10, 20);
console.log(`3 args: ${taxValue}`);
taxValue = calculateTax(100, 10, 20, 1, 30, 7);
console.log(`6 args: ${taxValue}`);
```

The code in listing 8.10 produces the following output when it is compiled and executed:

```
2 args: 120
1 arg: 120
3 args: 130
6 args: 168
```

APPLYING TYPE ANNOTATIONS TO FUNCTION PARAMETERS

By default, the TypeScript compiler assigns all function parameters to the any type, but more specific types can be declared using type annotations. Listing 8.11 applies type annotations to the calculateTax function to ensure that only number values can be used for its parameters.

Listing 8.11 Applying parameter type annotations in the index.ts file in the src folder

```
function calculateTax(amount: number,
        discount: number = 0, ...extraFees: number[]) {
    return (amount * 1.2) - discount
        + extraFees.reduce((total, val) => total + val, 0);
}

let taxValue = calculateTax(100, 0);
console.log(`2 args: ${taxValue}`);
taxValue = calculateTax(100);
console.log(`1 arg: ${taxValue}`);
taxValue = calculateTax(100, 10, 20);
console.log(`3 args: ${taxValue}`);
taxValue = calculateTax(100, 10, 20, 1, 30, 7);
console.log(`6 args: ${taxValue}`);
```

For parameters with default values, the type annotation comes before the value assignment. The type for a rest parameter is always an array. I return to the topic of typed arrays in chapter 9, and the annotation for the extraFees parameter tells the compiler that any additional arguments must be numbers. The code in listing 8.11 produces the following output:

```
2 args: 120
1 arg: 120
3 args: 130
6 args: 168
```

TIP Type annotations for optional parameters are applied after the question mark, like this: discount?: number.

CONTROLLING NULL PARAMETER VALUES

As explained in chapter 7, TypeScript allows null and undefined to be used as values for all types by default, which means that a function can receive null values for all of its parameters, as shown in listing 8.12.

Listing 8.12   Passing a null value to a function in the index.ts file in the src folder

```
function calculateTax(amount: number,
        discount: number = 0, ...extraFees: number[]) {
    return (amount * 1.2) - discount
        + extraFees.reduce((total, val) => total + val, 0);
}

let taxValue = calculateTax(null, 0);
console.log(`Tax value: ${taxValue}`);
```

If the null value is used for a default-initialized parameter, then its default value is used, as though the function had been called without an argument. But for required parameters, the function receives the null value, which can lead to unexpected results. In the example, the calculateTax function receives null for the amount parameter, which produces the following output:

```
Tax value: 0
```

The null value is coerced to the number 0 by the multiplication operator. For some projects, this may be a reasonable outcome, but it is the kind of outcome that silently swallows a null value and confuses the user at runtime. The strictNullChecks compiler option disables the use of null and undefined as values for all types, as described in chapter 7, and requires parameters that can accept null values to use a type union. Listing 8.13 enables the compiler option.

Listing 8.13   Changing the compiler option in the tsconfig.json file in the types folder

```
{
    "compilerOptions": {
        "target": "ES2022",
        "outDir": "./dist",
        "rootDir": "./src",
```

```
        "declaration": true,
        "strictNullChecks": true
    }
}
```

When the configuration file is saved, the compiler will run and produce the following error, flagging the use of the null argument:

```
src/index.ts(6,29): error TS2345: Argument of type 'null' is not assignable
to parameter of type 'number'.
```

When null values should be allowed, the parameter can be defined with a type union, as shown in listing 8.14.

> **Listing 8.14 Allowing a null parameter value in the index.ts file in the src folder**

```
function calculateTax(amount: number | null, discount: number = 0,
        ...extraFees: number[]) {
    if (amount != null) {
        return (amount * 1.2) - discount
            + extraFees.reduce((total, val) => total + val, 0);
    }
}

let taxValue = calculateTax(null , 0);
console.log(`Tax value: ${taxValue}`);
```

A type guard is required to prevent the null value from being used with the multiplication operator. This can feel like an arduous process when you start using TypeScript, but restricting nullable parameters can flush out problems that would otherwise produce unexpected results at runtime. The code in listing 8.14 produces the following result:

```
Tax value: undefined
```

8.2.3 *Understanding function results*

The TypeScript compiler will try to infer the result type from the code in the function and will automatically use type unions if a function can return multiple types. The easiest way to see what type the compiler infers for a function result is to enable the generation of type declaration files, using the declaration setting, which was enabled in listing 8.2. These files are used to provide type information when a package is used in another TypeScript project, and I describe their use in chapter 15.

Examine the contents of the index.d.ts file in the dist folder to see details of the types that the compiler has inferred or read from type annotations, as follows:

```
declare function calculateTax(amount: number | null, discount?: number,
    ...extraFees: number[]): number | undefined;
declare let taxValue: number | undefined;
```

The highlighted part of the type information for the calculateTax function shows the type inferred by the compiler for the function's result.

DISABLING IMPLICIT RETURNS

JavaScript has an unusually relaxed approach to function results, such that a function will return `undefined` for any path through the function's code that doesn't reach a statement with the `return` keyword, which is known as the *implicit return* feature.

The type guard used to filter out `null` values means that there is a path through the function's code that doesn't reach a `return` statement and so the function will return a `number` if the `amount` parameter isn't `null` and will return `undefined` if the `amount` parameter is `null`. The `strictNullChecks` compiler option was enabled in listing 8.14, so the compiler has inferred the result type to be `number | undefined`.

To prevent implicit returns, enable the compiler setting shown in listing 8.15.

> **Listing 8.15   Changing the compiler configuration in the tsconfig.json file in the types folder**

```
{
    "compilerOptions": {
        "target": "ES2022",
        "outDir": "./dist",
        "rootDir": "./src",
        "declaration": true,
        "strictNullChecks": true,
        "noImplicitReturns": true
    }
}
```

When the `noImplicitReturns` setting is `true`, the compiler will report an error when there are paths through functions that don't explicitly produce a result with the `result` keyword or throw an error. Save the change to the `tsconfig.json` file; you will see the following output from the compiler, and it builds the `index.ts` file using the new configuration:

```
src/index.ts(1,10): error TS7030: Not all code paths return a value.
```

Now every path through functions must produce a result. A function can still return `undefined`, but it must now be done explicitly, as shown in listing 8.16.

> **Listing 8.16   Returning a result in the index.ts file in the src folder**

```
function calculateTax(amount: number | null, discount: number = 0,
        ...extraFees: number[]) {
    if (amount != null) {
        return (amount * 1.2) - discount
            + extraFees.reduce((total, val) => total + val, 0);
    } else {
        return undefined;
    }
}

let taxValue = calculateTax(null, 0);
console.log(`Tax value: ${taxValue}`);
```

Disabling implicit returns ensures that functions have to be explicit about the results they produce. The change in listing 8.16 addresses the compiler error from listing 8.14 and produces the following result:

```
Tax value: undefined
```

USING TYPE ANNOTATIONS FOR FUNCTION RESULTS

The compiler infers a function result type by analyzing the code paths and creating a union of the types it encounters. I prefer to use a type annotation to explicitly specify the result type because it allows me to declare what I intended the function result to be, rather than what the code produces, ensuring that I do not accidentally use the wrong type. Annotations for function results appear at the end of the function signature, as shown in listing 8.17.

> **Listing 8.17 Annotating the function result type in the index.ts file in the src folder**

```
function calculateTax(amount: number, discount: number = 0,
        ...extraFees: number[]): number {
    return (amount * 1.2) - discount
        + extraFees.reduce((total, val) => total + val, 0);
}


let taxValue = calculateTax(100, 0);
console.log(`Tax value: ${taxValue}`);
```

I have set the result type to `number` and removed the `null` type from the `amount` parameter. Explicitly declaring the type means that the compiler will report an error if I accidentally return a different type from the function. The code in listing 8.17 produces the following output once it has been compiled and executed:

```
Tax value: 120
```

DEFINING VOID FUNCTIONS

Functions that do not produce results are declared using the `void` type, as shown in listing 8.18.

> **Listing 8.18 Defining a void function in the index.ts file in the src folder**

```
function calculateTax(amount: number, discount: number = 0,
        ...extraFees: number[]): number {
    return (amount * 1.2) - discount
        + extraFees.reduce((total, val) => total + val, 0);
}

function writeValue(label: string, value: number): void {
    console.log(`${label}: ${value}`);
}


writeValue("Tax value", calculateTax(100, 0));
```

The `writeValue` function doesn't return a result and has been annotated with the `void` type. Using `void` ensures that the compiler will warn you if the `result` keyword is used or if the function is used to assign a value.

NOTE   The `never` type can be used as the result type for functions that will never complete, such as functions that will always throw an exception, for example.

The code in listing 8.18 produces the following output:

```
Tax value: 120
```

8.2.4   *Overloading function types*

Type unions make it possible to define a range of types for function parameters and results, but they don't allow the relationship between them to be expressed accurately, as shown in listing 8.19.

> **Listing 8.19   Defining a function with unions in the index.ts file in the src folder**

```
function calculateTax(amount: number | null): number | null {
    if (amount != null) {
        return amount * 1.2;
    }
    return null;
}

function writeValue(label: string, value: number): void {
    console.log(`${label}: ${value}`);
}

let taxAmount: number | null = calculateTax(100);
if (typeof taxAmount === "number") {
    writeValue("Tax value",  taxAmount);
}
```

The type annotation in listing 8.19 describes the types that the `calculateTax` function will accept, telling users that the function will accept either a `number` or `null` and will return a `number` or `null`. The information provided by the type unions is correct but does not fully describe the situation. What's missing is the relationship between the parameter and result types: the function will always return a `number` result if the `amount` parameter is a `number` parameter and will always return `null` if `amount` is `null`. The missing details in the function's types mean that the user of the function has to use a type guard on the result to remove `null` values, even though the value `100` is a `number` and will always produce a `number` result.

To describe the relationships between the types used by a function, TypeScript supports type overloads, as shown in listing 8.20.

NOTE   This is not the function overloading supported by languages such as C# and Java. Only the type information is overloaded by this feature for the purposes of type checking. As listing 8.20 shows, there is only one implementation of the function, which is still responsible for dealing with all the types used in the overloads.

Listing 8.20 Overloading function types in the index.ts file in the src folder

```
function calculateTax(amount: number): number;
function calculateTax(amount: null): null;
function calculateTax(amount: number | null): number | null {
    if (amount != null) {
        return amount * 1.2;
    }
    return null;
}

function writeValue(label: string, value: number): void {
    console.log(`${label}: ${value}`);
}

let taxAmount: number = calculateTax(100);
//if (typeof taxAmount === "number") {
    writeValue("Tax value",  taxAmount);
//}
```

Each type overload defines a combination of types supported by the function, describing a mapping between the parameters and the result they produce, as illustrated in figure 8.4.

Figure 8.4 A function type overload

The type overloads replace the function definition as the type information used by the TypeScript compiler, which means that only those combinations of types can be used. When the function is invoked, the compiler can determine the result type based on the type of the arguments provided, allowing the taxAmount variable to be defined as a number and removing the need for the type guard to pass on the result to the writeValue function. The compiler knows that taxAmount can only be a number and doesn't require the type to be narrowed. The code in listing 8.20 produces the following output when it is compiled and executed:

```
Tax value: 120
```

> **TIP** You can also express the relationship between parameters and results using the conditional types feature, which is described in chapter 13.

8.2.5   Understanding assert functions

An assert function evaluates an expression condition and, typically, throws an error if the result isn't `true`. Assert functions are sometimes used as type guards in pure Java-Script, where the static types of TypeScript are not available. The problem with asset functions is that the TypeScript compiler cannot infer the effect of the assert function on types, as shown in listing 8.21.

Listing 8.21   Using an assert function in the index.ts file in the src folder

```
function check(expression: boolean) {
    if (!expression) {
        throw new Error("Expression is false");
    }
}

function calculateTax(amount: number | null): number {
    check(typeof amount == "number");
    return amount * 1.2;
}

let taxAmount: number = calculateTax(100);
console.log(`Tax value: ${taxAmount}`);
```

The `check` function defines a `boolean` parameter and throws an error if it is `false`. This is the basic pattern of an assert function.

The `calculateTax` function accepts a `number | null` argument and uses the `check` function to narrow the type so that `null` values cause errors and so `number` values are used to produce a result.

The problem with this code is that the TypeScript compiler doesn't understand that the `check` function means that only `number` values will be processed. When the code is compiled, the following error message is produced:

```
src/index.ts(9,12): error TS18047: 'amount' is possibly 'null'.
```

The `asserts` keyword can be used to denote an assert function, which lets the Type-Script compiler take the function into account, as shown in listing 8.22.

Listing 8.22   Denoting an assert function in the index.ts file in the src folder

```
function check(expression: boolean) : asserts expression   {
    if (!expression) {
        throw new Error("Expression is false");
    }
}

function calculateTax(amount: number | null): number {
    check(typeof amount == "number");
    return amount * 1.2;
}

let taxAmount: number = calculateTax(100);
console.log(`Tax value: ${taxAmount}`);
```

The `asserts` keyword is used like a result type and is followed by the name of the parameter that the function asserts, as shown in figure 8.5.

Figure 8.5 Denoting an assert function

The TypeScript compiler can take the effect of the `check` function into account and knows that the `calculateTax` function narrows the type of `amount` parameter to exclude `null` values.

There is a variation for assert functions that operate on types directly, rather than just evaluating an expression, as shown in listing 8.23.

Listing 8.23   Narrowing types directly in the index.ts file in the src folder

```
function checkNumber(val: any): asserts val is number {
    if (typeof val != "number") {
        throw new Error("Not a number");
    }
}

function calculateTax(amount: number | null): number {
    checkNumber(amount);
    return amount * 1.2;
}

let taxAmount: number = calculateTax(100);
console.log(`Tax value: ${taxAmount}`);
```

In this example, the `assets` keyword is followed by `val is number`, which tells the TypeScript compiler that the effect of the `checkNumber` function is to ensure that the `val` parameter is a `number` value.

Summary

In this chapter, I described the features that TypeScript provides for functions. I explained how duplicate function definitions are prevented, showed you the different ways to describe function parameters and results, and described how to override function types to create more specific mappings between parameter types and the results they produce.

- Functions are defined using the standard JavaScript syntax but can be annotated with static types for the parameters and the result.
- Optional parameters are denoted with the ? character and can be omitted when invoking the function.

- Default parameters are defined by assigning a value when defining the function.
- Rest parameters are denoted with an ellipsis and are used to capture an arbitrary number of parameters.
- The TypeScript compiler can be configured so that `null` and `undefined` can only be used for parameters or results whose type include those values in a union.
- The TypeScript compiler can be configured to require functions to explicitly return results if they define a result type.
- JavaScript doesn't support function overloading, but TypeScript can be used to define type overloads that describe specific combinations of parameter types and the result types they produce.
- Assert functions can be used to provide type information to the TypeScript compiler, similar to the way that type guards can be used for JavaScript types.

In the next chapter, I describe how TypeScript addresses simple data structures.

Using arrays, tuples, and enums

This chapter covers

- Restricting the types that an array can store
- Creating fixed-length arrays using tuples
- Using enums to group related values
- Using literal value types to specify a fixed set of acceptable values
- Creating a type alias to simplify working with complex type definitions

The examples so far in this part of the book have focused on primitive types, which has let me introduce the basic TypeScript features. In real projects, related data properties are grouped to create objects. In this chapter, I describe the TypeScript support for simple data structures, starting with arrays. Table 9.1 summarizes the chapter.

Table 9.1 Chapter summary

Problem	Solution	Listing
Restrict the range of types that an array can contain	Apply a type annotation or allow the compiler to infer the types from the value used to initialize the array	4–9
Define fixed-length arrays with specified types for each value	Use a tuple	10–14
Define variable-length arrays with specified types for each value	Use a tuple with a rest element	15

Table 9.1   Chapter summary *(continued)*

Problem	Solution	Listing
Refer to a collection of related values through a single name	Use an enum	16–25
Define a type that can be assigned only specific values	Use a literal value type	26–32
Avoid duplication when describing a complex type	Use a type alias	33

For quick reference, table 9.2 lists the TypeScript compiler options used in this chapter.

Table 9.2   The TypeScript compiler options used in this chapter

Name	Description
`target`	This option specifies the version of the JavaScript language that the compiler will target in its output.
`outDir`	This option specifies the directory in which the JavaScript files will be placed.
`rootDir`	This option specifies the root directory that the compiler will use to locate TypeScript files.
`declaration`	This option produces type declaration files when enabled, which can be useful in understanding how types have been inferred. These files are described in more detail in Chapter 14.
`strictNullChecks`	This option prevents `null` and `undefined` from being accepted as values for other types.

9.1   *Preparing for this chapter*

In this chapter, I continue to use the `types` project created in chapter 7. To prepare for this chapter, replace the contents of the `index.ts` file in the `src` folder with the code shown in listing 9.1.

> **TIP**   You can download the example project for this chapter—and for all the other chapters in this book—from https://github.com/manningbooks/essential-typescript-5.

Listing 9.1   The contents of the index.ts file in the src folder

```
function calculateTax(amount: number): number {
    return amount * 1.2;
}

function writePrice(product: string, price: number): void {
    console.log(`Price for ${product}: $${price.toFixed(2)}`);
}
```

```
let hatPrice = 100;
let glovesPrice = 75;
let umbrellaPrice = 42;

writePrice("Hat", calculateTax(hatPrice));
writePrice("Gloves", calculateTax(glovesPrice));
writePrice("Umbrella", calculateTax(umbrellaPrice));
```

Comment out the compiler options shown in listing 9.2 to reset the compiler configuration.

Listing 9.2   Disabling compiler options in the tsconfig.json file in the types folder

```
{
    "compilerOptions": {
        "target": "ES2022",
        "outDir": "./dist",
        "rootDir": "./src",
        "declaration": true,
        // "strictNullChecks": true,
        // "noImplicitReturns": true
    }
}
```

Open a new command prompt, navigate to the `types` folder, and run the command shown in listing 9.3 to start the TypeScript compiler so that the compiled code is executed automatically.

Listing 9.3   Starting the TypeScript compiler

```
npm start
```

The compiler will compile the code in the `index.ts` file, execute the output, and then enter watch mode, producing the following output:

```
6:58:20 AM - File change detected. Starting incremental compilation...
6:58:21 AM - Found 0 errors. Watching for file changes.
Price for Hat: $120.00
Price for Gloves: $90.00
Price for Umbrella: $50.40
```

9.2 *Working with arrays*

As explained in chapter 8, JavaScript arrays can contain any combination of types and have variable lengths, which means that values can be added and removed dynamically without the need to explicitly resize the array. TypeScript doesn't change the flexible sizing of arrays, but it does allow the data types they contain to be restricted through the use of type annotations, as shown in listing 9.4.

Listing 9.4   Using arrays in the index.ts file in the src folder

```
function calculateTax(amount: number): number {
    return amount * 1.2;
}
```

```
function writePrice(product: string, price: number): void {
    console.log(`Price for ${product}: $${price.toFixed(2)}`);
}

let prices: number[] = [100, 75, 42];
let names: string[] = ["Hat", "Gloves", "Umbrella"];

writePrice(names[0], calculateTax(prices[0]));
writePrice(names[1], calculateTax(prices[1]));
writePrice(names[2], calculateTax(prices[2]));
```

An array type is specified by putting square brackets after the type name in the annotation, as illustrated in figure 9.1.

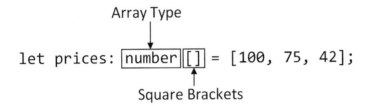

Figure 9.1   An array type annotation

TypeScript uses an annotation to restrict the operations that can be performed on the array to the specified type: one of the arrays in the listing is restricted to number values and the other to string values. In listing 9.5, I have used the JavaScript forEach method on the arrays, and you can see that the function I used to process the array values is typed to match the array types.

> **TIP**   You can use parentheses when describing an array that contains multiple types, such as when using a type union (described in chapter 8) or a type intersection (described in chapter 10). For example, an array whose elements can be number or string values can be annotated as (number | string)[], where the parentheses around the type union prevent the compiler from assuming that the union is between a single number or an array of strings.

Listing 9.5   Performing operations on typed arrays in the index.ts file in the src folder

```
function calculateTax(amount: number): number {
    return amount * 1.2;
}

function writePrice(product: string, price: number): void {
    console.log(`Price for ${product}: $${price.toFixed(2)}`);
}

let prices: number[] = [100, 75, 42];
let names: string[] = ["Hat", "Gloves", "Umbrella"];
```

```
prices.forEach((price: number, index: number) => {
    writePrice(names[index], calculateTax(price));
});
```

The first argument of the function passed to the `forEach` method receives a `number` value because that's the type of the array that is being processed. TypeScript will ensure that only operations that are allowed for number values are performed by the function. The code in listing 9.5 produces the following output when compiled and executed:

```
Price for Hat: $120.00
Price for Gloves: $90.00
Price for Umbrella: $50.40
```

9.2.1 *Using inferred typing for arrays*

I used type annotations in listing 9.5 to make it obvious that the arrays are typed, but the TypeScript compiler is adept at inferring types automatically, and the same example can be expressed without type annotations, as shown in listing 9.6.

> **Listing 9.6 Using inferred types in the index.ts file in the src folder**

```
function calculateTax(amount: number): number {
    return amount * 1.2;
}

function writePrice(product: string, price: number): void {
    console.log(`Price for ${product}: $${price.toFixed(2)}`);
}

let prices = [100, 75, 42];
let names = ["Hat", "Gloves", "Umbrella"];

prices.forEach((price, index) => {
    writePrice(names[index], calculateTax(price));
});
```

The compiler can determine the array types based on the set of values that are assigned when the arrays are initialized, and it uses the inferred types to follow through to the `forEach` method.

The compiler is skilled at inferring types, but if you don't get the results you expect, you can inspect the files that the compiler emits when the `declaration` option is enabled. This option generates type declaration files, which are used to provide type information when a package is used in another TypeScript project and which are described in detail in chapter 15.

Here are the types that the compiler has inferred for the arrays in listing 9.6, which are contained in the `index.d.ts` file in the `dist` folder:

```
...
declare let prices: number[];
declare let names: string[];
...
```

I explain the `declare` keyword in chapter 15. For the moment, it is enough to see that the compiler has correctly inferred the array types from the initial values.

9.2.2   Avoiding problems with inferred array types

The compiler infers array types using the values used to populate the array when it is created. This leads to type errors if the values used to populate an array are accidentally mixed, as shown in listing 9.7.

> **Listing 9.7   Mixing array types in the index.ts file in the src folder**

```
function calculateTax(amount: number): number {
    return amount * 1.2;
}

function writePrice(product: string, price: number): void {
    console.log(`Price for ${product}: $${price.toFixed(2)}`);
}

let prices = [100, 75, 42, "20"];
let names = ["Hat", "Gloves", "Umbrella", "Sunglasses"];

prices.forEach((price, index) => {
    writePrice(names[index], calculateTax(price));
});
```

The new value used to initialize the `price` array causes the following error when the code is compiled:

```
src/index.ts(13,43): error TS2345: Argument of type 'string | number' is
not assignable to parameter of type 'number'.
  Type 'string' is not assignable to type 'number'.
```

If you examine the `index.d.ts` file in the `dist` folder, you will see that the TypeScript compiler has inferred the smallest set of types that can describe the values used to initialize the array:

```
declare let prices: (string | number)[];
```

The change in the array type causes the error message because the function passed to the `forEach` method treats the values as `number` when they are now part of the `string | number` union. It is easy to see the cause of the problem in a simple example, but it becomes more difficult when the initial values for the array come from different parts of an application. I find it more useful to declare the array type explicitly, which means that problems like the one in listing 9.7 produce a compiler error that highlights my error in trying to add a `string` to a `number` array.

9.2.3   Avoiding problems with empty arrays

Another reason for using type annotations for arrays is that the compiler will infer the type `any` for arrays that are created empty, as shown in listing 9.8.

Listing 9.8   Creating an empty array in the index.ts file in the src folder

```
function calculateTax(amount: number): number {
    return amount * 1.2;
}

function writePrice(product: string, price: number): void {
    console.log(`Price for ${product}: $${price.toFixed(2)}`);
}

let prices = [];
prices.push(...[100, 75, 42, "20"]);
let names = ["Hat", "Gloves", "Umbrella", "Sunglasses"];

prices.forEach((price, index) => {
    writePrice(names[index], calculateTax(price));
});
```

There are no initial values for the compiler to use when selecting the type for the `prices` array. The only option available to the compiler is to use `any` since it has no other information to work with, which you can see by examining the `index.d.ts` file in the `dist` folder.

```
declare let prices: any[];
```

Even though the values added to the array mix `number` and `string` values, the code in listing 9.8 compiles without error and produces the following results:

```
Price for Hat: $120.00
Price for Gloves: $90.00
Price for Umbrella: $50.40
Price for Sunglasses: $24.00
```

The effect of allowing the compiler to infer the type of the empty array is to create a gap in the type-checking process. The code works because the JavaScript multiplication operator coerces `string` values to `number` values automatically. This can be useful behavior, but it is likely to be used accidentally, and it is for this reason that you should use explicit types.

UNDERSTANDING THE NEVER ARRAY TYPE PITFALL

TypeScript infers types for empty arrays differently when `null` and `undefined` values are not assignable to other types. To see the difference, change the compiler configuration as shown in listing 9.9.

Listing 9.9   Configuring the compiler in the tsconfig.json file in the types folder

```
{
    "compilerOptions": {
        "target": "ES2022",
        "outDir": "./dist",
        "rootDir": "./src",
        "declaration": true,
        "strictNullChecks": true,
    }
}
```

The `strictNullChecks` setting tells the compiler to restrict the use of `null` and `undefined` values and prevents the compiler from using `any` when inferring the type of an empty array. Instead, the compiler infers the `never` type, which means that nothing can be added to the array. When the code in listing 9.9 is compiled and executed, the following error is reported:

```
src/index.ts(10,13): error TS2345: Argument of type 'string | number' is
not assignable to parameter of type 'never'.
    Type 'string' is not assignable to type 'never'.
```

Inferring the `never` type ensures that the array doesn't escape the type-checking process and the code won't compile until a type is asserted for the array or the array is initialized using values that allow the compiler to infer a less restrictive type.

9.3   *Working with tuples*

Basic tuples are fixed-length arrays, where each element in the array can have a different type. Tuples are a data structure that is provided by the TypeScript compiler and implemented using regular JavaScript arrays in the compiled code. Listing 9.10 shows how tuples are defined and used. (There is a more complex type of tuple that I describe shortly.)

> **Listing 9.10   Using tuples in the index.ts file in the src folder**

```
function calculateTax(amount: number): number {
    return amount * 1.2;
}

function writePrice(product: string, price: number): void {
    console.log(`Price for ${product}: $${price.toFixed(2)}`);
}

let hat: [string, number] = ["Hat", 100];
let gloves: [string, number] = ["Gloves", 75];

writePrice(hat[0], hat[1]);
writePrice(gloves[0], gloves[1]);
```

Tuples are defined using square brackets containing the types for each element, separated by commas, as illustrated in figure 9.2.

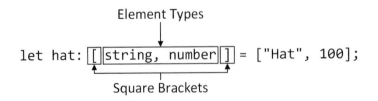

Figure 9.2   Defining a tuple

The type of the hat tuple in listing 9.10 is [string, number], which defines a tuple with two elements, where the first element is a string and the second value is a number. The elements in the tuple are accessed using the array index syntax so that the first element of the hat tuple is hat[0], for example.

The code in listing 9.10 produces the following output when compiled and executed:

```
Price for Hat: $100.00
Price for Gloves: $75.00
```

Tuples must be defined with type annotations; otherwise, the compiler will assume that a regular array with a type that is the union of each value used during initialization. Without the type annotation shown in figure 9.2, for example, the compiler would assume that the type of the value assigned to the hat variable is [string | number], which would denote a variable-length array in which every element can be either a string or number value.

9.3.1 Processing tuples

The restrictions on the number of elements and the element types are enforced entirely by the TypeScript compiler, and, at runtime, a tuple is implemented as a regular JavaScript array. This means tuples can be used with the standard JavaScript array features, as shown in listing 9.11.

> **Listing 9.11   Processing the elements in a tuple in the index.ts file in the src folder**

```
function calculateTax(amount: number): number {
    return amount * 1.2;
}

function writePrice(product: string, price: number): void {
    console.log(`Price for ${product}: $${price.toFixed(2)}`);
}

let hat: [string, number] = ["Hat", 100];
let gloves: [string, number] = ["Gloves", 75];

hat.forEach((h: string | number) => {
    if (typeof h === "string") {
        console.log(`String: ${h}`);
    } else {
        console.log(`Number: ${h.toFixed(2)}`);
    }
});
```

To process all the tuple values, the function passed to the forEach method must receive string | number values, which are then narrowed with a type guard. I used type annotations for clarity, but the compiler will correctly infer the type union based on the element types in the tuple. The code in listing 9.11 produces the following output when it is compiled and executed:

```
String: Hat
Number: 100.00
```

Since tuples are arrays, they can be destructured to access individual values, which can make tuples easier to work with, as shown in listing 9.12.

Listing 9.12   Destructuring tuples in the index.ts file in the src folder

```
function calculateTax(amount: number): number {
    return amount * 1.2;
}

function writePrice(product: string, price: number): void {
    console.log(`Price for ${product}: $${price.toFixed(2)}`);
}

let hat: [string, number] = ["Hat", 100];
let gloves: [string, number] = ["Gloves", 75];

let [hatname, hatprice] = hat;
console.log(`Name: ${hatname}`);
console.log(`Price: ${hatprice.toFixed(2)}`);
```

The `hat` tuple is destructured, and its values are assigned to `hatname` and `hatprice` variables, which are written to the console. There is no change in the output in this example; only the way the tuples values are accessed has changed.

9.3.2   *Using tuple types*

Tuples have a distinct type that can be used just like any type, which means you can create arrays of tuples, use tuples in type unions, and use type guards to narrow values to specific tuple types, all of which are shown in listing 9.13.

Listing 9.13   Using tuple types in the index.ts file in the src folder

```
function calculateTax(amount: number): number {
    return amount * 1.2;
}

function writePrice(product: string, price: number): void {
    console.log(`Price for ${product}: $${price.toFixed(2)}`);
}

let hat: [string, number] = ["Hat", 100];
let gloves: [string, number] = ["Gloves", 75];

let products: [string, number][] = [["Hat", 100], ["Gloves", 75]];
let tupleUnion: ([string, number] | boolean)[]
    = [true, false, hat, ...products];

tupleUnion.forEach((elem: [string, number] | boolean) => {
    if (elem instanceof Array) {
        let [str, num] = elem;
        console.log(`Name: ${str}`);
        console.log(`Price: ${num.toFixed(2)}`);
    } else if (typeof elem === "boolean") {
```

```
        console.log(`Boolean Value: ${elem}`);
    }
});
```

The profusion of square brackets can be confusing, and it can take a few attempts to describe the combination of types correctly, but the example shows how a tuple type can be used just like any other type, albeit with one important difference from the previous examples in this part of the book: I cannot use the `typeof` keyword in listing 9.13 to determine whether a value is a tuple. Tuples are implemented using standard JavaScript arrays, and the test for array types requires the `instanceof` keyword, which I described in chapter 4. The code in listing 9.13 produces the following output when it is compiled and executed:

```
Boolean Value: true
Boolean Value: false
String Value: Hat
Number Value: 100
String Value: Hat
Number Value: 100
String Value: Gloves
Number Value: 75
```

9.3.3 *Using tuples with optional elements*

Tuples can contain optional elements, which are denoted by the question mark (the `?` character). The tuple is still fixed-length, and the optional element will be `undefined` if no value has been defined, as shown in listing 9.14.

> **Listing 9.14   Using an optional element in the index.ts file in the src folder**

```
function calculateTax(amount: number): number {
    return amount * 1.2;
}

function writePrice(product: string, price: number): void {
    console.log(`Price for ${product}: $${price.toFixed(2)}`);
}

let hat: [string, number, number?] = ["Hat", 100];
let gloves: [string, number, number?] = ["Gloves", 75, 10];

[hat, gloves].forEach(tuple => {
    let [name, price, taxRate] = tuple;
    if (taxRate != undefined) {
        price += price * (taxRate / 100);
    }
    writePrice(name, price);
});
```

The tuple type in listing 9.14 has an optional `number` element. (A tuple can have multiple optional elements, but they must be the last elements defined by the tuple type.)

The type of the optional element is a union of the specified type and `undefined` so that in the example, the type is `number | undefined`. The value of the element will be `undefined` if no value has been provided, and it is the responsibility of the code that processes the tuple to narrow the type to exclude `undefined` values.

Defining an optional element means that the TypeScript compiler won't complain if there is no corresponding value, like this:

```
...
let hat: [string, number, number?] = ["Hat", 100];
...
```

There is no value for the third tuple element, but the compiler processes the code without complaint and produces the following output:

```
Price for Hat: $100.00
Price for Gloves: $82.50
```

9.3.4   *Defining tuples with rest elements*

Tuples can also contain a rest element, that can be used to match multiple values of a given type. This feature produces a variable-length tuple that lacks the rigidly defined structure of basic tuples. Listing 9.15 shows the use of a tuple with a rest element.

> **Listing 9.15   Using a rest element in the index.ts file in the src folder**

```
function calculateTax(amount: number): number {
    return amount * 1.2;
}

function writePrice(product: string, price: number): void {
    console.log(`Price for ${product}: $${price.toFixed(2)}`);
}

let hat: [string, number, number?, ...number[]]
    = ["Hat", 100, 10, 1.20, 3, 0.95];
let gloves: [string, number, number?, ...number[]]
    = ["Gloves", 75, 10];

[hat, gloves].forEach(tuple => {
    let [name, price, taxRate, ...coupons] = tuple;
    if (taxRate != undefined) {
        price += price * (taxRate / 100);
    }
    coupons.forEach(c => price -= c);
    writePrice(name, price);
});
```

In this example, I destructure the tuple rest element into an array named `coupons`, which is processed by a `forEach` loop, producing the following output:

```
Price for Hat: $104.85
Price for Gloves: $82.50
```

This is not a feature that I like because the variable lengths introduced by the rest elements undermine the fixed structure that makes tuples useful. The only time I use this feature is when describing JavaScript code, as described in chapter 15.

9.4 Using enums

An enum allows a collection of values to be used by name, which makes code easier to read and ensures that a fixed set of values is used consistently. Like tuples, enums are a feature that is provided by the TypeScript compiler. Listing 9.16 shows the definition and use of an enum.

Listing 9.16 Using an enum in the index.ts file in the src folder

```
function calculateTax(amount: number): number {
    return amount * 1.2;
}

function writePrice(product: string, price: number): void {
    console.log(`Price for ${product}: $${price.toFixed(2)}`);
}

enum Product { Hat, Gloves, Umbrella }

let products: [Product, number][] =
    [[Product.Hat, 100], [Product.Gloves, 75]];

products.forEach((prod: [Product, number]) => {
    switch (prod[0]) {
        case Product.Hat:
            writePrice("Hat", calculateTax(prod[1]));
            break;
        case Product.Gloves:
            writePrice("Gloves", calculateTax(prod[1]));
            break;
        case Product.Umbrella:
            writePrice("Umbrella", calculateTax(prod[1]));
            break;
    }
});
```

An enum is defined using the `enum` keyword, followed by a name, followed by a list of values in curly braces, as illustrated in figure 9.3.

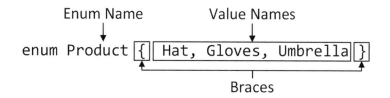

Figure 9.3 Defining an enum

The enum values are accessed in the form `<enum>.<value>` so that the `Hat` value defined by the `Product` enum is accessed as `Product.Hat`, like this:

```
...
case Product.Hat:
...
```

An enum is used like any other type, and the example shows the `Product` enum used in a tuple and a `switch` statement. The code in listing 9.16 produces the following output when it is compiled and executed:

```
Price for Hat: $120.00
Price for Gloves: $90.00
```

9.4.1 *Understanding how enums work*

Enums are implemented entirely by the TypeScript compiler, relying on type-checking during compilation and standard JavaScript features at runtime. Each enum value has a corresponding `number` value that is assigned automatically by the compiler and that starts at zero by default. This means that the numbers used for the `Hat`, `Gloves`, and `Umbrella` names for the `Product` enum are 0, 1, and 2, as demonstrated in listing 9.17.

> **Listing 9.17   Using an enum number value in the index.ts file in the src folder**

```
function calculateTax(amount: number): number {
    return amount * 1.2;
}

function writePrice(product: string, price: number): void {
    console.log(`Price for ${product}: $${price.toFixed(2)}`);
}

enum Product { Hat, Gloves, Umbrella }

[Product.Hat, Product.Gloves, Product.Umbrella].forEach(val => {
    console.log(`Number value: ${val}`);
});
```

The highlighted statements pass each value from the `Product` enum to the `console`
`.log` value. Each enum value is a `number`, and the code in listing 9.17 produces the following output:

```
Number value: 0
Number value: 1
Number value: 2
```

Because enums are implemented using JavaScript `number` values, an enum can be assigned a `number` and is displayed as a `number` value, as shown in listing 9.18.

> **Listing 9.18   Using enum and number values in the index.ts file in the src folder**

```
function calculateTax(amount: number): number {
    return amount * 1.2;
}

function writePrice(product: string, price: number): void {
    console.log(`Price for ${product}: $${price.toFixed(2)}`);
}
```

```
enum Product { Hat, Gloves, Umbrella }

let productValue: Product = 0;
let productName: string = Product[productValue];
console.log(`Value: ${productValue}, Name: ${productName}`);
```

The compiler enforces type checking for enums, which means that you will receive an error if you try to compare values from different enums, even when they have the same underlying `number` value. Enums provide an array-indexer style syntax that can be used to get the name of a value, like this:

```
...
let productName: string = Product[productValue];
...
```

The result from this operation is a `string` containing the name of the enum value, which is `Hat` in this example. The code in listing 9.18 produces the following output:

```
Value: 0, Name: Hat
```

USING SPECIFIC ENUM VALUES

By default, the TypeScript compiler starts assigning `number` values for an enum with zero and will compute the values by incrementing the previous value. For the `Product` enum in listing 9.18, the compiler starts by assigning `0` to `Hat`, `1` to `Gloves`, and `2` to `Umbrella`. If you want to see the values that have been assigned for an enum, then you can examine the type declaration files that are generated by the compiler when the `declarations` setting is `true`. If you examine the `index.d.ts` file in the `dist` folder, you will see the values the compiler computed for the `Product` enum:

```
...
declare enum Product {
    Hat = 0,
    Gloves = 1,
    Umbrella = 2
}
...
```

Enums can also be defined with literal values, where a specific value is used, as shown in listing 9.19. This is useful when the enum represents a real-world set of values.

> Listing 9.19   Using a constant enum value in the index.ts file in the src folder

```
function calculateTax(amount: number): number {
    return amount * 1.2;
}

function writePrice(product: string, price: number): void {
    console.log(`Price for ${product}: $${price.toFixed(2)}`);
}

enum Product { Hat, Gloves = 20, Umbrella }

let productValue: Product = 0;
let productName: string = Product[productValue];
console.log(`Value: ${productValue}, Name: ${productName}`);
```

I assigned `Gloves` a value of `20`. The compiler will still generate the remaining values required for the enum, and examining the `index.d.ts` file shows that the compiler has computed values for `Hat` and `Umbrella`.

```
...
declare enum Product {
    Hat = 0,
    Gloves = 20,
    Umbrella = 21
}
...
```

The previous value is used to generate enum values, regardless of whether it has been selected by the programmer or generated by the compiler. For the enum in listing 9.19, the compiler has used the value assigned to `Gloves` to generate the value for `Umbrella`. The code in listing 9.19 produces the following output:

```
Value: 0, Name: Hat
```

> **CAUTION** The compiler consults the previous value only when it generates a `number` value and doesn't check to see whether the value has already been used, which can lead to duplicate values in an enum.

The compiler will evaluate simple expressions for enum values, as shown in listing 9.20, which means that values can be based on other values in the same enum, another enum, or another value entirely.

Listing 9.20   Using expressions in an enum in the index.ts file in the src folder

```
function calculateTax(amount: number): number {
    return amount * 1.2;
}

function writePrice(product: string, price: number): void {
    console.log(`Price for ${product}: $${price.toFixed(2)}`);
}

enum OtherEnum { First = 10, Two = 20 }
enum Product { Hat = OtherEnum.First + 1, Gloves = 20,
    Umbrella = Hat + Gloves }

let productValue: Product = 11;
let productName: string = Product[productValue];
console.log(`Value: ${productValue}, Name: ${productName}`);
```

The `Hat` value is assigned using an expression that uses an `OtherEnum` value and the addition operator, and the `Umbrella` value is the sum of `Hat` and `Gloves`; examining the `index.d.ts` file in the `dist` folder shows the compiler has evaluated the expressions to determine the `Product` enum values.

```
...
declare enum Product {
    Hat = 11,
    Gloves = 20,
```

```
    Umbrella = 31
}
...
```

These features can be useful, but close attention is required to avoid accidentally creating duplicate values or unexpected results. My advice is to keep enums simple and leave the compiler to generate numbers wherever possible. The code in listing 9.20 produces the following output:

```
Value: 11, Name: Hat
```

9.4.2 Using string enums

The default implementation of enums represents each value with a `number`, but the compiler can also use `string` values for enums, as shown in listing 9.21.

> **TIP** An enum can contain both `string` and `number` values, although this is not a feature that is widely used.

Listing 9.21   Using a string enum in the index.ts file in the src folder

```
function calculateTax(amount: number): number {
    return amount * 1.2;
}

function writePrice(product: string, price: number): void {
    console.log(`Price for ${product}: $${price.toFixed(2)}`);
}

enum OtherEnum { First = 10, Two = 20 }
enum Product { Hat = OtherEnum.First + 1 , Gloves = 20,
    Umbrella = Hat + Gloves }

let productValue: Product = 11;
let productName: string = Product[productValue];
console.log(`Value: ${productValue}, Name: ${productName}`);

enum City { London = "London", Paris = "Paris", NY = "New York"}
console.log(`City: ${City.London}`);
```

A `string` value must be provided for every enum value name, but the advantage of using `string` values is that they are easier to recognize during debugging or in log files, as this output from listing 9.21 shows:

```
Value: 11, Name: Hat
City: London
```

9.4.3 Understanding the limitations of enums

Enums can be useful, but there are some limitations because they are a feature that is implemented entirely by the TypeScript compiler and then translated into pure JavaScript.

UNDERSTANDING THE VALUE-CHECKING LIMITATION

The compiler is excellent at checking types for enums, but it doesn't do anything to ensure that legal `number` values are used. In listing 9.21, I selected specific values for some of the `Product` enum values, which means this statement is a problem:

```
...
let productValue: Product = 0;
...
```

The compiler doesn't prevent the assignment of a number to a variable whose type is an enum when the number doesn't correspond to one of the enum values, which is why the output shown for listing 9.21 contains `undefined`, as the lookup fails to find a corresponding `Product` name for the number value. The same issue arises if a function uses an enum as its result type because the compiler will allow it to return any `number` value.

> **TIP** This isn't a problem with string enums, which are implemented differently behind the scenes and can be assigned values only from the enum.

UNDERSTANDING THE TYPE GUARD LIMITATION

A related problem arises when using a type guard. Testing types is done using the JavaScript `typeof` keyword, and since enums are implemented using JavaScript `number` values, `typeof` cannot be used to distinguish between `enum` and `number` values, as shown in listing 9.22.

> **Listing 9.22   Using a type guard in the index.ts file in the src folder**

```
function calculateTax(amount: number): number {
    return amount * 1.2;
}

function writePrice(product: string, price: number): void {
    console.log(`Price for ${product}: $${price.toFixed(2)}`);
}

enum OtherEnum { First = 10, Two = 20 }
enum Product { Hat = OtherEnum.First + 1 , Gloves = 20,
    Umbrella = Hat + Gloves }

let productValue: Product = Product.Hat;
if (typeof productValue === "number") {
    console.log("Value is a number");
}

let unionValue: number | Product = Product.Hat;
if (typeof unionValue === "number") {
    console.log("Value is a number");
}
```

The code in listing 9.22 produces the following output when it is compiled and executed:

```
Value is a number
Value is a number
```

USING CONSTANT ENUMS

The TypeScript compiler creates an object that provides the implementation for an enum. In some applications, the performance impact of using the object can be a problem, and a different approach can be used instead.

TIP   This is an advanced feature that is rarely required in most projects.

To demonstrate how the compiler uses an object to implement an enum, listing 9.23 simplifies the code in the `index.ts` file so that it defines an enum and contains a statement that assigns an enum value to a variable.

> **Listing 9.23   Simplifying the code in the index.ts file in the src folder**

```
enum Product { Hat, Gloves, Umbrella }
let productValue = Product.Hat;
```

To see how the enum is implemented, examine the `index.js` file in the `dist` folder, and you will see the following code:

```
...
var Product;
(function (Product) {
    Product[Product["Hat"] = 0] = "Hat";
    Product[Product["Gloves"] = 1] = "Gloves";
    Product[Product["Umbrella"] = 2] = "Umbrella";
})(Product || (Product = {}));
let productValue = Product.Hat;
...
```

You don't have to understand how this code works. What's important is that a `Product` object is created and that it is used when the value is assigned to the `productValue` variable.

To prevent the compiler from using an object to implement an enum, the `const` keyword can be used when the enum is defined in the TypeScript file, as shown in listing 9.24.

NOTE   Const enums are more restrictive than regular enums, and all of the values must be assigned constant expressions. The simplest way to do this is to allow the compiler to assign values or to explicitly assign values yourself.

> **Listing 9.24   Defining a const enum in the index.ts file in the src folder**

```
const enum Product { Hat, Gloves, Umbrella }
let productValue = Product.Hat;
```

When the code is compiled, the compiler will inline each reference to the enum, meaning that the numeric value will be used directly. If you examine the `index.js` file in the `dist` folder after the compilation is complete, you will see the following code:

```
...
let productValue = 0 /* Product.Hat */;
...
```

The comment is included by the compiler to indicate the relationship between the `number` value and the enum. The object that previously represented the enum is no longer included in the compiled code.

Const enums may offer a small performance improvement, but they do so by disabling the enum feature that allows a name to be looked up by value, as shown in listing 9.25.

Listing 9.25   Looking up an enum name in the index.ts file in the src folder

```
const enum Product { Hat, Gloves, Umbrella}
let productValue = Product.Hat;
let productName = Product[0];
```

The compiler will produce the following error when compiling the code:

```
src/index.ts(3,27): error TS2476: A const enum member can only be accessed
using a string literal.
```

The object used to represent a normal enum is responsible for providing the lookup feature and isn't available for const enums.

> **TIP**   There is a compiler option named `preserveConstEnums` that tells the compiler to generate the object even for const enums. This feature is only for debugging, and it doesn't restore the lookup feature.

9.5   *Using literal value types*

A literal value type specifies a specific set of values and allows only those values. The effect is to treat a set of values as a distinct type, which is a useful feature but can be difficult to understand because it blurs the separation between types and values. This feature is most easily understood with an example, as shown in listing 9.26.

Listing 9.26   Using a literal value type in the index.ts file in the src folder

```
let restrictedValue: 1 | 2 | 3 = 3;
console.log(`Value: ${restrictedValue}`);
```

A literal type looks similar to a type union, but literal values are used instead of data types, as illustrated in figure 9.4.

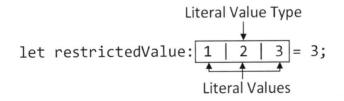

Figure 9.4   A literal value type

The literal value type in listing 9.26 tells the compiler that the `restrictedValue` variable can be assigned only 1, 2, or 3. The compiler will report an error if the variable is assigned any other value, including other `number` values, as shown in listing 9.27.

> **Listing 9.27 Assigning a different value in the index.ts file in the src folder**

```
let restrictedValue: 1 | 2 | 3 = 100;
console.log(`Value: ${restrictedValue}`);
```

The compiler determines that 100 isn't one of the allowed values and produces the following error:

```
src/index.ts(1,5): error TS2322: Type '100' is not assignable to type
'1 | 2 | 3'.
```

The combination of values is treated as a distinct type, and each combination of literal values is a different type, as shown in listing 9.28, but a value of one type can be assigned to a different type as long as it is one of the allowed values.

> **Listing 9.28 Defining a second literal value type in the index.ts file in the src folder**

```
let restrictedValue: 1 | 2 | 3 = 1;

let secondValue: 1 | 10 | 100 = 1;

restrictedValue = secondValue;
secondValue = 100;
restrictedValue = secondValue;

console.log(`Value: ${restrictedValue}`);
```

The first statement that assigns `secondValue` to `restrictedValue` is allowed because the value of `secondValue` is one of the `restrictedValue` literal values. The second assignment statement isn't allowed because the value falls outside the allowed set, producing the following error when the code is compiled:

```
src/index.ts(7,1): error TS2322: Type '100' is not assignable to type
'1 | 2 | 3'
```

9.5.1 Using literal value types in functions

Literal value types are most helpful when used with functions, allowing parameters or results to be restricted to a specific set of values, as shown in listing 9.29.

> **Listing 9.29 Restricting a function in the index.ts file in the src folder**

```
function calculatePrice(quantity: 1 | 2, price: number): number {
    return quantity * price;
}

let total = calculatePrice(2, 19.99);
console.log(`Price: ${total}`);
```

The function's `quantity` parameter will only accept `1` or `2`, and using any other value—even other `number` values—will produce a compiler error. The code in listing 9.29 produces the following output when it is compiled and executed:

```
Price: 39.98
```

9.5.2   *Mixing value types in a literal value type*

A literal value type can be made up of any combination of values that can be expressed literally, including enums. Listing 9.30 shows a mix of values in a literal value type.

> **Listing 9.30   Mixing values in a literal value type in the index.ts file in the src folder**

```typescript
function calculatePrice(quantity: 1 | 2, price: number): number {
    return quantity * price;
}

let total = calculatePrice(2, 19.99);
console.log(`Price: ${total}`);

function getRandomValue(): 1 | 2 | 3 | 4 {
    return Math.floor(Math.random() * 4) + 1 as 1 | 2 | 3 | 4;
}

enum City { London = "LON", Paris = "PAR", Chicago = "CHI" }

function getMixedValue(): 1 | "Hello" | true | City.London {
    switch (getRandomValue()) {
        case 1:
            return 1;
        case 2:
            return "Hello";
        case 3:
            return true;
        case 4:
            return City.London;
    }
}

console.log(`Value: ${getMixedValue()}`);
```

The `getRandomValue` function returns one of four values, which are used by the `getMixedValue` function to produce its result. The `getMixedValue` function shows how a literal value type can combine values that would usually be considered separate types, using a `number` value, a `string` value, a `boolean` value, and an enum value. The code in listing 9.30 produces the following output when it is compiled and executed, although you may see different output since the value from the `getMixedValue` function is selected using a random number:

```
Price: 39.98
Value: true
```

TIP Literal value types can be used in type unions with regular types, creating combinations that permit specific values of one type with any legal values for another. For example, the type union `string | true | 3` can be assigned any string value, the true `boolean` value, and the `number` value 3.

9.5.3 Using overrides with literal value types

In chapter 8, I explained how the relationship between a function's parameter and result types can be expressed using type overrides, restricting the effect of using type unions. Type overrides can also be applied to literal value types, as shown in listing 9.31, which are essentially unions for individual values.

Listing 9.31 Overriding literal value types in the index.ts file in the src folder

```
function calculatePrice(quantity: 1 | 2, price: number): number {
    return quantity * price;
}

let total = calculatePrice(2, 19.99);
console.log(`Price: ${total}`);

function getRandomValue(): 1 | 2 | 3 | 4 {
    return Math.floor(Math.random() * 4) + 1 as 1 | 2 | 3 | 4;
}

enum City { London = "LON", Paris = "PAR", Chicago = "CHI" }

function getMixedValue(input: 1): 1;
function getMixedValue(input: 2 | 3): "Hello" | true;
function getMixedValue(input: 4): City.London;
function getMixedValue(input: number): 1 | "Hello" | true | City.London {
    switch (input) {
        case 1:
            return 1;
        case 2:
            return "Hello";
        case 3:
            return true;
        case 4:
        default:
            return City.London;
    }
}

let first = getMixedValue(1);
let second = getMixedValue(2);
let third = getMixedValue(4);
console.log(`${ first}, ${second}, ${third}`);
```

Each mapping creates a relationship between parameter and result parameters, which can be expressed as one or more values. The TypeScript compiler can follow the overloads to determine the types for the `first`, `second`, and `third` variables, which can be seen by inspecting the contents of the `index.d.ts` file in the `dist` folder.

```
...
declare let first: 1;
declare let second: true | "Hello";
declare let third: City.London;
...
```

This isn't a feature that you will need in most projects, but I have demonstrated it here to show that literal value types are handled just like regular types and because it is an interesting insight into the way that the TypeScript compiler works. The code in listing 9.31 produces the following output:

```
Price: 39.98
1, Hello, LON
```

9.5.4   *Using template literal string types*

Literal string types can be used with the JavaScript template string feature to create template strings that only accept specific values, which can be a concise way to express complex combinations of values. Listing 9.32 creates a template string that uses a literal value type.

> **Listing 9.32   Using a literal value type in a template in the index.ts file in the src folder**

```
function calculatePrice(quantity: 1 | 2, price: number): number {
    return quantity * price;
}

let total = calculatePrice(2, 19.99);
console.log(`Price: ${total}`);

function getRandomValue(): 1 | 2 | 3 | 4 {
    return Math.floor(Math.random() * 4) + 1 as 1 | 2 | 3 | 4;
}

function getCityString(city: "London" | "Paris" | "Chicago")
        : `City: ${"London" | "Paris" | "Chicago"}` {
    return `City: ${city}`;
}

let str = getCityString("London");
console.log(str);
```

The `getCityString` function defines a parameter that is restricted to three string values with a literal value type. The function's result is expressed using a string template that uses the literal value type, like this:

```
...
`City: ${"London" | "Paris" | "Chicago"}`
...
```

To see why this is useful, inspect the contents of the `index.d.ts` file in the `dist` folder to see how the TypeScript compiler defines the type for the `str` variable:

```
...
declare let str: "City: London" | "City: Paris" | "City: Chicago";
...
```

The compiler has used the literal value type to expand the string template into the complete set of strings that can be assigned to the `str` variable. The code in listing 9.32 produces the following output:

```
Price: 39.98
City: London
```

9.6 Using type aliases

To avoid repetition, TypeScript provides the type alias feature, which allows a custom type combination to be assigned a name and applied where it is needed, as shown in listing 9.33.

> **Listing 9.33 Using type aliases in the index.ts file in the src folder**

```
function calculatePrice(quantity: 1 | 2, price: number): number {
    return quantity * price;
}

let total = calculatePrice(2, 19.99);
console.log(`Price: ${total}`);

type numVals = 1 | 2 | 3 | 4;

function getRandomValue(): numVals {
    return Math.floor(Math.random() * 4) + 1 as numVals;
}

type cities = "London" | "Paris" | "Chicago";
type cityResponse = `City: ${ cities }`;

function getCityString(city: cities): cityResponse {
    return `City: ${city}`;
}

let str = getCityString("London");
console.log(str);
```

Type aliases clean up TypeScript code by reducing duplication. Instead of having to define the same set of cities for the parameter and result of the `getCityString` function, for example, I can create a type alias that can be used for the function parameter and also in the template string:

```
...
type cities = "London" | "Paris" | "Chicago";
type cityResponse = `City: ${ cities }`;
...
```

Type aliases are defined using the `type` keyword, followed by a name for the alias, the equal sign, and the type that will be aliased, as shown in figure 9.5.

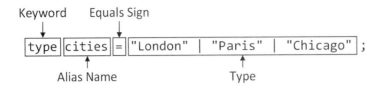

Figure 9.5   Defining a type alias

The name assigned to the alias is used in place of the full type description. Using a type alias allows a complex type or combination of types to be referred to more easily, but it doesn't change the way that the TypeScript compiler deals with the type, and the alias can be used in type annotations or assertions as normal. The code in listing 9.33 produces the following output when it is compiled and executed:

```
Price: 39.98
City: London
```

Summary

In this chapter, I explained how TypeScript can be used with arrays and introduced the tuples and enums features, which are implemented by the TypeScript compiler. I also showed you how to define literal value types and how to use aliases to describe types consistently.

- Annotations can be applied to arrays to restrict the types of values they contain.
- The TypeScript compiler can infer the type of an array based on its initial contents.
- The TypeScript compiler will allow empty arrays defined without a type annotation to accept any value.
- Basic tuples are fixed-length arrays where each element has its own type annotation, but tuples can also be defined with optional and rest elements.
- Enums allow collections of values to be used consistently. Enums are implemented entirely by the TypeScript compiler, which can lead to some oddities in the JavaScript code the compiler produces.
- Literal value types represent a specific set of values, such that only those values conform to the type.
- Type aliases allow a name to be assigned to a type, such as a union, to ensure consistency and avoid duplication.

In the next chapter, I describe the features that TypeScript provides for working with objects.

Working with objects

10

This chapter covers

- Using shape types to describe objects
- Making shape types easier to use with aliases
- Creating unions of shape types
- Guarding shape types
- Creating and using type intersections

In this chapter, I describe the way that TypeScript deals with objects. As explained in chapters 3 and 4, JavaScript has a fluid and flexible approach to dealing with objects, and TypeScript aims to strike a balance between preventing the most common mistakes while allowing useful features to be preserved. This is a theme that is continued in chapter 11, where I describe the TypeScript support for using classes. Table 10.1 summarizes the chapter.

Table 10.1 Chapter summary

Problem	Solution	Listing
Describe an object to the Type-Script compiler	Use a shape type	4-6, 8
Describe irregular shape types	Use optional properties	7, 9, 10
Use the same shape to describe multiple objects	Use a type alias	11
Combine shape types	Use type unions or intersections	12, 13, 17-23

Table 10.1   Chapter summary *(continued)*

Problem	Solution	Listing
Type guard for object types	Check the properties defined by an object using the `in` keyword	14, 15
Reuse a type guard	Define a predicate function	16

For quick reference, table 10.2 lists the TypeScript compiler options used in this chapter.

Table 10.2   The TypeScript compiler options used in this chapter

Name	Description
`target`	This option specifies the version of the JavaScript language that the compiler will target in its output.
`outDir`	This option specifies the directory in which the JavaScript files will be placed.
`rootDir`	This option specifies the root directory that the compiler will use to locate TypeScript files.
`declaration`	This option produces type declaration files when enabled, which can be useful in understanding how types have been inferred. These files are described in more detail in chapter 15.
`strictNullChecks`	This option prevents `null` and `undefined` from being accepted as values for other types.

10.1   Preparing for this chapter

In this chapter, I continue to use the `types` project created in chapter 7 and updated in the chapters since. To prepare for this chapter, replace the contents of the `index .ts` file in the `src` folder with the code shown in listing 10.1.

Listing 10.1   Replacing the contents of the index.ts file in the src folder

```
let hat = { name: "Hat", price: 100 };
let gloves = { name: "Gloves", price: 75 };

let products = [hat, gloves];

products.forEach(prod => console.log(`${prod.name}: ${prod.price}`));
```

Reset the configuration of the compiler by replacing the contents of the `tsconfig .json` file with those shown in listing 10.2.

Listing 10.2   Configuring the compiler in the tsconfig.json file in the types folder

```
{
    "compilerOptions": {
        "target": "ES2022",
        "outDir": "./dist",
```

```
        "rootDir": "./src",
        "declaration": true,
        //"strictNullChecks": true,
    }
}
```

The compiler configuration includes the `declaration` setting, which means that the compiler will create type declaration files alongside the JavaScript files. The real purpose of declaration files is explained in chapter 15, but they will be used in this chapter to explain how the compiler deals with data types.

Open a new command prompt, navigate to the `types` folder, and run the command shown in listing 10.3 to start the TypeScript compiler so that it automatically executes code after it has been compiled.

> **TIP** You can download the example project for this chapter—and for all the other chapters in this book—from https://github.com/manningbooks/essential-typescript-5.

Listing 10.3 Starting the TypeScript compiler

```
npm start
```

The compiler will compile the project, execute the output, and then enter watch mode, producing the following output:

```
7:10:34 AM - Starting compilation in watch mode...
7:10:35 AM - Found 0 errors. Watching for file changes.
Hat: 100
Gloves: 75
```

10.2 Working with objects

JavaScript objects are collections of properties that can be created using the literal syntax, constructor functions, or classes. Regardless of how they are created, objects can be altered once they have been created, adding or removing properties and receiving values of different types. To provide type features for objects, TypeScript focuses on an object's "shape," which is the combination of its property names and types.

The TypeScript compiler tries to make sure that objects are used consistently by looking for common shape characteristics. The best way to see how this works is to look at the declaration files that the compiler generates when its `declarations` option is enabled. If you examine the `index.d.ts` file in the `dist` folder, you will see that the compiler has used the shape of each object defined in listing 10.1 as its type, like this:

```
declare let hat:      { name: string; price: number; };
declare let gloves:   { name: string; price: number; };
declare let products: { name: string; price: number; }[];
```

I have formatted the contents of the declaration file to make it easier to see how the compiler has identified the type of each object using its shape. When the objects are placed into an array, the compiler uses the shape of the objects to set the type of the array to match.

This may not seem like a useful approach, but it prevents many common mistakes. Listing 10.4 adds an object with a different shape.

> Listing 10.4   Adding an object in the index.ts file in the src folder

```
let hat = { name: "Hat", price: 100 };
let gloves = { name: "Gloves", price: 75 };
let umbrella = { name: "Umbrella" };

let products = [hat, gloves, umbrella];

products.forEach(prod => console.log(`${prod.name}: ${prod.price}`));
```

Even though the objects in listing 10.1 are defined using the literal syntax, the Type-Script compiler can warn when the objects are used inconsistently. The `umbrella` object doesn't have a `price` property, and the compiler produces the following error when the file is compiled:

```
src/index.ts(9,60): error TS2339: Property 'price' does not exist on type
'{ name: string; }'.
```

The arrow function used with the `forEach` method reads a `price` property that isn't present on all of the objects in the `products` array, leading to an error. The compiler correctly identifies the shape of the objects in the example, which can be seen in the `index.d.ts` file in the `dist` folder.

```
declare let hat:      { name: string; price: number; };
declare let gloves:   { name: string; price: number; };
declare let umbrella: { name: string; };
declare let products: { name: string; }[];
```

Notice that the type for the `products` array has changed. When objects of different shapes are used together, such as in an array, the compiler creates a type that has the common properties of the objects it contains because they are the only properties that are safe to work with. In the example, the only property common to all the objects in the array is the `string` property `name`, which is why the compiler reports an error for the statement that tries to read the `price` property.

10.2.1 *Using object shape type annotations*

For object literals, the TypeScript compiler infers the type of each property using the value that it has been assigned. Types can also be explicitly specified using type annotations, which are applied to individual properties, as shown in listing 10.5.

> Listing 10.5   Using object shape type annotations in the index.ts file in the src folder

```
let hat = { name: "Hat", price: 100 };
let gloves = { name: "Gloves", price: 75 };
let umbrella = { name: "Umbrella" };

let products: { name: string, price: number }[] = [hat, gloves, umbrella];

products.forEach(prod => console.log(`${prod.name}: ${prod.price}`));
```

The type annotation restricts the contents of the `products` array to objects that have `name` and `price` properties that are `string` and `number` values, as shown in figure 10.1.

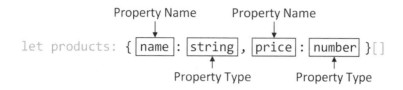

Figure 10.1 An object shape type

The compiler still reports an error for the code in listing 10.5, but now the problem is that the `umbrella` object doesn't conform to the shape specified by the type annotation for the `products` array, which provides a more useful description of the problem.

```
src/index.ts(5,64): error TS2741: Property 'price' is missing in type
'{ name: string; }' but required in type '{ name: string; price:
number; }'.
```

10.2.2 Understanding how shape types fit

To match a type, an object must define all the properties in the shape. The compiler will still match an object if it has additional properties that are not defined by the shape type, as shown in listing 10.6.

Listing 10.6   Adding properties in the index.ts file in the src folder

```
let hat = { name: "Hat", price: 100 };
let gloves = { name: "Gloves", price: 75 };
let umbrella = { name: "Umbrella", price: 30, waterproof: true };

let products: { name: string, price?: number }[] = [hat, gloves, umbrella];

products.forEach(prod => console.log(`${prod.name}: ${prod.price}`));
```

The new properties allow the `umbrella` object to match the shape of the array type because it now defines `name` and `price` properties. The `waterproof` property is ignored because it is not part of the shape type. The code in listing 10.6 produces the following code when it is compiled and executed:

```
Hat: 100
Gloves: 75
Umbrella: 30
```

Notice that type annotations are not required to indicate that individual objects have a specific shape. The TypeScript compiler automatically determines whether an object conforms to a shape by inspecting its properties and their values.

USING OPTIONAL PROPERTIES FOR IRREGULAR SHAPES

Optional properties make a shape type more flexible, allowing it to match objects that don't have those properties, as shown in listing 10.7. This can be important when dealing with a set of objects that don't share the same shape but where you need to use a property when it is available.

Listing 10.7   Using an optional property in the index.ts file in the src folder

```
let hat = { name: "Hat", price: 100 };
let gloves = { name: "Gloves", price: 75 };
let umbrella = { name: "Umbrella", price: 30, waterproof: true };

let products: { name: string, price?: number, waterproof?: boolean }[]
    = [hat, gloves, umbrella];

products.forEach(prod =>
    console.log(`${prod.name}: ${prod.price} `
        + `Waterproof: ${ prod.waterproof }`));
```

Optional properties are defined using the same syntax as optional function parameters, where a question mark follows the property name, as shown in figure 10.2.

Optional Property

```
let products: { name: string, price?: number, waterproof ?: boolean }[]
```

Figure 10.2   An optional property in a shape type

A shape type with optional properties can match objects that don't define those properties, as long the required properties are defined. When the optional property is used, such as in the `forEach` function in listing 10.7, the value of the optional property will be either the value defined by the object or `undefined`, as shown in the following output from the code when it is compiled and executed:

```
Hat: 100 Waterproof: undefined
Gloves: 75 Waterproof: undefined
Umbrella: 30 Waterproof: true
```

The `hat` and `gloves` objects don't define the optional `waterproof` property, so the value received in the `forEach` function is `undefined`. The `umbrella` object does define this property, and its value is displayed.

INCLUDING METHODS IN SHAPE TYPES

Shape types can include methods as well as properties, giving greater control over how objects are matched by the type, as shown in listing 10.8.

Listing 10.8   Including a method in a shape type in the index.ts file in the src folder

```
enum Feature { Waterproof, Insulated }

let hat = { name: "Hat", price: 100 };
```

```
let gloves = { name: "Gloves", price: 75 };
let umbrella = { name: "Umbrella", price: 30,
        hasFeature: (feature) => feature === Feature.Waterproof };

let products: { name: string, price?: number,
        hasFeature?(Feature): boolean }[]
    = [hat, gloves, umbrella];

products.forEach(prod => console.log(`${prod.name}: ${prod.price} `
    + `Waterproof: ${prod.hasFeature(Feature.Waterproof)}`));
```

The type annotation for the `products` array includes an optional property called `hasFeature` that represents a method. A method property is similar to a regular property with the addition of parentheses that describe the types of the parameters, followed by a colon and then the result type, as shown in figure 10.3.

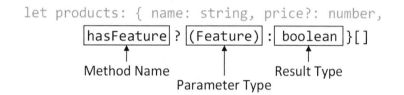

Figure 10.3   A method in a shape type

The method included in the shape type in listing 10.8 specifies a method called `hasFeature` that has one parameter, which must be a value from the `Feature` enum (also defined in listing 10.8) and which returns a `boolean` result.

> **TIP** Methods in shape types don't have to be optional, but when they are, as in listing 10.8, the question mark comes after the method name and before the parentheses that denote the start of the parameter types.

The `umbrella` object defines the `hasFeature` method with the correct types, but since the method is optional, the `hat` and `gloves` object are also matched by the shape type. As with regular properties, optional methods are `undefined` when they are not present on an object, which means that the code in listing 10.8 produces the following error when compiled and executed:

```
C:\types\dist\index.js:12
    + `Waterproof: ${prod.hasFeature(Feature.Waterproof)}`));
TypeError: prod.hasFeature is not a function
```

As with regular properties, you must ensure that a method is implemented before it is invoked.

Enforcing strict checking for methods

To help prevent errors like the one in the previous section, the TypeScript compiler can report errors when an optional method specified by a shape type is used without checking for `undefined` values. This check is enabled by the `strictNullChecks` setting, which has also been used in earlier chapters. Change the configuration of the compiler by enabling the settings as shown in listing 10.9.

Listing 10.9   Configuring the compiler in the tsconfig.json file in the types folder

```
{
    "compilerOptions": {
        "target": "ES2022",
        "outDir": "./dist",
        "rootDir": "./src",
        "declaration": true,
        "strictNullChecks": true,
    }
}
```

When the configuration file is saved, the compiler will rebuild the project and produce the following error:

```
src/index.ts(13,22): error TS2722: Cannot invoke an object which is
possibly 'undefined'.
```

This error prevents the use of optional methods until they are checked to make sure they exist on an object, as shown in listing 10.10.

Listing 10.10   Checking for an optional method in the index.ts file in the src folder

```
enum Feature { Waterproof, Insulated }

let hat = { name: "Hat", price: 100 };
let gloves = { name: "Gloves", price: 75 };
let umbrella = { name: "Umbrella", price: 30,
        hasFeature: (feature) => feature === Feature.Waterproof };

let products: { name: string, price?: number,
        hasFeature?(Feature): boolean }[]
    = [hat, gloves, umbrella];

products.forEach(prod => console.log(`${prod.name}: ${prod.price} ` +
    `${ prod.hasFeature ? prod.hasFeature(Feature.Waterproof) : "false" }`

));
```

The `hasFeature` method is invoked only if it has been defined, and the code in listing 10.10 produces the following output when it is compiled and executed:

```
Hat: 100 false
Gloves: 75 false
Umbrella: 30 true
```

10.2.3 *Using type aliases for shape types*

A type alias can be used to give a name to a specific shape, making it easier to refer to the shape in code consistently, as shown in listing 10.11.

Listing 10.11 Using an alias for a shape type in the index.ts file in the src folder

```
enum Feature { Waterproof, Insulated }

type Product = {
    name: string,
    price?: number,
    hasFeature?(Feature): boolean
};

let hat = { name: "Hat", price: 100 };
let gloves = { name: "Gloves", price: 75 };
let umbrella = { name: "Umbrella", price: 30,
        hasFeature: (feature) => feature === Feature.Waterproof };

let products: Product[] = [hat, gloves, umbrella];

products.forEach(prod => console.log(`${prod.name}: ${prod.price} ` +
    `${ prod.hasFeature ? prod.hasFeature(Feature.Waterproof) : "false" }`
));
```

The alias assigns a name to the shape, which can be used in type annotations. In the listing, an alias named `Product` is created and used as the type for the array. Using an alias doesn't change the output from the code when it is compiled and executed.

```
Hat: 100 false
Gloves: 75 false
Umbrella: 30 true
```

10.2.4 *Using shape type unions*

In chapter 7, I described the type union feature that allows multiple types to be expressed together so that, for example, arrays or function parameters can accept multiple types. As I explained, type unions are types in their own right and contain the properties that are defined by all of their constituent types. This isn't a useful feature when dealing with unions of primitive data types because there are few common properties, but it is a more useful feature when dealing with objects, as shown in listing 10.12.

Listing 10.12 Using a type union in the index.ts file in the src folder

```
type Product = {
    id: number,
    name: string,
    price?: number
};

type Person = {
    id: string,
    name: string,
    city: string
};
```

```
let hat = { id: 1, name: "Hat", price: 100 };
let gloves = { id: 2, name: "Gloves", price: 75 };
let umbrella = { id: 3, name: "Umbrella", price: 30 };
let bob = { id: "bsmith", name: "Bob", city: "London" };

let dataItems: (Product | Person)[] = [hat, gloves, umbrella, bob];

dataItems.forEach(item =>
    console.log(`ID: ${item.id}, Name: ${item.name}`));
```

The `dataItems` array in this example has been annotated with a union of the `Product` and `Person` types. These types have two properties in common, `id` and `name`, which means these properties can be used when processing the array without having to narrow to a single type.

```
...
dataItems.forEach(item =>
    console.log(`ID: ${item.id}, Name: ${item.name}`));
...
```

These are the only properties that can be accessed because they are the only properties shared by all types in the union. Any attempt to access the `price` property defined by the `Product` type or the `city` property defined by the `Person` type will produce an error because these properties are not part of the `Product | Person` union. The code in listing 10.12 produces the following output:

```
ID: 1, Name: Hat
ID: 2, Name: Gloves
ID: 3, Name: Umbrella
ID: bsmith, Name: Bob
```

10.2.5 *Understanding union property types*

When a union of shape types is created, the types of each common property are combined, also using a union. This effect can be more easily understood by creating a type that is equivalent to the union, as shown in listing 10.13.

> **Listing 10.13   Creating an equivalent type in the index.ts file in the src folder**

```
type Product = {
    id: number,
    name: string,
    price?: number
};

type Person = {
    id: string,
    name: string,
    city: string
};

type UnionType = {
    id: number | string,
    name: string
};
```

```
let hat = { id: 1, name: "Hat", price: 100 };
let gloves = { id: 2, name: "Gloves", price: 75 };
let umbrella = { id: 3, name: "Umbrella", price: 30 };
let bob = { id: "bsmith", name: "Bob", city: "London" };

let dataItems: UnionType[] = [hat, gloves, umbrella, bob];

dataItems.forEach(item =>
    console.log(`ID: ${item.id}, Name: ${item.name}`));
```

The UnionType shows the effect of the union between the Product and Person types. The id property type is a number | string union because the id property in the Product type is a number, but the id property in the Person type is a string. The name property in both types is a string, so this is the type for the name property in the union. The code in listing 10.13 produces the following output when it is compiled and executed:

```
ID: 1, Name: Hat
ID: 2, Name: Gloves
ID: 3, Name: Umbrella
ID: bsmith, Name: Bob
```

10.2.6 *Using type guards for objects*

The previous section demonstrated how unions of shape types can be useful in their own right, but type guards are still required to get to a specific type to access all of the features it defines.

In chapter 7, I demonstrated how the typeof keyword can be used to create type guards. The typeof keyword is a standard JavaScript feature that the TypeScript compiler recognizes and uses during the type-checking process. But the typeof keyword cannot be used with objects because it will always return the same result, as demonstrated in listing 10.14.

Listing 10.14 Type guarding in the index.ts file in the src folder

```
type Product = {
    id: number,
    name: string,
    price?: number
};

type Person = {
    id: string,
    name: string,
    city: string
};

let hat = { id: 1, name: "Hat", price: 100 };
let gloves = { id: 2, name: "Gloves", price: 75 };
let umbrella = { id: 3, name: "Umbrella", price: 30 };
let bob = { id: "bsmith", name: "Bob", city: "London" };
```

```
let dataItems: (Product | Person)[] = [hat, gloves, umbrella, bob];

dataItems.forEach(item =>
    console.log(`ID: ${item.id}, Type: ${typeof item}`));
```

This listing resets the type of the array to be a union of the `Product` and `Person` types and uses the `typeof` keyword in the `forEach` function to determine the type of each item in the array, producing the following results when the code is compiled and executed:

```
ID: 1, Type: object
ID: 2, Type: object
ID: 3, Type: object
ID: bsmith, Type: object
```

The shape type feature is provided entirely by TypeScript, and all objects have the type `object` as far as JavaScript is concerned, with the result that the `typeof` keyword isn't useful for determining whether an object conforms to the `Product` and `Person` shapes.

TYPE GUARDING BY CHECKING PROPERTIES

The simplest way to differentiate between shape types is to use the JavaScript `in` keyword to check for a property, as shown in listing 10.15.

Listing 10.15   Type guarding in the index.ts file in the src folder

```
type Product = {
    id: number,
    name: string,
    price?: number
};

type Person = {
    id: string,
    name: string,
    city: string
};

let hat = { id: 1, name: "Hat", price: 100 };
let gloves = { id: 2, name: "Gloves", price: 75 };
let umbrella = { id: 3, name: "Umbrella", price: 30 };
let bob = { id: "bsmith", name: "Bob", city: "London" };

let dataItems: (Product | Person)[] = [hat, gloves, umbrella, bob];

dataItems.forEach(item => {
    if ("city" in item) {
        console.log(`Person: ${item.name}: ${item.city}`);
    } else  {
        console.log(`Product: ${item.name}: ${item.price}`);
    }
});
```

The goal is to be able to determine each object in the array conforms to the `Product` shape or the `Person` shape. We know these are the only types that the array can contain because its type annotation is `(Product | Person)[]`.

A shape is a combination of properties, and a type guard must test for one or more properties that are included in one shape but not the other. In the case of listing 10.15, any object that has a `city` property must conform to the `Person` shape since this property is not part of the `Product` shape. To create a type guard that checks for a property, the property name is expressed as a `string` literal, followed by the `in` keyword, followed by the object to test, as shown in figure 10.4.

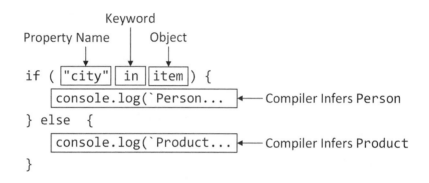

Figure 10.4   Using the in keyword

The `in` expression returns `true` for objects that define the specified property and `false` otherwise. The TypeScript compiler recognizes the significance of testing for a property and infers the type within the code blocks of the `if`/`else` statement. The code in listing 10.15 produces the following output when compiled and executed:

```
Product: Hat: 100
Product: Gloves: 75
Product: Umbrella: 30
Person: Bob: London
```

Avoiding common type guard problems

It is important to create type guard tests that definitively and accurately differentiate between types. If the compiler gives you unexpected errors when you have used a type guard, then the likely cause is an inaccurate test. There are two common problems to avoid. The first is creating an inaccurate test that doesn't reliably differentiate between types, such as this test:

```
dataItems.forEach(item => {
  if ("id" in item && "name" in item) {
      console.log(`Person: ${item.name}: ${item.city}`);
    } else {
      console.log(`Product: ${item.name}: ${item.price}`);
    }
});
```

(continued)

This test checks for `id` and `name` properties, but these are defined by both the `Person` and `Product` types, and the test doesn't give the compiler enough information to infer a type. The type inferred in the `if` block is the `Product | Person` union, which means the use of the `city` property will generate an error. The type inferred in the `else` block is `never`, since all the possible types have already been inferred, and the compiler will generate errors for the use of the `name` and `price` properties. A related problem is testing for an optional property, like this:

```
dataItems.forEach(item => {
    if ("price" in item) {
        console.log(`Product: ${item.name}: ${item.price}`);
    } else {
        console.log(`Person: ${item.name}: ${item.city}`);
    }
});
```

The test will match objects that define a `price` property, which means that the type inferred in the `if` block will be `Product`, as intended (notice that the statements in the code blocks are reversed in this example). The problem is that objects can still match the `Product` shape if they don't have a `price` property, which means the type inferred in the `else` block is `Product | Person` and the compiler will report an error for the use of the `city` property.

Writing effective tests for types can require careful thought and thorough testing, although the process becomes easier with experience.

TYPE GUARDING WITH A TYPE PREDICATE FUNCTION

The `in` keyword is a useful way to identify whether an object conforms to a shape, but it requires the same checks to be written each time types need to be identified. TypeScript also supports guarding object types using a function, as shown in listing 10.16.

Listing 10.16   Type guarding with a function in the index.ts file in the src folder

```
type Product = {
    id: number,
    name: string,
    price?: number
};

type Person = {
    id: string,
    name: string,
    city: string
};

let hat = { id: 1, name: "Hat", price: 100 };
let gloves = { id: 2, name: "Gloves", price: 75 };
let umbrella = { id: 3, name: "Umbrella", price: 30 };
let bob = { id: "bsmith", name: "Bob", city: "London" };
```

```
let dataItems: (Product | Person)[] = [hat, gloves, umbrella, bob];

function isPerson(testObj: any): testObj is Person {
    return testObj.city !== undefined;
}

dataItems.forEach(item => {
    if (isPerson(item)) {
        console.log(`Person: ${item.name}: ${item.city}`);
    } else  {
        console.log(`Product: ${item.name}: ${item.price}`);
    }
});
```

Type guarding for objects is done with a function that uses the is keyword, as shown in figure 10.5.

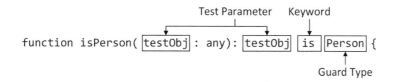

Figure 10.5   An object type guard function

The result of the function, which is a *type predicate*, tells the compiler which of the function's parameters is being tested and the type that the function checks for. In listing 10.16, the isPerson function tests its testObj parameter for the Person type. If the result of the function is true, then the TypeScript compiler will treat the object as the specified type.

Using a function for type guarding can be more flexible because the parameter type is any, allowing properties to be tested for without having to use string literals and the in keyword.

> **TIP**   There are no restrictions on the name of the type guard function, but the convention is to prefix the guarded type with is, such that a function that tests for the Person type is named isPerson and a function that tests for the Product type is named isProduct.

The code in listing 10.16 produces the following output when compiled and executed, showing that using the guard function has the same effect as the in keyword:

```
Product: Hat: 100
Product: Gloves: 75
Product: Umbrella: 30
Person: Bob: London
```

10.3   *Using type intersections*

Type intersections combine the features of multiple types, allowing all the features to be used. This is in contrast to type unions, which only allow the use of common features. Listing 10.17 shows an intersection type being defined and used.

Listing 10.17   Defining a type intersection in the index.ts file in the src folder

```typescript
type Person = {
    id: string,
    name: string,
    city: string
};

type Employee = {
    company: string,
    dept: string
};

let bob = { id: "bsmith", name: "Bob", city: "London",
    company: "Acme Co", dept: "Sales" };

let dataItems: (Person & Employee)[] = [bob];

dataItems.forEach(item => {
    console.log(`Person: ${item.id}, ${item.name}, ${item.city}`);
    console.log(`Employee: ${item.id}, ${item.company}, ${item.dept}`);
});
```

The type of the `dataItems` array is set to the intersection of the `Person` and `Employee` types. Intersections are defined using the ampersand between two or more types, as shown in figure 10.6.

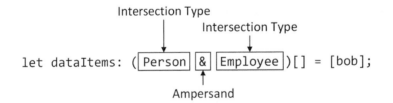

Figure 10.6   Defining an intersection type

An object will conform to the shape of a type intersection only if it defines the properties defined by merging all the types in that intersection, as shown in figure 10.7.

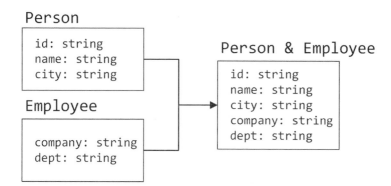

Figure 10.7   The effect of a type intersection

In listing 10.17, the intersection between `Person` and `Employee` types has the effect that the `dataItems` array can contain only objects that define `id`, `name`, `city`, `company`, and `dept` properties.

The contents of the array are processed using the `forEach` method, which demonstrates that the properties from both types in the intersection can be used. The code in the listing produces the following output when compiled and executed:

```
Person: bsmith, Bob, London
Employee: bsmith, Acme Co, Sales
```

10.3.1 Using intersections for data correlation

Intersections are useful when you receive objects from one source and need to introduce new functionality so they can be used elsewhere in the application or when objects from two data sources need to be correlated and combined. JavaScript makes it easy to introduce functionality from one object into another, and intersections allow the types that are used to be clearly described so they can be checked by the TypeScript compiler. Listing 10.18 shows a function that correlates two data arrays.

Listing 10.18   Correlating data in the index.ts file in the src folder

```
type Person = {
    id: string,
    name: string,
    city: string
};

type Employee = {
    id: string,
    company: string,
    dept: string
};

type EmployedPerson = Person & Employee;
```

```
function correlateData(peopleData: Person[], staff: Employee[])
        : EmployedPerson[] {
    const defaults = { company: "None", dept: "None"};
    return peopleData.map(p => ({ ...p,
        ...staff.find(e => e.id === p.id) || { ...defaults, id: p.id } }));
}

let people: Person[] =
    [{ id: "bsmith", name: "Bob Smith", city: "London" },
     { id: "ajones", name: "Alice Jones", city: "Paris"},
     { id: "dpeters", name: "Dora Peters", city: "New York"}];

let employees: Employee[] =
    [{ id: "bsmith", company: "Acme Co", dept: "Sales" },
     { id: "dpeters", company: "Acme Co", dept: "Development" }];

let dataItems: EmployedPerson[] = correlateData(people, employees);

dataItems.forEach(item => {
    console.log(`Person: ${item.id}, ${item.name}, ${item.city}`);
    console.log(`Employee: ${item.id}, ${item.company}, ${item.dept}`);
});
```

In this example, the `correlateData` function receives an array of `Person` objects and
an array of `Employee` objects and uses the `id` property they share to produce objects
that combine the properties of both shape types. As each `Person` object is processed
by the `map` method, the array `find` method is used to locate the `Employee` object with
the same `id` value, and the object spread operator is used to create objects that match
the intersection shape. Since the results from the `correlateData` function have to
define all the intersection properties, I use default values when there is no matching
`Employee` object.

```
...
const defaults = { company: "None", dept: "None"};
return peopleData.map(p => ({ ...p,
    ...staff.find(e => e.id === p.id) || { ...defaults, id: p.id } }));
...
```

I used type annotations in listing 10.18 to make the purpose of the code easier to
understand, but the code would work without them. The TypeScript compiler is adept
at understanding the effect of code statements and can understand the effect of this
statement is to create objects that conform to the shape of the type intersection.

The code in listing 10.18 produces the following output when it is compiled and
executed:

```
Person: bsmith, Bob Smith, London
Employee: bsmith, Acme Co, Sales
Person: ajones, Alice Jones, Paris
Employee: ajones, None, None
Person: dpeters, Dora Peters, New York
Employee: dpeters, Acme Co, Development
```

10.3.2 *Understanding intersection merging*

Because an intersection combines features from multiple types, an object that conforms to the intersection shape also conforms to each of the types in the intersection. For example, an object that conforms to `Person & Employee` can be used where the `Person` type or the `Employee` type is specified, as shown in listing 10.19.

> **Listing 10.19** **Using types in an intersection in the index.ts file in the src folder**

```
type Person = {
    id: string,
    name: string,
    city: string
};

type Employee = {
    id: string,
    company: string,
    dept: string
};

type EmployedPerson = Person & Employee;

function correlateData(peopleData: Person[], staff: Employee[])
        : EmployedPerson[] {
    const defaults = { company: "None", dept: "None"};
    return peopleData.map(p => ({ ...p,
        ...staff.find(e => e.id === p.id) || { ...defaults, id: p.id } }));
}

let people: Person[] =
    [{ id: "bsmith", name: "Bob Smith", city: "London" },
     { id: "ajones", name: "Alice Jones", city: "Paris"},
     { id: "dpeters", name: "Dora Peters", city: "New York"}];

let employees: Employee[] =
    [{ id: "bsmith", company: "Acme Co", dept: "Sales" },
     { id: "dpeters", company: "Acme Co", dept: "Development" }];

let dataItems: EmployedPerson[] = correlateData(people, employees);

function writePerson(per: Person): void {
    console.log(`Person: ${per.id}, ${per.name}, ${per.city}`);
}

function writeEmployee(emp: Employee): void {
    console.log(`Employee: ${emp.id}, ${emp.company}, ${emp.dept}`);
}

dataItems.forEach(item => {
    writePerson(item);
    writeEmployee(item);
});
```

The compiler matches an object to a shape by ensuring that it defines all the properties in the shape and doesn't care about excess properties (except when defining an object literal, as explained earlier in the chapter). The objects that conform to the `EmployedPerson` type can be used in the `writePerson` and `writeEmployee` functions because they conform to the types specified for the function's parameters. The code in listing 10.19 produces the following output:

```
Person: bsmith, Bob Smith, London
Employee: bsmith, Acme Co, Sales
Person: ajones, Alice Jones, Paris
Employee: ajones, None, None
Person: dpeters, Dora Peters, New York
Employee: dpeters, Acme Co, Development
```

It may seem obvious that an intersection type is compatible with each of its constituents, but it has an important effect when the types in the intersection define properties with the same name: the type of the property in the intersection is an intersection of the individual property types. That sentence is hard to make sense of, so the sections that follow provide a more useful explanation.

MERGING PROPERTIES WITH THE SAME TYPE

The simplest situation is where there are properties with the same name and the same type, such as the `id` properties defined by the `Person` and `Employee` types, which are merged into the intersection without any changes, as shown in figure 10.8.

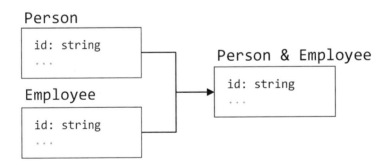

Figure 10.8   Merging properties with the same type

There are no issues to deal with in this situation because any value assigned to the `id` property will be a string and will conform to the requirements of the object and intersection types.

MERGING PROPERTIES WITH DIFFERENT TYPES

If there are properties with the same name but different types, the compiler keeps the property name but intersects the type. To demonstrate, listing 10.20 removes the functions and adds a `contact` property to the `Person` and `Employee` types.

Listing 10.20 Adding properties with different types in the index.ts file in the src folder

```
type Person = {
    id: string,
    name: string,
    city: string,
    contact: number
};

type Employee = {
    id: string,
    company: string,
    dept: string,
    contact: string
};

type EmployedPerson = Person & Employee;

let typeTest = ({} as EmployedPerson).contact;
```

The last statement in listing 10.20 is a useful trick for seeing what type the compiler assigns to a property in the intersection by looking at the declaration file created in the `dist` folder when the `declaration` compiler configuration option is `true`. The statement uses a type assertion to tell the compiler that an empty object conforms to the `EmployedPeson` type and assigns the `contact` property to the `typeTest` variable. When the changes to the `index.ts` file are saved, the compiler will compile the code, and the `index.d.ts` file in the `dist` folder will show the type for the `contact` property in the intersection.

```
declare let typeTest: never;
```

There is no intersection between the string and number types, so the compiler has used the never type for the merged property, as shown in figure 10.9.

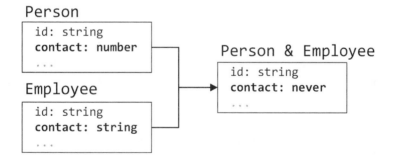

Figure 10.9 Merging properties with different types

Creating an intersection of the types is the only way the compiler can merge the properties, but it doesn't produce a useful result because there are no values that can be assigned to the intersection of the primitive `number` and `string` types, as shown in listing 10.21.

Listing 10.21   Assigning values to the intersection in the index.ts file in the src folder

```
type Person = {
    id: string,
    name: string,
    city: string,
    contact: number
};

type Employee = {
    id: string,
    company: string,
    dept: string,
    contact: string
};

type EmployedPerson = Person & Employee;

let typeTest = ({} as EmployedPerson).contact;

let person1: EmployedPerson = {
    id: "bsmith", name: "Bob Smith", city: "London",
    company: "Acme Co", dept: "Sales", contact: "Alice"
};

let person2: EmployedPerson = {
    id: "dpeters", name: "Dora Peters", city: "New York",
    company: "Acme Co", dept: "Development", contact: 6512346543
};
```

An object has to assign a value to the contact property to conform to the shape, but doing so creates the following errors:

```
src/index.ts(21,40): error TS2322: Type 'string' is not assignable to type
'never'.

src/index.ts(26,46): error TS2322: Type 'number' is not assignable to type
'never'.
```

The intersection of number and string is an impossible type. There is no way to work around this problem for primitive types, and the only solution is to adjust the types used in the intersection so that shape types are used instead of primitives, as shown in listing 10.22.

> **NOTE** It might seem odd that the TypeScript compiler allows impossible types to be defined, but the reason is that some of the advanced TypeScript features, described in later chapters, make it difficult for the compiler to deal with all situations consistently, and the Microsoft development team has chosen simplicity over exhaustively checking for every impossible type.

Listing 10.22   Using shape types in an intersection in the index.ts file in the src folder

```
type Person = {
    id: string,
    name: string,
```

```
        city: string,
        contact: { phone: number }
};

type Employee = {
        id: string,
        company: string,
        dept: string,
        contact: { name: string }
};

type EmployedPerson = Person & Employee;

let typeTest = ({} as EmployedPerson).contact;

let person1: EmployedPerson = {
        id: "bsmith", name: "Bob Smith", city: "London",
        company: "Acme Co", dept: "Sales",
        contact: { name: "Alice" , phone: 6512346543 }
};

let person2: EmployedPerson = {
        id: "dpeters", name: "Dora Peters", city: "New York",
        company: "Acme Co", dept: "Development",
        contact: { name: "Alice" , phone: 6512346543 }
};
```

The compiler handles the property merge in the same way, but the result of the intersection is a shape that has name and phone properties, as shown in figure 10.10.

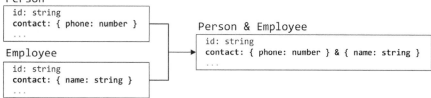

Figure 10.10   Merging properties with shape types

The intersection of an object with a phone property and an object with a name property is an object with phone and name properties, which makes it possible to assign contact values that conform to the Person and Employee types and their intersection.

MERGING METHODS

If the types in an intersection define methods with the same name, then the compiler will create a function whose signature is an intersection, as shown in listing 10.23.

Listing 10.23   Merging methods in the index.ts file in the src folder

```
type Person = {
    id: string,
    name: string,
    city: string,
    getContact(field: string): string
};

type Employee = {
    id: string,
    company: string,
    dept: string
    getContact(field: number): number
};

type EmployedPerson = Person & Employee;

let person: EmployedPerson = {
    id: "bsmith", name: "Bob Smith", city: "London",
    company: "Acme Co", dept: "Sales",
    getContact(field: string | number): any {
        return typeof field === "string" ? "Alice" : 6512346543;
    }
};

let typeTest = person.getContact;
let stringParamTypeTest = person.getContact("Alice");
let numberParamTypeTest = person.getContact(123);

console.log(`Contact: ${person.getContact("Alice")}`);
console.log(`Contact: ${person.getContact(12)}`);
```

The compiler will merge the functions by creating an intersection of their signatures, which can produce impossible types or functions that cannot be usefully implemented. In the example, the getContact methods in the Person and Employee types are intersected, as shown in figure 10.11.

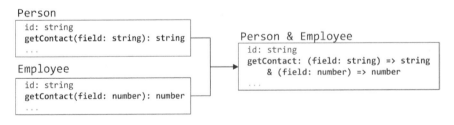

Figure 10.11   Merging methods

It can be difficult to work out the consequences of merging methods in an intersection, but the overall effect is similar to type overloading, described in chapter 8. I often rely on the type declaration file to make sure that I have achieved the intersection I want, and there are three statements in listing 10.23 that help show how the methods have been merged.

```
...
let typeTest = person.getContact;
let stringParamTypeTest = person.getContact("Alice");
let numberParamTypeTest = person.getContact(123);
...
```

When the `index.ts` file is saved and compiled, the `index.d.ts` file in the `dist` folder will contain statements that show the type the compiler has assigned to each of the variables:

```
declare let typeTest: ((field: string) => string)
    & ((field: number) => number);
declare let stringParamTypeTest: string;
declare let numberParamTypeTest: number;
```

The first statement shows the type of the intersected method, and the other statements show the type returned when `string` and `number` arguments are used. (I explain the intended purpose of the `index.d.ts` file in chapter 15, but taking advantage of this feature to see the types that the compiler is working with is often useful.)

The implementation of an intersected method must preserve compatibility with the methods in the intersection. Parameters are usually easy to deal with, and in listing 10.23, I used a type union to create a method that can receive `string` and `number` values. Method results are more difficult to deal with because it can be hard to find a type that preserves compatibility. I find the most reliable approach is to use `any` as the method result and use type guards to create the mappings between parameters and result types.

```
...
getContact(field: string | number): any {
    return typeof field === "string" ? "Alice" : 6512346543;
}
...
```

I try to avoid using `any` as much as possible, but there is no other type that can be specified in this example that allows an `EmployedPerson` object to be used both as a `Person` and an `Employee` object. The code in listing 10.23 produces the following output when compiled and executed:

```
Contact: Alice
Contact: 6512346543
```

Summary

In this chapter, I describe the way that TypeScript uses an object's shape to perform type checking. I explained how shapes are compared, how shapes can be used for aliases, and how shapes are combined into unions and intersections.

- The combination of types applied to properties and methods creates an object shape type.
- Objects conform to the shape type if they have properties and methods with the same names and types.
- Shape types can be defined with optional properties, which allows objects without these properties to match the type.
- Unions of shape types contain only the properties and methods which all types in the union define. Any member not defined by all the types is excluded.
- Intersections of shape types contain all the properties and methods defined by all the types in the union, even if they are not implemented by all the types.
- Intersections merge overlapping properties and methods based on their types.

In the next chapter, I explain how the shape features are used to provide type support for classes.

11

Working with
classes and interfaces

This chapter covers

- Working with types for constructor functions
- Defining classes with type annotations
- Restricting access to class members with access controls
- Simplifying classes by using the concise constructor syntax
- Creating properties that can only be modified in the class constructor
- Using accessors and auto-accessors
- Understanding class inheritance
- Using interfaces and abstract classes
- Dynamically creating properties with index signatures

In this chapter, I describe the features that TypeScript provides for working with classes and introduce the interface feature, which provides an alternative approach to describing the shape of objects. Table 11.1 summarizes the chapter.

Table 11.1   Chapter summary

Problem	Solution	Listing
Create objects consistently	Use a constructor function or define a class	4–6, 17–19
Prevent access to properties and methods	Use the TypeScript access control keywords or JavaScript private fields	7-9
Prevent properties from being modified	Use the `readonly` keyword	10
Receive a constructor parameter and create an instance property in a single step	Use the concise constructor syntax	11
Separate data access from storage	Use accessors or auto-accessors	12–16
Define partial common functionality that will be inherited by subclasses	Define an abstract class	20, 21
Define a shape that classes can implement	Define an interface	12–27
Define a property dynamically	Use an index signature	28-32

For quick reference, table 11.2 lists the TypeScript compiler options used in this chapter.

Table 11.2   The TypeScript compiler options used in this chapter

Name	Description
`target`	This option specifies the version of the JavaScript language that the compiler will target in its output.
`outDir`	This option specifies the directory in which the JavaScript files will be placed.
`rootDir`	This option specifies the root directory that the compiler will use to locate TypeScript files.
`declaration`	This option produces type declaration files when enabled, which can be useful in understanding how types have been inferred. These files are described in more detail in chapter 15.
`noUncheckedIndexedAccess`	This option does not allow properties accessed via an index signature to be accessed until they have been guarded against undefined values.

11.1   Preparing for this chapter

In this chapter, I continue to use the `types` project created in chapter 7 and used in the chapters since. To prepare for this chapter, replace the contents of the `index .ts` file in the `src` folder with the code shown in listing 11.1.

Listing 11.1   Replacing the contents of the index.ts file in the src folder

```ts
type Person = {
    id: string,
    name: string,
    city: string
};

let data: Person[] =
    [{ id: "bsmith", name: "Bob Smith", city: "London" },
     { id: "ajones", name: "Alice Jones", city: "Paris"},
     { id: "dpeters", name: "Dora Peters", city: "New York"}];

data.forEach(item => {
    console.log(`${item.id} ${item.name}, ${item.city}`);
});
```

Reset the configuration of the compiler by commenting out the configuration options shown in listing 11.2.

Listing 11.2   Configuring the compiler in the tsconfig.json file in the types folder

```json
{
    "compilerOptions": {
        "target": "ES2022",
        "outDir": "./dist",
        "rootDir": "./src",
        "declaration": true,
        // "strictNullChecks": true
    }
}
```

The compiler configuration includes the `declaration` setting, which means that the compiler will create type declaration files alongside the JavaScript files. The intended purpose for declaration files is explained in chapter 15, but they will be used in this chapter to explain how the compiler deals with data types.

Open a new command prompt, navigate to the `types` folder, and run the command shown in listing 11.3 to start the TypeScript compiler so that it automatically executes code after it has been compiled.

> **TIP** You can download the example project for this chapter—and for all the other chapters in this book—from https://github.com/manningbooks/essential-typescript-5.

Listing 11.3   Starting the TypeScript compiler

```
npm start
```

The compiler will compile the project, execute the output, and then enter watch mode, producing the following output:

```
7:16:33 AM - Starting compilation in watch mode...
7:16:35 AM - Found 0 errors. Watching for file changes.
```

```
bsmith Bob Smith, London
ajones Alice Jones, Paris
dpeters Dora Peters, New York
```

11.2   *Using constructor functions*

As explained in chapter 4, objects can be created using constructor functions and provide access to the JavaScript prototype system. Constructor functions can be used in TypeScript code, but the way they are supported is counterintuitive and not as elegant as the way that classes are handled, as explained later in this chapter. Listing 11.4 adds a constructor function to the example code.

> **Listing 11.4   Using a constructor function in the index.ts file in the src folder**

```
type Person = {
    id: string,
    name: string,
    city: string
};

let Employee = function(id: string, name: string, dept: string,
        city: string) {
    this.id = id;
    this.name = name;
    this.dept = dept;
    this.city = city;
};
Employee.prototype.writeDept = function() {
    console.log(`${this.name} works in ${this.dept}`);
};

let salesEmployee = new Employee("fvega", "Fidel Vega", "Sales", "Paris");

let data: (Person | Employee )[] =
    [{ id: "bsmith", name: "Bob Smith", city: "London" },
     { id: "ajones", name: "Alice Jones", city: "Paris"},
     { id: "dpeters", name: "Dora Peters", city: "New York"},
     salesEmployee];

data.forEach(item => {
    if (item instanceof Employee) {
        item.writeDept();
    } else {
        console.log(`${item.id} ${item.name}, ${item.city}`);
    }
});
```

The `Employee` constructor function creates objects with `id`, `name`, `dept`, and `city` properties, and there is a method named `writeDept` defined on the `Employee` prototype. The `data` array is updated to contain `Person` and `Employee` objects, and the function passed to the `forEach` method uses the `instanceof` operator to narrow the type of each object in the array. The code in listing 11.4 produces the following compiler errors:

```
src/index.ts(20,21): error TS2749: 'Employee' refers to a value, but is
    being used as a type here. Did you mean 'typeof Employee'?
```

```
src/index.ts(20,21): error TS4025: Exported variable 'data' has or is using
    private name 'Employee'.
```

```
src/index.ts(28,14): error TS2339: Property 'writeDept' does not exist on
    type '{}'.
```

TypeScript treats the `Employee` constructor function like any other function and looks at its parameter and result types to describe its shape. When the `Employee` function is used with the `new` keyword, the compiler uses the `any` type for the object assigned to the `salesEmployee` variable. The result is a series of errors as the compiler struggles to make sense of the way the constructor function is used.

The simplest way to solve this problem is to provide the compiler with additional information about the shapes of the objects that are used. Listing 11.5 adds a type alias that describes the objects created by the `Employee` constructor function.

> **Listing 11.5 Adding a type alias in the index.ts file in the src folder**

```
type Person = {
    id: string,
    name: string,
    city: string
};

type Employee = {
    id: string,
    name: string,
    dept: string,
    city: string,
    writeDept: () => void
};

let Employee = function(id: string, name: string, dept: string,
        city: string) {
    this.id = id;
    this.name = name;
    this.dept = dept;
    this.city = city;
};
Employee.prototype.writeDept = function() {
    console.log(`${this.name} works in ${this.dept}`);
};

let salesEmployee = new Employee("fvega", "Fidel Vega", "Sales", "Paris");

let data: (Person | Employee )[] =
    [{ id: "bsmith", name: "Bob Smith", city: "London" },
     { id: "ajones", name: "Alice Jones", city: "Paris"},
     { id: "dpeters", name: "Dora Peters", city: "New York"},
     salesEmployee];

data.forEach(item => {
```

```
    if ("dept" in item) {
        item.writeDept();
    } else {
        console.log(`${item.id} ${item.name}, ${item.city}`);
    }
});
```

The TypeScript compiler may not understand the significance of the constructor function, but it can match the objects it creates by shape. The listing adds a shape type that corresponds to those created by the constructor function, including the method that is accessed through the prototype. For convenience, I have given the shape type an alias that matches the name of the constructor function, but that is optional because the compiler keeps track of variable names and type names separately.

Notice that the type guard has changed in listing 11.5 so that the type is narrowed by checking for a property. The TypeScript compiler isn't able to use the `instanceof` operator as a type guard for objects created by a constructor function, so I have used one of the techniques described in chapter 10. The result is that the compiler can match the shape of the objects created by the `Employee` constructor function to the shape defined by the `Employee` type and differentiate between objects based on the presence of the `dept` property, producing the following output when the code is compiled and executed:

```
bsmith Bob Smith, London
ajones Alice Jones, Paris
dpeters Dora Peters, New York
Fidel Vega works in Sales
```

11.3 *Using classes*

TypeScript doesn't have good support for constructor functions, but that is because the focus has been on classes, building on the features provided by JavaScript to make them more familiar to programmers accustomed to languages such as C#. Listing 11.6 replaces the factory function with a class.

> **Listing 11.6   Using a class in the index.ts file in the src folder**

```
type Person = {
    id: string,
    name: string,
    city: string
};

class Employee {
    id: string;
    name: string;
    dept: string;
    city: string;

    constructor(id: string, name: string, dept: string, city: string) {
        this.id = id;
        this.name = name;
```

```
            this.dept = dept;
            this.city = city;
    }

    writeDept() {
        console.log(`${this.name} works in ${this.dept}`);
    }
}

let salesEmployee = new Employee("fvega", "Fidel Vega", "Sales", "Paris");

let data: (Person | Employee )[] =
    [{ id: "bsmith", name: "Bob Smith", city: "London" },
     { id: "ajones", name: "Alice Jones", city: "Paris"},
     { id: "dpeters", name: "Dora Peters", city: "New York"},
     salesEmployee];

data.forEach(item => {
    if (item instanceof Employee) {
        item.writeDept();
    } else {
        console.log(`${item.id} ${item.name}, ${item.city}`);
    }
});
```

The syntax for a TypeScript class requires the declaration of instance properties and their types. This leads to more verbose classes—although I demonstrate a feature that addresses this shortly—but it has the advantage of allowing the constructor parameter types to be different from the types of the instance properties to which they are assigned. Objects are created from classes using the standard `new` keyword, and the compiler understands the use of the `instanceof` keyword for type narrowing when classes are used.

As you will learn in the sections that follow, TypeScript provides powerful features for classes, and a TypeScript class can look different from the standard JavaScript classes described in chapter 4. But it is important to understand that the compiler generates standard classes that depend on the JavaScript constructor function and prototype features at runtime. You can see the class that is generated from listing 11.6 by looking at the contents of the `index.js` file in the `dist` folder, which will contain the following code:

```
...
class Employee {
    id;
    name;
    dept;
    city;
    constructor(id, name, dept, city) {
        this.id = id;
        this.name = name;
        this.dept = dept;
        this.city = city;
    }
```

```
    writeDept() {
        console.log(`${this.name} works in ${this.dept}`);
    }
}
...
```

As you start using more advanced class features, it can be useful to examine the classes that the compiler produces to see how the TypeScript features are translated into pure JavaScript. The code in listing 11.6 produces the following output when it is compiled and executed:

```
bsmith Bob Smith, London
ajones Alice Jones, Paris
dpeters Dora Peters, New York
Fidel Vega works in Sales
```

11.3.1 *Using the access control keywords*

JavaScript has only recently introduced private properties and methods in classes, using the # character, as described in chapter 4. TypeScript supports the # character, but also has a more comprehensive set of access control keywords that predate the introduction of the JavaScript features, as described in table 11.3.

Table 11.3   The TypeScript access control keywords

Name	Description
public	This keyword allows free access to a property or method and is the default if no keyword is used.
private	This keyword restricts access to the class that defines the property or method it is applied to.
protected	This keyword restricts access to the class that defines the property or method it is applied to and its subclasses.

TypeScript treats properties as `public` by default when no keyword is specified, although you can explicitly apply the `public` keyword to make the purpose of the code easier to understand. Listing 11.7 applies keywords to the properties defined by the `Employee` class.

Listing 11.7   Applying access control keywords in the index.ts file in the src folder

```
type Person = {
    id: string,
    name: string,
    city: string
};

class Employee {
    public id: string;
    public name: string;
    private dept: string;
```

```
    public city: string;

    constructor(id: string, name: string, dept: string, city: string) {
        this.id = id;
        this.name = name;
        this.dept = dept;
        this.city = city;
    }

    writeDept() {
        console.log(`${this.name} works in ${this.dept}`);
    }
}

let salesEmployee = new Employee("fvega", "Fidel Vega", "Sales", "Paris");
console.log(`Dept value: ${salesEmployee.dept}`);
```

The access control keywords are applied before the property name, as shown in figure 11.1.

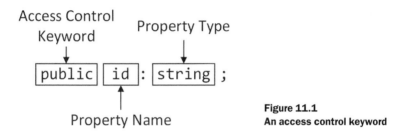

Figure 11.1
An access control keyword

In listing 11.7, I applied the public keyword to all the instance properties except dept, to which private has been applied. The effect of the private keyword is to restrict access to only within the Employee class, and the compiler generates the following error for the statement that attempts to read the value of the dept property from outside the class:

```
src/index.ts(26,42): error TS2341: Property 'dept' is private and only
accessible within class 'Employee'.
```

The only way that the dept property can be accessed is through the writeDept method, as used in listing 11.8, which is part of the Employee class and allowed by the private keyword.

> **CAUTION** The access protection features are enforced by the TypeScript compiler and are not part of the JavaScript code that the compiler generates. Do not rely on the private or protected keyword to shield sensitive data because it will be accessible to the rest of the application at runtime.

Listing 11.8   Using a method in the index.ts file in the src folder

```
type Person = {
    id: string,
    name: string,
    city: string
};

class Employee {
    public id: string;
    public name: string;
    private dept: string;
    public city: string;

    constructor(id: string, name: string, dept: string, city: string) {
        this.id = id;
        this.name = name;
        this.dept = dept;
        this.city = city;
    }

    writeDept() {
        console.log(`${this.name} works in ${this.dept}`);
    }
}

let salesEmployee = new Employee("fvega", "Fidel Vega", "Sales", "Paris");
salesEmployee.writeDept();
```

The code in listing 11.8 produces the following output when it compiled and executed:

```
Fidel Vega works in Sales
```

11.3.2 *Using JavaScript private fields*

TypeScript supports the JavaScript standard private fields, which have been recently added to the language specification, and which work in the same way as the `private` keyword, as shown in listing 11.9.

Listing 11.9   Using a private field in the index.ts file in the src folder

```
type Person = {
    id: string,
    name: string,
    city: string
};

class Employee {
    public id: string;
    public name: string;
    #dept: string;
    public city: string;
```

```
    constructor(id: string, name: string, dept: string, city: string) {
        this.id = id;
        this.name = name;
        this.#dept = dept;
        this.city = city;
    }

    writeDept() {
        console.log(`${this.name} works in ${this.#dept}`);
    }
}

let salesEmployee = new Employee("fvega", "Fidel Vega", "Sales", "Paris");
salesEmployee.writeDept();
```

Private fields are denoted with the # character, as shown in figure 11.2.

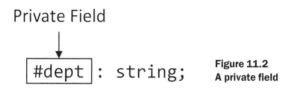

Figure 11.2
A private field

By prefixing the name of the dept variable, I restrict its access to the class that defines it. The # character is also required to get or set the value of the field, like this:

```
...
this.#dept = dept;
...
```

The key advantage over the TypeScript private keyword is that the # character is not removed during the compilation process, which means that access control is enforced by the JavaScript runtime. Like most TypeScript features, the private keyword is not included in the JavaScript code produced by the compiler, which means that access control is not enforced in the JavaScript code. The listing produces the same output as the previous example.

11.3.3 Defining read-only properties

The readonly keyword can be used to create instance properties whose value is assigned by the constructor but cannot otherwise be changed, as shown in listing 11.10.

Listing 11.10 Creating a read-only property in the index.ts file in the src folder

```
type Person = {
    id: string,
    name: string,
    city: string
};
```

```
class Employee {
    public readonly id: string;
    public name: string;
    #dept: string;
    public city: string;

    constructor(id: string, name: string, dept: string, city: string) {
        this.id = id;
        this.name = name;
        this.#dept = dept;
        this.city = city;
    }

    writeDept() {
        console.log(`${this.name} works in ${this.#dept}`);
    }
}

let salesEmployee = new Employee("fvega", "Fidel Vega", "Sales", "Paris");
salesEmployee.writeDept();
salesEmployee.id = "fidel";
```

The `readonly` keyword must come after the access control keyword if one has been used, as shown in figure 11.3.

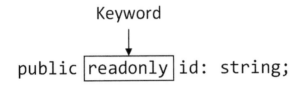

Figure 11.3   A read-only property

The application of the `readonly` keyword to the `id` property in listing 11.11 means the value assigned by the constructor cannot be changed subsequently. The statement that attempts to assign a new value to the `id` property causes the following compiler error:

```
src/index.ts(27,15): error TS2540: Cannot assign to 'id' because it is a
read-only property.
```

11.3.4 *Simplifying class constructors*

Pure JavaScript classes use constructors that create instance properties dynamically, but TypeScript requires properties to be explicitly defined. The TypeScript approach is the one that most programmers find familiar, but it can be verbose and repetitive, especially when most constructor parameters are assigned to properties that have the same name. TypeScript supports a more concise syntax for constructors that avoids the "define and assign" pattern, as shown in listing 11.11.

Listing 11.11   Simplifying the constructor in the index.ts file in the src folder

```
type Person = {
    id: string,
    name: string,
    city: string
};

class Employee {

    constructor(public readonly id: string, public name: string,
            private dept: string, public city: string) {
        // no statements required
    }

    writeDept() {
        console.log(`${this.name} works in ${this.dept}`);
    }
}

let salesEmployee = new Employee("fvega", "Fidel Vega", "Sales", "Paris");
salesEmployee.writeDept();
//salesEmployee.id = "fidel";
```

To simplify the constructor, access control keywords are applied to the parameters, as shown in figure 11.4.

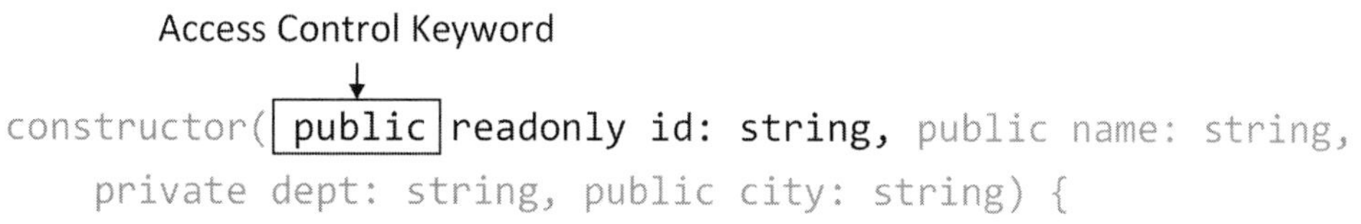

Access Control Keyword

```
constructor( public readonly id: string, public name: string,
        private dept: string, public city: string) {
```

Figure 11.4   Applying access control keywords to constructor parameters

The compiler automatically creates an instance property for each of the constructor arguments to which an access control keyword has been applied and assigns the parameter value. The use of the access control keywords doesn't change the way the constructor is invoked and is required only to tell the compiler that corresponding instance variables are required. The concise syntax can be mixed with conventional parameters if required, and the `readonly` keyword is carried over to the instance properties created by the compiler. The code in listing 11.11 produces the following output:

```
Fidel Vega works in Sales
```

11.3.5 Defining Accessors

Accessors are `get` and `set` functions that are used to mange access to a private class property, allowing additional logic to be introduced, separating the store data value from the way it is used. Listing 11.12 adds a `get` and `set` function, commonly referred to as the *getter* and *setter*, to a class.

Listing 11.12   Adding accessors in the index.ts file in the src folder

```typescript
type Person = {
    id: string,
    name: string,
    city: string
};

class Employee {
    private city: string;

    constructor(public readonly id: string, public name: string,
            private dept: string, city: string) {
        this.city = city;
    }

    writeDept() {
        console.log(`${this.name} works in ${this.dept}`);
    }

    get location() {
        return this.city;
    }

    set location(newCity) {
        this.city = newCity;
    }
}

let salesEmployee = new Employee("fvega", "Fidel Vega", "Sales", "Paris");

salesEmployee.writeDept();
console.log(`Location: ${salesEmployee.location}`);
salesEmployee.location = "London";
console.log(`Location: ${salesEmployee.location}`);
```

The property that is managed through the accessors is known as the *backing field*, which is the `city` property in this example. I have modified the constructor so the value received when the object is created is assigned to a `private` property.

The `get` and `set` keywords denote the accessors and are followed by a name, which is `location` in this case. The getter—the `get` accessor—is a function that returns a value, which is does by returning the value of the `city` property. The setter—the `set` accessor—is a function that receives a new `location` value, which is store using city property. The TypeScript compiler infers the type of the `location` value returned by the getter from the backing field and the overall effect is as if the Employee class defined a property named `location`. When I read the `location` value, I do so as though it were a property:

```typescript
...
console.log(`Location: ${salesEmployee.location}`);
salesEmployee.location = "London";
...
```

The code in listing 11.12 produces the following output:

```
Fidel Vega works in Sales
Location: Paris
Location: London
```

ADDING INDIRECTION IN ACCESSORS

The accessors in listing 11.12 manage access to a private property but the getter and setter are just functions, which means they can introduce additional logic, so that the stored value is only indirectly related to the value provided through the accessors, as shown in listing 11.13.

> **Listing 11.13 Adding accessor logic in the index.ts file in the src folder**

```typescript
type Person = {
    id: string,
    name: string,
    city: string
};

class Employee {
    private city: string;

    constructor(public readonly id: string, public name: string,
            private dept: string, city: string) {
        this.city = city;
    }

    writeDept() {
        console.log(`${this.name} works in ${this.dept}`);
    }

    get location() {
        switch (this.city) {
            case "Paris":
                return "France";
            case "London":
                return "UK";
            default:
                return this.city;
        }
    }

    set location(newCity) {
        this.city = newCity;
    }
}

let salesEmployee = new Employee("fvega", "Fidel Vega", "Sales", "Paris");

salesEmployee.writeDept();
console.log(`Location: ${salesEmployee.location}`);
salesEmployee.location = "London";
console.log(`Location: ${salesEmployee.location}`);
```

The getter uses the city value to determine the location value. These two values are linked, but the relationship between them is opaque outside of the class, where location is used just like a property. This example produces the following output, which shows the effect of the getter logic on the location value:

```
Fidel Vega works in Sales
Location: France
Location: UK
```

USING JUST A GET ACCESSOR

If the set accessor is omitted, the result is a value that behaves like a read-only property, as shown in listing 11.14.

> **Listing 11.14   Removing the setter in the index.ts file in the src folder**

```
type Person = {
    id: string,
    name: string,
    city: string
};

class Employee {
    private city: string;

    constructor(public readonly id: string, public name: string,
            private dept: string, city: string) {
        this.city = city;
    }

    writeDept() {
        console.log(`${this.name} works in ${this.dept}`);
    }

    get location() {
        switch (this.city) {
            case "Paris":
                return "France";
            case "London":
                return "UK";
            default:
                return this.city;
        }
    }

    // set location(newCity) {
    //     this.city = newCity;
    // }
}

let salesEmployee = new Employee("fvega", "Fidel Vega", "Sales", "Paris");

salesEmployee.writeDept();
console.log(`Location: ${salesEmployee.location}`);
// salesEmployee.location = "London";
// console.log(`Location: ${salesEmployee.location}`);
```

The `location` value is derived from the `city` property, but there is no longer any way to assign a new `location` value. This example produces the following output:

```
Fidel Vega works in Sales
Location: France
```

OMITTING THE BACKING FIELD

Accessors usually have a backing field, but that is not a requirement, getters and setters can be used to synthesize data values from other class features, as shown in listing 11.15.

> **Listing 11.15 A backing-free accessor in the index.ts file in the src folder**

```typescript
type Person = {
    id: string,
    name: string,
    city: string
};

class Employee {
    private city: string;

    constructor(public readonly id: string, public name: string,
            private dept: string, city: string) {
        this.city = city;
    }

    writeDept() {
        console.log(`${this.name} works in ${this.dept}`);
    }

    get location() {
        switch (this.city) {
            case "Paris":
                return "France";
            case "London":
                return "UK";
            default:
                return this.city;
        }
    }

    get details() {
        return `${this.name}, ${this.dept}, ${this.location}`;
    }
}

let salesEmployee = new Employee("fvega", "Fidel Vega", "Sales", "Paris");

salesEmployee.writeDept();
console.log(`Location: ${salesEmployee.location}`);
console.log(`Details: ${salesEmployee.details}`);
```

The `details` getter doesn't have its own backing field and the value it returns is derived from the `name` and `dept` properties, and the `location` accessor. The `details` value is still read like a regular property, but the value that is retuned is created using string composition, as the output from the example shows:

```
Fidel Vega works in Sales
Location: France
Details: Fidel Vega, Sales, France
```

11.3.6 *Using auto-accessors*

Most accessors are defined with backing fields and this is such a common requirement that the more concise auto-accessor feature has been introduced, as shown in listing 11.16.

> **Listing 11.16   Using an auto-accessor in the index.ts file in the src folder**

```typescript
type Person = {
    id: string,
    name: string,
    city: string
};

class Employee {
    private city: string;

    constructor(public readonly id: string, public name: string,
            private dept: string, city: string) {
        this.city = city;
    }

    writeDept() {
        console.log(`${this.name} works in ${this.dept}`);
    }

    get location() {
        switch (this.city) {
            case "Paris":
                return "France";
            case "London":
                return "UK";
            default:
                return this.city;
        }
    }

    get details() {
        return `${this.name}, ${this.dept}, ${this.location}`;
    }

    accessor salary: number = 100_000;
}

let salesEmployee = new Employee("fvega", "Fidel Vega", "Sales", "Paris");
```

```
salesEmployee.writeDept();
console.log(`Location: ${salesEmployee.location}`);
console.log(`Details: ${salesEmployee.details}`);
console.log(`Salary: ${salesEmployee.salary}`);
```

The `accessor` keyword denotes an auto-accessor, followed by a name and, optionally, an initial value. The TypeScript compiler will infer the accessor type from the initial value if one is provided, but a type annotation can be used as well.

Auto-accessors are not part of the JavaScript language specification yet, and so the TypeScript compiler translates the new statement in listing 11.16 into a backing field with a getter and setter, like this:

```
...
#salary_accessor_storage = 100000;
get salary() { return this.#salary_accessor_storage; }
set salary(value) { this.#salary_accessor_storage = value; }
...
```

The auto-accessor can be replaced with conventional accessors if additional logic is subsequently needed. This example produces the following output:

```
Fidel Vega works in Sales
Location: France
Details: Fidel Vega, Sales, France
Salary: 100000
```

11.3.7 *Using class inheritance*

TypeScript builds on the standard class inheritance features to make them more consistent and familiar, with some useful additions for commonly required tasks and for restricting some of the JavaScript characteristics that can cause problems. Listing 11.17 replaces the `Person` type alias with a class that provides the same features and uses it as the superclass for `Employee`.

> **NOTE** I have shown multiple classes in the same code file, but a common convention is to separate each class into its own file, which can make a project easier to navigate and understand. You can see more realistic examples in part 3, where I build a series of web applications.

Listing 11.17 Adding a class in the index.ts file in the src folder

```
class Person {

    constructor(public id: string, public name: string,
        public city: string) { }
}

class Employee extends Person {
    //private city: string;

    constructor(public readonly id: string, public name: string,
            private dept: string, public city: string) {
        super(id, name, city);
```

```
    }

    writeDept() {
        console.log(`${this.name} works in ${this.dept}`);
    }

    // get location() {
    //     switch (this.city) {
    //         case "Paris":
    //             return "France";
    //         case "London":
    //             return "UK";
    //         default:
    //             return this.city;
    //     }
    // }

    // get details() {
    //     return `${this.name}, ${this.dept}, ${this.location}`;
    // }

    // accessor salary: number = 100_000;
}

// let salesEmployee = new Employee("fvega", "Fidel Vega",
//     "Sales", "Paris");

// salesEmployee.writeDept();
// console.log(`Location: ${salesEmployee.location}`);
// console.log(`Details: ${salesEmployee.details}`);
// console.log(`Salary: ${salesEmployee.salary}`);

let data = [new Person("bsmith", "Bob Smith", "London"),
    new Employee("fvega", "Fidel Vega", "Sales", "Paris")];

data.forEach(item => {
    console.log(`Person: ${item.name}, ${item.city}`);
    if (item instanceof Employee) {
        item.writeDept();
    }
});
```

When using the extends keyword, TypeScript requires that the superclass constructor is invoked using the super keyword, ensuring that its properties are initialized. The code in listing 11.17 produces the following output:

```
Person: Bob Smith, London
Person: Fidel Vega, Paris
Fidel Vega works in Sales
```

UNDERSTANDING TYPE INFERENCE FOR SUBCLASSES

Caution is required when letting the compiler infer types from classes because it is easy to produce unexpected results by assuming the compiler has insight into the hierarchy of classes.

The data array in listing 11.17 contains a `Person` object and an `Employee` object, and if you examine the `index.d.ts` file in the `dist` folder, you will see that the compiler has inferred `Person[]` as the array type, like this:

```
...
declare let data: Person[];
...
```

If you are familiar with other programming languages, you might reasonably assume that the compiler has realized that `Employee` is a subclass of `Person` and that all the objects in the array can be treated as `Person` objects. In reality, the compiler creates a union of the types the array contains, which would be `Person | Employee`, and determines that this is equivalent to `Person` since a union only presents the features that are common to all types. It is important to remember that the compiler pays attention to object shapes, even if the developer is paying attention to classes. This can appear to be an unimportant difference, but it has consequences when using objects that share a common superclass, as shown in listing 11.18.

> **Listing 11.18 Using a common superclass in the index.ts file in the src folder**

```typescript
class Person {

    constructor(public id: string, public name: string,
        public city: string) { }
}

class Employee extends Person {

    constructor(public readonly id: string, public name: string,
            private dept: string, public city: string) {
        super(id, name, city);
    }

    writeDept() {
        console.log(`${this.name} works in ${this.dept}`);
    }
}

class Customer extends Person {
    constructor(public readonly id: string, public name: string,
            public city: string, public creditLimit: number) {
        super(id, name, city);
    }
}

class Supplier extends Person {
    constructor(public readonly id: string, public name: string,
            public city: string, public companyName: string) {
        super(id, name, city);
    }
}

let data = [new Employee("fvega", "Fidel Vega", "Sales", "Paris"),
```

```
            new Customer("ajones", "Alice Jones", "London", 500)];

data.push(new Supplier("dpeters", "Dora Peters", "New York", "Acme"));

data.forEach(item => {
    console.log(`Person: ${item.name}, ${item.city}`);
    if (item instanceof Employee) {
        item.writeDept();
    } else if (item instanceof Customer) {
        console.log(`Customer ${item.name} has ${item.creditLimit} limit`);
    } else if (item instanceof Supplier) {
        console.log(`Supplier ${item.name} works for ${item.companyName}`);
    }
});
```

This example won't compile because the TypeScript compiler has inferred the type for the `data` array based on the types of the objects it contains and has not reflected the shared superclass. Here is the statement from the `index.d.ts` file in the `dist` folder that shows the type the compiler inferred:

```
...
declare let data: (Employee | Customer)[];
...
```

The array can only contain `Employee` or `Customer` objects, and the errors are reported because a `Supplier` object is added. To resolve this problem, a type annotation can be used to tell the compiler that the array can contain `Product` objects, as shown in listing 11.19.

> **Listing 11.19   Using a type annotation in the index.ts file in the src folder**

```
...
let data: Person[] = [new Employee("fvega", "Fidel Vega", "Sales",
    "Paris"), new Customer("ajones", "Alice Jones", "London", 500)];

data.push(new Supplier("dpeters", "Dora Peters", "New York", "Acme"));
...
```

The compiler will allow the data array to store `Product` objects and objects created from its subclasses. The code in listing 11.19 produces the following output:

```
Person: Fidel Vega, Paris
Fidel Vega works in Sales
Person: Alice Jones, London
Customer Alice Jones has 500 limit
Person: Dora Peters, New York
Supplier Dora Peters works for Acme
```

11.3.8 *Using an abstract class*

Abstract classes cannot be instantiated directly and are used to describe common functionality that must be implemented by subclasses, forcing subclasses to adhere to a specific shape but allowing class-specific implementations of specific methods, as shown in listing 11.20.

Listing 11.20 Defining an abstract class in the index.ts file in the src folder

```typescript
abstract class Person {

    constructor(public id: string, public name: string,
        public city: string) { }

    getDetails(): string {
        return `${this.name}, ${this.getSpecificDetails()}`;
    }

    abstract getSpecificDetails(): string;
}

class Employee extends Person {

    constructor(public readonly id: string, public name: string,
            private dept: string, public city: string) {
        super(id, name, city);
    }

    getSpecificDetails() {
        return `works in ${this.dept}`;
    }
}

class Customer extends Person {

    constructor(public readonly id: string, public name: string,
            public city: string, public creditLimit: number) {
        super(id, name, city);
    }

    getSpecificDetails() {
        return `has ${this.creditLimit} limit`;
    }
}

class Supplier extends Person {

    constructor(public readonly id: string, public name: string,
            public city: string, public companyName: string) {
        super(id, name, city);
    }

    getSpecificDetails() {
        return `works for ${this.companyName}`;
    }
}

let data: Person[] = [new Employee("fvega", "Fidel Vega", "Sales",
    "Paris"), new Customer("ajones", "Alice Jones", "London", 500)];
data.push(new Supplier("dpeters", "Dora Peters", "New York", "Acme"));

data.forEach(item => console.log(item.getDetails()));
```

Abstract classes are created using the `abstract` keyword before the `class` keyword, as shown in figure 11.5.

Keyword

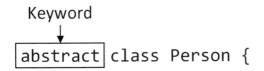

abstract class Person {

Figure 11.5   Defining an abstract class

The `abstract` keyword is also applied to individual methods, which are defined without a body, as shown in figure 11.6.

Keyword

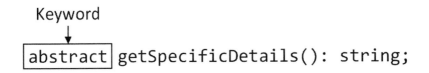

abstract getSpecificDetails(): string;

Figure 11.6   Defining an abstract method

When a class extends an abstract class, it must implement all the abstract methods. In the example, the abstract `Person` class defines an abstract method named `getSpecificDetails`, which must be implemented by the `Employee`, `Customer`, and `Supplier` classes. The `Person` class also defines a regular method named `getDetails`, which invokes the abstract method and uses its result.

Objects instantiated from classes derived from an `abstract` class can be used through the abstract class type, which means that the `Employee`, `Customer`, and `Supplier` objects can be stored in a `Person` array, although only the properties and methods defined by the `Person` class can be used unless objects are narrowed to a more specific type. The code in listing 11.20 produces the following output:

```
Fidel Vega, works in Sales
Alice Jones, has 500 limit
Dora Peters, works for Acme
```

TYPE GUARDING AN ABSTRACT CLASS

Abstract classes are implemented as regular classes in the JavaScript generated by the TypeScript compiler. The drawback of this approach is that it is the TypeScript compiler that prevents abstract classes from being instantiated, and this isn't carried over into the JavaScript code, potentially allowing objects to be created from the abstract class. However, this approach does mean that the `instanceof` keyword can be used to narrow types, as shown in listing 11.21.

Listing 11.21 Type guarding an abstract class in the index.ts file in the src folder

```typescript
abstract class Person {

    constructor(public id: string, public name: string,
        public city: string) { }

    getDetails(): string {
        return `${this.name}, ${this.getSpecificDetails()}`;
    }

    abstract getSpecificDetails(): string;
}

class Employee extends Person {

    constructor(public readonly id: string, public name: string,
            private dept: string, public city: string) {
        super(id, name, city);
    }

    getSpecificDetails() {
        return `works in ${this.dept}`;
    }
}

class Customer {

    constructor(public readonly id: string, public name: string,
            public city: string, public creditLimit: number) {
    }
}

let data: (Person | Customer)[] = [
        new Employee("fvega", "Fidel Vega", "Sales", "Paris"),
        new Customer("ajones", "Alice Jones", "London", 500)];

data.forEach(item => {
    if (item instanceof Person) {
        console.log(item.getDetails());
    } else {
        console.log(`Customer: ${item.name}`);
    }
});
```

In this listing, `Employee` extends the abstract `Person` class, but the `Customer` class does not. The `instanceof` operator can be used to identify any object instantiated from a class that extends the abstract class, which allows narrowing in the `Person | Customer` union used as the type for the array. The code in listing 11.21 produces the following output:

```
Fidel Vega, works in Sales
Customer: Alice Jones
```

11.4   *Using interfaces*

Interfaces are used to describe the shape of an object, which a class that implements
the interface must conform to, as shown in listing 11.22.

> **NOTE** Interfaces have a similar purpose to shape types, described in chapter
> 10, and successive versions of TypeScript have eroded the differences between
> these two features, to the point where they can often be used interchangeably
> to achieve the same effect, especially when dealing with simple types. Inter-
> faces do have some useful features, however, and they provide a development
> experience that is more consistent with other languages, such as C#.

Listing 11.22   Using an interface in the index.ts file in the src folder

```typescript
interface Person {
    name: string;
    getDetails(): string;
}

class Employee implements Person {

    constructor(public readonly id: string, public name: string,
            private dept: string, public city: string) {
        // no statements required
    }

    getDetails() {
        return `${this.name} works in ${this.dept}`;
    }
}

class Customer implements Person {

    constructor(public readonly id: string, public name: string,
            public city: string, public creditLimit: number) {
        // no statements required
    }

    getDetails() {
        return `${this.name} has ${this.creditLimit} limit`;
    }
}

let data: Person[] = [
        new Employee("fvega", "Fidel Vega", "Sales", "Paris"),
        new Customer("ajones", "Alice Jones", "London", 500)];
data.forEach(item => console.log(item.getDetails()));
```

Interfaces are defined by the `interface` keyword and contain the set of properties
and methods that a class must provide in order to conform to the interface, as shown
in figure 11.7.

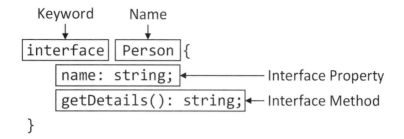

Figure 11.7 Defining an interface

Unlike abstract classes, interfaces don't implement methods or define a constructor and just define a shape. Interfaces are implemented by classes through the `implements` keyword, as shown in figure 11.8.

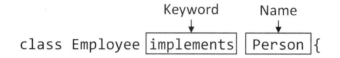

Figure 11.8 Implementing an interface

The `Person` interface defines a `name` property and a `getDetails` method, so the `Employee` and `Customer` classes must define the same property and method. These classes can define extra properties and methods, but they can only conform to the interface by providing `name` and `getDetails`. The interface can be used in type annotations, such as the array in the example.

```
...
let data: Person[] = [
        new Employee("fvega", "Fidel Vega", "Sales", "Paris"),
        new Customer("ajones", "Alice Jones", "London", 500)];
...
```

The data array can contain any object created from a class that implements the `Product` array, although the function passed to the `forEach` method can access only the features defined by the interface unless objects are narrowed to a more specific type. The code in listing 11.22 produces the following output:

```
Fidel Vega works in Sales
Alice Jones has 500 limit
```

> **Merging interface declarations**
>
> Interfaces can be defined in multiple `interface` declarations, which are merged by the compiler to form a single interface. This is an odd feature—and one that I have yet to find useful in my own projects. The declarations must be made in the same code file, and they must all be exported (defined with the `export` keyword) or defined locally (defined without the `export` keyword).

11.4.1 *Implementing multiple interfaces*

A class can implement more than one interface, meaning it must define the methods and properties defined by all of them, as shown in listing 11.23.

Listing 11.23   Implementing multiple interfaces in the index.ts file in the src folder

```typescript
interface Person {
    name: string;
    getDetails(): string;
}

interface DogOwner {
    dogName: string;
    getDogDetails(): string;
}

class Employee implements Person {

    constructor(public readonly id: string, public name: string,
            private dept: string, public city: string) {
        // no statements required
    }

    getDetails() {
        return `${this.name} works in ${this.dept}`;
    }
}

class Customer implements Person, DogOwner {

    constructor(public readonly id: string, public name: string,
            public city: string, public creditLimit: number,
            public dogName ) {
        // no statements required
    }

    getDetails() {
        return `${this.name} has ${this.creditLimit} limit`;
    }

    getDogDetails() {
        return `${this.name} has a dog named ${this.dogName}`;
    }
}

let alice = new Customer("ajones", "Alice Jones", "London", 500, "Fido");

let dogOwners: DogOwner[] = [alice];
dogOwners.forEach(item => console.log(item.getDogDetails()));

let data: Person[] = [new Employee("fvega", "Fidel Vega", "Sales",
    "Paris"), alice];
data.forEach(item => console.log(item.getDetails()));
```

Interfaces are listed after the `implements` keyword, separated with commas. In the listing, the `Customer` class implements the `Person` and `DogOwner` interfaces, which means that the `Person` object assigned to the variable named `alice` can be added to the arrays typed for `Person` and `DogOwner` objects. The code in listing 11.23 produces the following output:

```
Alice Jones has a dog named Fido
Fidel Vega works in Sales
Alice Jones has 500 limit
```

> **NOTE** A class can implement multiple interfaces only if there are no overlapping properties with conflicting types. For example, if the `Person` interface defined a `string` property named `id` and if the `DogOwner` interface defined a `number` property with the same name, the `Customer` class would not be able to implement both interfaces because there is no value that could be assigned to its `id` property that could represent both types.

11.4.2 Extending interfaces

Interfaces can be extended, just like classes. The same basic approach is used, and the result is an interface that contains the properties and methods inherited from its parent interfaces, along with any new features that are defined, as shown in listing 11.24.

Listing 11.24 Extending an interface in the index.ts file in the src folder

```
interface Person {
    name: string;
    getDetails(): string;
}

interface DogOwner extends Person {
    dogName: string;
    getDogDetails(): string;
}

class Employee implements Person {

    constructor(public readonly id: string, public name: string,
            private dept: string, public city: string) {
        // no statements required
    }

    getDetails() {
        return `${this.name} works in ${this.dept}`;
    }
}

class Customer implements DogOwner {

    constructor(public readonly id: string, public name: string,
            public city: string, public creditLimit: number,
            public dogName ) {
```

```
        // no statements required
    }

    getDetails() {
        return `${this.name} has ${this.creditLimit} limit`;
    }

    getDogDetails() {
        return `${this.name} has a dog named ${this.dogName}`;
    }
}

let alice = new Customer("ajones", "Alice Jones", "London", 500, "Fido");

let dogOwners: DogOwner[] = [alice];
dogOwners.forEach(item => console.log(item.getDogDetails()));

let data: Person[] = [new Employee("fvega", "Fidel Vega", "Sales",
    "Paris"), alice];
data.forEach(item => console.log(item.getDetails()));
```

The `extend` keyword is used to extend an interface. In the listing, the `DogOwner` interface extends the `Person` interface, which means that classes that implement `DogOwner` must define the properties and methods from both interfaces. Objects created from the `Customer` class can be treated as both `DogOwner` and `Person` objects, since they always define the shapes required by each interface. The code in listing 11.24 produces the following output:

```
Alice Jones has a dog named Fido
Fidel Vega works in Sales
Alice Jones has 500 limit
```

11.4.3 *Defining optional interface properties and methods*

Adding an optional property to an interface allows classes that implement the interface to provide the property without making it a requirement, as shown in listing 11.25.

> **Listing 11.25   Adding an Optional Property in the index.ts File in the src Folder**

```
interface Person {
    name: string;
    getDetails(): string;

    dogName?: string;
    getDogDetails?(): string;
}

class Employee implements Person {

    constructor(public readonly id: string, public name: string,
            private dept: string, public city: string) {
        // no statements required
    }
```

```
    getDetails() {
        return `${this.name} works in ${this.dept}`;
    }
}

class Customer implements Person {

    constructor(public readonly id: string, public name: string,
            public city: string, public creditLimit: number,
            public dogName) {
        // no statements required
    }

    getDetails() {
        return `${this.name} has ${this.creditLimit} limit`;
    }

    getDogDetails() {
        return `${this.name} has a dog named ${this.dogName}`;
    }
}

let alice = new Customer("ajones", "Alice Jones", "London", 500, "Fido");
let data: Person[] = [new Employee("fvega", "Fidel Vega", "Sales",
    "Paris"), alice];
data.forEach(item => {
    console.log(item.getDetails());
    if (item.getDogDetails) {
        console.log(item.getDogDetails());
    }
});
```

Declaring an optional property on an interface is done using the question mark character after the name, as shown in figure 11.9.

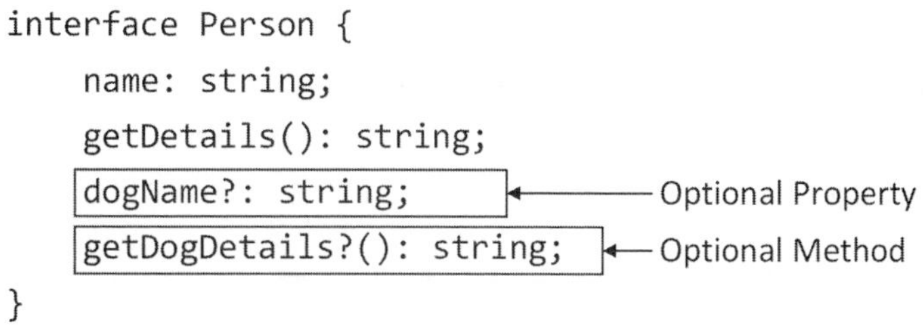

```
interface Person {
    name: string;
    getDetails(): string;
    dogName?: string;          ◄——————— Optional Property
    getDogDetails?(): string;  ◄—— Optional Method
}
```

Figure 11.9 Defining optional interface members

Optional interface features can be defined through the interface type without causing compiler errors, but you must check to ensure that you do not receive undefined values since objects may have been created from classes that have not implemented them, like this:

```
...
data.forEach(item => {
    console.log(item.getDetails());
    if (item.getDogDetails) {
        console.log(item.getDogDetails());
    }
});
...
```

Only one of the types in listing 11.25 that implements the `Person` interface defines the `getDogDetails` method. This method can be accessed through the `Person` type without narrowing to a specific class but may not have been defined, which is why I use type coercion in a conditional expression so that the method is only invoked on objects that have defined it. The code in listing 11.25 produces the following output:

```
Fidel Vega works in Sales
Alice Jones has 500 limit
Alice Jones has a dog named Fido
```

11.4.4 *Defining an abstract interface implementation*

Abstract classes can be used to implement some or all of the features described by an interface, as shown in listing 11.26. This can reduce code duplication when some of the classes that implement an interface would do so, in the same way, using the same code.

> **Listing 11.26   Creating an abstract implementation in the index.ts file in the src folder**

```
interface Person {
    name: string;
    getDetails(): string;

    dogName?: string;
    getDogDetails?(): string;
}

abstract class AbstractDogOwner implements Person {

    abstract name: string;
    abstract dogName?: string;

    abstract getDetails();

    getDogDetails() {
        if (this.dogName) {
            return `${this.name} has a dog called ${this.dogName}`;
        }
    }
}

class DogOwningCustomer extends AbstractDogOwner {

    constructor(public readonly id: string, public name: string,
```

```
              public city: string, public creditLimit: number,
              public dogName) {
            super();
        }

        getDetails() {
            return `${this.name} has ${this.creditLimit} limit`;
        }
    }

    let alice = new DogOwningCustomer("ajones", "Alice Jones", "London",
        500, "Fido");
    if (alice.getDogDetails) {
        console.log(alice.getDogDetails());
    }
```

`AbstractDogOwner` provides a partial implementation of the `Person` interface but declares the interface features that it doesn't implement as `abstract`, which forces subclasses to implement them. There is one subclass that extends `AbstractDogOwner`, which inherits the `getDogDetails` method from the abstract class. The code in listing 11.26 produces the following output:

```
Alice Jones has a dog called Fido
```

11.4.5 Type guarding an interface

There is no JavaScript equivalent to interfaces, and no details of interfaces are included in the JavaScript code generated by the TypeScript compiler. This means that the `instanceof` keyword cannot be used to narrow interface types, and type guarding can be done only by checking for one or more properties that are defined by the interface, as shown in listing 11.27.

> **Listing 11.27   Type guarding an interface in the index.ts file in the src folder**

```
interface Person {
    name: string;
    getDetails(): string;
}

interface Product {
    name: string;
    price: number;
}

class Employee implements Person {
    constructor(public name: string, public company: string) {
        // no statements required
    }

    getDetails() {
        return `${this.name} works for ${this.company}`;
    }
```

```
}

class SportsProduct implements Product {
    constructor(public name: string, public category: string,
            public price: number) {
        // no statements required
    }
}

let data: (Person | Product)[] = [new Employee("Bob Smith", "Acme"),
    new SportsProduct("Running Shoes", "Running", 90.50),
    new Employee("Dora Peters", "BigCo")];

data.forEach(item => {
    if ("getDetails" in item) {
        console.log(`Person: ${item.getDetails()}`);
    } else {
        console.log(`Product: ${item.name}, ${item.price}`);
    }
});
```

This listing uses the presence of the getDetails property to identify those objects that implement the Person interface, allowing the contents of the data array to be narrowed to the Person or Product type. Listing 11.27 produces the following output:

```
Person: Bob Smith works for Acme
Product: Running Shoes, 90.5
Person: Dora Peters works for BigCo
```

11.5   *Dynamically creating properties*

The TypeScript compiler only allows values to be assigned to properties that are part of an object's type, which means that interfaces and classes have to define all the properties that the application requires.

By contrast, JavaScript allows new properties to be created on objects simply by assigning a value to an unused property name. The TypeScript *index signature* feature bridges these two models, allowing properties to be defined dynamically while preserving type safety, as shown in listing 11.28.

> **Listing 11.28   Defining an index signature in the index.ts file in the src folder**

```
interface Product {
    name: string;
    price: number;
}

class SportsProduct implements Product {
    constructor(public name: string, public category: string,
            public price: number) {
        // no statements required
    }
}
```

```
class ProductGroup {
    constructor(...initialProducts: [string, Product][]) {
        initialProducts.forEach(p => this[p[0]] = p[1]);
    }

    [propertyName: string]: Product;
}

let group = new ProductGroup(["shoes", new SportsProduct("Shoes",
    "Running", 90.50)]);
group.hat = new SportsProduct("Hat", "Skiing", 20);
Object.keys(group).forEach(k => console.log(`Property Name: ${k}`));
```

The `ProductGroup` class receives an array of `[string, Product]` tuples through its
constructor, each of which is used to create a property using the `string` value as its
name and the `Product` as its value. The compiler will allow the constructor to create
the property and give it the `any` type, unless the `noImplicitAny` or `strict` compiler
options are enabled, when an error is thrown.

Classes can define an index signature to allow properties to be created dynamically
outside the constructor (and to prevent `noImplicitAny` compiler errors). An index
signature uses square brackets to specify the type of the property keys, followed by a
type annotation that restricts the types that can be used to create dynamic properties, as
shown in figure 11.10.

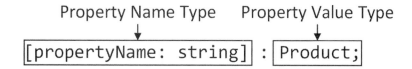

Figure 11.10 An index signature

The property name type can be only `string` or `number`, but the property value type
can be any type. The index signature in the figure tells the compiler to allow dynamic
properties that use `string` values for names and that are assigned `Product` values,
such as this property:

```
...
group.hat = new SportsProduct("Hat", "Skiing", 20);
...
```

This statement creates a property named `hat`. The code in listing 11.28 produces the
following output, showing the names of the properties created by the constructor and
by the subsequent statement:

```
Property Name: shoes
Property Name: hat
```

11.5.1 *Enabling index value checking*

One potential pitfall with index signatures is that the TypeScript compiler assumes that you will only access properties that exist, which is inconsistent with the broader approach taken by TypeScript to force assumptions into the open so they can be explicitly verified. In listing 11.29, I access a property that doesn't exist via an index signature.

> **Listing 11.29   Accessing a nonexistent property in the index.ts file in the src folder**

```
interface Product {
    name: string;
    price: number;
}

class SportsProduct implements Product {
    constructor(public name: string, public category: string,
            public price: number) {
        // no statements required
    }
}

class ProductGroup {
    constructor(...initialProducts: [string, Product][]) {
        initialProducts.forEach(p => this[p[0]] = p[1]);
    }

    [propertyName: string]: Product;
}

let group = new ProductGroup(["shoes", new SportsProduct("Shoes",
    "Running", 90.50)]);
group.hat = new SportsProduct("Hat", "Skiing", 20);

let total = group.hat.price + group.boots.price;
console.log(`Total: ${total}`);
```

The statement that assigns a value to `total` uses the index signature to access `hat` and `boots` properties. No `boots` property has been created, but the code still compiles, and the result is an error when the compiled code is executed.

```
let total = group.hat.price + group.boots.price;
                                    ^
```

```
TypeError: Cannot read properties of undefined (reading 'price')
```

To configure the compiler to check index signatures accesses, set the `noUnchecked-IndexedAccess` and `strictNullChecks` configuration options to `true`, as shown in listing 11.30.

> **Listing 11.30 Configuring the compiler in the tsconfig.json file in the types folder**

```
{
    "compilerOptions": {
        "target": "ES2022",
        "outDir": "./dist",
        "rootDir": "./src",
        "declaration": true,
        "strictNullChecks": true,
        "noUncheckedIndexedAccess": true
    }
}
```

Save the configuration changes, and the code will be recompiled. This time the Type-Script compiler generates an error.

```
src/index.ts(25,31): error TS18048: 'group.boots' is possibly 'undefined'.
```

To prevent the error, I must make sure that the property exists before attempting to use its value, as shown in listing 11.31, to guard against undefined values.

> **Listing 11.31 Checking a property in the index.ts file in the src folder**

```
interface Product {
    name: string;
    price: number;
}

class SportsProduct implements Product {
    constructor(public name: string, public category: string,
            public price: number) {
        // no statements required
    }
}

class ProductGroup {
    constructor(...initialProducts: [string, Product][]) {
        initialProducts.forEach(p => this[p[0]] = p[1]);
    }

    [propertyName: string]: Product;
}

let group = new ProductGroup(["shoes", new SportsProduct("Shoes",
    "Running", 90.50)]);
group.hat = new SportsProduct("Hat", "Skiing", 20);

if (group.hat && group.boots) {
    let total = group.hat.price + group.boots.price;
    console.log(`Total: ${total}`);
}
```

The `if` expression ensures that the `boots` property won't be used if it is `undefined`. An alternative approach is to use optional chaining and the nullish operator to provide a fallback value, as shown in listing 11.32.

Listing 11.32   Using a fallback value in the index.ts file in the src folder

```
interface Product {
    name: string;
    price: number;
}

class SportsProduct implements Product {
    constructor(public name: string, public category: string,
            public price: number) {
        // no statements required
    }
}

class ProductGroup {
    constructor(...initialProducts: [string, Product][]) {
        initialProducts.forEach(p => this[p[0]] = p[1]);
    }

    [propertyName: string]: Product;
}

let group = new ProductGroup(["shoes", new SportsProduct("Shoes",
    "Running", 90.50)]);
group.hat = new SportsProduct("Hat", "Skiing", 20);

let total = group.hat.price + (group.boots?.price ?? 0);
console.log(`Total: ${total}`);
```

This code produces the following output:

```
Total: 20
```

Summary

In this chapter, I explained the way that TypeScript enhances the JavaScript class feature, providing support for concise constructors, abstract classes, and access control keywords. I also described the interface feature, which is implemented by the compiler and provides an alternative way to describe the shape of objects so that classes can readily conform to them.

- TypeScript supports static types in constructor functions, but the feature is awkwardly implemented, and classes are easier to work with.
- TypeScript has good support for working with classes and infers types directly from the class definition.
- TypeScript simplifies class constructors by supporting a concise syntax that creates public properties for each public constructor argument.

- TypeScript supports the JavaScript syntax for private class members, but also supports the `public`, `private`, and `protected` keywords, which offer more granular control.
- The `readonly` keyword can be used to create a property that can be modified only by the constructor of the containing class.
- Class inheritance is managed by creating a type union, such that only the common features are included in the type.
- Abstract classes can be used to create base implementations of features, which are then inherited by subclasses.
- Interfaces describe the properties and methods a class must implement to conform to a type.
- TypeScript supports the JavaScript feature for dynamically creating properties on objects, which is handled through index signatures for type checking.

In the next chapter, I describe the TypeScript support for generic types.

Using generic types

This chapter covers

- Using generic type parameters as type placeholders
- Instantiating classes with generic type arguments
- Constraining generic type parameters
- Guarding generic types with predicate functions
- Defining interfaces with generic type parameters

Generic types are placeholders for types that are resolved when a class or function is used, allowing type-safe code to be written that can deal with a range of different types, such as collection classes. This is a concept that is more easily demonstrated than explained, so I start this chapter with an example of the problem that generic types solve and then describe the basic ways that generic types are used. In chapter 13, I describe the advanced generic type features that TypeScript provides. Table 12.1 summarizes the chapter.

Table 12.1 Chapter summary

Problem	Solution	Listing
Define a class or function that can safely operate on different types	Define a generic type parameter	6–8, 20, 21
Resolve a type for a generic type parameter	Use a generic type argument when instantiating the class or invoking the function	9–14
Extend a generic class	Create a class that passes on, restricts, or fixes the generic type parameter inherited from the superclass	15–17
Type guard a generic type	Use a type predicate function	18, 19
Describe a generic type without providing an implementation	Define an interface with a generic type parameter	22–26

For quick reference, table 12.2 lists the TypeScript compiler options used in this chapter.

Table 12.2 The TypeScript compiler options used in this chapter

Name	Description
declaration	This option produces type declaration files when enabled, which can be useful in understanding how types have been inferred. These files are described in more detail in chapter 15.
module	This option specifies the module format, as described in chapter 5.
outDir	This option specifies the directory in which the JavaScript files will be placed.
rootDir	This option specifies the root directory that the compiler will use to locate TypeScript files.
target	This option specifies the version of the JavaScript language that the compiler will target in its output.

12.1 Preparing for this chapter

In this chapter, I continue to use the `types` project created in chapter 7 and used in every chapter since. To prepare for this chapter, create a file called `dataTypes.ts` in the `src` folder, with the contents shown in listing 12.1.

> **TIP** You can download the example project for this chapter—and for all the other chapters in this book—from https://github.com/manningbooks/essential-typescript-5.

Listing 12.1   The contents of the dataTypes.ts file in the src folder

```
export class Person {
    constructor(public name: string, public city: string) {}
}

export class Product {
    constructor(public name: string, public price: number) {}
}

export class City  {
    constructor(public name: string, public population: number) {}
}

export class Employee {
    constructor(public name: string, public role: string) {}
}
```

Replace the contents of the index.ts file in the src folder with the code shown in listing 12.2.

Listing 12.2   Replacing the contents of the index.ts file in the src folder

```
import { Person, Product } from "./dataTypes.js";

let people = [new Person("Bob Smith", "London"),
    new Person("Dora Peters", "New York")];
let products = [new Product("Running Shoes", 100), new Product("Hat", 25)];


[...people, ...products].forEach(item =>
    console.log(`Item: ${item.name}`));
```

This listing uses an `import` statement to declare dependencies on the `Person` and `Product` classes defined in the `dataTypes` module. To configure the module format, as described in chapter 5, set the `type` configuration property in the `package.json` file, as shown in listing 12.3.

Listing 12.3   Configuring the module format in the package.json file in the types folder

```
{
  "name": "types",
  "version": "1.0.0",
  "description": "",
  "main": "index.js",
  "scripts": {
    "start": "tsc-watch --onsuccess \"node dist/index.js\""
  },
  "keywords": [],
  "author": "",
  "license": "ISC",
  "devDependencies": {
    "tsc-watch": "^6.0.0",
```

```
    "typescript": "^5.0.2"
  },
  "type": "module"
}
```

To configure the TypeScript compiler to use the `package.json` file to determine the module format, and disable features that are no longer required, change the configuration properties as shown in listing 12.4.

> **Listing 12.4　Configuring the compiler in the tsconfig.json file in the types folder**

```
{
    "compilerOptions": {
        "target": "ES2022",
        "outDir": "./dist",
        "rootDir": "./src",
        "declaration": true,
        // "strictNullChecks": true,
        // "noUncheckedIndexedAccess": true,
        "module": "Node16"
    }
}
```

Open a new command prompt, navigate to the `types` folder, and run the command shown in listing 12.5 to start the TypeScript compiler so that it automatically executes code after it has been compiled.

> **Listing 12.5　Starting the TypeScript compiler**

```
npm start
```

The compiler will compile the project, execute the output, and then enter watch mode, producing the following output:

```
7:22:32 AM - Starting compilation in watch mode...
7:22:34 AM - Found 0 errors. Watching for file changes.
Item: Bob Smith
Item: Dora Peters
Item: Running Shoes
Item: Hat
```

12.2　*Understanding the problem solved by generic types*

The best way to understand how generic types work—and why they are useful—is to work through a common scenario that shows when regular types become difficult to manage. Listing 12.6 defines a class that manages a collection of `Person` objects.

> **Listing 12.6　Defining a class in the index.ts file in the src folder**

```
import { Person, Product } from "./dataTypes.js";

let people = [new Person("Bob Smith", "London"),
    new Person("Dora Peters", "New York")];
```

```
let products = [new Product("Running Shoes", 100), new Product("Hat", 25)];

class PeopleCollection {
    private items: Person[] = [];

    constructor(initialItems: Person[]) {
        this.items.push(...initialItems);
    }

    add(newItem: Person) {
        this.items.push(newItem);
    }

    getNames(): string[] {
        return this.items.map(item => item.name);
    }

    getItem(index: number): Person {
        return this.items[index];
    }
}

let peopleData = new PeopleCollection(people);

console.log(`Names: ${peopleData.getNames().join(", ")}`);
let firstPerson = peopleData.getItem(0);
console.log(`First Person: ${firstPerson.name}, ${firstPerson.city}`);
```

The `PeopleCollection` class operates on `Person` objects, which are provided via the constructor or the `add` method. The `getNames` method returns an array containing the `name` value of each `Person` object, and the `getItem` method allows a `Person` object to be retrieved using an index. A new instance of the `PeopleCollection` class is created, and its methods are called to produce the following output:

```
Names: Bob Smith, Dora Peters
First Person: Bob Smith, London
```

12.2.1 Adding support for another type

The problem with the `PeopleCollection` class is that it works only on `Person` objects. If I want to perform the same set of operations on `Product` objects, then the obvious choices present compromises. I could create a new class that duplicates the functionality. This is easy to do, but there will always be another type to deal with in the future, and the classes will quickly become difficult to manage. Another approach is to take advantage of the TypeScript features and modify the existing class to support multiple types, as shown in listing 12.7.

> **Listing 12.7   Adding type support in the index.ts file in the src folder**

```
import { Person, Product } from "./dataTypes.js";

let people = [new Person("Bob Smith", "London"),
    new Person("Dora Peters", "New York")];
```

```
let products = [new Product("Running Shoes", 100), new Product("Hat", 25)];

type dataType = Person | Product;

class DataCollection {

    private items: dataType[] = [];

    constructor(initialItems: dataType[]) {
        this.items.push(...initialItems);
    }

    add(newItem: dataType) {
        this.items.push(newItem);
    }

    getNames(): string[] {
        return this.items.map(item => item.name);
    }

    getItem(index: number): dataType {
        return this.items[index];
    }
}

let peopleData = new DataCollection(people);

console.log(`Names: ${peopleData.getNames().join(", ")}`);
let firstPerson = peopleData.getItem(0);
if (firstPerson instanceof Person) {
    console.log(`First Person: ${firstPerson.name}, ${firstPerson.city}`);
}
```

The listing uses a type union to add support for the Product class. I could also have used an interface, an abstract class, or function type overrides, but the support for a wider range of types would require some form of type narrowing to get back to a specific type. The other problem is that the DataCollection class will accept both Person and Product objects. What I wanted was support for either Person or Product objects but not both. The code in listing 12.7 produces the following output:

```
Names: Bob Smith, Dora Peters
First Person: Bob Smith, London
```

12.3 Creating generic classes

A generic class is a class that has a generic type parameter, which is a placeholder for a type that is specified when the class is used to create a new object. Generic type parameters allow classes to be written that operate on a specific type without knowing what that type will be in advance, as shown in listing 12.8.

Listing 12.8   Using a generic type in the index.ts file in the src folder

```
import { Person, Product } from "./dataTypes.js";

let people = [new Person("Bob Smith", "London"),
    new Person("Dora Peters", "New York")];
let products = [new Product("Running Shoes", 100), new Product("Hat", 25)];

//type dataType = Person | Product;

class DataCollection<T> {

    private items: T[] = [];

    constructor(initialItems: T[]) {
        this.items.push(...initialItems);
    }

    add(newItem: T) {
        this.items.push(newItem);
    }

    // getNames(): string[] {
    //     return this.items.map(item => item.name);
    // }

    getItem(index: number): T {
        return this.items[index];
    }
}

let peopleData = new DataCollection<Person>(people);

//console.log(`Names: ${peopleData.getNames().join(", ")}`);
let firstPerson = peopleData.getItem(0);
//if (firstPerson instanceof Person) {
console.log(`First Person: ${firstPerson.name}, ${firstPerson.city}`);
//}
```

The `DataCollection` class has been defined with a generic type parameter, which is part of the class declaration, as shown in figure 12.1.

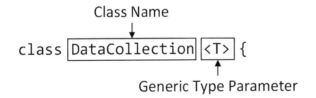

Class Name

class DataCollection <T> {

Generic Type Parameter

Figure 12.1   A generic type parameter

A generic type parameter is defined between angle brackets (the < and > characters), and only a name is specified. The convention is to start with the letter T as the name of the type parameter, although you are free to follow any naming scheme that makes sense in your project.

The result is known as a *generic class,* meaning a class that has at least one generic type parameter. The generic type parameter is named T in this example and can be used in place of a specific type. For example, the constructor can be defined to accept an array of T values, like this:

```
...
constructor(initialItems: T[]) {
    this.items.push(...initialItems);
}
...
```

As the constructor shows, generic types can be used in type annotations, even though we don't yet know the specific type for which it is a placeholder. The class in listing 12.8 defines a single type parameter named T and so is referred to as DataCollection<T>, clearly indicating that it is a generic class. The code in listing 12.8 produces the following output:

```
First Person: Bob Smith, London
```

12.3.1 *Understanding generic type arguments*

A generic type parameter is resolved to a specific type using a generic type argument when an instance of the DataCollection<T> class is created with the new keyword, as shown in figure 12.2.

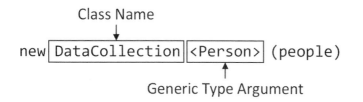

Figure 12.2   Creating an object with a generic type argument

The type argument uses angle brackets, and the argument in the example specifies the Person class.

```
...
let peopleData = new DataCollection<Person>(people);
...
```

This statement creates a DataCollection<T> object where the type parameter T will be Person. When an object is created from a generic class, its type incorporates the argument, such as DataCollection<Person>. The compiler enforces the TypeScript type rules using Person wherever it encounters T, which means that only Person objects can be passed to the constructor and the add method and that invoking the getItem method will return a `Person` object. TypeScript keeps track of the type argument used to create the `DataCollection<Person>` object, and no type assertions or type narrowing is required.

12.3.2 *Using different type arguments*

The value of a generic type parameter affects only a single object, and a different type can be used for the generic type argument for each use of the `new` keyword, producing a `DataCollection<T>` object that works with a different type, as shown in listing 12.9.

> **Listing 12.9   Using a different type argument in the index.ts file in the src folder**

```
import { Person, Product } from "./dataTypes.js";

let people = [new Person("Bob Smith", "London"),
    new Person("Dora Peters", "New York")];
let products = [new Product("Running Shoes", 100), new Product("Hat", 25)];

class DataCollection<T> {

    private items: T[] = [];

    constructor(initialItems: T[]) {
        this.items.push(...initialItems);
    }

    add(newItem: T) {
        this.items.push(newItem);
    }

    // getNames(): string[] {
    //     return this.items.map(item => item.name);
    // }

    getItem(index: number): T {
        return this.items[index];
    }
}

let peopleData = new DataCollection<Person>(people);
let firstPerson = peopleData.getItem(0);
console.log(`First Person: ${firstPerson.name}, ${firstPerson.city}`);

let productData = new DataCollection<Product>(products);
let firstProduct = productData.getItem(0);
console.log(`First Product: ${firstProduct.name}, ${firstProduct.price}`);
```

The new statements create a `DataCollection<Product>` object by using `Product` for the generic type argument. TypeScript keeps track of which type has been specified for each object and ensures only that the type can be used. The code in listing 12.9 produces the following output:

```
First Person: Bob Smith, London
First Product: Running Shoes, 100
```

12.3.3 Constraining generic type values

In listing 12.8 and listing 12.9, I commented out the getNames method. By default, any type can be used for a generic type argument, so the compiler treats generic types as any by default, meaning that it won't let me access the name property on which the getNames method depends without some kind of type narrowing.

I could do the type narrowing within the getNames method, but a more elegant approach is to restrict the range of types that can be used as the value for the generic type parameter so that the class can be instantiated only with types that define the features that the generic class relies on, as shown in listing 12.10.

Listing 12.10   Restricting generic types in the index.ts file in the src folder

```typescript
import { Person, Product } from "./dataTypes.js";

let people = [new Person("Bob Smith", "London"),
    new Person("Dora Peters", "New York")];
let products = [new Product("Running Shoes", 100), new Product("Hat", 25)];


class DataCollection<T extends (Person | Product)> {
    private items: T[] = [];

    constructor(initialItems: T[]) {
        this.items.push(...initialItems);
    }

    add(newItem: T) {
        this.items.push(newItem);
    }

    getNames(): string[] {
        return this.items.map(item => item.name);
    }

    getItem(index: number): T {
        return this.items[index];
    }
}

let peopleData = new DataCollection<Person>(people);
let firstPerson = peopleData.getItem(0);
console.log(`First Person: ${firstPerson.name}, ${firstPerson.city}`);
console.log(`Person Names: ${peopleData.getNames().join(", ")}`);

let productData = new DataCollection<Product>(products);
let firstProduct = productData.getItem(0);
console.log(`First Product: ${firstProduct.name}, ${firstProduct.price}`);
console.log(`Product Names: ${productData.getNames().join(", ")}`);
```

The extends keyword is used after the type parameter name to specify a constraint, as shown in figure 12.3.

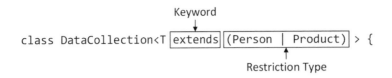

Figure 12.3   A generic type parameter restriction

The change in listing 12.10 can be thought of as creating two levels of restriction on the DataCollection<T> class: one applied when a new object is created and one that is applied when the object is used.

The first restriction constrains the types that can be used as the generic type argument to create a new DataCollection<Product | Person> object so that only types that can be assigned to Product | Person can be used as the type parameter value. Three types can meet that restriction: Person, Product, and the Person | Product union. These are the only types that can be assigned to the generic type parameter T.

The second restriction applies the value of the generic type parameter when the object is used. When a new object is created with Product as the type parameter, for example, Product is the value of T: the constructor and add methods will only accept Product objects, and the getItem method will only return a Product object. When Person is used as the type parameter, Person is the value of T and becomes the type used by the constructor and methods.

Put another way, the extends keyword constrains the types that can be assigned to the type parameter, and the type parameter restricts the types that can be used by a specific instance of the class. Since the compiler knows all the types that can be used for the generic type parameter to define a name property, it allows me to uncomment the getItem method and read the value of the name property without causing an error. The code in listing 12.10 produces the following output:

```
First Person: Bob Smith, London
Person Names: Bob Smith, Dora Peters
First Product: Running Shoes, 100
Product Names: Running Shoes, Hat
```

CONSTRAINING GENERIC TYPES USING A SHAPE

Using a type union to constrain generic type parameters is useful, but the union must be extended for each new type that is required. An alternative approach is to use a shape to constrain the type parameter, which will allow only the properties that the generic class relies on to be described, as shown in listing 12.11.

> **Listing 12.11   Using a shape type in the index.ts file in the src folder**

```
import { City, Person, Product } from "./dataTypes.js";

let people = [new Person("Bob Smith", "London"),
```

```
                    new Person("Dora Peters", "New York")];
let products = [new Product("Running Shoes", 100), new Product("Hat", 25)];
let cities = [new City("London", 8136000), new City("Paris", 2141000)];

class DataCollection<T extends { name: string }> {
    private items: T[] = [];

    constructor(initialItems: T[]) {
        this.items.push(...initialItems);
    }

    add(newItem: T) {
        this.items.push(newItem);
    }

    getNames(): string[] {
        return this.items.map(item => item.name);
    }

    getItem(index: number): T {
        return this.items[index];
    }
}

let peopleData = new DataCollection<Person>(people);
let firstPerson = peopleData.getItem(0);
console.log(`First Person: ${firstPerson.name}, ${firstPerson.city}`);
console.log(`Person Names: ${peopleData.getNames().join(", ")}`);

let productData = new DataCollection<Product>(products);
let firstProduct = productData.getItem(0);
console.log(`First Product: ${firstProduct.name}, ${firstProduct.price}`);
console.log(`Product Names: ${productData.getNames().join(", ")}`);

let cityData = new DataCollection<City>(cities);
console.log(`City  Names: ${cityData.getNames().join(", ")}`);
```

The shape specified in listing 12.11 tells the compiler that the DataCollection<T> class can be instantiated using any type that has a name property that returns a string. This allows DataCollection objects to be created to deal with Person, Product, and City objects without requiring individual types to be specified.

> **TIP** Generic type parameters can also be constrained using type aliases and interfaces. It is also possible to constrain generic types to those that define a specific constructor shape, which is done with the extends new keywords, which are demonstrated in chapter 13.

The code in listing 12.11 produces the following output:

```
First Person: Bob Smith, London
Person Names: Bob Smith, Dora Peters
First Product: Running Shoes, 100
Product Names: Running Shoes, Hat
City  Names: London, Paris
```

12.3.4 *Defining multiple type parameters*

A class can define multiple type parameters. Listing 12.12 adds a second type parameter to the `DataCollection<T>` class and uses it to correlate data values. (The listing also removes methods from the class that are no longer required for the examples.)

> **Listing 12.12   Defining another type parameter in the index.ts file in the src folder**

```
import { City, Person, Product } from "./dataTypes.js";

let people = [new Person("Bob Smith", "London"),
    new Person("Dora Peters", "New York")];
let products = [new Product("Running Shoes", 100), new Product("Hat", 25)];
let cities = [new City("London", 8136000), new City("Paris", 2141000)];

class DataCollection<T extends { name: string }, U> {
    private items: T[] = [];

    constructor(initialItems: T[]) {
        this.items.push(...initialItems);
    }

    collate(targetData: U[], itemProp: string,
            targetProp: string): (T & U)[] {
        let results = [];
        this.items.forEach(item => {
            let match = targetData.find(d =>
                d[targetProp] === item[itemProp]);
            if (match !== undefined) {
                results.push({ ...match, ...item });
            }
        });
        return results;
    }
}

let peopleData = new DataCollection<Person, City>(people);
let collatedData = peopleData.collate(cities, "city", "name");
collatedData.forEach(c =>
    console.log(`${c.name}, ${c.city}, ${c.population}`));
```

Additional type parameters are separated with commas, just like regular function or method parameters. The `DataCollection<T, U>` class defines two generic type parameters. The new parameter, named `U`, is used to define the type of an argument passed to the `collate` method, which compares the properties on an array of objects and intersections between those `T` and `U` objects that have the same property values.

When the generic class is instantiated, arguments must be supplied for each of the generic type parameters, separated by commas, like this:

```
...
let peopleData = new DataCollection<Person, City>(people);
...
```

This statement creates a `DataCollection<Person, City>` object that will store `Person` objects and compare them to `City` objects. An array of `City` objects is passed to the `collate` method, comparing the values of the `city` property of the `Person` objects and the `name` property of the `City` objects.

The properties of objects that have matching values are combined using the spread syntax to create an intersection.

```
...
results.push({ ...match, ...item });
...
```

There is one pair of objects with matching values, and the code in listing 12.12 produces the following result:

```
Bob Smith, London, 8136000
```

APPLYING A TYPE PARAMETER TO A METHOD

The second type parameter in listing 12.12 isn't as flexible as it could be because it requires the data type used by the `collate` method to be specified when the `DataCollection` object is created, meaning that's the only data type that can be used with that method.

When a type is used by only one method, the type parameter can be moved from the class declaration and applied directly to the method, allowing a different type to be specified each time the method is invoked, as shown in listing 12.13.

> **Listing 12.13   Applying a type parameter to a method in the index.ts file in the src folder**

```typescript
import { City, Person, Product, Employee } from "./dataTypes.js";

let people = [new Person("Bob Smith", "London"),
    new Person("Dora Peters", "New York")];
let products = [new Product("Running Shoes", 100), new Product("Hat", 25)];
let cities = [new City("London", 8136000), new City("Paris", 2141000)];
let employees = [new Employee("Bob Smith", "Sales"),
    new Employee("Alice Jones", "Sales")];

class DataCollection<T extends { name: string }> {
    private items: T[] = [];

    constructor(initialItems: T[]) {
        this.items.push(...initialItems);
    }

    collate<U>(targetData: U[], itemProp: string,
            targetProp: string): (T & U)[] {
        let results = [];
        this.items.forEach(item => {
            let match = targetData.find(d =>
                d[targetProp] === item[itemProp]);
            if (match !== undefined) {
                results.push({ ...match, ...item });
            }
        });
```

```
            return results;
    }
}

let peopleData = new DataCollection<Person>(people);
let collatedData = peopleData.collate<City>(cities, "city", "name");
collatedData.forEach(c =>
    console.log(`${c.name}, ${c.city}, ${c.population}`));
let empData = peopleData.collate<Employee>(employees, "name", "name");
empData.forEach(c => console.log(`${c.name}, ${c.city}, ${c.role}`));
```

The type parameter U is applied directly to the collate method, allowing a type to be provided when the method is invoked, like this:

```
...
let collatedData = peopleData.collate<City>(cities, "city", "name");
...
```

The method's type parameter allows the collate method to be invoked using City objects and then invoked again with Employee objects. The code in listing 12.13 produces the following output:

```
Bob Smith, London, 8136000
Bob Smith, London, Sales
```

12.3.5 *Allowing the compiler to infer type arguments*

The TypeScript compiler can infer generic type arguments based on the way that objects are created or methods are invoked. This can be a useful way to write concise code but requires caution because you must ensure that you initialize objects with the types that you would have specified explicitly. Listing 12.14 instantiates the DataCollection<T> class and invokes the collate method without type arguments, leaving the compiler to infer the type.

Listing 12.14   Using generic type inference in the index.ts file in the src folder

```
import { City, Person, Product, Employee } from "./dataTypes.js";

let people = [new Person("Bob Smith", "London"),
    new Person("Dora Peters", "New York")];
let products = [new Product("Running Shoes", 100), new Product("Hat", 25)];
let cities = [new City("London", 8136000), new City("Paris", 2141000)];
let employees = [new Employee("Bob Smith", "Sales"),
    new Employee("Alice Jones", "Sales")];

class DataCollection<T extends { name: string }> {
    private items: T[] = [];

    constructor(initialItems: T[]) {
        this.items.push(...initialItems);
    }

    collate<U>(targetData: U[], itemProp: string,
            targetProp: string): (T & U)[] {
        let results = [];
```

```
            this.items.forEach(item => {
                let match = targetData.find(d =>
                    d[targetProp] === item[itemProp]);
                if (match !== undefined) {
                    results.push({ ...match, ...item });
                }
            });
            return results;
        }
    }
```

```
export let peopleData = new DataCollection(people);
export let collatedData = peopleData.collate(cities, "city", "name");
collatedData.forEach(c =>
    console.log(`${c.name}, ${c.city}, ${c.population}`));
export let empData = peopleData.collate(employees, "name", "name");
empData.forEach(c => console.log(`${c.name}, ${c.city}, ${c.role}`));
```

The compiler is able to infer the type arguments based on the argument passed to the `DataCollection<T>` constructor and the first argument passed to the `collate` method. To check the types inferred by the complier, examine the `index.d.ts` file in the `dist` folder, which is created when the `declaration` option is enabled.

> **TIP** In a project that uses modules, the files created through the declaration option contain only those types that are exported outside a module, which is why I added the `export` keyword in listing 12.14.

Here are the types inferred by the compiler:

```
...
export declare let peopleData: DataCollection<Person>;
export declare let collatedData: (Person & City)[];
export declare let empData: (Person & Employee)[];
...
```

The code in listing 12.14 produces the following output:

```
Bob Smith, London, 8136000
Bob Smith, London, Sales
```

12.3.6 *Extending generic classes*

A generic class can be extended, and the subclass can choose to deal with the generic type parameters in several ways, as described in the following sections.

ADDING EXTRA FEATURES TO THE EXISTING TYPE PARAMETERS

The first approach is to simply add features to those defined by the superclass using the same generic types, as shown in listing 12.15.

> **Listing 12.15** Subclassing a generic class in the index.ts file in the src folder

```
import { City, Person, Product, Employee } from "./dataTypes.js";

let people = [new Person("Bob Smith", "London"),
    new Person("Dora Peters", "New York")];
```

```
let products = [new Product("Running Shoes", 100), new Product("Hat", 25)];
let cities = [new City("London", 8136000), new City("Paris", 2141000)];
let employees = [new Employee("Bob Smith", "Sales"),
    new Employee("Alice Jones", "Sales")];

class DataCollection<T extends { name: string }> {
    protected items: T[] = [];

    constructor(initialItems: T[]) {
        this.items.push(...initialItems);
    }

    collate<U>(targetData: U[], itemProp: string,
            targetProp: string): (T & U)[] {
        let results = [];
        this.items.forEach(item => {
            let match = targetData.find(d =>
                d[targetProp] === item[itemProp]);
            if (match !== undefined) {
                results.push({ ...match, ...item });
            }
        });
        return results;
    }
}

class SearchableCollection<T extends { name: string }>
        extends DataCollection<T> {

    constructor(initialItems: T[]) {
        super(initialItems);
    }

    find(name: string): T | undefined {
        return this.items.find(item => item.name === name);
    }
}

let peopleData = new SearchableCollection<Person>(people);
let foundPerson = peopleData.find("Bob Smith");
if (foundPerson !== undefined) {
    console.log(`Person ${ foundPerson.name }, ${ foundPerson.city}`);
}
```

The `SearchableCollection<T>` class is derived from `DataCollection<T>` and defines a `find` method that locates an object by its `name` property. The declaration of the `SearchableCollection<T>` class uses the `extends` keyword and includes type parameters, like this:

```
...
class SearchableCollection<T extends { name: string }>
    extends DataCollection<T> {
...
```

The type of a generic class includes its type parameters so that the superclass is DataCollection<T>. The type parameter defined by the SearchableCollection<T> class must be compatible with the type parameter of the superclass, so I have used the same shape type to specify types that defined a name property.

> **TIP** Notice I changed the access control keyword on the items property in listing 12.15 to protected, allowing it to be accessed by subclasses. See chapter 11 for details of the access control keywords provided by TypeScript.

The SearchableCollection<T> class is instantiated just like any other using a type argument (or allowing the compiler to infer the type argument). The code in listing 12.15 produces the following output:

```
Person Bob Smith, London
```

FIXING THE GENERIC TYPE PARAMETER

Some classes need to define functionality that is only available using a subset of the types that are supported by the superclass. In these situations, a subclass can use a fixed type for the superclass's type parameter, such that the subclass is not a generic class, as shown in listing 12.16.

> Listing 12.16 **Fixing a generic type parameter in the index.ts file in the src folder**

```
import { City, Person, Product, Employee } from "./dataTypes.js";

let people = [new Person("Bob Smith", "London"),
    new Person("Dora Peters", "New York")];
let products = [new Product("Running Shoes", 100), new Product("Hat", 25)];
let cities = [new City("London", 8136000), new City("Paris", 2141000)];
let employees = [new Employee("Bob Smith", "Sales"),
    new Employee("Alice Jones", "Sales")];

class DataCollection<T extends { name: string }> {
    protected items: T[] = [];

    constructor(initialItems: T[]) {
        this.items.push(...initialItems);
    }

    collate<U>(targetData: U[], itemProp: string,
            targetProp: string): (T & U)[] {
        let results = [];
        this.items.forEach(item => {
            let match = targetData.find(d =>
                d[targetProp] === item[itemProp]);
            if (match !== undefined) {
                results.push({ ...match, ...item });
            }
        });
        return results;
    }
}
```

```
class SearchableCollection extends DataCollection<Employee> {

    constructor(initialItems: Employee[]) {
        super(initialItems);
    }

    find(searchTerm: string): Employee[] {
        return this.items.filter(item =>
            item.name === searchTerm || item.role === searchTerm);
    }
}

let employeeData = new SearchableCollection(employees);
employeeData.find("Sales").forEach(e =>
    console.log(`Employee ${ e.name }, ${ e.role}`));
```

The `SearchableCollection` class extends `DataCollection<Employee>`, which fixes the generic type parameter so that the `SearchableCollection` can deal only with `Employee` objects. No type parameter can be used to create a `SearchableCollection` object, and the code in the `find` method can safely access the properties defined by the `Employee` class. The code in listing 12.16 produces the following output:

```
Employee Bob Smith, Sales
Employee Alice Jones, Sales
```

RESTRICTING THE GENERIC TYPE PARAMETER

The third approach strikes a balance between the previous two examples, providing a generic type variable but restricting it to specific types, as shown in listing 12.17. This allows functionality that can depend on features of particular classes without fixing the type parameter completely.

> **Listing 12.17   Restricting a type parameter in the index.ts file in the src folder**

```
import { City, Person, Product, Employee } from "./dataTypes.js";

let people = [new Person("Bob Smith", "London"),
    new Person("Dora Peters", "New York")];
let products = [new Product("Running Shoes", 100), new Product("Hat", 25)];
let cities = [new City("London", 8136000), new City("Paris", 2141000)];
let employees = [new Employee("Bob Smith", "Sales"),
    new Employee("Alice Jones", "Sales")];

class DataCollection<T extends { name: string }> {
    protected items: T[] = [];

    constructor(initialItems: T[]) {
        this.items.push(...initialItems);
    }

    collate<U>(targetData: U[], itemProp: string,
            targetProp: string): (T & U)[] {
        let results = [];
        this.items.forEach(item => {
            let match = targetData.find(d =>
```

```
                      d[targetProp] === item[itemProp]);
            if (match !== undefined) {
                results.push({ ...match, ...item });
            }
        });
        return results;
    }
}


class SearchableCollection<T
        extends Employee | Person> extends DataCollection<T> {

    constructor(initialItems: T[]) {
        super(initialItems);
    }

    find(searchTerm: string): T[] {
        return this.items.filter(item => {
            if (item instanceof Employee) {
                return item.name ===
                    searchTerm || item.role === searchTerm;
            } else if (item instanceof Person) {
                return item.name ===
                    searchTerm || item.city === searchTerm;
            }
        });
    }
}


let employeeData = new SearchableCollection<Employee>(employees);
employeeData.find("Sales").forEach(e =>
    console.log(`Employee ${ e.name }, ${ e.role}`));
```

The type parameter specified by the subclass must be assignable to the type parameter it inherits, meaning that only a more restrictive type can be used. In the example, the Employee | Person union can be assigned to the shape used to restrict the DataCollection<T> type parameter.

> **CAUTION** Bear in mind that when a union is used to constrain a generic type parameter, the union itself is an acceptable argument for that parameter. This means that the SearchableCollection class in listing 12.17 can be instantiated with a type parameter of Employee, Product, and Employee | Product. See chapter 13 for advanced features for restricting type arguments.

The find method uses the instanceof keyword to narrow objects to specific types to make property value comparisons. The code in listing 12.17 produces the following output:

```
Employee Bob Smith, Sales
Employee Alice Jones, Sales
```

12.3.7 *Type guarding generic types*

The `SearchableCollection<T>` class in listing 12.17 used the `instanceof` keyword to identify `Employee` and `Person` objects. This is manageable because the restriction applied to the type parameter means that there are only a small number of types to deal with. For classes with type parameters that are not restricted, narrowing to a specific type can be difficult, as shown in listing 12.18.

> **Listing 12.18   Narrowing a generic type in the index.ts file in the src folder**

```
import { City, Person, Product, Employee } from "./dataTypes.js";

let people = [new Person("Bob Smith", "London"),
    new Person("Dora Peters", "New York")];
let products = [new Product("Running Shoes", 100), new Product("Hat", 25)];
let cities = [new City("London", 8136000), new City("Paris", 2141000)];
let employees = [new Employee("Bob Smith", "Sales"),
    new Employee("Alice Jones", "Sales")];

class DataCollection<T> {
    protected items: T[] = [];

    constructor(initialItems: T[]) {
        this.items.push(...initialItems);
    }

    filter<V extends T>(): V[] {
        return this.items.filter(item => item instanceof V) as V[];
    }
}

let mixedData
    = new DataCollection<Person | Product >([...people, ...products]);
let filteredProducts = mixedData.filter<Product>();
filteredProducts.forEach(p =>
    console.log(`Product: ${ p.name}, ${p.price}`));
```

Listing 12.18 introduces a `filter` method that uses the `instanceof` keyword to select objects of a specific type from the array of data items. A `DataCollection<Person | Product>` object is created with an array that contains a mix of `Person` and `Product` objects, and the new `filter` method is used to select the `Product` objects.

> **TIP** Notice that the `filter` method's generic type parameter, named `V`, is defined with the `extend` keyword, telling the compiler that it can only accept types that can be assigned to the class generic type `T`, which prevents the compiler from treating `V` as `any`.

This example doesn't compile and produces the following error message:

```
src/index.ts(18,58): error TS2693: 'V' only refers to a type, but is being
used as a value here.
```

No JavaScript feature is equivalent to generic types, so they are removed from the Type-Script code during the compilation process, which means that there is no information available at runtime to use generic types with the `instanceof` keyword.

In situations where you need to identify objects by type, generic types are not helpful, and a predicate function must be used. Listing 12.19 adds a parameter to the `filter` method that accepts a type predicate function, which is then used to find objects of a specific type.

> **Listing 12.19 Using a type predicate function in the index.ts file in the src folder**

```
import { City, Person, Product, Employee } from "./dataTypes.js";

let people = [new Person("Bob Smith", "London"),
    new Person("Dora Peters", "New York")];
let products = [new Product("Running Shoes", 100), new Product("Hat", 25)];
let cities = [new City("London", 8136000), new City("Paris", 2141000)];
let employees = [new Employee("Bob Smith", "Sales"),
    new Employee("Alice Jones", "Sales")];

class DataCollection<T> {
    protected items: T[] = [];

    constructor(initialItems: T[]) {
        this.items.push(...initialItems);
    }

    filter<V extends T>(predicate: (target) => target is V): V[] {
        return this.items.filter(item => predicate(item)) as V[];
    }
}

let mixedData
    = new DataCollection<Person | Product >([...people, ...products]);
function isProduct(target): target is Product {
    return target instanceof Product;
}
let filteredProducts = mixedData.filter<Product>(isProduct);
filteredProducts.forEach(p =>
    console.log(`Product: ${ p.name}, ${p.price}`));
```

The predicate function for the required type is provided as an argument to the `filter` method using JavaScript features that are available when the code is executed; this provides the method with the means to select the required objects. The code in listing 12.19 produces the following results:

```
Product: Running Shoes, 100
Product: Hat, 25
```

12.3.8 *Defining a static method on a generic class*

Only instance properties and methods have a generic type, which can be different for each object. Static methods are accessed through the class, as shown in listing 12.20.

Listing 12.20   Defining a static method in the index.ts file in the src folder

```
import { City, Person, Product, Employee } from "./dataTypes.js";

let people = [new Person("Bob Smith", "London"),
    new Person("Dora Peters", "New York")];
let products = [new Product("Running Shoes", 100), new Product("Hat", 25)];
let cities = [new City("London", 8136000), new City("Paris", 2141000)];
let employees = [new Employee("Bob Smith", "Sales"),
    new Employee("Alice Jones", "Sales")];

class DataCollection<T> {
    protected items: T[] = [];

    constructor(initialItems: T[]) {
        this.items.push(...initialItems);
    }

    filter<V extends T>(predicate: (target) => target is V): V[] {
        return this.items.filter(item => predicate(item)) as V[];
    }

    static reverse(items: any[]) {
        return items.reverse();
    }
}

let mixedData
    = new DataCollection<Person | Product >([...people, ...products]);

function isProduct(target): target is Product {
    return target instanceof Product;
}

let filteredProducts = mixedData.filter<Product>(isProduct);
filteredProducts.forEach(p =>
    console.log(`Product: ${ p.name}, ${p.price}`));

let reversedCities: City[] = DataCollection.reverse(cities);
reversedCities.forEach(c =>
    console.log(`City: ${c.name}, ${c.population}`));
```

The `static reverse` method is accessed through the `DataCollection` class without the use of a type argument, like this:

```
...
let reversedCities: City[] = DataCollection.reverse(cities);
...
```

Static methods can define their own generic type parameters, as shown in listing 12.21.

Listing 12.21   Adding a type parameter in the index.ts file in the src folder

```
import { City, Person, Product, Employee } from "./dataTypes.js";

let people = [new Person("Bob Smith", "London"),
```

```
        new Person("Dora Peters", "New York")];
let products = [new Product("Running Shoes", 100), new Product("Hat", 25)];
let cities = [new City("London", 8136000), new City("Paris", 2141000)];
let employees = [new Employee("Bob Smith", "Sales"),
    new Employee("Alice Jones", "Sales")];

class DataCollection<T> {
    protected items: T[] = [];

    constructor(initialItems: T[]) {
        this.items.push(...initialItems);
    }

    filter<V extends T>(predicate: (target) => target is V): V[] {
        return this.items.filter(item => predicate(item)) as V[];
    }

    static reverse<ArrayType>(items: ArrayType[]): ArrayType[] {
        return items.reverse();
    }
}

let mixedData
    = new DataCollection<Person | Product >([...people, ...products]);

function isProduct(target): target is Product {
    return target instanceof Product;
}

let filteredProducts = mixedData.filter<Product>(isProduct);
filteredProducts.forEach(p =>
    console.log(`Product: ${ p.name}, ${p.price}`));

let reversedCities = DataCollection.reverse<City>(cities);
reversedCities.forEach(c =>
    console.log(`City: ${c.name}, ${c.population}`));
```

The `reverse` method defines a type parameter that specifies the array type it processes. When the method is invoked, it is done so through the `DataCollection` class, and a type argument is provided after the method name, like this:

```
...
let reversedCities = DataCollection.reverse<City>(cities);
...
```

The type parameters defined by static methods are separate from those defined by the class for use by its instance properties and methods. The code in listing 12.21 produces the following output:

```
Product: Running Shoes, 100
Product: Hat, 25
City: Paris, 2141000
City: London, 8136000
```

12.4   Defining generic interfaces

Interfaces can be defined with generic type parameters, allowing functionality to be defined without specifying individual types. Listing 12.22 defines an interface with a generic type parameter.

Listing 12.22   Defining a generic interface in the index.ts file in the src folder

```
import { City, Person, Product, Employee } from "./dataTypes.js";

type  shapeType = { name: string };

interface Collection<T extends shapeType> {

    add(...newItems: T[]): void;
    get(name: string): T;
    count: number;
}
```

The `Collection<T>` interface has a generic type parameter named `T`, following the same syntax used for class type parameters. The type parameter is used by the `add` and `get` methods, and it has been constrained to ensure that only types that have a `name` property can be used.

An interface with a generic type parameter describes a set of abstract operations but doesn't specify which types they can be performed on, leaving specific types to be selected by derived interfaces or implementation classes. The code in listing 12.22 produces no output.

12.4.1   Extending generic interfaces

Generic interfaces can be extended just like regular interfaces, and the options for dealing with its type parameters are the same as when extending a generic class. Listing 12.23 shows a set of interfaces that extend the `Collection<T>` interface.

Listing 12.23   Extending a generic interface in the index.ts file in the src folder

```
import { City, Person, Product, Employee } from "./dataTypes.js";

type  shapeType = { name: string };

interface Collection<T extends shapeType> {

    add(...newItems: T[]): void;
    get(name: string): T;
    count: number;
}

interface SearchableCollection<T extends shapeType> extends Collection<T> {

    find(name: string): T | undefined;
}
```

```
interface ProductCollection extends Collection<Product> {

    sumPrices(): number;
}

interface PeopleCollection<T extends Product | Employee>
        extends Collection<T> {

    getNames(): string[];
}
```

The code in listing 12.23 does not produce any output.

12.4.2 *Implementing a generic interface*

When a class implements a generic interface, it must implement all the interface properties and methods, but it has some choices about how to deal with type parameters, as described in the following sections. Some of these options are similar to those used when extending generic classes and interfaces.

PASSING ON THE GENERIC TYPE PARAMETER

The simplest approach is to implement the interface properties and methods without changing the type parameter, creating a generic class that directly implements the interface, as shown in listing 12.24.

Listing 12.24 Implementing an interface in the index.ts file in the src folder

```
import { City, Person, Product, Employee } from "./dataTypes.js";

type  shapeType = { name: string };

interface Collection<T extends shapeType> {

    add(...newItems: T[]): void;
    get(name: string): T;
    count: number;
}

class ArrayCollection<DataType extends shapeType>
        implements Collection<DataType> {
    private items: DataType[] = [];

    add(...newItems): void {
        this.items.push(...newItems);
    }

    get(name: string): DataType {
        return this.items.find(item => item.name === name);
    }

    get count(): number {
        return this.items.length;
    }
}
```

```
let peopleCollection: Collection<Person> = new ArrayCollection<Person>();
peopleCollection.add(new Person("Bob Smith", "London"),
    new Person("Dora Peters", "New York"));
console.log(`Collection size: ${peopleCollection.count}`);
```

The `ArrayCollection<DataType>` class uses the `implements` keyword to declare that it conforms to the interface. The interface has a generic type parameter, so the `ArrayCollection<DataType>` class must define a compatible parameter. Since the type parameter for the interface is required to have a `name` property, so must the type parameter for the class, and I used the same type alias for the interface and the class to ensure consistency.

The `ArrayCollection<DataType>` class requires a type argument when an object is created and can be operated on through the `Collection<T>` interface, like this:

```
...
let peopleCollection: Collection<Person> = new ArrayCollection<Person>();
...
```

The type argument resolves the generic type for the class and the interface it implements so that an `ArrayCollection<Person>` object implements the `Collection<Person>` interface. The code in listing 12.24 produces the following output:

```
Collection size: 2
```

RESTRICTING OR FIXING THE GENERIC TYPE PARAMETER

Classes can provide an implementation of an interface that is specific to a type or a subset of the types supported by the interface, as shown in listing 12.25.

Listing 12.25   Implementing an interface in the index.ts file in the src folder

```
import { City, Person, Product, Employee } from "./dataTypes.js";

type  shapeType = { name: string };

interface Collection<T extends shapeType> {

    add(...newItems: T[]): void;
    get(name: string): T;
    count: number;
}

class PersonCollection implements Collection<Person> {
    private items: Person[] = [];

    add(...newItems: Person[]): void {
        this.items.push(...newItems);
    }

    get(name: string): Person {
        return this.items.find(item => item.name === name);
    }

    get count(): number {
        return this.items.length;
```

```
        }
    }

let peopleCollection: Collection<Person> = new PersonCollection();
peopleCollection.add(new Person("Bob Smith", "London"),
    new Person("Dora Peters", "New York"));
console.log(`Collection size: ${peopleCollection.count}`);
```

The `PersonCollection` class implements the `Collection<Product>` interface, and the code in listing 12.25 produces the following output when compiled and executed:

```
Collection size: 2
```

CREATING AN ABSTRACT INTERFACE IMPLEMENTATION

An abstract class can provide a partial implementation of an interface, which can be completed by subclasses. The abstract class has the same set of options for dealing with type parameters as regular classes: pass it on to subclasses unchanged, apply further restrictions, or fix specific types. Listing 12.26 shows an abstract class that passed on the interface's generic type argument.

Listing 12.26   Defining an abstract class in the index.ts file in the src folder

```
import { City, Person, Product, Employee } from "./dataTypes.js";

type  shapeType = { name: string };

interface Collection<T extends shapeType> {

    add(...newItems: T[]): void;
    get(name: string): T;
    count: number;
}

abstract class ArrayCollection<T extends shapeType>
        implements Collection<T> {
    protected items: T[] = [];

    add(...newItems: T[]): void {
        this.items.push(...newItems);
    }

    abstract get(searchTerm: string): T;

    get count(): number {
        return this.items.length;
    }
}

class ProductCollection extends ArrayCollection<Product> {

    get(searchTerm: string): Product {
        return this.items.find(item => item.name === searchTerm);
    }
}
```

```
class PersonCollection extends ArrayCollection<Person> {

    get(searchTerm: string): Person {
        return this.items.find(item =>
            item.name === searchTerm || item.city === searchTerm);
    }
}

let peopleCollection: Collection<Person> = new PersonCollection();
peopleCollection.add(new Person("Bob Smith", "London"),
    new Person("Dora Peters", "New York"));
let productCollection: Collection<Product> = new ProductCollection();
productCollection.add(new Product("Running Shoes", 100),
    new Product("Hat", 25));
[peopleCollection, productCollection].forEach(c =>
    console.log(`Size: ${c.count}`));
```

The `ArrayCollection<T>` class is abstract and provides a partial implementation of the `Collection<T>` interface, leaving subclasses to provide the `get` method. The `ProductCollection` and `PersonCollection` classes extend `ArrayCollection<T>`, narrowing the generic type parameter to specific types and implementing the `get` method to use the properties of the type they operate on. The code in listing 12.26 produces the following output:

```
Size: 2
Size: 2
```

Summary

In this chapter, I introduced generic types and described the problem they solve. I showed you the relationship between generic type parameters and arguments and the different ways that generic types can be restricted or fixed. I explained that generic types can be used with regular classes, abstract classes, and interfaces, and showed you how functions and methods can have generic types that are resolved each time they are used.

- Generic type parameters are placeholders for types that are specified when a class is instantiated, using a type argument.
- Generic type parameters can be constrained so that classes can only be instantiated with type arguments that conform to the constraints.
- Generic types are guarded with predicate functions.
- Generic types can be used with interfaces and are inherited by the implementation classes.

In the next chapter, I describe the advanced generic type features that TypeScript provides.

Advanced generic types

In this chapter, I continue to describe the generic type features provided by TypeScript and focus on the advanced features. I explain how generic types can be used with collections and iterators, introduce the index types and type mapping features, and describe the most flexible of the generic type features: conditional types. Table 13.1 summarizes the chapter.

Table 13.1   Chapter summary

Problem	Solution	Listing
Use collection classes with type safety	Provide a generic type argument when creating the collection	3, 4
Use iterators with type safety	Use the interfaces that TypeScript provides that support generic type arguments	5–7
Define a type whose value can only be the name of a property	Use an index type query	8–14
Transform a type	Use a type mapping	15–22
Select types programmatically	Use conditional types	23–32

For quick reference, table 13.2 lists the TypeScript compiler options used in this chapter.

Table 13.2   The TypeScript compiler options used in this chapter

Name	Description
declaration	This option produces type declaration files when enabled, which can be useful in understanding how types have been inferred. These files are described in more detail in chapter 15.
downlevelIteration	This option enables support for iteration when targeting older versions of JavaScript.
outDir	This option specifies the directory in which the JavaScript files will be placed.
rootDir	This option specifies the root directory that the compiler will use to locate TypeScript files.
target	This option specifies the version of the JavaScript language that the compiler will target in its output.

13.1   *Preparing for this chapter*

In this chapter, I continue to use the `types` project created in chapter 7 and used in all the chapters since. To prepare for this chapter, replace the contents of the `index.ts` file in the `src` folder with the code shown in listing 13.1.

Listing 13.1   Replacing the contents of the index.ts file in the src folder

```
import { City, Person, Product, Employee } from "./dataTypes.js";

let products = [new Product("Running Shoes", 100), new Product("Hat", 25)];

type shapeType = { name: string };

class Collection<T extends shapeType> {

    constructor(private items: T[] = []) {}
```

```
    add(...newItems: T[]): void {
        this.items.push(...newItems);
    }

    get(name: string): T {
        return this.items.find(item => item.name === name);
    }

    get count(): number {
        return this.items.length;
    }
}

let productCollection: Collection<Product> = new Collection(products);
console.log(`There are ${ productCollection.count } products`);
let p = productCollection.get("Hat");
console.log(`Product: ${ p.name }, ${ p.price }`);
```

Open a new command prompt, navigate to the `types` folder, and run the command shown in listing 13.2 to start the TypeScript compiler so that it automatically executes code after it has been compiled.

> **TIP** You can download the example project for this chapter—and for all the other chapters in this book—from https://github.com/manningbooks/ essential-typescript-5.

> **Listing 13.2   Starting the TypeScript compiler**

```
npm start
```

The compiler will compile the project, execute the output, and then enter watch mode, producing the following output:

```
7:31:10 AM - Starting compilation in watch mode...
7:31:11 AM - Found 0 errors. Watching for file changes.
There are 2 products
Product: Hat, 25
```

13.2   *Using generic collections*

TypeScript provides support for using the JavaScript collections with generic type parameters, allowing a generic class to safely use collections, as described in table 13.3. The JavaScript collection classes are described in chapter 4.

Table 13.3   The generic collection types

Name	Description
`Map<K, V>`	This describes a `Map` whose key type is `K` and whose value type is `V`.
`ReadonlyMap<K, V>`	This describes a `Map` that cannot be modified.
`Set<T>`	This describes a `Set` whose value type is `T`.
`ReadonlySet<T>`	This describes a `Set` that cannot be modified.

Listing 13.3 shows how a generic class can use its type parameters with a collection.

Listing 13.3   Using a collection in the index.ts file in the src folder

```
import { City, Person, Product, Employee } from "./dataTypes.js";

let products = [new Product("Running Shoes", 100), new Product("Hat", 25)];

type shapeType = { name: string };

class Collection<T extends shapeType> {
    private items: Set<T>;

    constructor(initialItems: T[] = []) {
        this.items = new Set<T>(initialItems);
    }

    add(...newItems: T[]): void {
        newItems.forEach(newItem => this.items.add(newItem));
    }

    get(name: string): T {
        return [...this.items.values()].find(item => item.name === name);
    }

    get count(): number {
        return this.items.size;
    }
}

let productCollection: Collection<Product> = new Collection(products);
console.log(`There are ${ productCollection.count } products`);
let p = productCollection.get("Hat");
console.log(`Product: ${ p.name }, ${ p.price }`);
```

The `Collection<T>` class has been changed to `Set<T>` to store its items, which it does by using its generic type parameter for the collection. The TypeScript compiler uses the type parameter to prevent other data types from being added to the set, and no type guarding is required when retrieving objects from the collection. The same approach can be taken with a map, as shown in listing 13.4.

Listing 13.4   Using a map in the index.ts file in the src folder

```
import { City, Person, Product, Employee } from "./dataTypes.js";

let products = [new Product("Running Shoes", 100), new Product("Hat", 25)];

type shapeType = { name: string };

class Collection<T extends shapeType> {
    private items: Map<string, T>;

    constructor(initialItems: T[] = []) {
        this.items = new Map<string, T>();
```

```
        this.add(...initialItems);
    }

    add(...newItems: T[]): void {
        newItems.forEach(newItem => this.items.set(newItem.name, newItem));
    }

    get(name: string): T {
        return this.items.get(name);
    }

    get count(): number {
        return this.items.size;
    }
}

let productCollection: Collection<Product> = new Collection(products);
console.log(`There are ${ productCollection.count } products`);
let p = productCollection.get("Hat");
console.log(`Product: ${ p.name }, ${ p.price }`);
```

Generic classes don't have to provide generic type parameters for collections and can specify concrete types instead. In the example, a `Map` is used to store objects using the `name` property as a key. The `name` property can be used safely because it is part of the restriction applied to the type parameter named `T`. The code in listing 13.4 produces the following output:

```
There are 2 products
Product: Hat, 25
```

13.3 *Using generic iterators*

As explained in chapter 4, iterators allow a sequence of values to be enumerated, and support for iterators is a common feature for classes that operate on other types, such as collections. TypeScript provides the interfaces listed in table 13.4 for describing iterators and their results.

Table 13.4   The TypeScript iterator interface

Name	Description
`Iterator<T>`	This interface describes an iterator whose `next` method returns `IteratorResult<T>` objects.
`IteratorResult<T>`	This interface describes a result produced by an iterator, with `done` and `value` properties.
`Iterable<T>`	This interface defines an object that has a `Symbol.iterator` property and that supports iteration directly.
`IterableIterator<T>`	This interface combines the `Iterator<T>` and `Iterable<T>` interfaces to describe an object that has a `Symbol.iterator` property and that defines a `next` method and a `result` property.

Listing 13.5 shows the use of the `Iterator<T>` and `IteratorResult<T>` interfaces to provide access to the contents of the `Map<string, T>` used to store objects by the `Collection<T>` class.

Listing 13.5   Iterating objects in the index.ts file in the src folder

```
import { City, Person, Product, Employee } from "./dataTypes.js";

let products = [new Product("Running Shoes", 100), new Product("Hat", 25)];

type shapeType = { name: string };

class Collection<T extends shapeType> {
    private items: Map<string, T>;

    constructor(initialItems: T[] = []) {
        this.items = new Map<string, T>();
        this.add(...initialItems);
    }

    add(...newItems: T[]): void {
        newItems.forEach(newItem => this.items.set(newItem.name, newItem));
    }

    get(name: string): T {
        return this.items.get(name);
    }

    get count(): number {
        return this.items.size;
    }

    values(): Iterator<T> {
        return this.items.values();
    }
}

let productCollection: Collection<Product> = new Collection(products);
console.log(`There are ${ productCollection.count } products`);

let iterator: Iterator<Product> = productCollection.values();
let result: IteratorResult<Product> = iterator.next();
while (!result.done) {
    console.log(`Product: ${result.value.name}, ${ result.value.price}`);
    result = iterator.next();
}
```

The `values` method defined by the `Collection<T>` class returns an `Iterator<T>`. When this method is invoked on the `Collection<Product>` object, the iterator it returns will produce `IteratorResult<Product>` objects through its `next` method. The `result` property of each `IteratorResult<Product>` object will return a `Product`, allowing the objects managed by the collection to be iterated. The code in listing 13.5 produces the following output:

```
There are 2 products
Product: Running Shoes, 100
Product: Hat, 25
```

Using iterators with JavaScript ES5 and earlier

Iterators were introduced in the JavaScript ES6 standard. If you use iterators in your project and are targeting earlier versions of JavaScript, then you must set the TypeScript `downlevelIteration` compiler property to `true`.

13.3.1 *Combining an iterable and an iterator*

The `IterableIterator<T>` interface can be used to describe objects that can be iterated and that also define a `Symbol.iterator` property. Objects that implement this interface can be enumerated more elegantly, as shown in listing 13.6.

Listing 13.6   Using an iterable iterator in the index.ts file in the src folder

```
import { City, Person, Product, Employee } from "./dataTypes.js";

let products = [new Product("Running Shoes", 100), new Product("Hat", 25)];

type shapeType = { name: string };

class Collection<T extends shapeType> {
    private items: Map<string, T>;

    constructor(initialItems: T[] = []) {
        this.items = new Map<string, T>();
        this.add(...initialItems);
    }

    add(...newItems: T[]): void {
        newItems.forEach(newItem => this.items.set(newItem.name, newItem));
    }

    get(name: string): T {
        return this.items.get(name);
    }

    get count(): number {
        return this.items.size;
    }

    values(): IterableIterator<T> {
        return this.items.values();
    }
}

let productCollection: Collection<Product> = new Collection(products);
console.log(`There are ${ productCollection.count } products`);
```

```
[...productCollection.values()].forEach(p =>
    console.log(`Product: ${p.name}, ${ p.price}`));
```

The `values` method returns an `IterableIterator` object, which it can do because the result of the `Map` method defines all the members specified by the interface. The combined interface allows the result of the `values` method to be iterated directly, and the listing uses the spread operator to populate an array and then enumerates its contents with the `forEach` method. The code in listing 13.6 produces the following output:

```
There are 2 products
Product: Running Shoes, 100
Product: Hat, 25
```

13.3.2 *Creating an iterable class*

Classes that define a `Symbol.iterator` property can implement the `Iterable<T>` interface, which allows iteration without needing to call a method or read a property, as shown in listing 13.7.

> Listing 13.7   **Creating an iterable class in the index.ts file in the src folder**

```
import { City, Person, Product, Employee } from "./dataTypes.js";

let products = [new Product("Running Shoes", 100), new Product("Hat", 25)];

type shapeType = { name: string };

class Collection<T extends shapeType> implements Iterable<T> {
    private items: Map<string, T>;

    constructor(initialItems: T[] = []) {
        this.items = new Map<string, T>();
        this.add(...initialItems);
    }

    add(...newItems: T[]): void {
        newItems.forEach(newItem => this.items.set(newItem.name, newItem));
    }

    get(name: string): T {
        return this.items.get(name);
    }

    get count(): number {
        return this.items.size;
    }

    [Symbol.iterator](): Iterator<T> {
        return this.items.values();
    }
}

let productCollection: Collection<Product> = new Collection(products);
```

```
console.log(`There are ${ productCollection.count } products`);
```

```
[...productCollection].forEach(p =>
    console.log(`Product: ${p.name}, ${ p.price}`));
```

The new property implements the `Iterable<T>` interface, indicating that it defines a `Symbol.iterator` property that returns an `Iterator<T>` object that can be used for iteration. The code in listing 13.7 produces the following output:

```
There are 2 products
Product: Running Shoes, 100
Product: Hat, 25
```

13.4 Using index types

The `Collection<T>` class restricts the types it can accept using a shape type, which ensures that all the objects it deals with have a `name` property that can be used as the key to store and retrieve objects in the `Map`.

TypeScript provides a set of related features that allow any property defined by an object to be used as a key while preserving type safety. These features can be difficult to understand, so I show how they work in isolation and then use them to improve the `Collection<T>` class.

13.4.1 Using the index type query

The `keyof` keyword, known as the index type query operator, returns a union of the property names of a type, using the literal value type feature described in chapter 9. Listing 13.8 shows `keyof` applied to the `Product` class.

> **Listing 13.8 Using the index type query operator in the index.ts file in the src folder**

```
import { City, Person, Product, Employee } from "./dataTypes.js";

let myVar: keyof Product = "name";
myVar = "price";
myVar = "someOtherName";
```

The type annotation for the `myVar` variable is `keyof Product`, which will be the union of the property names defined by the `Product` class. The result is that `myVar` can be assigned only the string values `name` and `price` because these are the names of the only two properties defined by the `Product` class in the `dataTypes.ts` file, which was created in chapter 12.

```
...
export class Product {
    constructor(public name: string, public price: number) {}
}
...
```

Assigning any other value to `myVar`, as the final statement in listing 13.8 attempts to do, produces a compiler error.

```
src/index.ts(5,1): error TS2322: Type '"someOtherName"' is not assignable
to type 'keyof Product'.
```

The `keyof` keyword can be used to constrain generic type parameters so that they can only be typed to match the properties of another type, as shown in listing 13.9.

Listing 13.9   Constraining a generic type parameter in the index.ts file in the src folder

```
import { City, Person, Product, Employee } from "./dataTypes.js";

function getValue<T, K extends keyof T>(item: T, keyname: K) {
    console.log(`Value: ${item[keyname]}`);
}

let p = new Product("Running Shoes", 100);
getValue(p, "name");
getValue(p, "price");

let e = new Employee("Bob Smith", "Sales");
getValue(e, "name");
getValue(e, "role");
```

The example defines a function named `getValue`, whose type parameter K is constrained using `typeof` T, which means that K can be the name of only one of the properties defined by T, regardless of the type used for T when the function is invoked. When the `getValue` function is used with a `Product` object, the `keyname` parameter can be only name or price. And when the `getValue` function is used with an `Employee` object, the `keyname` parameter can be only name or role. In both cases, the `keyname` parameter can be used to safely get or set the value of the corresponding property from the `Product` or `Employee` object, and the code in listing 13.9 produces the following output:

```
Value: Running Shoes
Value: 100
Value: Bob Smith
Value: Sales
```

13.4.2   *Explicitly providing generic type parameters for index types*

The `getValue` method was invoked without generic type arguments in listing 13.9, allowing the compiler to infer the types from the function arguments. Explicitly stating the type arguments reveals an aspect of using the index type query operator that can be confusing, as shown in listing 13.10.

Listing 13.10   Using explicit type arguments in the index.ts file in the src folder

```
import { City, Person, Product, Employee } from "./dataTypes.js";

function getValue<T, K extends keyof T>(item: T, keyname: K) {
    console.log(`Value: ${item[keyname]}`);
}

let p = new Product("Running Shoes", 100);
getValue<Product, "name">(p, "name");
getValue(p, "price");
```

```
let e = new Employee("Bob Smith", "Sales");
getValue(e, "name");
getValue(e, "role");
```

It can appear as though the property that is required for the example is specified twice, but name has two different uses in the modified statement, as shown in figure 13.1.

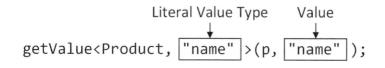

Figure 13.1 An index type and value

As a generic type argument, name is a literal value type that specifies one of the keyof Product types and is used by the TypeScript compiler for type checking. As a function argument, name is a string value that is used by the JavaScript runtime when the code is executed. The code in listing 13.10 produces the following output:

```
Value: Running Shoes
Value: 100
Value: Bob Smith
Value: Sales
```

13.4.3 *Using the indexed access operator*

The indexed access operator is used to get the type for one or more properties, as shown in listing 13.11.

Listing 13.11   Using the indexed access operator in the index.ts file in the src folder

```
import { City, Person, Product, Employee } from "./dataTypes.js";

function getValue<T, K extends keyof T>(item: T, keyname: K) {
    console.log(`Value: ${item[keyname]}`);
}

type priceType = Product["price"];
type allTypes = Product[keyof Product];

let p = new Product("Running Shoes", 100);
getValue<Product, "name">(p, "name");
getValue(p, "price");

let e = new Employee("Bob Smith", "Sales");
getValue(e, "name");
getValue(e, "role");
```

The indexed access operator is expressed using square brackets following a type so that Product["price"], for example, is number, since that is the type of the price property defined by the Product class. The indexed access operator works on literal value types, which means it can be used with index type queries, like this:

```
...
type allTypes = Product[keyof Product];
...
```

The `keyof Product` expression returns a literal value type union with the property names defined by the `Product` class, `"name"` | `"price"`. The indexed access operator returns the union of the types of those properties, such that `Product[keyof Product]` is `string` | `number`, which is the union of the types of the `name` and `price` properties.

TIP The types returned by the indexed access operator are known as *lookup types*.

The indexed access operator is most commonly used with generic types, which allows property types to be handled safely even though the specific types that will be used are unknown, as shown in listing 13.12.

Listing 13.12   Using the indexed access operator in the index.ts file in the src folder

```
import { City, Person, Product, Employee } from "./dataTypes.js";

function getValue<T, K extends keyof T>(item: T, keyname: K): T[K] {
    return item[keyname];
}

let p = new Product("Running Shoes", 100);
console.log(getValue<Product, "name">(p, "name"));
console.log(getValue(p, "price"));

let e = new Employee("Bob Smith", "Sales");
console.log(getValue(e, "name"));
console.log(getValue(e, "role"));
```

The indexed access operator is expressed using a regular type, its `keyof` type, and square brackets, as shown in figure 13.2.

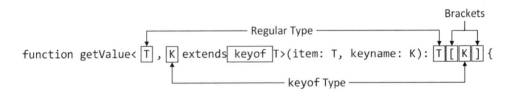

Figure 13.2   The indexed access operator

The indexed access operator in listing 13.12, `T[K]`, tells the compiler that the result of the `getValue` function will have the type of the property whose name is specified by the `keyof` type argument, leaving the compiler to determine the result types based on the generic type arguments used to invoke the function. For the `Product` object, that means a `name` argument will produce a `string` result, and a `price` argument will produce a `number` result. The code in listing 13.12 produces the following output:

```
Running Shoes
100
Bob Smith
Sales
```

13.4.4 *Using an index type for the collection<t> class*

Using an index type allows me to change the `Collection<T>` class so that it can store any type of object and not just those that define a `name` property. Listing 13.13 shows the changes to the class, which uses an index type query to restrict the `propertyName` constructor property to the names of the properties defined by the generic type parameter `T`, providing the key by which objects can be stored in the `Map`.

Listing 13.13 **Using an index type in a collection class in the index.ts file in the src folder**

```
import { City, Person, Product, Employee } from "./dataTypes.js";

let products = [new Product("Running Shoes", 100), new Product("Hat", 25)];

//type shapeType = { name: string };

class Collection<T, K extends keyof T> implements Iterable<T> {
    private items: Map<T[K], T>;

    constructor(initialItems: T[] = [], private propertyName: K) {
        this.items = new Map<T[K], T>();
        this.add(...initialItems);
    }

    add(...newItems: T[]): void {
        newItems.forEach(newItem =>
            this.items.set(newItem[this.propertyName], newItem));
    }

    get(key: T[K]): T {
        return this.items.get(key);
    }

    get count(): number {
        return this.items.size;
    }

    [Symbol.iterator](): Iterator<T> {
        return this.items.values();
    }
}

let productCollection: Collection<Product, "name">
    = new Collection(products, "name");
console.log(`There are ${ productCollection.count } products`);

let itemByKey = productCollection.get("Hat");
console.log(`Item: ${ itemByKey.name}, ${ itemByKey.price}`);
```

The class has been rewritten with an additional generic type parameter, K, that is restricted to keyof T, which is the data type of the objects stored by the collection. A new instance of the Collection<T, K> is created like this:

```
. . .
let productCollection: Collection<Product, "name">
    = new Collection(products, "name");
. . .
```

The code in listing 13.13 produces the following output:

```
There are 2 products
Item: Hat, 25
```

The dense chains of angle and square brackets in listing 13.13 can be difficult to make sense of when you first start using index types. To help make sense of the code, table 13.5 describes the significant type and constructor parameters and the types they are resolved to for the Collection<Product, "name"> object that is created in the example.

Table 13.5   The significant types used by the Collection<T> class

Name	Description
T	This is the type of the objects stored in the collection class, which is provided by the first generic type argument, which is Product for the object created in the listing.
K	This is the key property name, which is restricted to the property names defined by T. The value for this type is provided by the second generic type argument, which is name for the object created in the listing.
T[K]	This is the type of the key property, which is obtained using the indexed access operator and which is used to specify the key type when creating the Map object and to restrict the type for the parameters. This is the type of the Product.name property for the object created in the listing, which is string.
propertyName	This is the key property name, which is required as a value that can be used by the JavaScript runtime after the TypeScript generic type information has been removed. For the object created in the listing, this value is name, corresponding to the generic type K.

The results of the index type in listing 13.13 are that any property can be used to store objects and that any type of object can be stored. Listing 13.14 changes the way that the Collection<T, K> class is instantiated so that the price property is used as the key. The listing also omits the generic type arguments and allows the compiler to infer the types that are required.

Listing 13.14   Changing the key property in the index.ts file in the src folder

```
...
let productCollection = new Collection(products, "price");
console.log(`There are ${ productCollection.count } products`);

let itemByKey = productCollection.get(100);
console.log(`Item: ${ itemByKey.name}, ${ itemByKey.price}`);
...
```

The type of the argument to the `get` method changes to match the type of the key property so that objects can be obtained using a `number` argument. The code in listing 13.14 produces the following output:

```
There are 2 products
Item: Running Shoes, 100
```

13.5   *Using type mapping*

Mapped types are created by applying a transformation to the properties of an existing type. The best way to understand how mapped types work is to create one that processes a type but doesn't make any changes, as shown in listing 13.15.

Listing 13.15   Using a mapped type in the index.ts file in the src folder

```
import { City, Person, Product, Employee } from "./dataTypes.js";

type MappedProduct = {
    [P in keyof Product] : Product[P]
};

let p: MappedProduct = { name: "Kayak", price: 275};
console.log(`Mapped type: ${p.name}, ${p.price}`);
```

A type mapping is an expression that selects property names to be included in the mapped type and the type for each of them, as shown in figure 13.3.

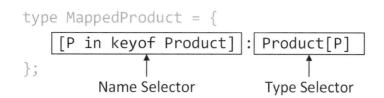

Figure 13.3   A mapped type

The property name selector defines a type parameter, named P in this example, and uses the `in` keyword to enumerate the types in a literal value union. The type union can be expressed directly, such as `"name"|"price"`, or obtained using `keyof`.

The TypeScript compiler creates a new property in the mapped type for each of the types in the union. The type of each property is determined by the type selector, which can be obtained from the source type using the indexed access operator with `P` as the literal value type to look up.

The `MappedProduct` type in listing 13.15 uses `keyof` to select the properties defined by the `Product` class and uses the indexed type operator to get the type of each of those properties. The result is equivalent to this type:

```
type MappedProduct = {
    name: string;
    price: number;
}
```

The code in listing 13.15 produces the following output:

```
Mapped type: Kayak, 275
```

13.5.1 *Changing mapping names and types*

The previous example preserved the names and types of the properties during the mapping. But type mapping is more flexible and there is support for changing both the name and the type of the properties in the new type, as shown in listing 13.16.

> **Listing 13.16   Changing mappings names and types in the index.ts file in the src folder**

```
import { City, Person, Product, Employee } from "./dataTypes.js";

type MappedProduct = {
    [P in keyof Product] : Product[P]
};

let p: MappedProduct = { name: "Kayak", price: 275};
console.log(`Mapped type: ${p.name}, ${p.price}`);

type AllowStrings = {
    [P in keyof Product] : Product[P] | string
}
let q: AllowStrings = { name: "Kayak",  price: "apples" };
console.log(`Changed type # 1: ${q.name}, ${q.price}`);

type ChangeNames = {
    [P in keyof Product as `${P}Property`] : Product[P]
}

let r: ChangeNames = { nameProperty: "Kayak",  priceProperty: 12 };
console.log(`Changed type # 2: ${r.nameProperty}, ${r.priceProperty}`);
```

The `AllowStrings` type is created with a mapping that creates a type union between `string` and the property's original type, like this:

```
...
[P in keyof Product] : Product[P] | string
...
```

The result is a type that is equivalent to this type:

```
type AllowStrings = {
    name: string;
```

```
    price: number | string;
}
```

The `ChangeNames` type is created with a mapping that alters the name of each property by adding `Property`.

```
...
[P in keyof Product as `${P}Property`] : Product[P]
...
```

The `as` keyword is combined with an expression that defines the property name. In this case, a template string is used to modify the existing name, with the result that is equivalent to this type:

```
type ChangeNames = {
    nameProperty: string;
    priceProperty: number;
}
```

The code in listing 13.16 produces the following output when it is compiled and executed:

```
Mapped type: Kayak, 275
Changed type # 1: Kayak, apples
Changed type # 2: Kayak, 12
```

13.5.2 *Using a generic type parameter with a mapped type*

Mapped types become more useful when they define a generic type parameter, as shown in listing 13.17, which allows the transformation they describe to be applied to a broader range of types.

> **Listing 13.17 Using a generic type parameter in the index.ts file in the src folder**

```
import { City, Person, Product, Employee } from "./dataTypes.js";

type Mapped<T> = {
    [P in keyof T] : T[P]
};

let p: Mapped<Product> = { name: "Kayak", price: 275};
console.log(`Mapped type: ${p.name}, ${p.price}`);

let c: Mapped<City> = { name: "London", population: 8136000};
console.log(`Mapped type: ${c.name}, ${c.population}`);
```

The `Mapped<T>` type defines a generic type parameter named `T`, which is the type to be transformed. The type parameter is used in the name and type selectors, meaning that any type can be mapped using a generic type parameter. In listing 13.17, the `Mapped<T>` mapped type is used on the `Product` and `City` classes and produces the following output:

```
Mapped type: Kayak, 275
Mapped type: London, 8136000
```

13.5.3   *Changing property optionality and mutability*

Mapped types can change properties to make them optional or required and to add or remove the `readonly` keyword, as shown in listing 13.18.

> **Listing 13.18   Changing properties in the index.ts file in the src folder**

```
import { City, Person, Product, Employee } from "./dataTypes.js";

type MakeOptional<T> = {
    [P in keyof T]? : T[P]
};

type MakeRequired<T> = {
    [P in keyof T]-? : T[P]
};

type MakeReadOnly<T> = {
    readonly [P in keyof T] : T[P]
};

type MakeReadWrite<T> = {
    -readonly [P in keyof T] : T[P]
};

type optionalType = MakeOptional<Product>;
type requiredType = MakeRequired<optionalType>;
type readOnlyType = MakeReadOnly<requiredType>;
type readWriteType = MakeReadWrite<readOnlyType>;

let p: readWriteType = { name: "Kayak", price: 275};
console.log(`Mapped type: ${p.name}, ${p.price}`);
```

A question mark (the ? character) is placed after the name selector to make the properties in the mapped type optional, and a minus sign and a question mark (the -? characters) are used to make properties required. Properties are made read-only and read-write by preceding the name selector with `readonly` and `-readonly`.

Mapped types change all the properties defined by the type they transform so that the type produced by `MakeOptional<T>` when applied to the `Product` class, for example, is equivalent to this type:

```
type optionalType = {
    name?: string;
    price?: number;
}
```

The types produced by mappings can be fed into other mappings, creating a chain of transformations. In the listing, the type produced by the `MakeOptional<T>` mapping is then transformed by the `MakeRequired<T>` mapping, the output of which is then fed to the `MakeReadOnly<T>` mapping and then the `MakeReadWrite<T>` mapping. The result is that properties are made optional and then required and then read-only and, finally, read-write. The code in listing 13.18 produces the following output:

```
Mapped type: Kayak, 275
```

13.5.4 *Using the basic built-in mappings*

TypeScript provides built-in mapped types, some of which correspond to the transformations in listing 13.18 and some that are described in later sections. Table 13.6 describes the basic built-in mappings.

Table 13.6 **The basic type mappings**

Name	Description
Partial<T>	This mapping makes properties optional.
Required<T>	This mapping makes properties required.
Readonly<T>	This mapping adds the readonly keyword to properties.
Pick<T, K>	This mapping selects specific properties to create a new type, as described in the "Mapping Specific Properties" section.
Omit<T, keys>	This mapping selects specific properties to create a new type, as described in the "Mapping Specific Properties" section.
Record<T, K>	This mapping creates a type without transforming an existing one, as explained in the "Creating Types with a Type Mapping" section.

There is no built-in mapping to remove the readonly keyword, but listing 13.19 replaces my custom mappings with those provided by TypeScript.

Listing 13.19   Using the built-in mappings in the index.ts file in the src folder

```
import { City, Person, Product, Employee } from "./dataTypes.js";

// type MakeOptional<T> = {
//     [P in keyof T]? : T[P]
// };

// type MakeRequired<T> = {
//     [P in keyof T]-? : T[P]
// };

// type MakeReadOnly<T> = {
//     readonly [P in keyof T] : T[P]
// };

type MakeReadWrite<T> = {
    -readonly [P in keyof T] : T[P]
};

type optionalType = Partial<Product>;
type requiredType = Required<optionalType>;
type readOnlyType = Readonly<requiredType>;
type readWriteType = MakeReadWrite<readOnlyType>;
```

```
let p: readWriteType = { name: "Kayak", price: 275};
console.log(`Mapped type: ${p.name}, ${p.price}`);
```

The built-in mappings have the same effect as the ones defined in listing 13.19, and the code in listing 13.19 produces the following output:

```
Mapped type: Kayak, 275
```

MAPPING SPECIFIC PROPERTIES

The index type query for a mapped type can be expressed as a generic type parameter, which can then be used to select specific properties to map by name, as shown in listing 13.20.

> **Listing 13.20   Mapping specific properties in the index.ts file in the src folder**

```
import { City, Person, Product, Employee } from "./dataTypes.js";

type SelectProperties<T, K extends keyof T> = {
    [P in K]: T[P]
};

let p1: SelectProperties<Product, "name"> = { name: "Kayak" };
let p2: Pick<Product, "name"> = { name: "Kayak" };
let p3: Omit<Product, "price"> = { name: "Kayak"};
console.log(`Custom mapped type: ${p1.name}`);
console.log(`Built-in mapped type (Pick): ${p2.name}`);
console.log(`Built-in mapped type (Omit): ${p3.name}`);
```

The `SelectProperties` mapping defines an additional generic type parameter named `K` that is restricted using `keyof` so that only types that correspond to properties defined by the type parameter `T` can be specified. The new type parameter is used in the mapping's name selector, with the result that individual properties can be selected for inclusion in the mapped type, like this:

```
...
let p1: SelectProperties<Product, "name"> = { name: "Kayak" };
...
```

This mapping selects the `name` property defined by the `Product` class. Multiple properties can be expressed as a type union, and TypeScript provides the built-in `Pick<T, K>` mapping that performs the same role.

```
...
let p2: Pick<Product, "name"> = { name: "Kayak" };
...
```

The `Pick` mapping specifies the keys that are to be kept in the mapped type. The `Omit` mapping works in the opposite way and excludes one or more keys.

```
...
let p3: Omit<Product, "price"> = { name: "Kayak"};
...
```

The result of all three mappings is the same, and the code in listing 13.20 produces the following output:

```
Custom mapped type: Kayak
Built-in mapped type (Pick): Kayak
Built-in mapped type (Omit): Kayak
```

13.5.5 Combining transformations in a single mapping

Listing 13.19 showed how mappings can be combined to create a chain of transformations, but mappings can apply multiple changes to properties, as shown in listing 13.21.

> **Listing 13.21 Combining transformations in the index.ts file in the src folder**

```
import { City, Person, Product, Employee } from "./dataTypes.js";

type CustomMapped<T, K extends keyof T> = {
    readonly[P in K]?: T[P]
};

type BuiltInMapped<T, K extends keyof T> = Readonly<Partial<Pick<T, K>>>;

let p1: CustomMapped<Product, "name"> = { name: "Kayak" };
let p2: BuiltInMapped<Product, "name"| "price">
    = { name: "Lifejacket", price: 48.95};
console.log(`Custom mapped type: ${p1.name}`);
console.log(`Built-in mapped type: ${p2.name}, ${p2.price}`);
```

For custom type mappings, the question mark and the `readonly` keyword can be applied in the same transformation, which can be constrained to allow properties to be selected by name. Mappings can also be chained together, as shown by the combination of the `Pick`, partial, and `Readonly` mappings. The code in listing 13.21 produces the following results:

```
Custom mapped type: Kayak
Built-in mapped type: Lifejacket, 48.95
```

13.5.6 Creating types with a type mapping

The final feature provided by type mappings is the ability to create new types, rather than transform a specific one. Listing 13.22 shows the basic use of this feature, which creates a type that contains `name` and `city` properties.

> **Listing 13.22 Creating a type in the index.ts file in the src folder**

```
import { City, Person, Product, Employee } from "./dataTypes.js";

type CustomMapped<K extends keyof any, T> = {
    [P in K]: T
};

let p1: CustomMapped<"name" | "city", string>
    = { name: "Bob",  city: "London"};
let p2: Record<"name"| "city", string> = { name: "Alice", city: "Paris"};

console.log(`Custom mapped type: ${p1.name}, ${p1.city}`);
console.log(`Built-in mapped type: ${p2.name}, ${p2.city}`);
```

The first generic type parameter is restricted using `keyof any`, which means that a literal value type union can be specified and that it can contain the property names required for the new type. The second generic type parameter is used to specify the type for the properties that are created and is used like this:

```
...
let p1: CustomMapped<"name" | "city", string>
    = { name: "Bob",  city: "London"};
...
```

The mapping produces a type with two `string` properties: `name` and `city`. TypeScript provides the built-in `Record` mapping, which performs the same task.

```
...
let p2: Record<"name"| "city", string> = { name: "Alice", city: "Paris"};
...
```

This is the mapping feature that I use the least in my own projects, but it does serve to show that mappings are more flexible than they might appear and that literal value types restricted by `keyof  any` can accept any combination of property names. The code in listing 13.22 produces the following output:

```
Custom mapped type: Bob, London
Built-in mapped type: Alice, Paris
```

13.6   *Using conditional types*

Conditional types are expressions containing generic type parameters that are evaluated to select new types. Listing 13.23 shows a basic conditional type.

Listing 13.23   Using a conditional type in the index.ts file in the src folder

```
import { City, Person, Product, Employee } from "./dataTypes.js";

type resultType<T extends boolean> = T extends true ? string : number;

let firstVal: resultType<true> = "String Value";
let secondVal: resultType<false> = 100;

let mismatchCheck: resultType<false> = "String Value";
```

Conditional types have a generic type parameter and a ternary expression that selects a result type, as illustrated in figure 13.4.

Figure 13.4   A conditional type

A conditional type is a placeholder for one of its result types, which isn't chosen until the generic type parameter is used, which allows the expression to be evaluated using one of the result types selected.

In the listing, the `resultType<T>` conditional type is a placeholder for the `string` and `number` types, meaning that the argument for the generic type `T` will determine whether the conditional type resolves to `string` or `number`. The generic type parameter `T` is restricted so that it can only accept `boolean` values, and the expression will evaluate as `true` if the argument provided for `T` is the literal value type `true`. The effect is that `resultType<T>` resolves to `string` when `T` is `true`.

```
...
let firstVal: resultType<true> = "String Value";
let stringTypeCheck: string = firstVal;
...
```

The compiler resolves the conditional type and knows that the type annotation for `firstVal` resolves to `string`, allowing a string literal value to be assigned to `firstVal`. When the generic type argument is `false`, the conditional type resolves to `number`.

```
...
let secondVal: resultType<false> = 100;
let numberTypeCheck: number = secondVal;
...
```

The compiler enforces type safety with conditional types. In the final statement in listing 13.23, the conditional type resolves to `number` but is assigned a `string` value, which produces the following compiler error:

```
error TS2322: Type 'string' is not assignable to type 'number'.
```

The danger of conditional types

Conditional types are an advanced feature that should be used carefully. Writing conditional types can be a tortured process and can often feel like a sleight of hand as you lead the compiler through a series of expressions to get the results you require.

As the complexity of a conditional type increases, so does the danger that you won't capture all of the permutations of types correctly and create a result that is too lax, creating a type-checking hole, or too restrictive, causing compiler errors for valid uses.

When using conditional types, remember that you are only describing combinations of types to the TypeScript compiler and that the type information will be removed during compilation. And, as a conditional type becomes more complex and encompasses more combinations, you should take a moment to consider if there is a simpler way to achieve the same result.

13.6.1 *Nesting conditional types*

More complex combinations of types can be described by nesting conditional types. A conditional type's result type can be another conditional type, and the compiler will follow the chain of expressions until it reaches a result that isn't conditional, as shown in listing 13.24.

```
import { City, Person, Product, Employee } from "./dataTypes.js";

type resultType<T extends boolean> = T extends true ? string : number;

type references = "London" | "Bob" | "Kayak";

type nestedType<T extends references>
    = T extends "London" ? City : T extends "Bob" ? Person : Product;

let firstVal: nestedType<"London"> = new City("London", 8136000);
let secondVal: nestedType<"Bob"> = new Person("Bob", "London");
let thirdVal: nestedType<"Kayak"> = new Product("Kayak", 275);
```

The type `nestedType<T>` is a nested conditional type to select between three result types, based on the value of the generic type parameter. As noted in the sidebar, complex conditional types can be difficult to understand, and this is especially true when they are nested.

13.6.2 *Using conditional types in generic classes*

Conditional types can be used to express the relationship between a method or function's parameter types and the results it produces, as shown in listing 13.25. This is a more concise alternative to the function type overloading I described in chapter 8, although conditional types can be harder to understand.

```
import { City, Person, Product, Employee } from "./dataTypes.js";

type resultType<T extends boolean> = T extends true ? string : number;

class Collection<T> {
    private items: T[];

    constructor(...initialItems: T[]) {
        this.items = initialItems || [];
    }

    total<P extends keyof T, U extends boolean>(propName: P, format: U)
            : resultType<U> {
        let totalValue = this.items.reduce((t, item) =>
            t += Number(item[propName]), 0);
        return format ? `$${totalValue.toFixed()}` : totalValue as any;
    }
}

let data = new Collection<Product>(new Product("Kayak", 275),
    new Product("Lifejacket", 48.95));

let firstVal: string = data.total("price", true);
```

```
console.log(`Formatted value: ${firstVal}`);
let secondVal: number = data.total("price", false);
console.log(`Unformatted value: ${secondVal}`);
```

The `Collection<T>` class uses an array to store objects whose type is specified by the generic type parameter named `T`. The `total` method defines two generic type parameters: `P`, which specifies a property to use to create a total, and `U`, which specifies whether the result should be formatted. The result of the `total` method is a conditional type, which is resolved using the value provided for the type parameter `U`.

```
...
total<P extends keyof T, U extends boolean>(propName: P, format: U)
    : resultType<U> {
...
```

The use of the conditional type means that the result of the `total` method is determined by the argument provided for the type parameter `U`. And since the compiler can infer `U` from the value provided for the argument `format`, as explained in chapter 12, the method can be invoked like this:

```
...
let firstVal: string = data.total("price", true);
...
```

When the argument for the `format` parameter is `true`, the conditional type resolves to set the result type of the `total` method to `string`. This matches the data type produced by the method implementation.

```
...
return format ? `$${totalValue.toFixed()}` : totalValue as any;
...
```

When the argument for the format parameter is `false`, the conditional type resolves to set the type of the total method to `number`, allowing the method to return the unformatted number `value`.

```
...
return format ? `$${totalValue.toFixed()}` : totalValue as any;
...
```

> ### Returning values in methods that use a conditional type
>
> At the time of writing, the TypeScript compiler has difficulty correlating the data type of values returned by methods and functions when conditional types are used. It is for this reason that listing 13.25 uses a type assertion in the `total` method to tell the compiler to treat the result as `any`. Without the type annotation, the compiler will report an error.

The code in listing 13.25 produces the following output:

```
Formatted value: $324
Unformatted value: 323.95
```

13.6.3 *Using conditional types with type unions*

Conditional types can be used to filter type unions, allowing types to be easily selected or excluded from the set that the union contains, as shown in listing 13.26.

Listing 13.26   Filtering a type union in the index.ts file in the src folder

```
import { City, Person, Product, Employee} from "./dataTypes.js";

type Filter<T, U> = T extends U ? never : T;

function FilterArray<T, U>(data: T[],
        predicate: (item) => item is U): Filter<T, U>[] {
    return data.filter(item => !predicate(item)) as any;
}

let dataArray = [new Product("Kayak", 275), new Person("Bob", "London"),
    new Product("Lifejacket", 27.50)];

function isProduct(item: any): item is Product {
    return item instanceof Product;
}

let filteredData: Person[] = FilterArray(dataArray, isProduct);
filteredData.forEach(item => console.log(`Person: ${item.name}`));
```

When a conditional type is provided with a type union, the TypeScript compiler distributes the condition over each type in the union, creating what is known as a *distributive conditional type*. This effect is applied when a conditional type is used like a type union, like this, for example:

```
...
type filteredUnion = Filter<Product | Person, Product>
...
```

The TypeScript compiler applies the conditional type to each type in the union separately and then creates a union of the results, like this:

```
...
type filteredUnion = Filter<Product, Product> | Filter<Person, Product>
...
```

The `Filter<T, U>` conditional type evaluates to `never` when the first type parameter is the same as the second, producing this result:

```
...
type filteredUnion = never | Person
...
```

It isn't possible to have a union with `never`, so the compiler omits it from the union, with the result that `Filter<Product | Person, Product>` is equivalent to this type:

```
...
type filteredUnion = Person
...
```

The conditional type filters out any type that cannot be assigned to `Person` and returns the remaining types in the union. The `FilterArray<T, U>` method does the work of filtering an array using a predicate function and returns the `Filter<T, U>` type. The code in listing 13.26 produces the following result:

```
Person: Bob
```

USING THE BUILT-IN DISTRIBUTIVE CONDITIONAL TYPES

TypeScript provides a set of built-in conditional types that are used to filter unions, as described in table 13.7, allowing common tasks to be performed without the need to define custom types.

Table 13.7   The built-in distributive conditional types

Name	Description
`Exclude<T, U>`	This type excludes the types that can be assigned to U from T, equivalent to the `Filter<T, U>` type in listing 13.26.
`Extract<T, U>`	This type selects the types that can be assigned to U from T.
`NonNullable<T>`	This type excludes `null` and `undefined` from T.

13.6.4 *Using conditional types in type mappings*

Conditional types can be combined with type mappings, allowing different transformations to be applied to the properties in a type, which can provide greater flexibility than using either feature alone. Listing 13.27 shows a type mapping that uses a conditional type.

> **Listing 13.27   A mapping with a conditional type in the index.ts file in the src folder**

```
import { City, Person, Product, Employee} from "./dataTypes.js";

type changeProps<T, U, V> = {
    [P in keyof T]: T[P] extends U ? V: T[P]
};

type modifiedProduct = changeProps<Product, number, string>;

function convertProduct(p: Product): modifiedProduct {
    return { name: p.name, price: `$${p.price.toFixed(2)}` };
}

let kayak = convertProduct(new Product("Kayak", 275));
console.log(`Product: ${kayak.name}, ${kayak.price}`);
```

The `changeProps<T, U, V>` mapping selects the properties of type U and changes them to type V in the mapped type. This statement applies the mapping to the `Product` class, specifying that `number` properties should be made into `string` properties:

```
...
type modifiedProduct = changeProp<Product, number, string>;
...
```

The mapped type defines `name` and `price` properties, both of which are typed as `string`. The `modifiedProduct` type is used as the result of the `convertProduct` function, which accepts a `Product` object and returns an object that conforms to the shape of the mapped type by formatting the `price` property. The code in listing 13.27 produces the following output:

```
Product: Kayak, $275.00
```

13.6.5 *Identifying properties of a specific type*

A common requirement is to limit a type parameter so that it can be used only to specify a property that has a specific type. For example, the `Collection<T>` class in listing 13.25 defined a `total` method that accepts a property name and that should be restricted to `number` properties. This type of restriction can be achieved by combining the features described in the previous sections, as shown in listing 13.28.

> **Listing 13.28 Identifying properties in the index.ts file in the src folder**

```
import { City, Person, Product, Employee} from "./dataTypes.js";

type unionOfTypeNames<T, U> = {
    [P in keyof T] : T[P] extends U ? P : never;
};

type propertiesOfType<T, U> = unionOfTypeNames<T, U>[keyof T];

function total<T, P extends propertiesOfType<T, number>>(data: T[],
        propName: P): number {
    return data.reduce((t, item) => t += Number(item[propName]), 0);
}

let products = [new Product("Kayak", 275),
    new Product("Lifejacket", 48.95)];
console.log(`Total: ${total(products, "price")}`);
```

The method for identifying the properties is unusual, so I have broken the process into two statements to make it easier to explain. The first step is to use a type mapping that has a conditional statement.

```
...
type unionOfTypeNames<T, U> = {
    [P in keyof T] : T[P] extends U ? P : never;
};
...
```

The conditional statement checks the type of each property. If a property doesn't have the target type, then its type is changed to `never`. If a property does have the expected type, then its type is changed to the literal value that is the property name. This means that the mapping `unionOfTypeNames<Product, number>` produces the following mapped type:

```
...
{
    name: never,
    price: "price"
}
...
```

This odd mapped type provides the input to the second stage in the process, which is to use the indexed access operator to get a union of the types of the properties defined by the mapped type, like this:

```
...
type propertiesOfType<T, U> = unionOfTypeNames<T, U>[keyof T];
...
```

For the mapped type created by `unionOfTypeNames<Product, number>`, the indexed access operator produces the following union:

```
...
never | "price"
...
```

As noted previously, `never` is automatically removed from unions, leaving a union of literal value types that are the properties of the required type. The union of property names can then be used to restrict generic type parameters.

```
...
function total<T, P extends propertiesOfType<T, number>>(data: T[],
        propName: P): number {
    return data.reduce((t, item) => t += Number(item[propName]), 0);
}
...
```

The `propName` parameter of the `total` function can be used only with the names of the `number` properties in the type `T`, like this:

```
...
console.log(`Total: ${total(products, "price")}`);
...
```

This example shows how flexible the TypeScript generic type features can be but also illustrates how unusual steps can be required to achieve a specific effect. The code in listing 13.28 produces the following output:

```
Total: 323.95
```

13.6.6 *Inferring additional types in conditions*

There can be tension between the need to accept a wide range of types through a generic type parameter and the need to know the details of those types. As an example, listing 13.29 shows a function that accepts an array or a single object of a given type.

> **Listing 13.29** Defining a function in the index.ts file in the src folder

```
import { City, Person, Product, Employee} from "./dataTypes.js";

function getValue<T, P extends keyof T>(data: T, propName: P): T[P] {
    if (Array.isArray(data)) {
```

```
            return data[0][propName];
        } else {
            return data[propName];
        }
    }

    let products = [new Product("Kayak", 275),
        new Product("Lifejacket", 48.95)];
    console.log(`Array Value: ${getValue(products, "price")}`);
    console.log(`Single Total: ${getValue(products[0], "price")}`);
```

This code won't compile because the generic parameters don't correctly capture the relationship between the types. If the `total` function receives an array through the `data` parameter, it returns the value of the property specified by the `propName` parameter for the first item in the array. If the function receives a single object through `data`, then it returns the `propName` value for that object. The `propName` parameter is constrained using `keyof`, which is a problem when an array is used because `keyof` returns a union of the property names defined by the JavaScript array object and not the properties of the type contained in the array, which can be seen in the compiler error message.

```
src/index.ts(13,48): error TS2345: Argument of type '"price"' is not
assignable to parameter of type 'keyof Product[]'.
```

The TypeScript `infer` keyword can be used to infer types that are not explicitly expressed in the parameters of a conditional type. For the example, this means I can ask the compiler to infer the type of the objects in an array, as shown in listing 13.30.

> **Listing 13.30 Inferring the array type in the index.ts file in the src folder**

```
import { City, Person, Product, Employee} from "./dataTypes.js";

type targetKeys<T> = T extends (infer U)[] ? keyof U: keyof T;

function getValue<T, P extends targetKeys<T>>(data: T, propName: P): T[P] {
    if (Array.isArray(data)) {
        return data[0][propName];
    } else {
        return data[propName];
    }
}

let products = [new Product("Kayak", 275),
    new Product("Lifejacket", 48.95)];
console.log(`Array Value: ${getValue(products, "price")}`);
console.log(`Single Total: ${getValue(products[0], "price")}`);
```

Types are inferred with the `infer` keyword, and they introduce a generic type whose type will be inferred by the compiler when the conditional type is resolved, as shown in figure 13.5.

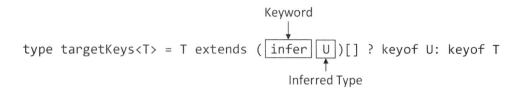

Figure 13.5 Inferring a type in a conditional type

In listing 13.30, the type U is inferred if T is an array. The type of U is inferred by the compiler from the generic type parameter T when the type is resolved. The effect is that the type of targetKeys<Product> and targetKeys<Product[]> both produce the "name" | "price" union. The conditional type can be employed to constrain the property of the getValue<T, P> function, providing consistent typing for both single objects and arrays. The code in listing 13.30 produces the following output:

```
Array Value: 275
Single Total: 275
```

INFERRING TYPES OF FUNCTIONS

The compiler can also infer types in generic types that accept functions, as shown in listing 13.31.

Listing 13.31 Using type inference for a function in the index.ts file in the src folder

```
import { City, Person, Product, Employee} from "./dataTypes.js";

type Result<T> = T extends (...args: any) => infer R ? R : never;

function processArray<T,
        Func extends (T) => any>(data: T[], func: Func): Result<Func>[] {
    return data.map(item => func(item));
}

let selectName = (p: Product) => p.name;

let products = [new Product("Kayak", 275),
    new Product("Lifejacket", 48.95)];
let names: string[] = processArray(products, selectName);
names.forEach(name => console.log(`Name: ${name}`));
```

The Result<T> conditional type uses the infer keyword to obtain the result type for a function that accepts an object of type T and produces an any result. The use of type inference allows functions that process a specific type to be used while ensuring that the result of the processArray function is a specific type, based on the result of the function provided for the func parameter. The selectName function returns the string value of the name property of a Product object, and the inference means that Result<(...args:Product) => string)> is correctly identified as string, allowing the processArray function to return a string[] result. The code in listing 13.31 produces the following output:

```
Name: Kayak
Name: Lifejacket
```

Type inference in conditional types can be difficult to figure out, and TypeScript provides a series of built-in conditional types that are useful for dealing with functions, as described in table 13.8.

Table 13.8   The built-in conditional types with inference

Name	Description
Parameters<T>	This conditional type selects the types of each function parameter, expressed as a tuple.
ReturnType<T>	This conditional type selects the function result type, equivalent to Result<T> in listing 13.31.
ConstructorParameters<T>	The conditional type selects the types of each parameter of a constructor function, expressed as a tuple, as demonstrated after the table.
InstanceType<T>	This conditional type returns the result type of a constructor function.

The ConstructorParameters<T> and InstanceType<T> conditional types operate on constructor functions and are most useful when describing the types of functions that create objects whose type is specified as a generic type parameter, as shown in listing 13.32.

> **Listing 13.32   Using the built-in conditional types in the index.ts file in the src folder**

```
import { City, Person, Product, Employee} from "./dataTypes.js";

function makeObject<T extends new (...args: any) => any>
        (constructor: T, ...args: ConstructorParameters<T>)
            : InstanceType<T> {
    return  new constructor(...args as any[]);
}

let prod: Product = makeObject(Product, "Kayak", 275);
let city: City = makeObject(City, "London", 8136000);

[prod, city].forEach(item => console.log(`Name: ${item.name}`));
```

The makeObject function creates objects from classes without advanced knowledge of which class is required. The ConstructorParameters<T> and InstanceType<T> conditional types infer the parameters and result for the constructor of the class provided as the first generic type parameter, ensuring that the makeObject function receives the correct types for creating an object and whose type accurately reflects the type of the object that is created. The code in listing 13.32 produces the following output:

```
Name: Kayak
Name: London
```

Summary

In this chapter, I described the advanced generic type features that TypeScript provides. These are not required in every project, but they are invaluable when the more basic features cannot describe the types that an application requires.

- TypeScript supports JavaScript collections with generic type parameters and provides iterators that enforce type safety.
- Index types allow an object property to be used as a key.
- Mapped types transform the properties of an existing type. TypeScript provides a set of built-in transformations for creating mapped types.
- Conditional types are expressions evaluated to select one type based on another and give fine-grained control over generic types.

In the next chapter, I introduce decorators, which allow the behavior of class features, such as methods and properties, to be transformed without altering their implementation.

Using decorators

14

This chapter covers

- Defining and applying decorators
- Decorating classes, methods, properties, accessors, and auto-accessors
- Using decorator context data
- Creating decorators with a factory function
- Accumulating state data in decorators

Decorators are a forthcoming addition to the JavaScript language that transform features defined by classes. TypeScript has long supported an experimental version of decorators, used mainly in Angular development, but TypeScript 5 has added support for the version of decorators that will be adopted in a future release of the JavaScript specification. Table 14.1 summarizes the chapter.

Table 14.1 Chapter summary

Problem	Solution	Listing
Transform a class feature	Define and apply a decorator	9–12, 16–30, 38–41
Get details of the feature to be transformed	Use the decorator context object	13–15
Configure each application of a decorator	Use a factory function	31–37
Perform initial setup for a decorator	Use an initializer function	42–44
Accumulate state data	Define a variable outside of the decorator function or factory function	45, 46

For quick reference, table 14.2 lists the TypeScript compiler options used in this chapter.

Table 14.2 The TypeScript compiler options used in this chapter

Name	Description
`module`	This option specifies the module format, as described in chapter 5.
`outDir`	This option specifies the directory in which the JavaScript files will be placed.
`rootDir`	This option specifies the root directory that the compiler will use to locate TypeScript files.
`target`	This option specifies the version of the JavaScript language that the compiler will target in its output.

14.1 Preparing for this chapter

To prepare the project for this chapter, open a new command prompt, navigate to a convenient location, and create a folder named `decorators`. Run the commands shown in listing 14.1 to navigate into the new folder and tell the Node Package Manager (NPM) to create a `package.json` file, which will track the packages added to the project.

> **TIP** You can download the example project for this chapter—and for all the other chapters in this book—from https://github.com/manningbooks/essential-typescript-5.

Listing 14.1 Creating the package.json file

```
cd decorators
npm init --yes
```

Run the commands shown in listing 14.2 in the `decorators` folder to download and install the packages required for this chapter.

Listing 14.2   Adding packages

```
npm install --save-dev typescript@5.0.2
npm install --save-dev tsc-watch@6.0.0
```

To create a configuration file for the TypeScript compiler, add a file called `tsconfig.json` to the `decorators` folder with the content shown in listing 14.3.

Listing 14.3   The contents of the tsconfig.json file in the decorators folder

```
{
    "compilerOptions": {
        "target": "ES2022",
        "outDir": "./dist",
        "rootDir": "./src",
        "module": "Node16"
    }
}
```

These configuration settings tell the TypeScript compiler to generate code for the most recent JavaScript implementations, using the `src` folder to look for TypeScript files and using the `dist` folder for its outputs. The `module` setting tells the compiler to use the same mechanism that Node.js uses to determine the module format.

To configure NPM so that it can start the compiler, and to specify the module format, add the configuration entry shown in listing 14.4 to the `package.json` file.

Listing 14.4   Configuring NPM in the package.json file in the decorators folder

```
{
  "name": "decorators",
  "version": "1.0.0",
  "description": "",
  "main": "index.js",
  "scripts": {
    "start": "tsc-watch --onsuccess \"node dist/index.js\""
  },
  "keywords": [],
  "author": "",
  "license": "ISC",
  "devDependencies": {
    "tsc-watch": "^6.0.0",
    "typescript": "^5.0.2"
  },
  "type": "module"
}
```

Create the `decorators/src` folder and add to it a file named `product.ts`, with the contents shown in listing 14.5.

Listing 14.5   The contents of the product.ts file in the src folder

```
export class Product {

    constructor(public name: string, public price: number) {}
```

```
getDetails(): string {
    return `Name: ${this.name}, Price: $$${this.price}`;
}
```
}

Add a file named `city.ts` to the `src` folder with the content shown in listing 14.6.

Listing 14.6   The contents of the city.ts file in the src folder

```
export class City {

    constructor(public name: string, public population: number) {}

    getSummary(): string {
        return `Name: ${this.name}, Population: ${this.population}`;
    }
}
```

To create the entry point for the example project, add a file named `index.ts` to the `src` folder, with the content shown in listing 14.7.

Listing 14.7   The contents of the index.ts file in the src folder

```
import { City } from "./city.js";
import { Product } from "./product.js";

let city = new City("London", 8_982_000);
let product = new Product("Kayak", 275);

console.log(city.getSummary());
console.log(product.getDetails());
```

Run the command shown in listing 14.8 in the `decorators` folder to start the compiler so that the compiled code is executed automatically.

Listing 14.8   Starting the compiler

```
npm start
```

The compiler will start and produce the following output:

```
08:12:02 - Starting compilation in watch mode...
08:12:04 - Found 0 errors. Watching for file changes.
Name: London, Population: 8982000
Name: Kayak, Price: $275
```

14.2 *Understanding decorators*

There are different types of decorators. They all work in largely the same way, but each type is responsible for transforming a different aspect of a class. Each type of decorator transforms a different part of the class:

- *Class decorators* transform the entire class.
- *Method decorators* transform a method.
- *Field decorators* transform a class field.
- *Accessor decorators* transform a class accessor or auto-accessor.

Decorators get their name from the way they are applied because they are used to decorate class features without otherwise modifying them. Listing 14.9 applies a decorator to the `Product` class. This decorator doesn't exist yet, so the TypeScript will report an error for this code.

```
import { time } from "./methodDecorator.js";

export class Product {

    constructor(public name: string, public price: number) {}

    @time
    getDetails(): string {
        return `Name: ${this.name}, Price: $${this.price}`;
    }
}
```

Decorators are written using standard TypeScript/JavaScript features and are imported like any other module. In this case, I have imported a feature named `time` from the `methodDecorator.js` file. The syntax for applying a decorator is unlike any other language feature and uses the @ character, followed by the name of the decorator, which is `time` in this example, as shown in figure 14.1. This is an example of a *method decorator* because it has been applied to a method.

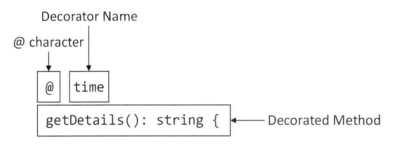

Figure 14.1   Applying a method decorator

Decorators work by replacing the feature to which they are applied. For a method decorator, this means providing the JavaScript runtime with a replacement method that will be used instead of the one to which the decorator has been applied. The job of the `time` decorator applied in listing 14.9 is to provide a replacement for the `getDetails` method.

To define the decorator, add a file named `methodDecorator.ts` to the `src` folder with the content shown in listing 14.10.

```
export function time(...args) {
    return function() : string {
        return "Hello, Decorator!"
    }
}
```

Decorators are functions, and the decorator defined in listing 14.10 is named `time` and is exported like any TypeScript or JavaScript feature so that it can be used in other code files.

When the decorator is applied to a method, the `time` function will be invoked and the function it returns will be used as a replacement. There are two functions listing 14.10: the outer decorator function that defines the decorator, and the inner function that will be used as the replacement method, as shown in figure 14.2.

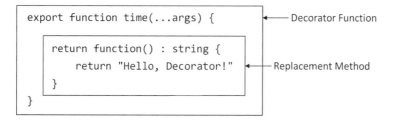

Figure 14.2   The basic structure of a method decorator

Save the changes, and you will see the following output once the code is compiled and executed:

```
Name: London, Population: 8982000
Hello, Decorator!
```

Decorators can be applied to multiple classes, and each will receive its replacement method from the decorator function. Listing 14.11 applies the test decorator to the `City` class.

Listing 14.11   Applying a decorator in the city.ts file in the src folder

```
import { time } from "./methodDecorator.js";

export class City {

    constructor(public name: string, public population: number) {}

    @time
    getSummary(): string {
        return `Name: ${this.name}, Population: ${this.population}`;
    }
}
```

The `time` decorator has been applied to two methods. The `time` function will be called once for each decorated method, and the replacements that are returned will be used instead of the method defined by the classes, producing the following results:

```
Hello, Decorator!
Hello, Decorator!
```

The replacement class features produced by decorators must be suitable replacements. The replacement method produced by the `time` decorator takes no arguments and returns a `string` value, which means that it matches the signature of the decorated methods. The compiler will report an error if there is a mismatch between the types used by the decorated method and the replacement method. Listing 14.12 adds a new method to the `Product` class that returns a number value.

> **Listing 14.12   Adding a method in the product.ts file in the src folder**

```
import { time } from "./methodDecorator.js";

export class Product {

    constructor(public name: string, public price: number) {}

    @time
    getDetails(): string {
        return `Name: ${this.name}, Price: $${this.price}`;
    }

    @time
    getPrice(): number {
        return this.price;
    }
}
```

The compiler will report the following error for this change:

```
src/product.ts(12,6): error TS1270: Decorator function return type '() =>
string' is not assignable to type 'void | (() => number)'.
  Type '() => string' is not assignable to type '() => number'.
    Type 'string' is not assignable to type 'number'.
```

The TypeScript compiler has realized that the decorator doesn't produce a suitable replacement for the `getPrice` method.

14.2.1   *Using decorator context data*

The `time` decorator demonstrates the basic functionality, but it works by replacing every method with a function that always does the same thing, which isn't useful in a real project.

When a method decorator function is invoked, it is provided with two arguments, which I ignored in the previous section. The first argument is the original method to which the decorator has been applied, which allows the replacement method to invoke the original method. The second argument is an object that implements the `Class-MethodDecoratorContext` interface, and which provides helpful context about the method to which the decorator has been applied. The most useful `ClassMethod-DecoratorContext` members are described in table 14.3.

Table 14.3 Useful ClassMethodDecoratorContext Members

Name	Description
`kind`	This property returns the string `method`, indicating that the decorator has been applied to a method. The context objects provided for other types of decorators define this property but return different values, as demonstrated in later examples.
`name`	This property returns a `string	symbol` value that contains the name of the method to which the decorator has been applied.
`static`	This `boolean` property returns `true` if the decorator has been applied to a static method and `false` otherwise.
`private`	This `boolean` property returns `true` if the decorator has been applied to a private method and `false` otherwise.
`addInitializer()`	This method is used to register an initialization function, as explained in the "Using an initializer" section.

These arguments allow the decorator function to build on the features of the original method, as shown in listing 14.13. (All of the statements in this listing have changed, so I have not marked any of them in bold).

Listing 14.13 Using decorator context in the methodDecorator.ts file in the src folder

```
export function time(method: any, ctx: ClassMethodDecoratorContext) {
    const methodName = String(ctx.name);
    return function(this: any, ...args: any[]) {
        const start = performance.now();
        console.log(`${methodName} started`);
        const result = method.call(this, ...args);
        const duration = (performance.now() - start).toFixed(2);
        console.log(`${methodName} ended ${duration} ms`);
        return result;
    }
}
```

There is a lot to unpack here, so I'll go through and explain what the key statements do, starting with the declaration for the decorator function:

```
...
export function time(method: any, ctx: ClassMethodDecoratorContext) {
...
```

Using type annotations for decorators can be complex, as I demonstrate in the next example, and it is often easier to use the `any` type when a decorator is written so it can be applied to all methods, as in this example.

The next statement creates a constant `string` value containing the name of the method:

```
...
const methodName = String(ctx.name);
...
```

The `name` property defined by the `ClassMethodDecoratorContext` returns a `string | symbol` value, which accommodates the fact that method names can be defined using the `symbol` type, which is often done in automatically generated code to ensure that a method name is unique. I want a `string` value, so I use the `String` value and assign the result to a constant. I placed this statement outside of the replacement method so that the conversion to a string is performed only once for each method to which the decorator has been applied.

The next statement defines the replacement method, which will be invoked instead of the original method defined by the class:

```
...
return function(this: any, ...args: any[]) {
...
```

The parameters allow me to invoke the original method, passing along any arguments that are received and preserving context with the `this` value, with this statement within the replacement method:

```
...
const result = method.call(this, ...args);
...
```

I described the use of the `method.call` function in chapter 3, and the effect is that the decorator can be applied to any method, and the replacement method will invoke the original using whatever arguments and context are received. The results are assigned to a constant, which is used as the result of the replacement method, ensuring that the replacement is compatible with the original method.

The rest of the statements in the replacement method write messages that indicate when the replacement method is invoked and time how long it takes to invoke the original method, using the JavaScript `performance` API, which provides a high-resolution timer. Save the changes and you will see output similar to the following once the code is compiled and executed:

```
getSummary started
getSummary ended 4.03 ms
Name: London, Population: 8982000
getDetails started
getDetails ended 0.15 ms
Name: Kayak, Price: $275
```

The output shows that the `getSummary` method is invoked first, and took 4.03 milliseconds, followed by the `getDetails` method, which took 0.15 milliseconds.

The `time` decorator has been applied to three methods in the example, but there is only output from two methods because only the `getSummary` and `getDetails` methods are invoked when the code is executed. The decorator has also been applied to the `getPrice` method defined in listing 14.12, but this method is never invoked and so generates no output.

> **NOTE** The difference in the durations reported arises because there is some initial setup that is being included in the timings. This example is about defining decorators and the numbers reported don't matter, but as a rule, you should measure performance only once the runtime tasks have been completed and take repeated measurements. See the "Accumulating state data" section for a revised decorator that separates the initialization overhead from its timings.

14.2.2 Using specific types in a decorator

I used the `any` type so widely in listing 14.13 because it makes it easy to write decorators that can be applied to any method, regardless of the defining class, parameter types, and result type. This technique is well-suited to decorators that will invoke the original method, which ensures that the types are preserved.

A different approach is required for decorators that need some knowledge of the methods to which they are applied, as shown in listing 14.14, which defines a decorator with generic type parameters.

Listing 14.14 Adding type parameters in the methodDecorator.ts file in the src folder

```
interface HasGetPrice {
    getPrice(): number;
}

export function time<This extends HasGetPrice, Args extends any[], Result>(
        method: (This, Args) => Result,
        ctx: ClassMethodDecoratorContext<This, (This, Args) => Result>) {
    const methodName = String(ctx.name);
    return function(this: This, ...args: Args) : Result {
        const start = performance.now();
        console.log(`${methodName} started`);
        const result = method.call(this, ...args);
        const duration = (performance.now() - start).toFixed(2);
        console.log(`${methodName} ended ${duration} ms`);
        return result;
    }
}
```

The decorator function has three generic type parameters, which represent the type of the class that has been decorated, the argument types, and the result:

```
...
export function time<This extends HasGetPrice, Args extends any[], Result>(
        method: (This, Args) => Result,
        ctx: ClassMethodDecoratorContext<This, (This, Args) => Result>) {
...
```

The generic type parameters affect the decorator function parameters so that the `method` parameter is a function annotated with the generic types:

```
...
export function time<This extends HasGetPrice, Args, Result>(
        method: (This, Args) => Result,
        ctx: ClassMethodDecoratorContext<This, (This, Args) => Result>) {
...
```

The `ClassMethodDecoratorContext` parameter has two generic type parameters, which specify the decorated class and the decorated method signature:

```
...
export function test<This extends HasGetPrice, Args, Result>(
        method: (This, Args) => Result,
        ctx: ClassMethodDecoratorContext<This, (This, Args) => Result>) {
...
```

The final change is to apply the same types to the replacement method, which ensures that the original method and its replacement use the same types:

```
...
return function(this: This, ...args: Args) : Result {
...
```

In this example, I constrained the `This` type so that the decorator can only be applied to classes that have a `getPrice` method that returns a `number`, which I have defined using an interface. Only one of the two classes to which the decorator has been applied conforms to the interface, and so the compiler produces the following error:

```
src/city.ts(7,6): error TS1241: Unable to resolve signature of method
decorator when called as an expression.
```

The compiler uses the decorator's generic types and determines that the `City` class doesn't conform to the generic type constraint.

Method decorators don't typically constrain the classes to which they can be applied, and it is more common to define restrictions that are specific to the method signature, as shown in listing 14.15.

Listing 14.15   Constraining the result type in the methodDecorator.ts file in the src folder

```
// interface HasGetPrice {
//     getPrice(): number;
// }

export function time<This, Args extends any[],
            Result extends string | number>(
        method: (This, Args) => Result,
        ctx: ClassMethodDecoratorContext<This, (This, Args) => Result>) {
    const methodName = String(ctx.name);
    return function(this: This, ...args: Args) : Result {
        const start = performance.now();
        console.log(`${methodName} started`);
        const result = method.call(this, ...args);
        const duration = (performance.now() - start).toFixed(2);
        console.log(`${methodName} ended ${duration} ms`);
        return result;
    }
}
```

The generic type parameters allow the decorator to be applied to any method that returns a `string` or a `number`, with no restriction on other class features. Save the changes and you will see results similar to the following:

```
getSummary started
getSummary ended 3.90 ms
Name: London, Population: 8982000
getDetails started
getDetails ended 0.12 ms
Name: Kayak, Price: $275
```

14.3 Using the other decorator types

Methods are only one of the class features for which decorators can be created. All types of decorator work in much the same way, but each has its type of context object, as shown in table 14.4.

Table 14.4   The Decorator Types and Context Interfaces

Class Feature	Context Type
Class	ClassDecoratorContext
Methods	ClassMethodDecoratorContext
Fields	ClassFieldDecoratorContext
Accessors	ClassGetterDecoratorContext, ClassSetterDecoratorContext
Auto-accessors	ClassAccessorDecoratorContext

There is also a `DecoratorContext` interface, which is the union of all the context types and can be used in decorators that are applied to different class features.

In the sections that follow, I create each type of decorator and show how it can be used to transform a class feature.

14.3.1 Creating a class decorator

Class constructors are applied to entire classes, and the most common use of this type of decorator is to perform a transformation by creating a subclass that adds new features. Class decorators require generic type parameters to provide the TypeScript compiler with enough information to avoid errors. Add a file named `classDecorator.ts` to the `src` folder with the content shown in listing 14.16.

Listing 14.16   The contents of the classDecorator.ts file in the src folder

```
export function serialize<T extends new (...args: any) => any>(
    originalClass: T, ctx: ClassDecoratorContext) {

    const className = String(ctx.name);

    return class extends originalClass {

        serialize() {
```

```
                console.log(`${className}: ${JSON.stringify(this)}`);
            }
        };
    }
```

The important part of the generic type parameter is the constraint, without which the TypeScript compiler generates an error because the type of the replacement class doesn't match the original. The decorator adds a method named `serialize`, which writes out the class name and a JSON representation of the object on which the method is called.

The name of the method is obtained from the `ClassDecoratorContext` parameter, which defines the properties and method shown in table 14.5.

Table 14.5   The ClassDecoratorContext Properties and Method

Name	Description
kind	This property returns the string `class`, indicating that the decorator has been applied to a class.
name	This property returns a `string	symbol` value that contains the name of the class to which the decorator has been applied.
addInitializer()	This method is used to register an initialization function, as explained in the Using an initializer section.

Listing 14.17 applies the decorator to the `Product` class.

Listing 14.17   Applying a decorator in the product.ts file in the src folder

```
import { time } from "./methodDecorator.js";
import { serialize } from "./classDecorator.js";

@serialize
export class Product {

    constructor(public name: string, public price: number) {}

    @time
    getDetails(): string {
        return `Name: ${this.name}, Price: $${this.price}`;
    }

    @time
    getPrice(): number {
        return this.price;
    }
}
```

One drawback of class decorators is they don't change the definition of the type they transform, which means that the `serialize` method added by the decorator in listing 14.16 doesn't become part of the `Product` type, as shown in listing 14.18.

Listing 14.18   Invoking an additional method in the index.ts file in the src folder

```
import { City } from "./city.js";
import { Product } from "./product.js";

let city = new City("London", 8_982_000);
let product = new Product("Kayak", 275);

console.log(city.getSummary());
console.log(product.getDetails());
```

(product as any).serialize();

I have to use the `any` type to invoke the method added by the decorator, producing the following output, which includes a JSON representation of the `Product` object:

```
getSummary started
getSummary ended 4.43 ms
Name: London, Population: 8982000
getDetails started
getDetails ended 0.16 ms
Name: Kayak, Price: $275
```
Product: {"name":"Kayak","price":275}

One way to improve the decorator types is to introduce an interface and a predicate function for type guarding, as shown in listing 14.19.

Listing 14.19   Adding a type guard in the classDecorator.ts file in the src folder

```
export function serialize<T extends new (...args: any) => any>(
    originalClass: T, ctx: ClassDecoratorContext) {

    const className = String(ctx.name);

    return class extends originalClass implements Serializeable {

        serialize() {
            console.log(`${className}: ${JSON.stringify(this)}`);
        }
    };
}

export interface Serializeable {
    serialize();
}

export function isSerializeable(target): target is Serializeable {
    return typeof target.serialize === "function";
}
```

The `Serializeable` interface and its type guard allow type-safe access to the `serialize` method on objects created from the class transformed by the decorator, as shown in listing 14.20.

Listing 14.20   Using a type guard in the index.ts file in the src folder

```
import { City } from "./city.js";
import { Product } from "./product.js";
import { isSerializeable } from "./classDecorator.js";

let city = new City("London", 8_982_000);
let product = new Product("Kayak", 275);

console.log(city.getSummary());
console.log(product.getDetails());

if (isSerializeable(product)) {
    product.serialize();
}
```

This code produces the same output as the previous example but doesn't require the use of the `any` type.

14.3.2 *Creating a field decorator*

Field decorators can change the initial value of a class property. Add a class named `fieldDecorator.ts` to the `src` folder with the content shown in listing 14.21.

Listing 14.21   The contents of the fieldDecorator.ts file in the src folder

```
export function double(notused: any, ctx: ClassFieldDecoratorContext) {
    return function(initialValue) {
        return initialValue * 2;
    }
}
```

Field decorators return a function that receives the initial value of the field and returns the transformed value. The `double` decorator multiples the initial value by 2 and returns the result.

Field decorator functions define two parameters for consistency with other decorator types, but the first parameter isn't used. The second parameter is a context object that implements the `ClassFieldDecoratorContext` interface, with the most useful features described in table 14.6.

Table 14.6   Useful ClassFieldDecoratorContext Members

Name	Description
kind	This property returns the string `field`, indicating that the decorator has been applied to a field.
name	This property returns a `string	symbol` value that contains the name of the field to which the decorator has been applied.
static	This `boolean` property returns `true` if the decorator has been applied to a static field and `false` otherwise.

Table 14.6 Useful ClassFieldDecoratorContext Members *(continued)*

Name	Description
`private`	This `boolean` property returns `true` if the decorator has been applied to a private field and `false` otherwise.
`addInitializer()`	This method is used to register an initialization function, as explained in the Using an initializer section.

Listing 14.22. Adds a field to the `Product` class and applies the `double` decorator.

Listing 14.22 Adding a decorated field in the product.ts file in the src folder

```
import { time } from "./methodDecorator.js";
import { serialize } from "./classDecorator.js";
import { double } from "./fieldDecorator.js";

@serialize
export class Product {
    @double
    private taxRate: number = 20;

    constructor(public name: string, public price: number) {}

    @time
    getDetails(): string {
        return `Name: ${this.name}, Price: $${this.getPrice()}`;
    }

    @time
    getPrice(): number {
        return this.price * (1 + (this.taxRate/100));
    }
}
```

I have added a `taxRate` property, which is used in the `getPrice` method to calculate the product price, based on the value of the `price` property. The initial value assigned to the field is 20, but the `double` decorator will change this value, which can be seen in the output:

```
getSummary started
getSummary ended 4.03 ms
Name: London, Population: 8982000
getDetails started
getPrice started
getPrice ended 0.15 ms
getDetails ended 0.44 ms
Name: Kayak, Price: $385
Product: {"name":"Kayak","price":275,"taxRate":40}
```

Bear in mind that field decorators are transforming the class, which means that any value assigned by the constructor when an object is created will replace the value set by the decorator.

Listing 14.23 revises the field decorator to introduce generic type parameters.

Listing 14.23   Using generic type parameters in the fieldDecorator.ts file in the src folder

```
export function double<This, FieldType extends number>(
        notused: any, ctx: ClassFieldDecoratorContext<This, FieldType>) {
    return function (initialValue: FieldType) {
        return initialValue * 2;
    }
}
```

The `This` and `FieldType` generic parameters allow constraints to be applied to both the classes and the fields to which the decorator can be applied. In listing 14.23, I constrained the decorator so that it can only be applied to `number` fields. The decorator in listing 14.23 produces the same output as the one in listing 14.22.

14.3.3   *Creating an accessor decorator*

Accessor decorators are similar to method decorators because getters and setters are functions. Add a file named `accessorDecorator.ts` to the `src` folder with the content shown in listing 14.24.

Listing 14.24   The contents of the accessorDecorator.ts file in the src folder

```
export function log(accessor: any,
        ctx: ClassSetterDecoratorContext | ClassGetterDecoratorContext) {
    const name = String(ctx.name);
    return function(this: any, ...args: any[]) {
        if (ctx.kind === "getter") {
            const result = accessor.call(this, ...args);
            console.log(`${name} get returned ${result}`);
            return result;
        } else {
            console.log(`${name} set to ${args}`);
            return accessor.call(this, ...args);
        }
    }
}
```

Accessor decorator functions receive two arguments, providing the original accessor function and a context object. The type of the context object will be `ClassSetter-DecoratorContext` when setters are decorated and `ClassGetterDecoratorContext` when getters are decorated. These two context types are similar, and the most useful members are shown in table 14.7.

Table 14.7 Useful Accessor Context Type Members

Name	Description
kind	This property returns the string `getter` or `setter`, indicating which part of the accessor has been decorated.
name	This property returns a `string	symbol` value that contains the name of the accessor to which the decorator has been applied.
static	This `boolean` property returns `true` if the decorator has been applied to a static accessor and `false` otherwise.
private	This `boolean` property returns `true` if the decorator has been applied to a private accessor and `false` otherwise.
addInitializer()	This method is used to register an initialization function, as explained in the Using an initializer section.

The decorator defined in listing 14.24 uses the `kind` property to determine whether a getter or a setter has been decorated. For getters, the replacement function calls the original and writes out the result to the console. For setters, the replacement function writes out the arguments it has received and passes them on to the original setter function. Listing 14.25 adds a getter and a setter to the `Product` class and decorates both of them.

Listing 14.25 Using an accessor decorator in the product.ts file in the src folder

```
import { time } from "./methodDecorator.js";
import { serialize } from "./classDecorator.js";
import { double } from "./fieldDecorator.js";
import { log } from "./accessorDecorator.js";

@serialize
export class Product {
    @double
    private taxRate: number = 20;

    constructor(public name: string, public price: number) {}

    @time
    getDetails(): string {
        return `Name: ${this.name}, Price: $${this.getPrice()}`;
    }

    @time
    getPrice(): number {
        return this.price * (1 + (this.taxRate/100));
    }

    @log
```

```
    get tax() { return this.taxRate };

    @log
    set tax(newValue) { this.taxRate = newValue};
}
```

Listing 14.26 uses the new `Product` features so the output generated by the decorator will be produced.

Listing 14.26   Using a class feature in the index.ts file in the src folder

```
import { City } from "./city.js";
import { Product } from "./product.js";
import { isSerializeable } from "./classDecorator.js";

let city = new City("London", 8_982_000);
let product = new Product("Kayak", 275);

console.log(city.getSummary());
console.log(product.getDetails());

console.log(`Get Product tax: ${product.tax}`);
product.tax = 30;

if (isSerializeable(product)) {
    product.serialize();
}
```

This code produces the following output when it is executed, showing the messages created by the accessor decorator as the getter and setter are used:

```
getSummary started
getSummary ended 4.08 ms
Name: London, Population: 8982000
getDetails started
getPrice started
getPrice ended 0.23 ms
getDetails ended 0.72 ms
Name: Kayak, Price: $385
tax get returned 40
Get Product tax: 40
tax set to 30
Product: {"name":"Kayak","price":275,"taxRate":30}
```

Listing 14.27 revises the accessor decorator to introduce generic type parameters.

Listing 14.27   Using type parameters in the accessorDecorator.ts file in the src folder

```
export function log<This, ValueType extends number>(
    setter: (ValueType) => void,
    ctx: ClassSetterDecoratorContext<This, ValueType>)
        : ((ValueType) => void);
export function log<This, ValueType extends number>(
    getter: () => ValueType,
```

```
    ctx: ClassGetterDecoratorContext<This, ValueType>) : () => ValueType;

export function log(accessor: any, ctx: any) {
    const name = String(ctx.name);
    return function(this: any, ...args: any[]) {
        if (ctx.kind === "getter") {
            const result = accessor.call(this, ...args);
            console.log(`${name} get returned ${result}`);
            return result;
        } else {
            console.log(`${name} set to ${args}`);
            return accessor.call(this, ...args);
        }
    }
}
```

The decorator can be applied to getters and setters, each of which requires a different combination of types. The simplest way to describe those types to the TypeScript compiler is to use function overloads, which allow me to describe the type of accessor and the context object.

As part of the function type overloads in listing 14.27, I constrained the getter and setter types so the decorator can only be applied to `number` accessors. The decorator produces the same output as the one in listing 14.26.

14.3.4 *Creating an auto-accessor decorator*

The last type of decorator is applied to auto-accessors and combines the getter and setter in a single parameter. Add a file named `autoAccessorDecorator.ts` to the `src` folder with the content shown in listing 14.28.

> **Listing 14.28 The contents of the autoAccessorDecorator.ts in the src folder**

```
export function autolog(
        accessor: any,
        ctx: ClassAccessorDecoratorContext)  {
    const name = String(ctx.name);
    return {
        get() {
            const result = accessor.get.call(this);
            console.log(`Auto-accessor ${name} get returned ${result}`);
            return result;
        },
        set(value) {
            console.log(`Auto-accessor ${name} set to ${value}`);
            return accessor.set.call(this, value);
        },
        init(value) {
            console.log(`Auto-accessor initialized to ${value}`);
            return value;
        }
    }
}
```

The first argument received by the decorator is an object with `get` and `set` functions, which correspond to the getter and setter created by the auto-accessor. The second argument is an object that implements the `ClassAccessorDecoratorContext` interface, which provides the properties and method described in table 14.8.

Table 14.8   Useful ClassAccessorDecoratorContext properties and method

Name	Description
kind	This property returns the string `accessor`, indicating that an accessor has been decorated.
name	This property returns a `string	symbol` value that contains the name of the accessor to which the decorator has been applied.
static	This `boolean` property returns `true` if the decorator has been applied to a static accessor and `false` otherwise.
private	This `boolean` property returns `true` if the decorator has been applied to a private accessor and `false` otherwise.
addInitializer()	This method is used to register an initialization function, as explained in the Using an initializer section.

The result from the decorator is an object that defines `get` and `set` properties with replacement getter and setter functions, along with an `init` property that is invoked when the decorated accessor is initialized and whose result is used to replace the initial value. The `get`, `set`, and `init` properties are all optional, which means that the decorator can define only the properties for the features it wishes to transform.

The decorator in listing 14.28 logs calls to the getter and setter and also writes a message during initialization. Listing 14.29 replaces the existing getter and setter in the `Product` class with a decorated auto-accessor.

Listing 14.29   Adding an auto-accessor in the product.ts file in the src folder

```
import { time } from "./methodDecorator.js";
import { serialize } from "./classDecorator.js";
import { double } from "./fieldDecorator.js";
import { log } from "./accessorDecorator.js";
import { autolog } from "./autoAccessorDecorator.js";

@serialize
export class Product {
    // @double
    // private taxRate: number = 20;

    constructor(public name: string, public price: number) {}

    @time
    getDetails(): string {
        return `Name: ${this.name}, Price: $${this.getPrice()}`;
```

```
    }

    @time
    getPrice(): number {
        return this.price * (1 + (this.tax/100));
    }

    // @log
    // get tax() { return this.taxRate };

    // @log
    // set tax(newValue) { this.taxRate = newValue};

    @autolog
    accessor tax: number = 20;
}
```

Save the changes and the output will show the messages produced by the new decorator, like this:

```
Auto-accessor initialized to 20
getSummary started
getSummary ended 0.32 ms
Name: London, Population: 8982000
getDetails started
getPrice started
Auto-accessor tax get returned 20
getPrice ended 0.48 ms
getDetails ended 0.93 ms
Name: Kayak, Price: $330
Auto-accessor tax get returned 20
Get Product tax: 20
Auto-accessor tax set to 30
Product: {"name":"Kayak","price":275}
```

Typescript provides built-in interface types for describing auto-accessors with generic type parameters, as shown in listing 14.30.

Listing 14.30 Adding type parameters in the autoAccessorDecorator.ts file in the src folder

```
export function autolog<This, ValueType extends number>(
        accessor: ClassAccessorDecoratorTarget<This, ValueType>,
        ctx: ClassAccessorDecoratorContext<This, ValueType>)
            : ClassAccessorDecoratorResult<This, ValueType> {
    const name = String(ctx.name);
    return {
        get() {
            const result = accessor.get.call(this);
            console.log(`Auto-accessor ${name} get returned ${result}`);
            return result;
        },
        set(value) {
            console.log(`Auto-accessor ${name} set to ${value}`);
            return accessor.set.call(this, value);
        },
        init(value) {
```

```
                console.log(`Auto-accessor initialized to ${value}`);
                return value;
            }
        }
    }
```

The `ClassAccessorDecoratorTarget` interface is used to represent the original accessor and defines `get` and `set` properties, which return typed functions. The `ClassAccessorDecoratorResult` interface represents the decorator result, with the optional `get`, `set`, and `init` properties. In listing 14.30, I used the generic type parameters to restrict the decorator so that it can only be applied to `number` auto-accessors. The decorator produces the same output as the one in listing 14.29.

14.4   *Passing an additional argument to a decorator*

Decorators can be created within a factory function, which receives an additional configuration argument when the decorator is applied. This allows the behavior of decorators to be customized when they are applied to class features. Listing 14.31 shows the addition of a factory function to the method decorator.

> Listing 14.31   Adding a factory function in the methodDecorator.ts file in the src folder

```
export function time(label? : string) {
    return function<This, Args extends any[],
            Result extends string | number>(
        method: (This, Args) => Result,
        ctx: ClassMethodDecoratorContext<This,
            (This, Args) => Result>) {
      const methodName = label ?? String(ctx.name);
      return function(this: This, ...args: Args) : Result {
          const start = performance.now();
          console.log(`${methodName} started`);
          const result = method.call(this, ...args);
          const duration = (performance.now() - start).toFixed(2);
          console.log(`${methodName} ended ${duration} ms`);
          return result;
      }
    }
}
```

The factory function defines an optional `string` parameter that is used to override the name of the method to which the decorator has been applied in the messages written to the console. The generic types make the decorator difficult to read, so I removed them in listing 14.32, which also removes the constraint on the result of the method to which the decorator is applied.

> Listing 14.32   Removing type parameters in the methodDecorator.ts file in the src folder

```
export function time(label? : string) {
    return function(method, ctx: ClassMethodDecoratorContext) {
        const methodName = label ?? String(ctx.name);
        return function(this, ...args: any[]) {
```

```
                const start = performance.now();
                console.log(`${methodName} started`);
                const result = method.call(this, ...args);
                const duration = (performance.now() - start).toFixed(2);
                console.log(`${methodName} ended ${duration} ms`);
                return result;
            }
        }
    }
```

There are now three nested functions, as shown in figure 14.3. The outer function is the factory responsible for receiving an optional string and returns the original decorator function. The decorator function receives the original method and the context object and is responsible for returning the replacement method.

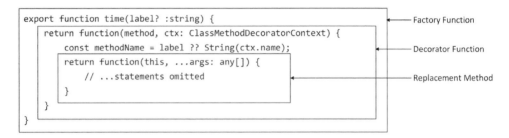

Figure 14.3 A decorator with a wrapper function

When a factory function is used, the decorator must be applied with parentheses, even if a value for the optional parameter isn't provided, as shown in listing 14.33.

Listing 14.33 Applying a wrapped decorator in the product.ts file in the src folder

```
import { time } from "./methodDecorator.js";
import { serialize } from "./classDecorator.js";
import { double } from "./fieldDecorator.js";
import { log } from "./accessorDecorator.js";
import { autolog } from "./autoAccessorDecorator.js";

@serialize
export class Product {

    constructor(public name: string, public price: number) {}

    @time("Product.getDetails")
    getDetails(): string {
        return `Name: ${this.name}, Price: $${this.getPrice()}`;
    }

    @time()
    getPrice(): number {
        return this.price * (1 + (this.tax/100));
    }
}
```

```
@autolog
accessor tax: number = 20;
}
```

The parentheses are required wherever the decorator is applied, which means that the `City` class must also be updated, as shown in listing 14.34.

Listing 14.34   Applying a wrapped decorator in the city.ts file in the src folder

```
import { time } from "./methodDecorator.js";

export class City {

    constructor(public name: string, public population: number) {}

    @time()
    getSummary(): string {
        return `Name: ${this.name}, Population: ${this.population}`;
    }
}
```

Save the changes and you will see output similar to the following when the code is compiled and executed, showing how the argument provided to the decorator has been used:

```
Auto-accessor initialized to 20
getSummary started
getSummary ended 0.19 ms
Name: London, Population: 8982000
Product.getDetails started
getPrice started
Auto-accessor tax get returned 20
getPrice ended 0.32 ms
Product.getDetails ended 0.64 ms
Name: Kayak, Price: $330
Auto-accessor tax get returned 20
Get Product tax: 20
Auto-accessor tax set to 30
Product: {"name":"Kayak","price":275}
```

Decorator factory functions can accept multiple arguments, but a common technique is to accept an object whose properties are used to configure the decorator, as shown in listing 14.35.

Listing 14.35   Receiving a config object in the methodDecorator.ts file in the src folder

```
type Config = {
    label?: string,
    time?: boolean,
    replacement?: Function,
}

export function time(config? : Config) {
    return function(method, ctx: ClassMethodDecoratorContext) {
```

```
        const methodName = config?.label ?? String(ctx.name);
        return function(this, ...args: any[]) {
            const start = performance.now();
            if (config?.time) {
                console.log(`${methodName} started`);
            }
            let result;
            if (config?.replacement) {
                result = config.replacement.call(this, args);
            } else {
                result = method.call(this, args);
            }
            if (config?.time) {
                const duration = (performance.now() - start).toFixed(2);
                console.log(`${methodName} ended ${duration} ms`);
            }
            return result;
        }
    }
}
```

The `Config` type defines a `label` property to use instead of the method name, a `time` property that controls whether the method execution is timed, and a `replacement` property that can be used to replace the original method entirely. All the `Config` properties are optional, so that any configuration setting that is not required can be omitted.

Listing 14.36 uses configuration objects when applying the decorator in the `Product` class.

Listing 14.36 Configuring the decorator in the product.ts file in the src folder

```
import { time } from "./methodDecorator.js";
import { serialize } from "./classDecorator.js";
import { double } from "./fieldDecorator.js";
import { log } from "./accessorDecorator.js";
import { autolog } from "./autoAccessorDecorator.js";

@serialize
export class Product {

    constructor(public name: string, public price: number) {}

    @time({
        replacement: () => "Hello, Decorator"
    })
    getDetails(): string {
        return `Name: ${this.name}, Price: $${this.getPrice()}`;
    }

    @time({
        label: "Product.getPrice",
        time: true
    })
```

```
getPrice(): number {
    return this.price * (1 + (this.tax/100));
}

@autolog
accessor tax: number = 20;
}
```

In isolation, and a small example project, using an object to configure a decorator may seem overkill, but this is a powerful technique because it allows fine-grained control over how a decorator behaves, specific to the decorated method. You will see this style of decorator configuration in part 3 when I demonstrate how to create a web application using the Angular framework.

Listing 14.37 adds a call to the `getPrice` method in the `index.ts` file so that the effect of both decorators in listing 14.36 is shown.

Listing 14.37   Adding a method call in the index.ts file in the src folder

```
import { City } from "./city.js";
import { Product } from "./product.js";
import { isSerializeable } from "./classDecorator.js";

let city = new City("London", 8_982_000);
let product = new Product("Kayak", 275);

console.log(city.getSummary());
console.log(product.getDetails());
console.log(`Price: ${product.getPrice()}`);

// console.log(`Get Product tax: ${product.tax}`);
// product.tax = 30;

// if (isSerializeable(product)) {
//     product.serialize();
// }
```

When the code is compiled and executed, it will produce results similar to the following:

```
Auto-accessor initialized to 20
Name: London, Population: 8982000
Hello, Decorator
Product.getPrice started
Auto-accessor tax get returned 20
Product.getPrice ended 0.31 ms
Price: 330
```

14.5   *Applying multiple decorators*

Multiple decorators can be applied to a class feature, but care must be taken to ensure that the order in which they are executed is understood. Add a file named `multiples.ts` to the `src` folder with the content shown in listing 14.38.

Listing 14.38 The contents of the multiples.ts file in the src folder

```
export function message(message: string) {
    console.log(`Factory function: ${message}`);
    return function (method: any, ctx: ClassMemberDecoratorContext) {
        console.log(`Get replacement: ${message}`);
        return function(this: any, ...args: any[]) {
            console.log(`Message: ${message}`);
            return method.call(this, ...args);
        }
    }
}
```

This method decorator returns a function that writes out a message before calling the original method. Listing 14.39 applies the decorator to the `City` class.

Listing 14.39 Applying a decorator in the city.ts file in the src folder

```
import { time } from "./methodDecorator.js";
import { message } from "./multiples.js";

export class City {

    constructor(public name: string, public population: number) {}

    @message("First Decorator")
    @message("Second Decorator")
    getSummary(): string {
        return `Name: ${this.name}, Population: ${this.population}`;
    }

}
```

Listing 14.40 simplifies the code in the `index.ts` file so that the output from the decorator is easier to locate.

Listing 14.40 Simplifying code in the index.ts file in the src folder

```
import { City } from "./city.js";
import { Product } from "./product.js";
import { isSerializeable } from "./classDecorator.js";

let city = new City("London", 8_982_000);
let product = new Product("Kayak", 275);

console.log(city.getSummary());
// console.log(product.getDetails());
// console.log(`Price: ${product.getPrice()}`);
```

Decorators are evaluated from the outside-in so that the decorator closest to the class feature is executed last. You can see the execution order in the output produced by this example:

```
Factory function: First Decorator
Factory function: Second Decorator
```

```
Get replacement: Second Decorator
Get replacement: First Decorator
Auto-accessor initialized to 20
Message: First Decorator
Message: Second Decorator

Name: London, Population: 8982000
```

To create the replacement method, the decorators are applied inside-out, so that the function returned by the decorator closest to the class feature is applied first and the result is passed to the next decorator. Listing 14.41 alters the decorator so that the replacement method adds a message to the string result.

Listing 14.41   Using string composition in the multiples.ts file in the src folder

```
export function message(message: string) {
    console.log(`Factory function: ${message}`);
    return function (method: any, ctx: ClassMemberDecoratorContext) {
        console.log(`Get replacement: ${message}`);
        return function(this: any, ...args: any[]) {
            // console.log(`Message: ${message}`);
            // return method.call(this, ...args);
            return `${message} (${method.call(this, ...args)})`;
        }
    }
}
```

Save the changes, and you can see how the replacement method created by the inner-most decorator is passed as the input to the outermost decorator:

```
Factory function: First Decorator
Factory function: Second Decorator
Get replacement: Second Decorator
Get replacement: First Decorator
Auto-accessor initialized to 20
```

First Decorator (Second Decorator (Name: London, Population: 8982000))

14.6   *Using an initializer*

The context objects provided to decorators define an `addInitializer` method, which can be used to register an initialization function, as shown in listing 14.42.

Listing 14.42   Adding an initializer in the methodDecorator.ts file in the src folder

```
type Config = {
    label?: string,
    time?: boolean,
    replacement?: Function,
}

export function time(config? : Config) {
    return function(method, ctx: ClassMethodDecoratorContext) {
        let start;
        ctx.addInitializer(() => start = performance.now());
        const methodName = config?.label ?? String(ctx.name);
```

```
        return function(this, ...args: any[]) {
            const start = performance.now();
            if (config?.time) {
                console.log(`${methodName} started`);
            }
            let result;
            if (config?.replacement) {
                result = config.replacement.call(this, args);
            } else {
                result = method.call(this, args);
            }
            if (config?.time) {
                const duration = (performance.now() - start).toFixed(2);
                console.log(`${methodName} ended ${duration} ms`);
            }
            return result;
        }
    }
}
```

The initializer function is passed to the context object's `addInitializer` method and is invoked when the class that has been decorated will be instantiated. In this example, I use the initializer to call the `performance.now` method, which allows me to incur the costs of setting up the timer from the measurements made by the decorator. Listing 14.43 configures decorator on the `Product` class.

Listing 14.43 Configuring the decorator in the product.ts file in the src folder

```
import { time } from "./methodDecorator.js";
import { serialize } from "./classDecorator.js";
import { double } from "./fieldDecorator.js";
import { log } from "./accessorDecorator.js";
import { autolog } from "./autoAccessorDecorator.js";

@serialize
export class Product {

    constructor(public name: string, public price: number) {}

    @time({
        //replacement: () => "Hello, Decorator"
        time: true
    })
    getDetails(): string {
        return `Name: ${this.name}, Price: $${this.getPrice()}`;
    }

    @time({
        label: "Product.getPrice",
        time: true
    })
    getPrice(): number {
        return this.price * (1 + (this.tax/100));
    }
```

```
  @autolog
  accessor tax: number = 20;
}
```

And, finally, listing 14.44 changes the code in the index.ts file so that the methods decorated in listing 14.43 are invoked.

```
import { City } from "./city.js";
import { Product } from "./product.js";
import { isSerializeable } from "./classDecorator.js";

//let city = new City("London", 8_982_000);
let product = new Product("Kayak", 275);

//console.log(city.getSummary());
console.log(product.getDetails());

console.log(`Price: ${product.getPrice()}`);
```

The output shows the effect of the initializer, with the time taken to initialize the timer now being separated from measuring individual methods:

```
Auto-accessor initialized to 20
getDetails started
Product.getPrice started
Auto-accessor tax get returned 20
Product.getPrice ended 0.32 ms
getDetails ended 0.65 ms
Name: Kayak, Price: $330
Product.getPrice started
Auto-accessor tax get returned 20
Product.getPrice ended 0.40 ms
Price: 330
```

14.7 Accumulating state data

Decorators can accumulate data, which is useful when the effect of decorators on multiple features must be combined, as shown in listing 14.45.

```
type Config = {
    label?: string,
    time?: boolean,
    replacement?: Function,
}

const timings = new Map<string, { count: number, elapsed : number}>();

export function writeTimes() {
    [...timings.entries()].forEach(t => {
        const average = (t[1].elapsed / t[1].count).toFixed(2);
        console.log(`${t[0]}, count: ${t[1].count}, time: ${average}ms`);
```

```
    });
}

export function time(config? : Config) {
    return function(method, ctx: ClassMethodDecoratorContext) {
        let start;
        ctx.addInitializer(() => start = performance.now());
        const methodName = config?.label ?? String(ctx.name);
        return function(this, ...args: any[]) {
            start = performance.now();
            // if (config?.time) {
            //     console.log(`${methodName} started`);
            // }
            let result;
            if (config?.replacement) {
                result = config.replacement.call(this, args);
            } else {
                result = method.call(this, args);
            }
            if (config?.time) {
                //const duration = (performance.now() - start).toFixed(2);
                const duration = (performance.now() - start);
                //console.log(`${methodName} ended ${duration} ms`);
                if (timings.has(methodName)) {
                    const data = timings.get(methodName);
                    data.count++;
                    data.elapsed += duration;
                } else {
                    timings.set(methodName, {
                        count: 1, elapsed: duration
                    });
                }
            }
            return result;
        }
    }
}
```

The decorator uses a `Map` to keep track of timing data for each method to which it is applied. Each replacement method created by the decorator adds its performance data to the `Map`, accumulating data every time the replacement method is called. The `Map` is defined outside of the factory, decorator, and replacement method functions, with the effect that a single `Map` is used for all the data.

The data is written out by calling the `writeTimes` function, which is exported so it can be used elsewhere in the application, as shown in listing 14.46.

> **Listing 14.46 Writing data in the index.ts file in the src folder**

```
import { City } from "./city.js";
import { Product } from "./product.js";
import { isSerializeable } from "./classDecorator.js";
import { writeTimes } from "./methodDecorator.js";
```

```
//let city = new City("London", 8_982_000);
let product = new Product("Kayak", 275);

//console.log(city.getSummary());
console.log(product.getDetails());
console.log(`Price: ${product.getPrice()}`);
```

writeTimes();

This example produces output similar to the following, showing the accumulation of data:

```
Auto-accessor initialized to 20
Auto-accessor tax get returned 20
Name: Kayak, Price: $330
Auto-accessor tax get returned 20
Price: 330
Product.getPrice, count: 2, time: 0.15ms
getDetails, count: 1, time: 0.24ms
```

Two of the replacement methods created by the decorator were invoked a total of three times.

Summary

In this chapter, I described how decorators can be applied to classes to transform the features they define. Decorators are not widely used outside of Angular development, but this is likely to change now that they are on track to be added to the JavaScript language specification.

- Decorators are a proposed addition to the JavaScript language that allows classes to be transformed.
- Decorators are applied using the @ character, followed by the decorator name.
- Decorators can be applied to classes, methods, properties, accessors, and auto-accessors.
- Decorators are functions that are invoked with a context object and produce a replacement for the feature to which they have been applied.
- Decorators can be defined with a factory function that supports additional configuration settings.
- Decorators can accumulate state data, which allows multiple instances of a decorator—or multiple types of decorator—to work together.

In the next chapter, I explain how TypeScript deals with JavaScript code, both when it is directly part of the project and when it is in third-party packages on which the application depends.

Working with JavaScript

This chapter covers

- Adding pure JavaScript code to a TypeScript project
- Providing type definitions for JavaScript code
- Enabling type checking for JavaScript code
- Defining types for third-party packages
- Using publicly available type definitions
- Generating type declarations for use in other projects

TypeScript projects generally incorporate some amount of pure JavaScript code, either because the application is written in both TypeScript and JavaScript or because the project relies on third-party JavaScript packages installed using NPM. In this chapter, I describe the features that TypeScript provides for working with JavaScript. Table 15.1 summarizes the chapter.

Table 15.1   Chapter summary

Problem	Solution	Listing
Incorporate JavaScript files in a project	Enable the `allowJs` and `checkJs` compiler options	9–13
Control whether a JavaScript file is checked by the TypeScript compiler	Use the `@ts-check` and `@ts-nocheck` comments	14
Describe JavaScript types	Use JSDoc comments or create a declaration file	15–22
Describe third-party JavaScript code	Update the compiler configuration and create a declaration file	22–26
Describe third-party code without creating a declaration file	Use a package that contains a declaration file or install a publicly available type declaration package	27–34
Generate declaration files for use in other projects	Enable the declaration compiler option	35–38

For quick reference, table 15.2 lists the TypeScript compiler options used in this chapter.

Table 15.2   The TypeScript compiler options used in this chapter

Name	Description
`allowJs`	This option includes JavaScript files in the compilation process.
`baseUrl`	This option specifies the root location used to resolve module dependencies.
`checkJs`	This option tells the compiler to check JavaScript code for common errors.
`declaration`	This option produces type declaration files when enabled, which describe the types for use in other projects.
`outDir`	This option specifies the directory in which the JavaScript files will be placed.
`paths`	This option specifies the locations used to resolve module dependencies.
`rootDir`	This option specifies the root directory that the compiler will use to locate TypeScript files.
`target`	This option specifies the version of the JavaScript language that the compiler will target in its output.

15.1   *Preparing for this chapter*

To prepare the project for this chapter, open a new command prompt, navigate to a convenient location, and create a folder named `usingjs`. Run the commands shown in listing 15.1 to navigate into the new folder and tell the Node Package Manager (NPM) to create a `package.json` file, which will track the packages added to the project.

TIP You can download the example project for this chapter—and for all the other chapters in this book—from https://github.com/manningbooks/essential-typescript-5.

Listing 15.1 Creating the package.json file

```
cd usingjs
npm init --yes
```

Run the commands shown in listing 15.2 in the `usingjs` folder to download and install the packages required for this chapter.

Listing 15.2 Adding packages

```
npm install --save-dev typescript@5.0.2
npm install --save-dev tsc-watch@6.0.0
```

To create a configuration file for the TypeScript compiler, add a file called `tsconfig.json` to the `usingjs` folder with the content shown in listing 15.3.

Listing 15.3 The contents of the tsconfig.json file in the usingjs folder

```
{
    "compilerOptions": {
        "target": "ES2022",
        "outDir": "./dist",
        "rootDir": "./src",
        "module": "Node16"
    }
}
```

These configuration settings tell the TypeScript compiler to generate code for the most recent JavaScript implementations, using the `src` folder to look for TypeScript files and using the `dist` folder for its outputs. The `module` setting tells the compiler to select the module format based on the content of the `package.json` file.

To configure NPM so that it can start the compiler, and to specify the module format, add the configuration entries shown in listing 15.4 to the `package.json` file.

Listing 15.4 Configuring NPM in the package.json file in the usingjs folder

```
{
  "name": "usingjs",
  "version": "1.0.0",
  "description": "",
  "main": "index.js",
  "scripts": {
    "start": "tsc-watch --onsuccess \"node dist/index.js\""
  },
  "keywords": [],
  "author": "",
```

```
    "license": "ISC",
    "devDependencies": {
      "tsc-watch": "^6.0.0",
      "typescript": "^5.0.2"
    },
    "type": "module"

}
```

15.1.1 *Adding TypeScript code to the example project*

Create the `usingjs/src` folder and add to it a file called `product.ts` with the code shown in listing 15.5.

Listing 15.5   The contents of the product.ts file in the src folder

```
export class Product {

    constructor(public id: number,
            public name: string,
            public price: number) {
        // no statements required
    }
}

export enum SPORT {
    Running, Soccer, Watersports, Other
}

export class SportsProduct extends Product {
    private _sports: SPORT[];

    constructor(public id: number,
            public name: string,
            public price: number,
            ...sportArray: SPORT[]) {
        super(id, name, price);
        this._sports = sportArray;
    }

    usedForSport(s: SPORT): boolean {
        return this._sports.includes(s);
    }

    get sports(): SPORT[] {
        return this._sports;
    }
}
```

This file is used to define a basic `Product` class, which is extended by the `Sports-Product` class that adds features specific to sporting goods. Next, add a file called `cart.ts` to the `src` folder with the code shown in listing 15.6.

Listing 15.6   The contents of the cart.ts file in the src folder

```
import { SportsProduct } from "./product.js";

class CartItem {

    constructor(public product: SportsProduct,
            public quantity: number) {
        // no statements required
    }

    get totalPrice(): number {
        return this.quantity * this.product.price;
    }
}

export class Cart {
    private items = new Map<number, CartItem>();

    constructor(public customerName: string) {
        // no statements required
    }

    addProduct(product: SportsProduct, quantity: number): number {
        if (this.items.has(product.id)) {
            let item = this.items.get(product.id);
            item.quantity += quantity;
            return item.quantity;
        } else {
            this.items.set(product.id, new CartItem(product, quantity));
            return quantity;
        }
    }

    get totalPrice(): number {
        return [...this.items.values()].reduce((total, item) =>
            total += item.totalPrice, 0);
    }

    get itemCount(): number {
        return [...this.items.values()].reduce((total, item) =>
            total += item.quantity, 0);
    }
}
```

This file defines the `Cart` class, which tracks a customer's selection of `SportProduct` objects using a `Map`. To create the entry point for the project, add a file called `index.ts` to the `src` folder with the code shown in listing 15.7.

Listing 15.7   The contents of the index.ts file in the src folder

```
import { SportsProduct, SPORT } from "./product.js";
import { Cart } from "./cart.js";

let kayak = new SportsProduct(1, "Kayak", 275, SPORT.Watersports);
```

```
let hat =  new SportsProduct(2, "Hat", 22.10, SPORT.Running,
    SPORT.Watersports);
let ball = new SportsProduct(3, "Soccer Ball", 19.50, SPORT.Soccer);

let cart = new Cart("Bob");
cart.addProduct(kayak, 1);
cart.addProduct(hat, 1);
cart.addProduct(hat, 2);

console.log(`Cart has ${cart.itemCount} items`);
console.log(`Cart value is $${cart.totalPrice.toFixed(2)}`);
```

The code in the index.ts file creates some SportsProduct objects, uses them to populate a Cart, and writes details of the Cart contents to the console.

Run the command shown in listing 15.8 in the usingjs folder to start the compiler so that the compiled code is executed automatically.

Listing 15.8   Starting the compiler

```
npm start
```

The compiler will start and produce the following output:

```
7:23:34 AM - Starting compilation in watch mode...7:23:36 AM - Found
0 errors. Watching for file changes.
Cart has 4 items
Cart value is $341.30
```

15.2   *Working with JavaScript*

The examples in this book have all assumed that you are working purely in TypeScript. Often, this won't be possible, either because TypeScript is introduced partway through a project or because you need to work with JavaScript code that has already been developed in earlier projects.

A project can contain TypeScript and JavaScript code side by side, requiring only changes to the TypeScript compiler and some optional steps to describe the types used by the JavaScript code. To demonstrate the process, some JavaScript code is required. Add a file called formatters.js to the src folder with the code shown in listing 15.9.

NOTE   The file extension for the file in listing 15.9 is js because this is a pure JavaScript file. It is important to use the right extension for the examples in this section.

Listing 15.9   The contents of the formatters.js file in the src folder

```
export function sizeFormatter(thing, count) {
    writeMessage(`The ${thing} has ${count} items`);
}

export function costFormatter(thing, cost) {
    writeMessage(`The ${thing} costs $${cost.toFixed(2)}`, true);
}
```

```
function writeMessage(message) {
    console.log(message);
}
```

The JavaScript file exports two formatting functions that write messages to the console. To incorporate the JavaScript code into the application, add the statements shown in listing 15.10 to the `index.ts` file.

Listing 15.10 Using JavaScript functions in the index.ts file in the src folder

```
import { SportsProduct, SPORT } from "./product.js";
import { Cart } from "./cart.js";
import { sizeFormatter, costFormatter } from "./formatters.js";

let kayak = new SportsProduct(1, "Kayak", 275, SPORT.Watersports);
let hat =  new SportsProduct(2, "Hat", 22.10, SPORT.Running,
    SPORT.Watersports);
let ball = new SportsProduct(3, "Soccer Ball", 19.50, SPORT.Soccer);

let cart = new Cart("Bob");
cart.addProduct(kayak, 1);
cart.addProduct(hat, 1);
cart.addProduct(hat, 2);

sizeFormatter("Cart", cart.itemCount);
costFormatter("Cart", cart.totalPrice);
```

When the changes to the `index.ts` file are saved, the compiler will run without reporting any problems, but the following message will be displayed when the code is executed:

```
Error [ERR_MODULE_NOT_FOUND]: Cannot find module 'formatters.js' imported
from index.js
```

The TypeScript compiler locates the JavaScript code without difficulty but doesn't copy the code into the `dist` folder, which means that the Node.js runtime can't locate the JavaScript code at runtime.

15.2.1 Including JavaScript in the compilation process

The TypeScript compiler uses JavaScript files to resolve dependencies during compilation but doesn't include them in the output it generates. To change this behavior, set the `allowJs` option in the `tsconfig.json` file to `true`, as shown in listing 15.11.

Listing 15.11 Changing the configuration in the tsconfig.json file in the usingjs folder

```
{
    "compilerOptions": {
        "target": "ES2022",
        "outDir": "./dist",
        "rootDir": "./src",
        "module": "Node16",
        "allowJs": true
    }
}
```

This setting includes the JavaScript files in the `src` folder in the compilation process. The JavaScript files don't contain TypeScript features, but the compiler will transform the JavaScript files to match the JavaScript version specified by the `target` setting and the module format specified by the `module` property.

For this example, no code features used in the `formatters.js` file will change because the `target` property is set to ES2022 and the `module` property tells the compiler to read the module format from the `package.json` file. But configuring the TypeScript compiler to include JavaScript files allows code to be easily mixed and ensures that JavaScript features are versioned consistently.

15.2.2 *Type-checking JavaScript code*

The TypeScript compiler will check JavaScript code for common errors when the `checkJs` configuration option is `true`, as shown in listing 15.12. This is not as comprehensive as the features applied to TypeScript files, but it can highlight potential problems.

Listing 15.12 Configuring the compiler in the tsconfig.json file in the usingjs folder

```
{
    "compilerOptions": {
        "target": "ES2022",
        "outDir": "./dist",
        "rootDir": "./src",
        "module": "Node16",
        "allowJs": true,
        "checkJs": true
    }
}
```

The compiler doesn't always detect the change to the `checkJs` property until it is restarted. Once you have saved the `tsconfig.json` file, use Control+C to stop the compiler; run the command shown in listing 15.13 in the `usingjs` folder to start it again.

Listing 15.13 Starting the compiler

```
npm start
```

The `costFormatter` function in the `formatters.js` file calls the `writeMessage` function defined in the same file with more arguments than there are parameters. This is legal JavaScript, which doesn't enforce restrictions on the number of arguments used to invoke a function, but the TypeScript compiler reports an error because this is a common error.

```
src/formatters.js(6,60): error TS2554: Expected 0-1 arguments, but got 2.
```

This feature is useful only if you can modify the JavaScript files to address the problems the compiler reports. You may have code that causes the TypeScript compiler to report an error but that can't be changed because it conforms to the requirements of a third-party library. If you have a mix of JavaScript files you can edit and those you cannot, you can add comments to control which JavaScript files are checked. Table 15.3 describes the comments, which are applied to the top of JavaScript files.

Table 15.3   The comments controlling JavaScript checking

Name	Description
`//@ts-check`	This comment tells the compiler to check the contents of a JavaScript file even when the `checkJs` property in the `tsconfig.json` file is `false`.
`//@ts-nocheck`	This comment tells the compiler to ignore the contents of a JavaScript file, even when the `checkJs` property in the `tsconfig.json` file is `true`.

Listing 15.14 adds a comment to the `formatters.js` file to tell the compiler not to check the contents of the file. Any other JavaScript files in the project will still be checked unless the same comment is applied.

Listing 15.14   Disabling JavaScript checks in the formatters.js file in the src folder

```
// @ts-nocheck

export function sizeFormatter(thing, count) {
    writeMessage(`The ${thing} has ${count} items`);
}

export function costFormatter(thing, cost) {
    writeMessage(`The ${thing} costs $${cost.toFixed(2)}`, true);
}

function writeMessage(message) {
    console.log(message);
}
```

The compiler will detect the change and run without checking the statements in the JavaScript file, producing the following output:

```
The Cart has 4 items
The Cart costs $341.30
```

15.3   *Describing types used in JavaScript code*

The TypeScript compiler will incorporate JavaScript code into a project, but there won't be static type information available. The compiler will do its best to infer the types used in the JavaScript code but will struggle and fall back to using `any`, especially for function parameters and results. The `costFormatter` function defined in the `formatters.js` file, for example, will be treated as though it had been defined with these type annotations:

```
...
export function costFormatter(thing: any, cost: any): any {
...
```

Adding JavaScript to a project can create holes in type checking that undermine the benefits of using TypeScript. The compiler can't determine that the costFormatter function assumes that it will receive a number value, which can be seen by adding a statement to the index.ts file that provides a string value, as shown in listing 15.15.

```
import { SportsProduct, SPORT } from "./product.js";
import { Cart } from "./cart.js";
import { sizeFormatter, costFormatter } from "./formatters.js";

let kayak = new SportsProduct(1, "Kayak", 275, SPORT.Watersports);
let hat =   new SportsProduct(2, "Hat", 22.10, SPORT.Running,
    SPORT.Watersports);
let ball = new SportsProduct(3, "Soccer Ball", 19.50, SPORT.Soccer);

let cart = new Cart("Bob");
cart.addProduct(kayak, 1);
cart.addProduct(hat, 1);
cart.addProduct(hat, 2);

sizeFormatter("Cart", cart.itemCount);
costFormatter("Cart", `${cart.totalPrice}`);
```

The new statement invokes the costFormatter function with two string arguments. The TypeScript compiler doesn't understand this will cause a problem and compiles the code without error. But when the code is executed, the costFormatter function invokes the toFixed method without checking that it has received a number value, which causes the following runtime error:

```
writeMessage(`The ${thing} costs $$${cost.toFixed(2)}`, true);
                                          ^
```

```
TypeError: cost.toFixed is not a function
```

This issue can be resolved by providing the compiler with type information that describes the JavaScript code so that its use can be checked during compilation. There are two approaches to describing types in JavaScript code, which I demonstrate in the following sections.

15.3.1 *Using comments to describe types*

The TypeScript compiler can obtain type information when it is included in JSDoc comments. JSDoc is a popular markup language used to annotate JavaScript code as comments. Listing 15.16 adds JSDoc comments to the formatters.js file.

> **TIP** Many code editors will help generate JSDoc comments. Visual Studio Code, for example, responds when a comment is created and automatically generates a list of function parameters.

Listing 15.16   Using JSDoc in the formatters.js file in the src folder

```
// @ts-nocheck

export function sizeFormatter(thing, count) {
    writeMessage(`The ${thing} has ${count} items`);
}

/**
 * Format something that has a money value
 * @param { string } thing - the name of the item
 * @param { number} cost - the value associated with the item
 */
export function costFormatter(thing, cost) {
    writeMessage(`The ${thing} costs $${cost.toFixed(2)}`, true);
}

function writeMessage(message) {
    console.log(message);
}
```

The JSDoc specification allows types to be indicated for function parameters. The JSDoc comment in listing 15.16 indicates that the `costFormatter` function expects to receive `string` and `number` parameters. The type information is a standard part of JSDoc, but it is usually just to provide guidance.

The TypeScript compiler reads the JSDoc comments to get type information about the JavaScript code. When the JSDoc comment in listing 15.16 is saved, the compiler will run and report the following error:

```
Argument of type 'string' is not assignable to parameter of type 'number'.
```

The compiler has read the JSDoc comment for the `costFormatter` function and determined that the value used to invoke the function in the `index.ts` file doesn't use the right data type.

> **TIP** See https://github.com/Microsoft/TypeScript/wiki/JSDoc-support-in-Java Script for a complete list of the JSDoc tags that the TypeScript compiler understands.

JSDoc comments can use the TypeScript syntax to describe more complex types, as shown in listing 15.17, which uses a type union.

Listing 15.17   Describing a type union in the formatters.js file in the src folder

```
// @ts-nocheck

export function sizeFormatter(thing, count) {
    writeMessage(`The ${thing} has ${count} items`);
}

/**
 * Format something that has a money value
 * @param { string } thing - the name of the item
```

```
 * @param { number | string } cost - the value associated with the item
 */
export function costFormatter(thing, cost) {
    if (typeof cost === "number") {
        writeMessage(`The ${thing} costs $$${cost.toFixed(2)}`, true);
    } else {
        writeMessage(`The ${thing} costs $$${cost}`);
    }
}

function writeMessage(message) {
    console.log(message);
}
```

The `costFormatter` function has been modified so that it can accept `number` and `string` values for its `cost` parameter, which is reflected in the updated JSDoc comment, which specifies the type as `number | string`. When the changes are saved, the code will be compiled, and the following output will be produced:

```
The Cart has 4 items
The Cart costs $341.3
```

15.3.2 Using type declaration files

Declaration files, also referred to as type *definition files*, provide a way to describe Java-Script code to the TypeScript file without having to change the source code file. Type declaration files have the `d.ts` extension, and the name of the file corresponds to the JavaScript file. To create a declaration file for the `formatters.js` file, a file named `formatters.d.ts` must be created. Add a file named `formatters.d.ts` to the `src` folder with the contents shown in listing 15.18.

> **Listing 15.18   The contents of the formatters.d.ts file in the src folder**

```
export declare function sizeFormatter(thing: string, count: number): void;
export declare function
    costFormatter(thing: string, cost: number | string ): void;
```

The contents of a type declaration file mirror those of the code file it describes. Each statement contains the `declare` keyword, which tells the compiler that the statement describes the types defined elsewhere. Listing 15.18 describes the parameters and result types of the functions that are exported from the `formatters.js` file.

> **TIP** Type declaration files take precedence over JSDoc comments when both are used to describe JavaScript code.

When a type declaration file is used, it must describe all the features defined in the corresponding JavaScript file that is used by the application because it is the only source of information used by the TypeScript compiler, which no longer examines the JavaScript file. For the example project, this means that the type declaration in listing 15.18 must describe the `sizeFormatter` and `costFormatter` functions since both are used in the `index.ts` file. Any feature that is not described in the type declaration file will not be visible to the TypeScript compiler. To demonstrate, listing 15.19 changes the `write-Message` function in the `formatters.js` file so that is exported for use in the rest of the application.

> **TIP** The TypeScript compiler trusts that the contents of a type declaration file are accurate, which means you are responsible for ensuring the types you select are supported by the JavaScript code and that all of the features in the Java-Script code are implemented as you describe.

Listing 15.19 Exporting a function in the formatters.js file in the src folder

```javascript
// @ts-nocheck

export function sizeFormatter(thing, count) {
    writeMessage(`The ${thing} has ${count} items`);
}

/**
 * Format something that has a money value
 * @param { string } thing - the name of the item
 * @param { number | string } cost - the value associated with the item
 */
export function costFormatter(thing, cost) {
    if (typeof cost === "number") {
        writeMessage(`The ${thing} costs $${cost.toFixed(2)}`, true);
    } else {
        writeMessage(`The ${thing} costs $${cost}`);
    }
}

export function writeMessage(message) {
    console.log(message);
}
```

Listing 15.20 uses the newly exported function in the `index.ts` file to display a simple message.

Listing 15.20 Using a function in the index.ts file in the src folder

```javascript
import { SportsProduct, SPORT } from "./product.js";
import { Cart } from "./cart.js";
import { sizeFormatter, costFormatter, writeMessage }
    from "./formatters.js";

let kayak = new SportsProduct(1, "Kayak", 275, SPORT.Watersports);
let hat =  new SportsProduct(2, "Hat", 22.10, SPORT.Running,
    SPORT.Watersports);
let ball = new SportsProduct(3, "Soccer Ball", 19.50, SPORT.Soccer);

let cart = new Cart("Bob");
cart.addProduct(kayak, 1);
cart.addProduct(hat, 1);
cart.addProduct(hat, 2);
```

```
sizeFormatter("Cart", cart.itemCount);
costFormatter("Cart", `${cart.totalPrice}`);
writeMessage("Test message");
```

The compiler will process the changes to the index.ts file when they are saved and report the following error:

```
Module '"/usingjs/src/formatters"' has no exported member 'writeMessage'.
```

The compiler relies entirely on the type declaration file to describe the contents of the formatters module. A declaration statement in the formatters.d.ts file is required to make the writeMessage function visible to the compiler, as shown in listing 15.21.

> **Listing 15.21   Adding a statement in the formatters.d.ts file in the src folder**

```
export declare function sizeFormatter(thing: string, count: number): void;
export declare function
    costFormatter(thing: string, cost: number | string ): void;
export declare function writeMessage(message: string): void;
```

Once the declaration file includes the function, the code in the project will compile and produce the following output:

```
The Cart has 4 items
The Cart costs $341.3
Test message
```

15.3.3 *Describing third-party JavaScript code*

Declaration files can also be used to describe JavaScript code added to the project in third-party packages that have been added to the project using NPM. Open a new command prompt, navigate to the usingjs folder, and run the command shown in listing 15.22 to install a new package in the example project.

> **Listing 15.22   Adding a package to the example project**

```
npm install debug@4.3.4
```

The debug package is a utility package that provides decorated debugging output to the JavaScript console. I have chosen it for this chapter because it is small but well-written and widely used in JavaScript development.

The compiler will try to infer types for third-party packages but will have the same limited success as for JavaScript files in the project. A type declaration file can be created for packages installed in the node_modules folder, although the technique is awkward; a better approach is to use publicly available definitions, as described in the next section.

The first step is to reconfigure the way that the TypeScript compiler resolves dependencies on modules, as shown in listing 15.23.

Listing 15.23 Configuring the compiler in the tsconfig.json file in the usingjs folder

```
{
    "compilerOptions": {
        "target": "ES2022",
        "outDir": "./dist",
        "rootDir": "./src",
        "module": "Node16",
        "allowJs": true,
        "checkJs": true,
        "baseUrl": ".",
        "paths": {
            "*": ["types/*.d.cts", "types/*.d.mts", "types/*.d.ts"]
        },
    }
}
```

The `paths` property is used to specify locations that the TypeScript compiler will use as it tries to resolve `import` statements for modules. The configuration used in the listing tells the compiler to look for all packages in a folder called `types`. I have specified the `cts`, `mts` and `ts` file extensions, which is important because type declarations have to match the module formats of the package they are applied to. (As I explained in chapter 5, the `mts` file extension denotes a TypeScript file that uses ECMAScript modules and the `cts` extension denotes CommonJS modules. Files with these extensions are compiled to output files with `mjs` and `cjs` extensions, and provide an alternative to the `package.json` file for specifying the module format.

When the `paths` property is used, the `baseUrl` property must also be specified, and the value used in the listing tells the compiler that the location specified by the `path` property can be found in the same folder as the `tsconfig.json` file.

The next step is to create the `usingjs/types` folder and add to it a file called `debug.d.cts`. I used the `cts` file extension because the debug package is published as CommonJS modules, which I determined by examining the `package.json` file and the JavaScript files in the project's GitHub repository.

Once you have created the file, add the contents shown in listing 15.24.

Listing 15.24 The contents of the debug.d.cts file in the types folder

```
declare interface Debug {
    (namespace: string): Debugger
}
declare interface Debugger {
    (...args: string[]): void;
    enabled: boolean;
}

declare var debug: Debug & { default: Debug };

export = debug;
```

The process for describing a third-party module can be complicated, not least because the package authors may not have anticipated that someone would try to describe their code using static types. To further complicate matters, the wide range of JavaScript language versions and module formats means that arcane incantations can be required to present TypeScript with descriptions that are useful and accurately represent the code in the module.

The two interfaces in listing 15.24 describe the most basic features of the debug package, allowing a simple debugger to be set up and used. The last two statements are required to represent the exports from the package to TypeScript.

> **TIP** See https://github.com/debug-js/debug for details of the full API provided by the debug package.

To make use of the debug package, add the statements shown in listing 15.25 to the index.ts file in the src folder.

> **Listing 15.25 Using a package in the index.ts file in the src folder**

```
import { SportsProduct, SPORT } from "./product.js";
import { Cart } from "./cart.js";
import { sizeFormatter, costFormatter, writeMessage }
    from "./formatters.js";
import debug from "debug";

let kayak = new SportsProduct(1, "Kayak", 275, SPORT.Watersports);
let hat =  new SportsProduct(2, "Hat", 22.10, SPORT.Running,
    SPORT.Watersports);
let ball = new SportsProduct(3, "Soccer Ball", 19.50, SPORT.Soccer);

let cart = new Cart("Bob");
cart.addProduct(kayak, 1);
cart.addProduct(hat, 1);
cart.addProduct(hat, 2);

sizeFormatter("Cart", cart.itemCount);
costFormatter("Cart", `${cart.totalPrice}`);

let db = debug("Example App", true);
db.enabled = true;
db("Message: %s", "Test message");
```

The TypeScript compiler will locate the declaration file and determine that the debug function has been invoked with too many arguments, producing the following error message:

```
...
src/index.ts(20,31): error TS2554: Expected 1 arguments, but got 2.
...
```

This error would not have been reported without the declaration file because pure JavaScript doesn't require that the number of arguments used to invoke a function matches the number of parameters it defines, as explained in chapter 8.

You don't have to create a deliberate error to check that the compiler has found the declaration file. Instead, open a new command prompt, navigate to the `usingjs` folder, and run the command shown in listing 15.26.

Listing 15.26 Running the compiler

```
tsc --traceResolution
```

The `traceResolution` argument, which can also be used as a configuration setting in the `tsconfig.json` file, tells the compiler to report on its progress as it attempts to locate each module. The output can be verbose—especially in complex projects—but the trace for the example project will contain this message:

```
======== Module name 'debug' was successfully resolved to 'C:/usingjs/types/
debug.d.cts'. ========
```

You may see different locations reported on your development machine, but the message will confirm that the compiler has located the custom declaration file and will use it to resolve dependencies on the `debug` package.

> ### Don't write declarations for third-party packages
>
> The declaration file in listing 15.24 shows that it is possible to describe publicly available packages, but it is not a process that I recommend and I don't provide any detail about the different ways that package contents can be described.
>
> First, it can be difficult to accurately represent someone else's code, and creating an accurate type declaration file can require a detailed analysis of a package and a solid understanding of what it does and how it works. Second, custom declarations tend to focus on just the features that are immediately required, and declaration files get patched up and extended as further features are needed, producing results that are difficult to understand and manage. Third, each new release means that the declaration file must be revisited to ensure that it still accurately reflects the API presented by the package.
>
> But, the most compelling reason not to create declaration files is that there is an excellent library of high-quality declarations for thousands of JavaScript packages available through the Definitely Typed project, as described in the next section. And the increased popularity of TypeScript means that more packages come with type declaration files built in.
>
> If you are determined to write your own files—or you want to contribute to the Definitely Typed project—then Microsoft has produced a dedicated guide to describing packages, which can be found at https://www.typescriptlang.org/docs/handbook/declaration-files/introduction.html.

15.3.4 Using Definitely Typed declaration files

The Definitely Typed project provides declaration files for thousands of JavaScript packages and is a more reliable—and quicker—way to use TypeScript with third-party packages than creating your own declaration files. Definitely Typed declaration files are installed using the `npm install` command. To install the declaration file for the `debug` package, run the command shown in listing 15.27 in the `usingjs` folder.

Listing 15.27   Installing a type declaration package

```
npm install --save-dev @types/debug
```

The name used for the Definitely Typed package is @types/ followed by the name of the package for which a description is required. For the debug package, for example, the Definitely Typed package is called @types/debug.

> **TIP** Notice that a version number for the @types/debug package is not specified in listing 15.27. When installing @types packages, I let NPM select the package version.

The compiler won't use the Definitely Typed declarations until the configuration is changed to stop the compiler from looking in the types folder, as shown in listing 15.28.

> **NOTE** The configuration change is required because the project contains custom and Definitely Typed declarations for the same package. This won't be a problem in real projects, and you can use the configuration settings to choose between custom and Definitely Typed declarations for each package you use.

Listing 15.28   Configuring the compiler in the tsconfig.json file in the usingjs folder

```
{
    "compilerOptions": {
        "target": "ES2022",
        "outDir": "./dist",
        "rootDir": "./src",
        "module": "Node16",
        "allowJs": true,
        "checkJs": true,
        // "baseUrl": ".",
        // "paths": {
        //      "*": ["types/*.d.cts", "types/*.d.mts", "types/*.d.ts"]
        // },
    }
}
```

Open a new command prompt, navigate to the usingjs folder, and run the command shown in listing 15.29 to see the effect of using the Definitely Typed package.

Listing 15.29   Running the compiler

```
tsc --traceResolution
```

The new trace shows that the compiler has located a different declaration file.

```
======== Type reference directive 'debug' was successfully resolved to
'C:/usingjs/node_modules/@types/debug/index.d.ts' with Package ID

'@types/debug/index.d.ts@4.1.7', primary: true. ========
```

The compiler looks in the `node_modules/@types` folder, which contains folders that correspond to each of the packages for which there are declaration files, following the same pattern as for custom files. (No configuration changes are required to tell the compiler to look in the `node_modules@types` folder.)

The result is that the Definitely Typed declaration file is used, which provides a full description of the API presented by the `debug` package. Listing 15.30 corrects the number of arguments used to invoke the `debug` function.

Listing 15.30   Using package features in the index.ts file in the src folder

```
import { SportsProduct, SPORT } from "./product.js";
import { Cart } from "./cart.js";
import { sizeFormatter, costFormatter, writeMessage }
    from "./formatters.js";
import debug from "debug";

let kayak = new SportsProduct(1, "Kayak", 275, SPORT.Watersports);
let hat =  new SportsProduct(2, "Hat", 22.10, SPORT.Running,
    SPORT.Watersports);
let ball = new SportsProduct(3, "Soccer Ball", 19.50, SPORT.Soccer);

let cart = new Cart("Bob");
cart.addProduct(kayak, 1);
cart.addProduct(hat, 1);
cart.addProduct(hat, 2);

sizeFormatter("Cart", cart.itemCount);
costFormatter("Cart", `${cart.totalPrice}`);

let db = debug("Example App");
db.enabled = true;
db("Message: %s", "Test message");
```

Save the changes and start the TypeScript compiler using the `npm start` command if it isn't already running. The compiler will run using the new declaration file, which includes a description of the `debug` method used in the listing. The compiled code produces the following output:

```
The Cart has 4 items
The Cart costs $341.3
Example App Message: Test message +0ms
```

15.3.5   *Using packages that include type declarations*

As TypeScript has become more popular, packages have started to include declaration files so that no additional downloads are required. The easiest way to see whether a project includes a declaration file is to install the package and look in the `node_modules` folder. As a demonstration, open a new command prompt, navigate to the `usingjs` folder, and run the command shown in listing 15.31 to add a package to the example project.

> **Listing 15.31   Adding a package to the project**

```
npm install chalk@4.1.2
```

The `Chalk` package provides styles for console output. Examine the contents of the `node_modules/chalk` folder, and you will see that it contains an `index.d.ts` file, which contains the type declarations for the package.

To confirm that the TypeScript compiler can find the `Chalk` declaration file, add the statements shown in listing 15.32 to the `index.ts` file in the `src` folder to confirm.

> **Listing 15.32   Adding statements in the index.ts file in the src folder**

```
import { SportsProduct, SPORT } from "./product.js";
import { Cart } from "./cart.js";
import { sizeFormatter, costFormatter, writeMessage }
    from "./formatters.js";
import debug from "debug";
import chalk from "chalk";

let kayak = new SportsProduct(1, "Kayak", 275, SPORT.Watersports);
let hat =  new SportsProduct(2, "Hat", 22.10, SPORT.Running,
    SPORT.Watersports);
let ball = new SportsProduct(3, "Soccer Ball", 19.50, SPORT.Soccer);

let cart = new Cart("Bob");
cart.addProduct(kayak, 1);
cart.addProduct(hat, 1);
cart.addProduct(hat, 2);

sizeFormatter("Cart", cart.itemCount);
costFormatter("Cart", `${cart.totalPrice}`);

console.log(chalk.greenBright("Formatted message"));
console.log(chalk.notAColor("Formatted message"));
```

One of the features provided by the `Chalk` package is coloring for text written to the console. The first statement tells `Chalk` to apply the `greenBright` color, and the second statement uses a nonexistent property. When the changes to the `index.ts` file are saved, the compiler will use the declaration file and report the following error:

```
src/index.ts(22,19): error TS2339: Property 'notAColor' does not exist on
type 'Chalk & ChalkFunction & { supportsColor: false | ColorSupport; Level:
Level; Color: Color; ForegroundColor: ForegroundColor; BackgroundColor:
BackgroundColor; Modifiers: Modifiers; stderr: Chalk & { ...; }; }'.
```

To see the process by which the compiler locates the declaration file, use the command prompt to run the command shown in listing 15.33 in the `usingjs` folder.

> **Listing 15.33   Running the compiler**

```
tsc --traceResolution
```

The output from the `traceResolution` argument is verbose, but if you read through the messages, you will see the different locations the compiler checks for declaration files and the effect of the settings in the `Chalk package.json` file:

```
======== Module name 'chalk' was successfully resolved to 'C:
/usingjs/node_modules/chalk/index.d.ts' with Package ID
'chalk/index.d.ts@4.1.2'. ========
```

Listing 15.34 removes the statement that deliberately caused a compiler error so the example application can be compiled and executed.

> **Listing 15.34 Removing a statement in the index.ts file in the src folder**

```
import { SportsProduct, SPORT } from "./product.js";
import { Cart } from "./cart.js";
import { sizeFormatter, costFormatter, writeMessage }
    from "./formatters.js";
import debug from "debug";
import chalk from "chalk";

let kayak = new SportsProduct(1, "Kayak", 275, SPORT.Watersports);
let hat =  new SportsProduct(2, "Hat", 22.10, SPORT.Running,
    SPORT.Watersports);
let ball = new SportsProduct(3, "Soccer Ball", 19.50, SPORT.Soccer);

let cart = new Cart("Bob");
cart.addProduct(kayak, 1);
cart.addProduct(hat, 1);
cart.addProduct(hat, 2);

sizeFormatter("Cart", cart.itemCount);
costFormatter("Cart", `${cart.totalPrice}`);

console.log(chalk.greenBright("Formatted message"));

//console.log(chalk.notAColor("Formatted message"));
```

The code will be compiled and executed, with the statement formatted by `Chalk` displayed in bright green

15.4 *Generating declaration files*

If your code is going to be used by other projects, you can ask the compiler to generate declaration files alongside the pure JavaScript, which has the effect of preserving the type information for other TypeScript programmers but still allows the project to be used as regular JavaScript.

The compiler won't generate declaration files when the `allowJS` option is enabled, which means I have to remove the dependency on the `formatters.js` file so that the project is all TypeScript. Add a file called `tsFormatters.ts` to the `src` folder and add the code shown in listing 15.35.

> **Listing 15.35 The contents of the tsformatters.ts file in the src folder**

```
export function sizeFormatter(thing: string, count: number): void {
    writeMessage(`The ${thing} has ${count} items`);
}
```

```
export function costFormatter(thing: string, cost: number | string): void {
    if (typeof cost === "number") {
        writeMessage(`The ${thing} costs $$${cost.toFixed(2)}`);
    } else {
        writeMessage(`The ${thing} costs $$${cost}`);
    }
}

export function writeMessage(message: string): void {
    console.log(message);
}
```

This is the JavaScript code from the `formatters.js` file but with type annotations. Listing 15.36 updates the `index.ts` file to depend on the TypeScript file instead of the JavaScript file.

> **CAUTION**   It is important to follow through with the changes in this process because disabling the `allowJS` option only prevents the compiler from adding the JavaScript file to the output folder. It doesn't prevent any of the TypeScript code from depending on the JavaScript file, which can lead to runtime errors because the JavaScript runtime won't be able to find all the files it needs.

Listing 15.36   Updating a dependency in the index.ts file in the src folder

```
import { SportsProduct, SPORT } from "./product.js";
import { Cart } from "./cart.js";
import { sizeFormatter, costFormatter, writeMessage }
    from "./tsFormatters.js";
import debug from "debug";
import chalk from "chalk";

let kayak = new SportsProduct(1, "Kayak", 275, SPORT.Watersports);
let hat =  new SportsProduct(2, "Hat", 22.10, SPORT.Running,
    SPORT.Watersports);
let ball = new SportsProduct(3, "Soccer Ball", 19.50, SPORT.Soccer);

let cart = new Cart("Bob");
cart.addProduct(kayak, 1);
cart.addProduct(hat, 1);
cart.addProduct(hat, 2);

sizeFormatter("Cart", cart.itemCount);
costFormatter("Cart", `${cart.totalPrice}`);

console.log(chalk.greenBright("Formatted message"));

//console.log(chalk.notAColor("Formatted message"));
```

Listing 15.37 changes the configuration of the compiler to disable the `allowJS` and `checkJS` properties and to enable the automatic generation of declaration files.

Listing 15.37 Configuring the compiler in the tsconfig.json file in the usingjs folder

```
{
    "compilerOptions": {
        "target": "ES2022",
        "outDir": "./dist",
        "rootDir": "./src",
        "module": "Node16",
        // "allowJs": true,
        // "checkJs": true,
        "declaration": true
    }
}
```

The compiler won't reliably generate the declaration files until it is restarted. Use Control+C to stop the compiler and run the command shown in listing 15.38 in the usingjs folder to start it again.

Listing 15.38 Starting the compiler

```
npm start
```

When the declaration property is true, the compiler will generate declaration files in the dist folder that describe the features exported from each TypeScript file, as shown in figure 15.1.

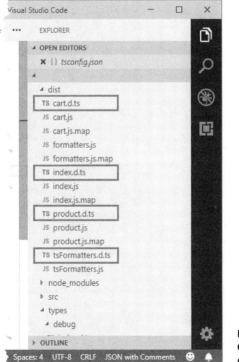

**Figure 15.1
Generating
declaration files**

Summary

In this chapter, I showed you how to work with JavaScript in a TypeScript project. I explained how to configure the compiler to process and type check JavaScript files and how declaration files can be used to describe JavaScript code to the compiler. Type-Script projects can include pure JavaScript code.

- The TypeScript compiler can check types for pure JavaScript code but can only infer basic types without type declarations.
- Type declarations can be provided for JavaScript code in the project and third-party packages.
- Public type declarations are available for most popular JavaScript packages and many packages include type declarations.
- The TypeScript compiler can generate type declarations for the JavaScript code it produces, allowing the compiled code to be used in other TypeScript projects.

In the next part of the book, I build a series of web applications that rely on Type-Script, starting with a standalone application and then using the Angular and React frameworks.

Part 3

Creating a stand-alone web app, part 1

This chapter covers

- Setting up a bundler to create files that can be efficiently delivered to browsers
- Setting up the TypeScript compiler for the JSX workflow
- Using JSX files to combine HTML markup and TypeScript code
- Starting a simple web application without using a web application framework

In this part of the book, I show you how TypeScript fits into the development process for the most popular web application frameworks: Angular and React. In both cases, I go through the process of creating the project, setting up a web service, and writing a simple web application. In this chapter, I create the same web application without using any of these frameworks, providing a baseline for understanding the features they provide and context for how TypeScript features are used.

I don't recommend creating real applications without using a framework, but working on a stand-alone application reveals much about TypeScript and its role in modern development and is worthwhile simply to learn. For quick reference, table 16.1 lists the TypeScript compiler options used in this chapter.

Table 16.1   The Typescript compiler options used in this chapter

Name	Description
jsx	This option specifies how HTML elements in TSX files are processed.
jsxFactory	This option specifies the name of the factory function that is used to replace HTML elements in TSX files.
outDir	This option specifies the directory in which the JavaScript files will be placed.
rootDir	This option specifies the root directory that the compiler will use to locate TypeScript files.
target	This option specifies the version of the JavaScript language that the compiler will target in its output.

16.1   *Preparing for this chapter*

To prepare for this chapter, open a new command prompt, navigate to a convenient location, and create a folder called `webapp`. Run the commands shown in listing 16.1 to move to the `webapp` folder and to tell the Node Package Manager (NPM) to create a file named `package.json`.

> **TIP**   You can download the example project for this chapter—and for all the other chapters in this book—from https://github.com/manningbooks/essential-typescript-5.

Listing 16.1   Creating the package.json file

```
cd webapp
npm init --yes
```

I will be building a toolchain that incorporates the TypeScript compiler in this chapter to show the workflow common in web application development. This requires the TypeScript package to be installed locally in the project; you cannot rely on the globally installed package from chapter 1. Run the command shown in listing 16.2 in the `webapp` folder to install the TypeScript package.

Listing 16.2   Adding packages using the node package manager

```
npm install --save-dev typescript@5.0.2
```

I will install further packages as the application takes shape, but the TypeScript package is enough for now. To configure the TypeScript compiler, add a file named `tsconfig.json` to the `webapp` folder with the content shown in listing 16.3.

Listing 16.3   The contents of the tsconfig.json file in the webapp folder

```
{
    "compilerOptions": {
        "target": "es2022",
        "outDir": "./dist",
        "rootDir": "./src"
    }
}
```

The configuration tells the compiler to target the ES2022 version of JavaScript, to find the code files in the `src` folder, and to put the generated files in the `dist` folder. To prepare the entry point for the application, create the `src` folder and add to it a file called `index.ts` with the content shown in listing 16.4.

Listing 16.4   The contents of the index.ts file in the src folder

```
console.log("Web App");
```

Run the commands shown in listing 16.5 in the `webapp` folder to compile the `index.ts` file and execute the contents of the JavaScript file that is produced.

Listing 16.5   Compiling and executing the result

```
tsc
node dist/index.js
```

The compiled code will generate the following output:

```
Web App
```

16.2   *Creating the toolchain*

Web application development relies on a chain of tools that compile the code and prepare it for the delivery and execution of the application by the JavaScript runtime. The TypeScript compiler is the only development tool in the project at present, as shown in figure 16.1.

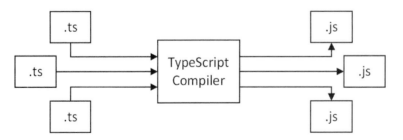

Figure 16.1   The initial project toolchain

The development tools are hidden when you use a framework like Angular or React, as demonstrated in later chapters, but for this chapter, I am going to install and configure each tool and show you how they work together.

16.3 *Adding a bundler*

When the application is executed using Node.js in the project folder, any `import` statements can be resolved using the JavaScript generated by the TypeScript compiler or by the packages installed in the `node_modules` folder.

The JavaScript runtime starts with the application entry point—the `index.js` file that is compiled from the `index.ts` file—and processes the `import` statements it contains. For each `import` statement, the runtime resolves the dependency and loads the required module, which will be another JavaScript file. Any `import` statements declared in the new JavaScript file are processed in the same way, allowing all the dependencies in the application to be resolved so the code can be executed.

The JavaScript runtime doesn't know in advance what `import` statements each code file may contain and so it doesn't know which JavaScript files are required. But it doesn't matter because looking for files to resolve dependencies is a relatively quick operation since all the local files are easily accessible.

This approach doesn't work as well for web applications, which don't have direct access to the file system. Instead, files have to be requested over HTTP, which can be a slow and expensive operation and doesn't lend itself to easily checking multiple locations to resolve dependencies on files. Instead, a bundler is used, which resolves the dependencies during compilation and packages all the files that the application uses into a single file. One HTTP request delivers all the JavaScript required to run the application, and other content types, such as CSS, can be included in the file produced by the bundler, which is known as a *bundle*. During the bundling process, the code and content can be minified and compressed, reducing the amount of bandwidth required to deliver the application to the client. Large applications can be split into multiple bundles so that optional code or content can be loaded separately and only when it is required.

The most widely used bundler is webpack, and it forms a key part of the toolchains used by React and Angular, although you don't usually need to work with it directly, as you will see in later chapters. Webpack can be complex to work with, but it is supported by a wide range of add-on packages that allow development toolchains to be created for just about any type of project. Run the commands shown in listing 16.6 in the `webapp` folder to add webpack packages to the example project.

> **Listing 16.6   Adding packages to the example project**

```
npm install --save-dev webpack@5.76.3
npm install --save-dev webpack-cli@5.0.1
npm install --save-dev ts-loader@9.4.2
```

The `webpack` package contains the main bundler features, and the `webpack-cli` package adds command-line support. Webpack uses packages known as *loaders* to deal with different content types, and the `ts-loader` package adds support for compiling TypeScript files and feeding the compiled code into the bundle created by webpack.

To configure webpack, add a file named `webpack.config.js` to the `webapp` folder with the contents shown in listing 16.7.

Listing 16.7   The contents of the webpack.config.js file in the webapp folder

```
module.exports = {
    mode: "development",
    devtool: "inline-source-map",
    entry: "./src/index.ts",
    output: { filename: "bundle.js" },
    resolve: { extensions: [".ts", ".js"] },
    module: {
        rules: [
            { test: /\.ts/, use: "ts-loader", exclude: /node_modules/ }
        ]
    }
};
```

This `entry` and `output` settings tell webpack to start with the `src/index.ts` file when resolving the application's dependencies and to give the bundle file the name `bundle.js`. The other settings configure webpack to use the `ts-loader` package to process files with the `ts` file extension.

> **TIP**   See https://webpack.js.org for details of the full range of configuration options that webpack supports.

Run the command shown in listing 16.8 in the `webapp` folder to run webpack and create the bundle file.

Listing 16.8   Creating a bundle file

```
npx webpack
```

Webpack works its way through the dependencies in the project and uses the `ts-loader` package to compile the TypeScript files it encounters, producing the following output:

```
asset bundle.js 788 bytes [emitted] (name: main)
./src/index.ts 25 bytes [built] [code generated]
webpack 5.17.0 compiled successfully in 1865 ms
```

The `bundle.js` file is created in the `dist` folder. Run the command shown in listing 16.9 in the `webapp` folder to execute the code in the bundle.

Listing 16.9   Executing the bundle file

```
node dist/bundle.js
```

There is only one TypeScript file in the project, but the bundle is self-contained and will remain so even as the example application becomes more complex. Executing the bundle produces the following output:

```
Web App
```

The addition of webpack and its supporting packages has changed the development toolchain, as shown in figure 16.2.

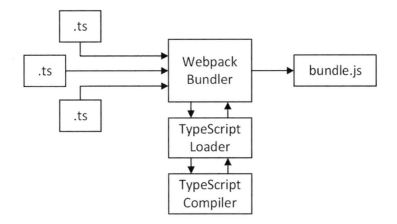

Figure 16.2   Adding a bundle to the toolchain

16.4   *Adding a development web server*

A web server is required to deliver the bundle file to the browser so it can be executed. The Webpack Dev Server (WDS) is an HTTP server that is integrated into webpack and includes support for triggering automatic browser reloads when a code file changes and a new bundle file is produced. Run the command shown in listing 16.10 in the webapp folder to install the WDS package.

Listing 16.10   Adding the wds package

```
npm install --save-dev webpack-dev-server@4.13.1
```

Change the webpack configuration to set up the basic configuration for WDS, as shown in listing 16.11.

Listing 16.11   Server configuration in the webpack.config.js file in the webapp folder

```
module.exports = {
    mode: "development",
    devtool: "inline-source-map",
    entry: "./src/index.ts",
    output: { filename: "bundle.js" },
    resolve: { extensions: [".ts", ".js"] },
    module: {
        rules: [
            { test: /\.ts/, use: "ts-loader", exclude: /node_modules/ }
        ]
    },
    devServer: {
        static: "./assets",
```

```
        port: 4500
    }
};
```

The new configuration settings tell WDS to look for any file that is not a bundle in a folder named `assets` and to listen for HTTP requests on port 4500. To provide WDS with an HTML file that can be used to respond to browsers, create a `webapp/assets` folder and add to it a file named `index.html` with the content shown in listing 16.12.

Listing 16.12   The contents of the index.html file in the assets folder

```html
<!DOCTYPE html>
<html>
<head>
    <title>Web App</title>
    <script src="bundle.js"></script>
</head>
<body>
    <div id="app">Web App Placeholder</div>
</body>
</html>
```

When the browser receives the HTML file, it will process the contents and encounter the `script` element, which will trigger an HTTP request for the `bundle.js` file, which contains the application's JavaScript code.

To start the server, run the command shown in listing 16.13 in the `webapp` folder.

Listing 16.13   Starting the development web server

```
npx webpack serve
```

The HTTP server will start, and the bundle will be created. However, the `dist` folder is no longer used to store the files—the output from the bundling process is held in memory and used to respond to HTTP requests without needing to create a file on disk. As the server starts and the application is bundled, you will see the following output:

```
<i> [webpack-dev-server] Project is running at:
<i> [webpack-dev-server] Loopback: http://localhost:4500/
<i> [webpack-dev-server] On Your Network (IPv4): http://192.168.1.13:4500/
<i> [webpack-dev-server] Content not from webpack is served from './assets'
directory
asset bundle.js 609 KiB [emitted] (name: main)
runtime modules 27.3 KiB 12 modules
modules by path ./node_modules/ 173 KiB
  modules by path ./node_modules/webpack-dev-server/client/ 68.9 KiB 16
modules
  modules by path ./node_modules/webpack/hot/*.js 4.59 KiB
 ./node_modules/webpack/hot/dev-server.js 1.88 KiB [built] [code generated]
 ./node_modules/webpack/hot/log.js 1.34 KiB [built] [code generated]
    + 2 modules
  modules by path ./node_modules/html-entities/lib/*.js 81.3 KiB
   ./node_modules/html-entities/lib/index.js 7.74 KiB [built]
[code generated]
```

```
    ./node_modules/html-entities/lib/named-references.js 72.7 KiB [built]
[code generated]
    ./node_modules/html-entities/lib/numeric-unicode-map.js 339 bytes
[built] [code generated]
    ./node_modules/html-entities/lib/surrogate-pairs.js 537 bytes [built]
[code generated]
  ./node_modules/ansi-html-community/index.js 4.16 KiB [built] [code
generated]
  ./node_modules/events/events.js 14.5 KiB [built] [code generated]
./src/index.ts 24 bytes [built] [code generated]

webpack 5.76.3 compiled successfully in 3883 ms
```

The detail of the messages isn't important other than to give you a sense of the overall progress. Once the server has started, open a new web browser and navigate to
http://locahost:4500, which is the port on which WDS was configured to listen for
HTTP requests. The contents of the index.html file will be displayed by the browser,
as shown in figure 16.3.

Figure 16.3   Displaying the HTML file

Open the browser's F12 development tools and switch to the Console tab to see the
output from the console.log statement in the index.ts file:

Web App

When WDS is started, webpack is put into a watch mode that builds a new bundle when
a change to the code files is detected. During the bundling process, WDS injects additional code into the JavaScript file that opens a connection back to the server and waits
for a signal to reload the browser, which is sent for each new bundle. The effect is that
the browser is reloaded automatically each time a change is detected and processed,
which can be seen by adding a statement to the index.ts file, as shown in listing 16.14.

> **TIP** The reload feature works only for code files and doesn't apply to the
> HTML file in the assets folder. Changes to the HTML file take effect only
> when WDS is restarted.

Listing 16.14   Adding a statement to the index.ts file in the src folder

```
console.log("Web App");
console.log("This is a new statement");
```

As soon as the index.ts file is saved, webpack builds a new bundle, and the signal is
sent to the browser to trigger a reload, producing the following output in the browser's
F12 developer tool console:

```
Web App
This is a new statement
```

Adding WDS extends the chain of development tools and links the application to the JavaScript runtime provided by the browser, as shown in figure 16.4.

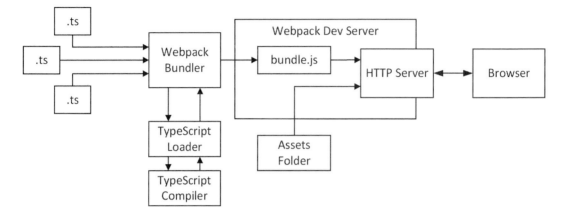

Figure 16.4   Adding WDS to the development toolchain

This toolchain contains the key elements that you will see in most web application projects, although the individual parts are often hidden from sight. Notice how the TypeScript compiler is just one part of the chain, allowing TypeScript code to be integrated into a set of broader JavaScript development tools.

16.5   *Creating the data model*

The application will retrieve its list of products from a web service using an HTTP request. The user will be able to select products to assemble an order, which will be sent back to the web service using another HTTP request. To start the data model, I created the src/data folder and added to it a file called entities.ts with the code shown in listing 16.15.

> **Listing 16.15   The contents of the entities.ts file in the src/data folder**

```
export type Product = {
    id: number,
    name: string,
    description: string,
    category: string,
    price: number
};

export class OrderLine {
    constructor(public product: Product, public quantity: number) {
        // no statements required
    }
```

```
    get total(): number {
        return this.product.price * this.quantity;
    }
}

export class Order {
    private lines = new Map<number, OrderLine>();

    constructor(initialLines?: OrderLine[]) {
        if (initialLines) {
            initialLines.forEach(ol => this.lines.set(ol.product.id, ol));
        }
    }

    public addProduct(prod: Product, quantity: number) {
        if (this.lines.has(prod.id)) {
            if (quantity === 0) {
                this.removeProduct(prod.id);
            } else {
                this.lines.get(prod.id)!.quantity += quantity;
            }
        } else {
            this.lines.set(prod.id, new OrderLine(prod, quantity));
        }
    }

    public removeProduct(id: number) {
        this.lines.delete(id);
    }

    get orderLines(): OrderLine[] {
        return [...this.lines.values()];
    }

    get productCount(): number {
        return [...this.lines.values()]
            .reduce((total, ol) => total += ol.quantity, 0);
    }

    get total(): number {
        return [...this.lines.values()]
            .reduce((total, ol) => total += ol.total, 0);
    }
}
```

The `Product`, `Order`, and `OrderLine` types are all exported so they can be used outside of the code file. The `Order` class represents the user's product selections, each of which is expressed as an `OrderLine` object that combines a `Product` and a quantity. I have defined `Product` as a type alias because this will simplify working with data obtained remotely when I introduce a web service in chapter 17. The `Order` and `OrderLine` types are defined as classes because they define additional features beyond being a collection of related properties.

16.5.1 Creating the data source

I will introduce the web service later in the chapter. For the moment, I will create a class that provides access to some local test data. To ease the transition from local to remote data, I will define an abstract class that provides the basic features and create concrete implementations for each data source. I added a file called `abstractDataSource.ts` to the `src/data` folder and used it to define the class shown in listing 16.16.

> **CAUTION** Notice that the import statements in this chapter do not include the `js` file extensions. The requirement for file extensions is specific to Node.js and their interpretation of the JavaScript language specification. This chapter uses a browser to execute the compiled JavaScript code, and this does requires file extensions to be omitted. I hope that this kind of incompatibility will be resolved but the history of JavaScript modules has been messy, and I do not expect consistency any time soon.

Listing 16.16 The contents of the abstractdatasource.ts file in the src/data folder

```typescript
import { Product, Order } from "./entities";

export type ProductProp = keyof Product;

export abstract class AbstractDataSource {
    private _products: Product[];
    private _categories: Set<string>;
    public order: Order;
    public loading: Promise<void>;

    constructor() {
        this._products = [];
        this._categories = new Set<string>();
        this.order = new Order();
        this.loading = this.getData();
    }

    async getProducts(sortProp: ProductProp = "id",
            category? : string): Promise<Product[]> {
        await this.loading;
        return this.selectProducts(this._products, sortProp, category);
    }

    protected async getData(): Promise<void> {
        this._products = [];
        this._categories.clear();
        const rawData = await this.loadProducts();
        rawData.forEach(p => {
            this._products.push(p);
            this._categories.add(p.category);
        });
    }

    protected selectProducts(prods: Product[],
```

```
                sortProp: ProductProp, category?: string): Product[] {
            return prods.filter(p=> category === undefined
                        || p.category === category)
                    .sort((p1, p2) => p1[sortProp] < p2[sortProp]
                        ? -1 : p1[sortProp] > p2[sortProp] ? 1: 0);
        }

        async getCategories(): Promise<string[]> {
            await this.loading;
            return [...this._categories.values()];
        }

        protected abstract loadProducts(): Promise<Product[]>;
        abstract storeOrder(): Promise<number>;
    }
```

The AbstractDataSource class uses the JavaScript Promise features to fetch data in the background and uses the async/await keywords to express the code that depends on those operations. The class in listing 16.16 invokes the abstract loadProducts method in the constructor, and the getProducts and getCategories methods wait for the background operation to produce data before returning any responses. To create an implementation of the data source class that uses local test data, I added a file called localDataSource.ts to the src/data folder and added the code shown in listing 16.17.

> **Listing 16.17 The contents of the localdatasource.ts file in the src/data folder**

```
import { AbstractDataSource } from "./abstractDataSource";
import { Product } from "./entities";

export class LocalDataSource extends AbstractDataSource {

        loadProducts(): Promise<Product[]> {
            return Promise.resolve([
                { id: 1, name: "P1", category: "Watersports",
                    description: "P1 (Watersports)", price: 3 },
                { id: 2, name: "P2", category: "Watersports",
                    description: "P2 (Watersports)", price: 4 },
                { id: 3, name: "P3", category: "Running",
                    description: "P3 (Running)", price: 5 },
                { id: 4, name: "P4", category: "Chess",
                    description: "P4 (Chess)", price: 6 },
                { id: 5, name: "P5", category: "Chess",
                    description: "P6 (Chess)", price: 7 },
            ]);
        }

        storeOrder(): Promise<number> {
            console.log("Store Order");
            console.log(JSON.stringify(this.order));
            return Promise.resolve(1);
        }
    }
```

This class uses the `Promise.resolve` method to create a `Promise` that immediately produces a response and allows test data to be easily used. In chapter 17, I introduce a data source that performs real background operations to request data from a web service. To check that the basic features of the data model are working, I replaced the code in the `index.ts` file with the statements shown in listing 16.18.

Listing 16.18   Replacing the contents of the index.ts file in the src folder

```
import { LocalDataSource } from "./data/localDataSource";

async function displayData(): Promise<string> {
    let ds = new LocalDataSource();
    let allProducts = await ds.getProducts("name");
    let categories = await ds.getCategories();
    let chessProducts = await ds.getProducts("name", "Chess");

    let result = "";

    allProducts
        .forEach(p => result += `Product: ${p.name}, ${p.category}\n`);
    categories.forEach(c => result += (`Category: ${c}\n`));
    chessProducts.forEach(p => ds.order.addProduct(p, 1));
    result += `Order total: $${ds.order.total.toFixed(2)}`;
    return result;
}

displayData().then(res => console.log(res));
```

When the changes to the `index.ts` file are saved, the code will be compiled, and the chain of `import` statements is resolved to include all the JavaScript required by the application in the webpack bundle. A browser reload will be triggered, and the following output will be displayed in the browser's JavaScript console:

```
Product: P1, Watersports
Product: P2, Watersports
Product: P3, Running
Product: P4, Chess
Product: P5, Chess
Category: Watersports
Category: Running
Category: Chess
Order total: $13.00
```

16.6   Rendering HTML content using the DOM API

Few users will want to look in the browser's JavaScript console window to see the output. Browsers provide the Domain Object Model (DOM) API to allow applications to interact with the HTML document displayed to the user, generate content dynamically, and respond to user interaction. To create a class that will produce an HTML element, I added a file called `domDisplay.ts` to the `src` folder and used it to define the class shown in listing 16.19.

Listing 16.19 The contents of the domDisplay.ts file in the src folder

```typescript
import { Product, Order } from "./data/entities";

export class DomDisplay {

    props: {
        products: Product [],
        order: Order
    }

    getContent(): HTMLElement {
        let elem = document.createElement("h3");
        elem.innerText = this.getElementText();
        elem.classList.add("bg-primary", "text-center",
            "text-white", "p-2");
        return elem;
    }

    getElementText() {
        return `${this.props.products.length} Products, `
            + `Order total: $${ this.props.order.total }`;
    }
}
```

The `DomDisplay` class defines a `getContent` method whose result is an `HTMLElement` object, which is the type used by the DOM API to represent an HTML element. The `getContent` method creates an H3 element and uses a template string to set its content. The element is added to four classes, which will be used to manage the appearance of the element when it is displayed. The data values used in the template string are provided through a property named `props`. This is a convention that was adopted from the React framework.

16.6.1 Adding support for Bootstrap CSS styles

The three classes to which the `h3` element is assigned in listing 16.19 correspond to styles defined by Bootstrap, which is a high-quality, open-source CSS framework that makes it easy to consistently style HTML content.

The webpack configuration can be extended with loaders for additional content types that are included in the bundle file, which means that the development toolchain can be extended to include support for CSS stylesheets, such as the one that defines the Bootstrap styles applied to the `h3` element.

Stop the WDS process using Control+C and run the commands shown in listing 16.20 in the `webapp` folder to install the CSS loaders and Bootstrap packages.

> **NOTE** I use the Bootstrap CSS framework in most of my projects because it is easy to work with and produces good results. See https://getbootstrap.com for details of the styles available and of the optional JavaScript features that are available.

Listing 16.20   Adding packages to the project

```
npm install bootstrap@5.2.3
npm install --save-dev css-loader@6.7.3
npm install --save-dev style-loader@3.3.2
```

The `bootstrap` package contains the CSS styles that I want to apply to the example project. The `css-loader` and `style-loader` packages contain the loaders that deal with CSS styles (both are required to incorporate CSS into the webpack bundle). Make the changes shown in listing 16.21 to the webpack configuration to add support for including CSS in the bundle file.

```
module.exports = {
    mode: "development",
    devtool: "inline-source-map",
    entry: "./src/index.ts",
    output: { filename: "bundle.js" },
    resolve: { extensions: [".ts", ".js", ".css"] },
    module: {
        rules: [
            { test: /\.ts/, use: "ts-loader", exclude: /node_modules/ },
            { test: /\.css$/, use: ["style-loader", "css-loader"] },
        ]
    },
    devServer: {
        static: "./assets",
        port: 4500
    }
};
```

In listing 16.22, I have revised the code in the `index.ts` file to declare a dependency on the CSS stylesheet from the Bootstrap package and to use the `DomHeader` class to render HTML content in the browser.

```
import { LocalDataSource } from "./data/localDataSource";
import { DomDisplay } from "./domDisplay";
import "bootstrap/dist/css/bootstrap.css";

let ds = new LocalDataSource();

async function displayData(): Promise<HTMLElement> {
    let display = new DomDisplay();
    display.props = {
        products: await ds.getProducts("name"),
        order: ds.order
    }
    return display.getContent();
}
```

```
document.onreadystatechange = () => {
    if (document.readyState === "complete") {
        displayData().then(elem => {
            let rootElement = document.getElementById("app");
            rootElement.innerHTML = "";
            rootElement.appendChild(elem);
        });
    }
};
```

The DOM API provides a complete set of features to work with the HTML document displayed by the browser, but the result can be verbose code that is difficult to read, especially when the content to be displayed depends on the result of background tasks, such as getting data from a web service.

The code in listing 16.22 has to wait for two tasks to be completed before it can display any content. The browser has to complete processing the HTML document contained in the `index.html` file before the DOM API can be used to manipulate its contents. Browsers process HTML elements in the order in which they are defined in the HTML document, which means that the JavaScript code will be executed before the browser has processed the elements in the `body` section of the document. Any attempt to modify the document before it has been fully processed can lead to inconsistent results.

TIP The default settings for the TypeScript compiler include type declaration files for the DOM API, which allows type-safe use of the browser features.

The code in listing 16.22 also has to wait for the data source to obtain its data. The `LocalDataSource` class uses local test data that is immediately available, but there may be a delay when the data is retrieved from a web service, which I implement in chapter 17.

When both tasks are complete, the placeholder element in the `index.html` file is removed and replaced with the `HTMLElement` object obtained by creating a `DomDisplay` object and calling its `getContent` method.

Save the changes to the `index.ts` file and run the command shown in listing 16.23 in the `webapp` folder to start the Webpack Development Server using the configuration created in listing 16.21.

Listing 16.23 Starting the development tools

```
npx webpack serve
```

A new bundle that includes the CSS styles will be created. Use the browser to navigate to http://localhost:4500, and the styled HTML content will be displayed, as shown in figure 16.5.

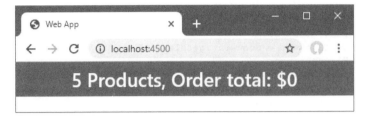

Figure 16.5   Generating HTML elements

> **TIP** The loaders added to the project deal with CSS by adding JavaScript code
> that is executed when the contents of the bundle file are processed. This code
> uses an API provided by the browser to create the CSS styles. This approach
> means that the bundle file contains only JavaScript even though it delivers dif-
> ferent types of content to the client.

16.7   *Using JSX to create HTML content*

Expressing HTML elements using JavaScript statements is awkward, and using the
DOM API directly produces verbose code that is difficult to understand and prone to
errors, even with the static type support that TypeScript provides.

The problem isn't the DOM API itself—although it hasn't always been designed with
ease of use in mind—but the difficulty in using code statements to create declarative
content like HTML elements. A more elegant approach is to use JSX, which stands for
JavaScript XML and which allows declarative content such as HTML elements to be easily mixed with code statements. JSX is most closely associated with React development
but the TypeScript compiler provides features that allow it to be used in any project.

> **NOTE** JSX isn't the only way to simplify working with HTML elements, but I
> have used it in this chapter because the TypeScript compiler supports it. If you
> don't like JSX, you can use one of the many JavaScript template packages avail-
> able (search for *mustache templates* to get started).

The best way to understand JSX is to start by writing some JSX code. TypeScript files
that contain JSX content are defined in files with the `tsx` extension, reflecting the
combination of TypeScript and JSX features. Add a file called `htmlDisplay.tsx` to
the `src` folder and add the content shown in listing 16.24.

Listing 16.24   The contents of the htmlDisplay.tsx file in the src folder

```
import { Product, Order } from "./data/entities";

export class HtmlDisplay {

    props: {
        products: Product[],
        order: Order
```

```
    }

    getContent(): HTMLElement {
        return <h3 className="bg-secondary text-center text-white p-2">
                { this.getElementText() }
            </h3>
    }

    getElementText() {
        return `${this.props.products.length} Products, `
            + `Order total: $${ this.props.order.total }`;
    }
}
```

This file uses JSX to create the same result as the regular TypeScript class. The difference is the `getContent` method, which returns an HTML element expressed directly as an element, instead of using the DOM API to create an object and configure it through its properties. The `h3` element returned by the `h3` element is expressed in a way that is similar to an element in an HTML document, with the addition of fragments of JavaScript that allow expressions to generate content dynamically based on the values provided through the `props` property.

This file won't compile because the project has not yet been configured for JSX, but you can see how this format can be used to create content more naturally. In the sections that follow, I will explain how JSX files are processed and configure the example project to support them.

16.7.1 *Understanding the JSX workflow*

When a TypeScript JSX file is compiled, the compiler processes the HTML elements it contains to transform them into JavaScript statements. Each element is parsed and separated into the tag that defines the element type, the attributes applied to the element, and the element's content.

The compiler replaces each HTML element with a call to a function, known as the *factory function,* that will be responsible for creating the HTML content at runtime. The factory function is conventionally named `createElement` because that's the name used by the React framework, and it means that the class in listing 16.24 is transformed into this code:

```
...
import { Product, Order } from "./data/entities";

export class HtmlDisplay {

    props: {
        products: Product[],
        order: Order
    }

    getContent() {
        return createElement("h3",
            { className: "bg-secondary text-center text-white p-2" },
```

```
                      this.getElementText());
    }

    getElementText() {
        return `${this.props.products.length} Products, `
            + `Order total: $${ this.props.order.total }`;
    }
}
...
```

The compiler doesn't know anything about the factory function other than its name. The result of the transformation is that the HTML content is replaced with code statements that can be compiled normally and executed by a regular JavaScript runtime, as shown in figure 16.6.

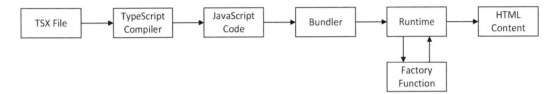

Figure 16.6   Transforming JSX

When the application runs, each call to the factory function is responsible for using the tag name, attribute, and content parsed by the compiler to create the HTML element the application requires.

Understanding props versus attributes

The elements in a JSX file are not standard HTML. The key difference is that the attributes on the elements use the JavaScript property names defined by the DOM API instead of the corresponding attribute names from the HTML specification. Many of the properties and attributes share the same name, but there are some important differences, and the one that causes the most confusion is the `class` attribute, which is used to assign elements to one or more classes, typically so they can be styled.

The DOM API can't use `class` because it is a reserved JavaScript word and so elements are assigned to classes using the `className` property, like this:

```
...
<h3 className="bg-secondary text-center text-white p-2">
...
```

This is the reason that TypeScript JSX classes receive their data values through the property named `props`, because each prop corresponds to a property that must be set on the `HTMLElement` object created by the factory function. Forgetting to use property names in a JSX file is a common mistake and is a good place to start checking when you don't get the results you expect.

16.7.2 Configuring the compiler and the loader

The TypeScript compiler won't process TSX files by default and requires two configuration settings to be set, as described in table 16.2. There are other compiler options for JSX, but these are the two that are required to get started.

Table 16.2 The compiler settings for JSX

Name	Description
jsx	This option determines the way that the compiler handles elements in a TSX file. The react setting replaces HTML elements with calls to the factory function and emits a JavaScript file. The react-native setting emits a JavaScript file that leaves the HTML elements intact. The preserve setting emits a JSX file that leaves the HTML elements intact. The react-jsx and react-jsx settings use __jsx as the name of the function that creates elements.
jsxFactory	This option specifies the name of the factory function, which the compiler will use when the jsx option is set to react.

For this project, I am going to define a factory function called createElement and select the react option for the jsx setting so the compiler will replace HTML content with calls to the factory function, as shown in listing 16.25.

Listing 16.25 Configuring the compiler in the tsconfig.json file in the webapp folder

```
{
    "compilerOptions": {
        "target": "es2022",
        "outDir": "./dist",
        "rootDir": "./src",
        "jsx": "react",
        "jsxFactory": "createElement"
    }
}
```

The webpack configuration must be updated so that TSX files will be included in the bundling process, as shown in listing 16.26.

Listing 16.26 Configuring webpack in the webpack.config.js file in the webapp folder

```
module.exports = {
    mode: "development",
    devtool: "inline-source-map",
    entry: "./src/index.ts",
    output: { filename: "bundle.js" },
    resolve: { extensions: [".ts", ".tsx", ".js", ".css"] },
    module: {
        rules: [
            { test: /\.tsx?$/, use: "ts-loader", exclude: /node_modules/ },
```

```
            { test: /\.css$/, use: ["style-loader", "css-loader"] },
        ]
    },
    devServer: {
        static: "./assets",
        port: 4500
    }
};
```

The change to the `resolve` setting tells webpack that TSX files should be included in the bundle, and the other change specifies that TSX files will be handled by the `ts-loader` package, which will use the TypeScript compiler.

16.7.3 *Creating the factory function*

The code generated by the compiler replaces HTML content with calls to the factory function, which allows JSX code to be transformed into standard JavaScript. The implementation of the factory function depends on the environment in which the application is being run so that React applications, for example, will use the factory function that generates content that React can manage. For the example application, I am going to create a factory function that simply uses the DMO API to create an `HTMLElement` object. This is nowhere near as elegant or efficient as the way that React and the other frameworks handle dynamic content, but it is enough to allow the use of JSX in the application without getting bogged down in the details. To define the factory function, I created the `src/tools` folder and added to it a file named `jsxFactory.ts` with the code shown in listing 16.27.

> **Listing 16.27   The contents of the jsxFactory.ts file in the src/tools folder**

```
export function createElement(tag: any, props: Object,
        ...children : Object[]) : HTMLElement {

    function addChild(elem: HTMLElement, child: any) {
        elem.appendChild(child instanceof Node ? child
            : document.createTextNode(child.toString()));
    }

    if (typeof tag === "function") {
        return Object.assign(new tag(), { props: props || {}}).getContent();
    }

    const elem = Object.assign(document.createElement(tag), props || {});
    children.forEach(child => Array.isArray(child)
        ? child.forEach(c => addChild(elem, c)) : addChild(elem, child));
    return elem;
}

declare global {
    namespace JSX {
        interface ElementAttributesProperty { props; }
    }
}
```

The `createElement` function in listing 16.27 does the bare minimum to create HTML elements using the DOM API without any of the sophisticated features provided by the frameworks used in later chapters. The `tag` parameter can be a function, in which case another class that uses JSX has been specified as the element type.

> **TIP** The last section of code in listing 16.27 is a specific incantation that tells the TypeScript compiler that it should use the `props` property to perform type checking on the values assigned to JSX element attributes in TSX files. This relies on the TypeScript namespace feature, which I have not described in this chapter because it has been superseded by the introduction of standard Java-Script modules and is no longer recommended for use.

16.7.4 Using the JSX class

JSX classes are transformed into standard JavaScript code, which means they can be used in the same way as any TypeScript class. In listing 16.28, I have removed the dependency on the DOM API class and replaced it with a JSX class.

> **Listing 16.28 Using a JSX class in the index.ts file in the src folder**

```
import { LocalDataSource } from "./data/localDataSource";
import { HtmlDisplay } from "./htmlDisplay";
import "bootstrap/dist/css/bootstrap.css";

let ds = new LocalDataSource();

async function displayData(): Promise<HTMLElement> {
    let display = new HtmlDisplay();
    display.props = {
        products: await ds.getProducts("name"),
        order: ds.order
    }
    return display.getContent();
}

document.onreadystatechange = () => {
    if (document.readyState === "complete") {
        displayData().then(elem => {
            let rootElement = document.getElementById("app");
            rootElement.innerHTML = "";
            rootElement.appendChild(elem);
        });
    }
};
```

The JSX class is a drop-in replacement for the class that uses the DOM API directly. In later sections, you will see how classes that use JSX can be combined using only elements, but there is always a boundary between a regular class and one that contains HTML elements. For the example application, that boundary will be between the `index` file and `HtmlDisplay` class.

16.7.5 *Importing the factory function in the JSX class*

The final change to complete the JSX configuration is to add an `import` statement for the factory function to the JSX class, as shown in listing 16.29. The TypeScript compiler will convert HTML elements into calls to the factory function, but an `import` statement is required to allow the converted code to be compiled.

> **Listing 16.29 Adding an import statement in the htmlDisplay.tsx file in the src folder**

```
import { createElement } from "./tools/jsxFactory";
import { Product, Order } from "./data/entities";

export class HtmlDisplay {

    props: {
        products: Product[],
        order: Order
    }

    getContent(): HTMLElement {
        return <h3 className="bg-secondary text-center text-white p-2">
                { this.getElementText() }
            </h3>
    }

    getElementText() {
        return `${this.props.products.length} Products, `
            + `Order total: $${ this.props.order.total }`;
    }
}
```

An `import` statement for the factory function is required in every TSX file. Use Control+C to stop the webpack development tools and use the command prompt to run the command shown in listing 16.30 in the `webapp` folder to start them again using the new configuration.

> **Listing 16.30 Starting the development tools**

```
npx webpack serve
```

Once the bundle has been re-created, use the browser to navigate to http://localhost:4500, and you will see the content shown in figure 16.7, which is styled using a different color from the previous example.

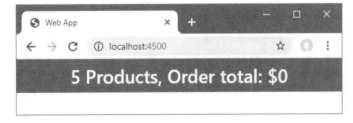

Figure 16.7 Rendering content using JSX

16.8 *Adding features to the application*

Now that the basic structure of the application is in place, I can add features, starting
with a display of products that can be filtered by category.

16.8.1 *Displaying a filtered list of products*

Add a file called `productItem.tsx` in the `src` folder and add the code shown in listing
16.31 to create a class that will display details of a single product.

> **Listing 16.31 The contents of the productItem.tsx file in the src folder**

```
import { createElement } from "./tools/jsxFactory";
import { Product } from "./data/entities";

export class ProductItem {
    private quantity: number = 1;

    props: {
        product: Product,
        callback: (product: Product, quantity: number) => void
    }

    getContent(): HTMLElement {
        return <div className="card card-outline-primary m-1 p-1 bg-light">
            <h4>
                { this.props.product.name }
                <span className="badge rounded-pill bg-primary text-white"
                        style="float:right">
                    <small>${ this.props.product.price.toFixed(2) }</small>
                </span>
            </h4>
            <div className="card-text bg-white p-1">
                { this.props.product.description }
                <button className="btn btn-success btn-sm float-end"
                        onclick={ this.handleAddToCart } >
                    Add To Cart
                </button>
                <select className="form-control-inline float-end m-1"
                        onchange={ this.handleQuantityChange }>
                    <option>1</option>
                    <option>2</option>
                    <option>3</option>
                </select>
            </div>
        </div>
    }

    handleQuantityChange = (ev: Event): void => {
        this.quantity = Number((ev.target as HTMLSelectElement).value);
    }

    handleAddToCart = (): void => {
        this.props.callback(this.props.product, this.quantity);
    }
}
```

The `ProductItem` class receives a `Product` object and a callback function through its props. The `getContent` method renders HTML elements that display the details of the `Product` object, along with a `select` element that allows a quantity to be selected and a `button` that the user will click to add items to the order.

The `select` and `button` elements are configured with event-handling functions using the `onchange` and `onclick` props. The methods that handle the events are defined using the fat arrow syntax, like this:

```
...
handleQuantityChange = (ev: Event): void => {
    this.quantity = Number((ev.target as HTMLSelectElement).value);
}
...
```

The fat arrow syntax ensures that the `this` keyword refers to the `ProductItem` object, which allows the `props` and `quantity` properties to be used. If a conventional method is used to handle an event, `this` refers to the object that describes the event.

The TypeScript type declarations for DOM API event handling are awkward and require a type assertion for the target of the event before its features can be accessed.

```
...
handleQuantityChange = (ev: Event): void => {
    this.quantity = Number((ev.target as HTMLSelectElement).value);
}
...
```

To read the `value` property from the `select` element, I have to apply an assertion to tell the TypeScript compiler that the `event.target` property will return an `HTMLSelectElement` object.

> **TIP** The `HTMLSelectElement` type is one of the standard DOM API types, which are described in detail at https://developer.mozilla.org/en-US/docs/Web/API/HTMLElement.

To display a list of category buttons allowing the user to filter the content, add a file called `categoryList.tsx` to the `src` folder with the contents shown in listing 16.32.

Listing 16.32   The contents of the categoryList.tsx file in the src folder

```
import { createElement } from "./tools/jsxFactory";

export class CategoryList {

    props: {
        categories: string[];
        selectedCategory: string,
        callback: (selected: string) => void
    }

    getContent(): HTMLElement {
        return <div className="d-grid gap-2">
            { ["All", ...this.props.categories]
                .map(c => this.getCategoryButton(c))}
```

```
        </div>
    }

    getCategoryButton(cat?: string): HTMLElement {
        let selected = this.props.selectedCategory === undefined
            ? "All": this.props.selectedCategory;
        let btnClass = selected === cat ? "btn-primary": "btn-secondary";
        return <button className={ `btn btn-block ${btnClass}` }
                onclick={ () => this.props.callback(cat)}>
            { cat }
        </button>
    }
}
```

This class displays a list of `button` elements that are styled using Bootstrap classes. The props for this class provide the list of categories for which buttons should be created, the currently selected category, and a callback function to invoke when the user clicks a button.

```
...
return <button className={ `btn btn-block ${btnClass}` }
    onclick={ () => this.props.callback(cat) }>
...
```

This pattern is common when JSX is used so that classes render HTML elements using data received via props; this props also includes callback functions that are invoked in response to events. In this case, the `onclick` attribute is used to invoke the function received through the `callback` prop.

To display a list of products and the category buttons, add a file called `productList` `.tsx` to the `src` folder with the contents shown in listing 16.33.

> **Listing 16.33 The contents of the productList.tsx file in the src folder**

```
import { createElement } from "./tools/jsxFactory";
import { Product } from "./data/entities";
import { ProductItem } from "./productItem";
import { CategoryList } from "./categoryList";

export class ProductList {
    props: {
        products: Product[],
        categories: string[],
        selectedCategory: string,
        addToOrderCallback?: (product: Product, quantity: number) => void,
        filterCallback?: (category: string) => void;
    }

    getContent(): HTMLElement {
        return <div className="container-fluid">
            <div className="row">
                <div className="col-3 p-2">
                    <CategoryList categories={ this.props.categories }
                        selectedCategory={ this.props.selectedCategory }
```

```
                        callback={ this.props.filterCallback } />
            </div>
            <div className="col-9 p-2">
                {
                    this.props.products.map(p =>
                        <ProductItem product={ p }
                            callback={
                                this.props.addToOrderCallback } />)
                }
            </div>
        </div>
    </div>
    }
}
```

The `getContent` method in this class relies on one of the most useful JSX features, which is the ability to apply other JSX classes as HTML elements, like this:

```
...
<div className="col-3 p-2">
    <CategoryList categories={ this.props.categories }
        selectedCategory={ this.props.selectedCategory }
        callback={ this.props.filterCallback } />
</div>
...
```

When it parses the TSX file, the TypeScript compiler detects that the custom tag creates a statement that invokes the factory function with the corresponding class. At runtime, a new instance of the class is created, the attributes of the element are assigned to the `props` property, and the `getContent` method is called to get the content to include in the HTML presented to the user.

16.8.2 *Displaying content and handling updates*

I need to create a bridge between the features of the data store and the JSX classes that display content to the user, ensuring that the content is updated to reflect changes in the application state. The frameworks demonstrated in later chapters take care of handling updates efficiently and minimizing the amount of work the browser does to display changes.

I am going to take the simplest approach for the example application, which is to deal with changes by destroying and re-creating the HTML elements displayed by the browser, as shown in listing 16.34, which revises the `HtmlDisplay` class so that it receives a data source and manages the state data required to display a list of products filtered by category.

> **Listing 16.34   Displaying content in the htmlDisplay.tsx file in the src folder**

```
import { createElement } from "./tools/jsxFactory";
import { Product, Order } from "./data/entities";
import { AbstractDataSource } from "./data/abstractDataSource";
import { ProductList } from "./productList";

export class HtmlDisplay {
```

```
private containerElem: HTMLElement;
private selectedCategory: string;

constructor() {
    this.containerElem = document.createElement("div");
}

props: {
    dataSource: AbstractDataSource;
}

async getContent(): Promise<HTMLElement> {
    await this.updateContent();
    return this.containerElem;
}

async updateContent() {
    let products = await this.props.dataSource.getProducts("id",
        this.selectedCategory);
    let categories = await this.props.dataSource.getCategories();
    this.containerElem.innerHTML = "";
    let content = <div>
        <ProductList products={ products } categories={ categories }
            selectedCategory={ this.selectedCategory }
            addToOrderCallback={ this.addToOrder }
            filterCallback={ this.selectCategory} />
    </div>
    this.containerElem.appendChild(content);
}

addToOrder = (product: Product, quantity: number) => {
    this.props.dataSource.order.addProduct(product, quantity);
    this.updateContent();
}

selectCategory = (selected: string) => {
    this.selectedCategory = selected === "All" ? undefined : selected;
    this.updateContent();
}
}
```

The methods defined by the `HtmlDisplay` class are used as the callback functions for the `ProductList` class, which passes them on to the `ProductItem` and `CategoryList` classes. When these methods are invoked, they update the properties that keep track of the application state and then call the `updateContent` method, which replaces the HTML rendered by the class.

To provide the `HtmlDisplay` class with the props it requires, update the `index.ts` file, as shown in listing 16.35.

> **Listing 16.35 Changing props in the index.ts file in the src folder**

```
import { LocalDataSource } from "./data/localDataSource";
import { HtmlDisplay } from "./htmlDisplay";
import "bootstrap/dist/css/bootstrap.css";
```

```
let ds = new LocalDataSource();

async function displayData(): Promise<HTMLElement> {
    let display = new HtmlDisplay();
    display.props = {
        // products: await ds.getProducts("name"),
        // order: ds.order
        dataSource: ds
    }
    return display.getContent();
}

document.onreadystatechange = () => {
    if (document.readyState === "complete") {
        displayData().then(elem => {
            let rootElement = document.getElementById("app");
            rootElement.innerHTML = "";
            rootElement.appendChild(elem);
        });
    }
};
```

A new bundle will be created when the changes are saved, triggering a browser reload and displaying the content shown in figure 16.8. As the figure shows, clicking a category button filters the products shown to the user.

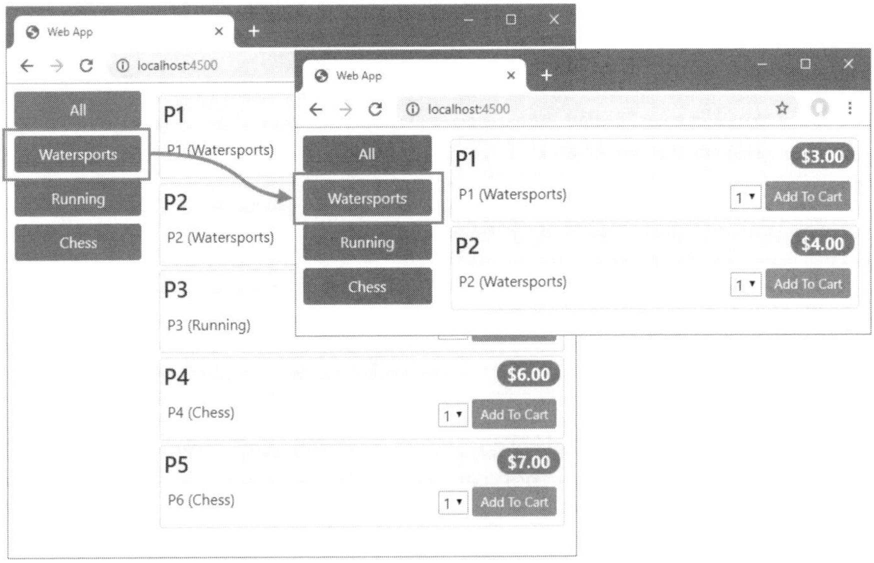

Figure 16.8   Displaying products

Summary

In this chapter, I showed you how to create a simple but effective development tool-chain for web application development using the TypeScript compiler and webpack. I showed you how the output from the TypeScript compiler can be incorporated into a webpack bundle and how the support for JSX can be used to simplify working with HTML elements.

- Bundlers are tools that combine project assets into files that can be efficiently delivered to the browser.
- JSX is a file format that combines code and markup, which makes it easier to generate content for a web application.
- JSX elements are not standard HTML and adaptions have been made to avoid using reserved JavaScript keywords, such as class.
- A factory function is used to transform JSX content into JavaScript code. The factory function is usually provided by a web application framework, but custom factories can be used.
- Content generated from JSX files can include CSS styles, where the stylesheets are included in the bundles delivered to the browser.

In the next chapter, I complete the standalone web application and prepare it for deployment.

Creating a stand-alone web app, part 2

This chapter covers

- Creating and consuming a web service
- Completing the basic application features
- Creating a deployment server and persistent data storage
- Deploying the application in a container

In this chapter, I complete the stand-alone web application and prepare it for deployment, demonstrating the way that a TypeScript project dovetails with standard development processes for deployment. For quick reference, table 17.1 lists the TypeScript compiler options used in this chapter.

Table 17.1   The TypeScript compiler options used in this chapter

Name	Description
`jsx`	This option specifies how HTML elements in TSX files are processed.
`jsxFactory`	This option specifies the name of the factory function that is used to replace HTML elements in TSX files.
`moduleResolution`	This option specifies the style of module resolution that should be used to resolve dependencies.

Table 17.1   The TypeScript compiler options used in this chapter *(continued)*

Name	Description
`outDir`	This option specifies the directory in which the Java-Script files will be placed.
`rootDir`	This option specifies the root directory that the compiler will use to locate TypeScript files.
`target`	This option specifies the version of the JavaScript language that the compiler will target in its output.

17.1   *Preparing for this chapter*

In this chapter, I continue to use the project created in chapter 16. To prepare for this chapter, open a new command prompt, navigate to the `webapp` folder, and run the commands shown in listing 17.1 to add new packages to the project.

> **TIP** You can download the example project for this chapter—and for all the other chapters in this book—from https://github.com/manningbooks/essential-typescript-5.

Listing 17.1   Adding packages to the project

```
npm install --save-dev json-server@0.17.3
npm install --save-dev npm-run-all@4.1.5
```

The `json-server` package is a RESTful web service that will provide data for the application, replacing the local test data used in chapter 16. The `npm-run-all` package is a useful tool for running multiple NPM packages from a single command.

To provide the web service with its data, create a file called `data.js` in the `webapp` folder with the contents shown in listing 17.2.

Listing 17.2   The contents of the data.js file in the webapp folder

```
module.exports = function () {
    return {
        products: [
            { id: 1, name: "Kayak", category: "Watersports",
                description: "A boat for one person", price: 275 },
            { id: 2, name: "Lifejacket", category: "Watersports",
              description: "Protective and fashionable", price: 48.95 },
            { id: 3, name: "Soccer Ball", category: "Soccer",
                description: "FIFA-approved size and weight",
                price: 19.50 },
            { id: 4, name: "Corner Flags", category: "Soccer", description:
                "Give your playing field a professional touch",
                price: 34.95 },
            { id: 5, name: "Stadium", category: "Soccer",
                description: "Flat-packed 35,000-seat stadium",
                price: 79500 },
```

```
        { id: 6, name: "Thinking Cap", category: "Chess",
            description: "Improve brain efficiency by 75%", price: 16 },
        { id: 7, name: "Unsteady Chair", category: "Chess",
            description: "Secretly give your opponent a disadvantage",
            price: 29.95 },
        { id: 8, name: "Human Chess Board", category: "Chess",
            description: "A fun game for the family", price: 75 },
        { id: 9, name: "Bling Bling King", category: "Chess",
            description: "Gold-plated, diamond-studded King",
            price: 1200 }
    ],
    orders: []
  }

}
```

The `json-server` package will be configured to use the data in listing 17.2, which will cause it to reset each time it is restarted. (The package can also store data persistently, but that is not as useful for example projects where a known baseline is more useful.)

To configure the development tools, update the `scripts` section of the `package` `.json` file, as shown in listing 17.3.

Listing 17.3   Configuring the development tools in the package.json file in the webapp folder

```
...
  "scripts": {
    "json": "json-server data.js -p 4600",
    "wds": "webpack serve",
    "start": "npm-run-all -p json wds"
  },
...
```

These entries allow both the web service that will provide the data and the webpack HTTP server to be started with a single command. Use the command prompt to run the command shown in listing 17.4 in the `webapp` folder.

Listing 17.4   Starting the development tools

```
npm start
```

The web service will start, although the data has yet to be integrated into the application. To test the web service, use the browser to navigate to http://localhost:4600/products, which will produce the response shown in figure 17.1.

Figure 17.1 Getting data from the web service

The TypeScript files will be compiled, a bundle will be created, and the development HTTP server will start listening for HTTP requests. Open a new browser window and navigate to http://localhost:4500 to see the content shown in figure 17.2.

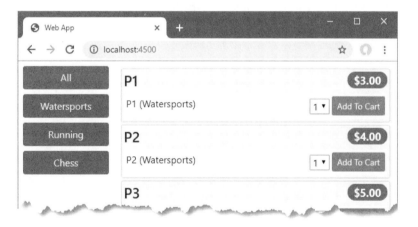

Figure 17.2 Running the example application

17.2 *Adding a web service*

In chapter 16, I used local test data to get started. I find this a useful approach to laying the foundation for a project, without getting bogged down in the details of getting the data from a server. But now that the application is taking shape, it is time to add a web service and start working with remote data. Open a new command prompt, navigate to the `webapp` folder, and run the command shown in listing 17.5 to add a new package to the project.

Listing 17.5   Adding a package to the project

```
npm install axios@1.3.4
```

Many packages are available for making HTTP requests in JavaScript applications, all of which use APIs provided by the browser. In this chapter, I am using the Axios package, which is a popular choice because it is easy to work with and comes complete with TypeScript declarations. To create a data source that uses HTTP requests, add a file called `remoteDataSource.ts` in the `src/data` folder and add the code shown in listing 17.6.

> **TIP** There are two APIs provided by browsers for making HTTP requests. The traditional API is `XmlHttpRequest` and is supported by all browsers, but it is difficult to work with. There is a new API, named Fetch, that is easier to work with but is not supported by older browsers. You can use either API directly, but packages like Axios provide an API that is easy to work with while preserving support for older browsers.

Listing 17.6   The contents of the remotedatasource.ts file in the src/data folder

```
import { AbstractDataSource } from "./abstractDataSource";
import { Product, Order } from "./entities";
import Axios from "axios";

const protocol = "http";
const hostname = "localhost";
const port = 4600;

const urls = {
    products: `${protocol}://${hostname}:${port}/products`,
    orders: `${protocol}://${hostname}:${port}/orders`
};

export class RemoteDataSource extends AbstractDataSource {

    loadProducts(): Promise<Product[]> {
        return Axios.get(urls.products).then(response => response.data);
    }

    storeOrder(): Promise<number> {
        let orderData = {
            lines: [...this.order.orderLines.values()].map(ol => ({
                productId: ol.product.id,
                productName: ol.product.name,
                quantity: ol.quantity
            }))
        }
        return Axios.post(urls.orders, orderData)
            .then(response => response.data.id);
    }
}
```

The Axios package provides `get` and `post` methods that send HTTP requests with the corresponding verbs. The implementation of the `loadProducts` method sends a GET request to the web service to get the product data. The `storeOrder` method transforms the details of the order to a shape that can be easily stored and sends the data to the web service as a POST request. The web service will respond with the object that has been stored, which includes an `id` value that uniquely identifies the stored object.

17.2.1 *Incorporating the data source into the application*

A configuration change is required so that the TypeScript compiler can resolve the dependency on the Axios package, as shown in listing 17.7.

Listing 17.7   Configuring the TypeScript compiler in the tsconfig.json file in the webapp folder

```
{
    "compilerOptions": {
        "target": "ES2022",
        "outDir": "./dist",
        "rootDir": "./src",
        "jsx": "react",
        "jsxFactory": "createElement",
        "moduleResolution": "bundler"
    }
}
```

This change tells the compiler that it can resolve dependencies by looking in the node_modules folder, using the `bundler` setting, which is intended for use with bundlers like webpack. Listing 17.8 updates the `index.ts` file to use the new data source.

Listing 17.8   Changing the data source in the index.ts file in the src folder

```
//import { LocalDataSource } from "./data/localDataSource";
import { RemoteDataSource } from "./data/remoteDataSource";
import { HtmlDisplay } from "./htmlDisplay";
import "bootstrap/dist/css/bootstrap.css";

let ds = new RemoteDataSource();

function displayData(): Promise<HTMLElement> {
    let display = new HtmlDisplay();
    display.props = {
        dataSource: ds
    }
    return display.getContent();
}

document.onreadystatechange = () => {
    if (document.readyState === "complete") {
        displayData().then(elem => {
            let rootElement = document.getElementById("app");
            rootElement.innerHTML = "";
```

```
                rootElement.appendChild(elem);
        });
    }
};
```

The development tools must be restarted to apply the configuration change in listing 17.7. Use Control+C to stop the combined web service and webpack process, and run the command shown in listing 17.9 in the `webapp` folder to start them again.

Listing 17.9   Starting the development tools

```
npm start
```

Use a browser to navigate to http://localhost:4500, and you will see the data that has been retrieved from the web service, as shown in figure 17.3.

Figure 17.3   Using remote data

17.3   *Completing the application*

Much of chapter 16 was spent setting up the development tools and configuring the project to deal with JSX, which makes it easier to work with HTML content in code files. Now that the basic structure of the application is in place, adding new features is relatively simple. There are no new TypeScript features in this section of the chapter, which just completes the application.

17.3.1   *Adding a header class*

To display a header that provides the user with a summary of their selections, add a file called `header.tsx` to the `src` folder with the contents shown in listing 17.10.

Listing 17.10 The contents of the header.tsx file in the src folder

```
import { createElement } from "./tools/jsxFactory";
import { Order } from "./data/entities";

export class Header {

    props: {
        order: Order,
        submitCallback: () => void
    }

    getContent(): HTMLElement {
        let count = this.props.order.productCount;
        return <div className="p-1 bg-secondary text-white text-end">
            { count === 0 ? "(No Selection)"
                : `${ count } product(s), $`
                    + `${ this.props.order.total.toFixed(2)}` }
            <button className="btn btn-sm btn-primary m-1"
                    onclick={ this.props.submitCallback }>
                Submit Order
            </button>
        </div>
    }

}
```

This class receives an `Order` object and a callback function through its props. A simple summary of the `Order` is displayed, along with a button that invokes the callback function when it is clicked.

17.3.2 Adding an order details class

To display details of the order, add a file called `orderDetails.tsx` to the `src` folder and add the code shown in listing 17.11.

Listing 17.11 The contents of the orderDetails.tsx file in the src folder

```
import { createElement } from "./tools/jsxFactory";
import { Product, Order } from "./data/entities";

export class OrderDetails {

    props: {
        order: Order
        cancelCallback: () => void,
        submitCallback: () => void
    }

    getContent(): HTMLElement {
        return <div>
            <h3 className="text-center bg-primary text-white p-2">
                Order Summary
            </h3>
            <div className="p-3">
```

```
            <table className="table table-sm table-striped">
                <thead>
                    <tr>
                        <th>Quantity</th><th>Product</th>
                        <th className="text-right">Price</th>
                        <th className="text-right">Subtotal</th>
                    </tr>
                </thead>
                <tbody>
                    { this.props.order.orderLines.map(line =>
                        <tr>
                            <td>{ line.quantity }</td>
                            <td>{ line.product.name }</td>
                            <td className="text-right">
                                ${ line.product.price.toFixed(2) }
                            </td>
                            <td className="text-right">
                                ${ line.total.toFixed(2) }
                            </td>
                        </tr>
                    )}
                </tbody>
                <tfoot>
                    <tr>
                        <th className="text-right" colSpan="3">
                            Total:
                        </th>
                        <th className="text-right">
                            ${ this.props.order.total.toFixed(2) }
                        </th>
                    </tr>
                </tfoot>
            </table>
        </div>
        <div className="text-center">
            <button className="btn btn-secondary m-1"
                    onclick={ this.props.cancelCallback }>
                Back
            </button>
            <button className="btn btn-primary m-1"
                    onclick={ this.props.submitCallback }>
                Submit Order
            </button>
        </div>
    </div>
    }
}
```

The `OrderDetails` class displays a table containing the details of the order, along with buttons to return to the product list or to submit the order.

17.3.3 *Adding a confirmation class*

To display a message when an order has been submitted, add a file called `summary.tsx` to the `src` folder and add the code shown in listing 17.12.

```
Listing 17.12  The contents of the summary.tsx file in the src folder
```

```tsx
import { createElement } from "./tools/jsxFactory";

export class Summary {

    props: {
        orderId: number,
        callback: () => void
    }

    getContent(): HTMLElement {
        return <div className="m-2 text-center">
            <h2>Thanks!</h2>
            <p>Thanks for placing your order.</p>
            <p>Your order is #{ this.props.orderId }</p>
            <p>We'll ship your goods as soon as possible.</p>
            <button className="btn btn-primary"
                    onclick={ this.props.callback }>
                OK
            </button>
        </div>
    }
}
```

This class displays a simple message that contains the unique ID assigned by the web service and a button that invokes a callback received as a prop when it is clicked.

17.3.4 Completing the application

The final step is to add the code that will combine the classes created in the earlier sections, provide them with the data and callback functions they require through their props, and display the HTML content they generate, as shown in listing 17.13.

```
Listing 17.13  Completing the application in the htmlDisplay.tsx file in the src folder
```

```tsx
import { createElement } from "./tools/jsxFactory";
import { Product, Order } from "./data/entities";
import { AbstractDataSource } from "./data/abstractDataSource";
import { ProductList } from "./productList";
import { Header } from "./header";
import { OrderDetails } from "./orderDetails";
import { Summary } from "./summary";

enum DisplayMode {
    List, Details, Complete
}

export class HtmlDisplay {
    private containerElem: HTMLElement;
    private selectedCategory: string;
    private mode: DisplayMode = DisplayMode.List;
    private orderId: number;

    constructor() {
```

```
            this.containerElem = document.createElement("div");
    }

    props: {
        dataSource: AbstractDataSource;
    }

    async getContent(): Promise<HTMLElement> {
        await this.updateContent();
        return this.containerElem;
    }

    async updateContent() {
        let products = await this.props.dataSource
            .getProducts("id", this.selectedCategory);
        let categories = await this.props.dataSource.getCategories();
        this.containerElem.innerHTML = "";
        let contentElem: HTMLElement;
        switch (this.mode) {
            case DisplayMode.List:
                contentElem = this.getListContent(products, categories);
                break;
            case DisplayMode.Details:
                contentElem = <OrderDetails
                    order={ this.props.dataSource.order }
                    cancelCallback={ this.showList }
                    submitCallback={ this.submitOrder } />
                break;
            case DisplayMode.Complete:
                contentElem = <Summary orderId={ this.orderId }
                    callback= { this.showList } />
                break;
        }
        this.containerElem.appendChild(contentElem);
    }

    getListContent(products: Product[], categories: string[])
            : HTMLElement {
        return <div>
            <Header order={ this.props.dataSource.order }
                submitCallback={ this.showDetails } />
            <ProductList products={ products } categories={ categories }
                selectedCategory={ this.selectedCategory }
                addToOrderCallback={ this.addToOrder }
                filterCallback={ this.selectCategory} />
        </div>
    }

    addToOrder = (product: Product, quantity: number) => {
        this.props.dataSource.order.addProduct(product, quantity);
        this.updateContent();
    }

    selectCategory = (selected: string) => {
        this.selectedCategory = selected === "All" ? undefined : selected;
        this.updateContent();
    }
```

```
showDetails = () => {
    this.mode = DisplayMode.Details;
    this.updateContent();
}

showList = () => {
    this.mode = DisplayMode.List;
    this.updateContent();
}

submitOrder = () => {
    this.props.dataSource.storeOrder().then(id => {
        this.orderId = id;
        this.props.dataSource.order = new Order();
        this.mode = DisplayMode.Complete;
        this.updateContent();
    });
}
}
```

The additions to the `HtmlDisplay` class are used to determine which JSX classes are used to display content to the user. The key is the `mode` property, which uses the values of the `DisplayMode` enum to select content, combined with the `showDetails`, `showList`, and `submitOrder` methods, which change the `mode` value and update the display.

There can often be a single class in a web application that becomes a point where complexity is concentrated, even in a simple application like this one. Using one of the frameworks described in the chapters that follow can help but simply expresses it in a different way, most often in a complex set of mappings between the URLs the application supports and the content classes that they correspond to.

When all the changes are saved and the browser has loaded the new bundle, you will be able to make product selections, review those selections, and submit them to the server, as shown in figure 17.4.

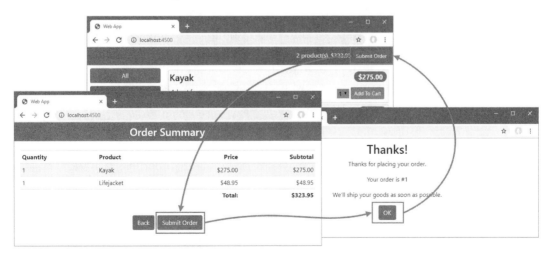

Figure 17.4   Using the example application

When you submit an order, you can see the data that the server has stored by navigating to http://localhost:4600/orders, as shown in figure 17.5.

> **NOTE** The orders are not stored persistently and will be lost when the web service is stopped or restarted. Persistent storage is added in the next section.

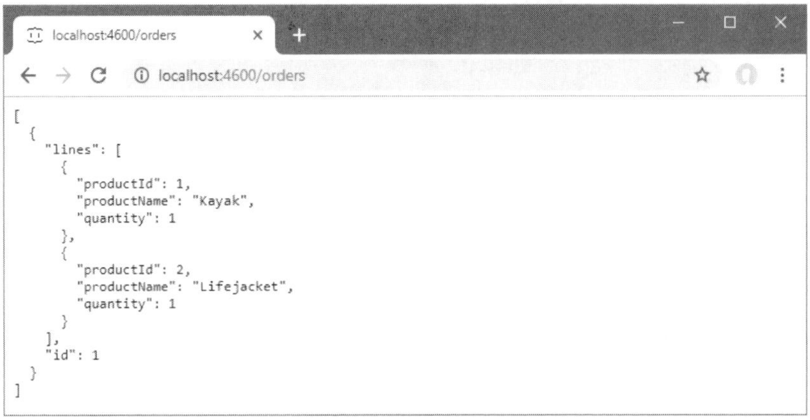

Figure 17.5   Inspecting the submitted orders

17.4   *Deploying the application*

The Webpack Development Server and the toolchain that provides it with the bundle cannot be used in production, so some additional work is required to prepare an application for deployment, as described in the following sections.

17.4.1   *Adding the production HTTP server package*

The Webpack Development Server should not be used in production because the features it provides are focused on creating bundles dynamically based on changes in the source code. For production, a regular HTTP server is required to deliver the HTML, CSS, and JavaScript files to the browser, and a good choice for simple projects is the open-source Express server, which is a JavaScript package that is executed by the Node.js runtime. Use Control+C to stop the development tools, and use the command prompt to run the command shown in listing 17.14 in the webapp folder to install the express package.

> **NOTE** The express package may already be installed because it is used by other tools. Even so, it is good practice to add the package because it adds a dependency in the project.json file.

Listing 17.14   Adding a package for deployment

```
npm install --save-dev express@4.18.2
```

17.4.2 Creating the persistent data file

The `json-server` package will store its data persistently when configured to use a JSON file, rather than the JavaScript file that allows the data to be reset during development. Add a file called `data.json` to the `webapp` folder and add the content shown in listing 17.15.

> **Listing 17.15   The contents of the data.json file in the webapp folder**

```
{
    "products": [
        { "id": 1, "name": "Kayak", "category": "Watersports",
          "description": "A boat for one person", "price": 275 },
        { "id": 2, "name": "Lifejacket", "category": "Watersports",
          "description": "Protective and fashionable", "price": 48.95 },
        { "id": 3, "name": "Soccer Ball", "category": "Soccer",
          "description": "FIFA-approved size and weight",
          "price": 19.50 },
        { "id": 4, "name": "Corner Flags", "category": "Soccer",
          "description": "Give your playing field a professional touch",
          "price": 34.95 },
        { "id": 5, "name": "Stadium", "category": "Soccer",
          "description": "Flat-packed 35,000-seat stadium",
          "price": 79500 },
        { "id": 6, "name": "Thinking Cap", "category": "Chess",
          "description": "Improve brain efficiency by 75%",
          "price": 16 },
        { "id": 7, "name": "Unsteady Chair", "category": "Chess",
          "description": "Secretly give your opponent a disadvantage",
          "price": 29.95 },
        { "id": 8, "name": "Human Chess Board", "category": "Chess",
          "description": "A fun game for the family", "price": 75 },
        { "id": 9, "name": "Bling Bling King", "category": "Chess",
          "description": "Gold-plated, diamond-studded King",
          "price": 1200 }
    ],
    "orders": []
}
```

This is the same product information I added to the JavaScript file in listing 17.2, but it is expressed in JSON format, which means that the stored order data won't be lost when the application is stopped or restarted.

17.4.3 Creating the server

To create the server that will deliver the application and its data to the browser, create a file called `server.js` in the `webapp` folder and add the code shown in listing 17.16.

> **Listing 17.16   The contents of the server.js file in the webapp folder**

```
const express = require("express");
const jsonServer = require("json-server");

const app = express();
```

```
app.use("/", express.static("dist"));
app.use("/", express.static("assets"));

const router = jsonServer.router("data.json");
app.use(jsonServer.bodyParser)
app.use("/api", (req, resp, next) => router(req, resp, next));

const port = process.argv[3] || 4000;
app.listen(port, () => console.log(`Running on port ${port}`));
```

The statements in the `server.js` file configure the `express` and `json-server` packages so that the contents of the `dist` and `assets` folders are used to deliver static files and so URLs prefixed with `/api` will be handled by the web service.

> **TIP** You can write server code like this in TypeScript and then compile it to generate the JavaScript that will be executed in production. This is a good idea if you have especially complex server code, but I find working directly in JavaScript easier for simple projects that are only combining the features provided by different packages.

17.4.4 *Using relative URLs for data requests*

The web service that provided the application with data has been running alongside the Webpack Development Server. In deployment, I am going to listen for both types of HTTP requests in a single port. In preparation, a change is required to the URLs used by the `RemoteDataSource` class, as shown in listing 17.17.

> **Listing 17.17   Using relative URLs in the remoteDataSource.ts file in the src/data folder**

```
import { AbstractDataSource } from "./abstractDataSource";
import { Product, Order } from "./entities";
import Axios from "axios";

// const protocol = "http";
// const hostname = "localhost";
// const port = 4600;

const urls = {
    // products: `${protocol}://${hostname}:${port}/products`,
    // orders: `${protocol}://${hostname}:${port}/orders`
    products: "/api/products",
    orders: "/api/orders"
};

export class RemoteDataSource extends AbstractDataSource {

    loadProducts(): Promise<Product[]> {
        return Axios.get(urls.products).then(response => response.data);
    }

    storeOrder(): Promise<number> {
        let orderData = {
            lines: [...this.order.orderLines.values()].map(ol => ({
```

```
                    productId: ol.product.id,
                    productName: ol.product.name,
                    quantity: ol.quantity
                }))
        }
        return Axios.post(urls.orders, orderData)
            .then(response => response.data.id);
    }
}
```

The URLs are specified relative to the one used to request the HTML document, following the common convention that data requests are prefixed with `/api`.

17.4.5 Building the application

Run the command shown in listing 17.18 in the `webapp` folder to create a bundle that
can be used in production.

Listing 17.18 Creating the production bundle

```
npx webpack --mode "production"
```

When the `mode` argument is `production`, webpack creates a bundle whose contents
are minified, meaning that they are optimized for size instead of code readability. The
build process can take a few moments to complete and will produce the following output, which shows which files have been incorporated into the bundle:

```
asset bundle.js 2.23 MiB [emitted] [minimized] [big] (name: main)
orphan modules 99.8 KiB [orphan] 55 modules
runtime modules 1.09 KiB 5 modules
cacheable modules 956 KiB
  asset modules 4.4 KiB
    data:image/svg+xml,%3csvg xmlns=%27.. 281 bytes [built] [code generated]
    data:image/svg+xml,%3csvg xmlns=%27.. 279 bytes [built] [code generated]
    data:image/svg+xml,%3csvg xmlns=%27.. 161 bytes [built] [code generated]
    data:image/svg+xml,%3csvg xmlns=%27.. 271 bytes [built] [code generated]
    + 12 modules
  javascript modules 952 KiB

    modules by path ./node_modules/style-loader/dist/runtime/*.js
        5.84 KiB 6 modules

    modules by path ./node_modules/css-loader/dist/runtime/*.js
        3.33 KiB 3 modules
    ./src/index.ts + 53 modules 99.7 KiB [built] [code generated]

    ./node_modules/css-
loader/dist/cjs.js!./node_modules/bootstrap/dist/css/bootstrap.css
        843 KiB [built] [code generated]

WARNING in asset size limit: The following asset(s) exceed the recommended
size limit (244 KiB).
This can impact web performance.
Assets:
  bundle.js (2.23 MiB)

WARNING in entrypoint size limit: The following entrypoint(s) combined
```

```
asset size exceeds the recommended limit (244 KiB). This can impact web
performance.
Entrypoints:
  main (2.23 MiB)
      bundle.js


WARNING in webpack performance recommendations:
You can limit the size of your bundles by using import() or require.ensure
to lazy load some parts of your application.
For more info visit https://webpack.js.org/guides/code-splitting/


webpack 5.76.3 compiled with 3 warnings in 4690 microservice
```

The TypeScript files are compiled into JavaScript, just as they were in development, and the bundle file is written to the `dist` folder. The warnings about the size of the files that have been created can be ignored.

17.4.6   *Testing the production build*

To make sure that the build process has worked and the configuration changes have taken effect, run the command shown in listing 17.19 in the `webapp` folder.

> **Listing 17.19   Starting the production server**

```
node server.js
```

The code will be executed and will produce the following output:

```
Running on port 4000
```

Open a new web browser and navigate to http://localhost:4000, which will show the application, as illustrated in figure 17.6.

Figure 17.6   Running the production build

17.5 Containerizing the application

To complete this chapter, I am going to create a container for the example application so that it can be deployed into production. At the time of writing, Docker is the most popular way to create a container, which is a pared-down version of Linux with just enough functionality to run the application. Most cloud platforms or hosting engines have support for Docker, and its tools run on the most popular operating systems.

17.5.1 Installing Docker

The first step is to download and install Docker on your development machine, which is available from https://www.docker.com/products/docker. There are versions for macOS, Windows, and Linux, and there are some specialized versions to work with the Amazon and Microsoft cloud platforms. The free edition is sufficient for this chapter.

> **CAUTION** One drawback of using Docker is that the company that produces the software has gained a reputation for making breaking changes. This may mean that the example that follows may not work as intended with later versions. If you have problems, check the repository for this book for updates (https://github.com/manningbooks/essential-typescript-5) or contact me at adam@adam-freeman.com.

17.5.2 Preparing the application

The first step is to create a configuration file for NPM that will be used to download the additional packages required by the application for use in the container. I created a file called `deploy-package.json` in the `webapp` folder with the content shown in listing 17.20.

> **Listing 17.20   The contents of the deploy-package.json file in the webapp folder**

```
{
    "name": "webapp",
    "description": "Stand-Alone Web App",
    "repository": "https://github.com/manningbooks/essential-typescript-5",
    "license": "0BSD",
    "devDependencies": {
        "express": "4.18.2",
        "json-server": "0.17.3"
    }
}
```

The `devDependencies` section specifies the packages required to run the application in the container. All of the packages for which there are `import` statements in the application's code files will have been incorporated into the bundle created by webpack and are listed. The other fields describe the application, and their main use is to prevent a warning when the container is created.

17.5.3 *Creating the Docker container*

To define the container, I added a file called `Dockerfile` (with no extension) to the `webapp` folder and added the content shown in listing 17.21.

> **Listing 17.21   The contents of the Dockerfile file in the webapp folder**

```
FROM node:18.14.0

RUN mkdir -p /usr/src/webapp

COPY dist /usr/src/webapp/dist
COPY assets /usr/src/webapp/assets

COPY data.json /usr/src/webapp/
COPY server.js /usr/src/webapp/
COPY deploy-package.json /usr/src/webapp/package.json

WORKDIR /usr/src/webapp

RUN echo 'package-lock=false' >> .npmrc
RUN npm install

EXPOSE 4000

CMD ["node", "server.js"]
```

The contents of the `Dockerfile` use a base image that has been configured with Node.js and copies the files required to run the application, including the bundle file containing the application and the file that will be used to install the NPM packages required to run the application in deployment.

To speed up the containerization process, I created a file called `.dockerignore` in the `webapp` folder with the content shown in listing 17.22. This tells Docker to ignore the `node_modules` folder, which is not required in the container and takes a long time to process.

> **Listing 17.22   The contents of the .dockerignore file in the webapp folder**

```
node_modules
```

Run the command shown in listing 17.23 in the `webapp` folder to create an image that will contain the example application, along with all the packages it requires.

> **Listing 17.23   Building the Docker image**

```
docker build . -t webapp -f Dockerfile
```

An image is a template for containers. As Docker processes the instructions in the Docker file, the NPM packages will be downloaded and installed, and the configuration and code files will be copied into the image.

17.5.4 *Running the application*

Once the image has been created, create and start a new container using the command shown in listing 17.24.

Listing 17.24 Starting the Docker container

```
docker run -p 4000:4000 webapp
```

You can test the application by opening http://localhost:4000 in the browser, which will display the response provided by the web server running in the container, as shown in figure 17.7.

Figure 17.7 Running the containerized application

To stop the container, run the command shown in listing 17.25.

Listing 17.25 Listing the containers

```
docker ps
```

You will see a list of running containers, like this (I have omitted some fields for brevity):

```
CONTAINER ID    IMAGE      COMMAND                 CREATED
4b9b82772197    webapp     "docker-entrypoint.s…"  33 seconds ago
```

Using the value in the Container ID column, run the command shown in listing 17.26.

Listing 17.26 Stopping the container

```
docker stop 4b9b82772197
```

The application is ready to deploy to any platform that supports Docker.

Summary

In this chapter, I completed the development of the standalone web application by adding a data source that consumed a web service and by adding JSX classes that displayed different content to the user. I finished by preparing the application for deployment and creating a Docker container image.

- RESTful web services can be consumed using standard HTTP requests, which is made easier with a package such as Axios.
- The TypeScript compiler has a `bundler` setting for the `moduleResolution` configuration property, which can be used to find modules in the `node_modules` folder and ensures that module imports are processed in a way that works with bundlers such as webpack.
- TypeScript applications are compiled to pure JavaScript, which means they can be packages and deployed so they are served from containers.

In the next chapter, I build a web application using the Angular framework.

18

Creating
an Angular app, part 1

This chapter covers

- Creating and configuring an Angular project
- Understanding the Angular TypeScript configuration
- Building a data model for the Angular application
- Creating Angular components for basic application features
- Configuring the Angular application

In this chapter, I start the process of creating an Angular web application that has the same set of features as the example in chapters 16 and 17 Unlike other frameworks, where using TypeScript is an option, Angular puts TypeScript at the heart of web application development and relies on its features, especially decorators. For quick reference, table 18.1 lists the TypeScript compiler options used in this chapter.

Table 18.1   The TypeScript Compiler Options Used in This chapter

Name	Description
baseUrl	This option specifies the root location used to resolve module dependencies.
declaration	This option produces type declaration files when enabled, which describe the types for use in other projects.
downlevelIteration	This option enables support for iterators when targeting older versions of JavaScript.
experimentalDecorators	This option determines whether decorators are enabled.
forceConsistentCasing-InFileNames	This option requires files to be imported using correctly-cased names.
importHelpers	This option determines whether helper code is added to the JavaScript to reduce the amount of code that is produced overall.
lib	This option selects the type declaration files the compiler uses.
module	This option determines the style of module that is used.
moduleResolution	This option specifies how modules are resolved.
noFallthroughCasesInSwitch	This option enables errors when switch statements are allowed to fall through without a break statement.
noImplicitOverride	This option enables errors when a subclass redefines a member defined by the base class without using the override keyword.
noImplicitReturns	This option enables errors for functions and methods that return undeclared results.
noPropertyAccessFromIndex-Signature	This option enables errors when attempting to access existent properties on objects.
outDir	This option specifies the directory in which the JavaScript files will be placed.
sourceMap	This option determines whether the compiler generates source maps for debugging.
strict	This option enables stricter type checking, including preventing the implicit use of any.
target	This option specifies the version of the JavaScript language that the compiler will target in its output.
useDefineForClassFields	This option determines how class fields are defined in the output JavaScript.

18.1 Preparing for this chapter

Angular projects are most easily created using the `angular-cli` package. Open a command prompt and run the command shown in listing 18.1 to install the `angular-cli` package.

> **TIP** You can download the example project for this chapter—and for all the other chapters in this book—from https://github.com/manningbooks/essential-typescript-5.

Listing 18.1   Installing the project creation package

```
npm install --global @angular/cli@15.2.4
```

The Angular package names are prefixed with `@`. Once you have installed the package, navigate to a convenient location and run the command shown in listing 18.2 to create a new Angular project.

Listing 18.2   Creating a new project

```
ng new angularapp
```

The Angular development tools are used through the `ng` command, and `ng new` creates a new project. During the setup process, you will be asked to make choices about the way the new project is configured. Use the answers from table 18.2 to prepare the example project for this chapter.

Table 18.2   The project setup questions and answers

Question	Answer
Would you like to add Angular routing?	Yes
Which stylesheet format would you like to use?	CSS

It can take a few minutes for the project to be created because a large number of Java-Script packages must be downloaded.

18.1.1 Configuring the web service

Once the creation process is complete, run the commands shown in listing 18.3 to navigate to the project folder and add the packages that will provide the web service, and allow multiple packages to be started with a single command.

Listing 18.3   Adding packages to the project

```
cd angularapp
npm install --save-dev json-server@0.17.3
npm install --save-dev npm-run-all@4.1.5
```

To provide the data for the web service, add a file called `data.js` to the `angularapp` folder with the content shown in listing 18.4.

Listing 18.4   The contents of the data.js file in the angularapp folder

```
module.exports = function () {
    return {
        products: [
            { id: 1, name: "Kayak", category: "Watersports",
                description: "A boat for one person", price: 275 },
            { id: 2, name: "Lifejacket", category: "Watersports",
                description: "Protective and fashionable", price: 48.95 },
            { id: 3, name: "Soccer Ball", category: "Soccer",
                description: "FIFA-approved size and weight",
                price: 19.50 },
            { id: 4, name: "Corner Flags", category: "Soccer",
                description:
                    "Give your playing field a professional touch",
                price: 34.95 },
            { id: 5, name: "Stadium", category: "Soccer",
                description: "Flat-packed 35,000-seat stadium",
                price: 79500 },
            { id: 6, name: "Thinking Cap", category: "Chess",
                description: "Improve brain efficiency by 75%",
                price: 16 },
            { id: 7, name: "Unsteady Chair", category: "Chess",
                description: "Secretly give your opponent a disadvantage",
                price: 29.95 },
            { id: 8, name: "Human Chess Board", category: "Chess",
                description: "A fun game for the family", price: 75 },
            { id: 9, name: "Bling Bling King", category: "Chess",
                description: "Gold-plated, diamond-studded King",
                price: 1200 }
        ],
        orders: []
    }
}
```

Update the scripts section of the package.json file to configure the development tools so that the Angular toolchain and the web service are started at the same time, as shown in listing 18.5.

Listing 18.5   Configuring tools in the package.json file in the angularapp folder

```
...
"scripts": {
  "ng": "ng",
  "json": "json-server data.js -p 4600",
  "serve": "ng serve",
  "start": "npm-run-all -p serve json",
  "build": "ng build",
  "test": "ng test",
  "lint": "ng lint",
  "e2e": "ng e2e"
},
...
```

These entries allow both the web service that will provide the data and the Angular development tools to be started with a single command.

18.1.2 Configuring the Bootstrap CSS package

Use the command prompt to run the command shown in listing 18.6 in the `angularapp` folder to add the Bootstrap CSS framework to the project.

Listing 18.6   Adding the package

```
npm install bootstrap@5.2.3
```

The Angular development tools require a configuration change to incorporate the Bootstrap CSS stylesheet in the application. Open the `angular.json` file in the `angularapp` folder and add the item shown in listing 18.7 to the `build/styles` section.

> **CAUTION**   There are two `styles` settings in the `angular.json` file, and you must take care to change the one in the `build` section and not the `test` section. If you don't see styled content when you run the example application, the likely cause is that you have edited the wrong section.

Listing 18.7   Adding a stylesheet in the angular.json file in the angularapp folder

```
...
"build": {
    "builder": "@angular-devkit/build-angular:browser",
    "options": {
    "outputPath": "dist/angularapp",
    "index": "src/index.html",
    "main": "src/main.ts",
    "polyfills": "src/polyfills.ts",
    "tsConfig": "src/tsconfig.app.json",
    "assets": [
        "src/favicon.ico",
        "src/assets"
    ],
    "styles": [
        "src/styles.css",
        "node_modules/bootstrap/dist/css/bootstrap.min.css"
    ],
    "scripts": [],
    "es5BrowserSupport": true
    },
...
```

18.1.3 Starting the example application

Use the command prompt to run the command shown in listing 18.8 in the `angularapp` folder.

Listing 18.8   Starting the development tools

```
npm start
```

The Angular development tools take a moment to start and perform the initial compilation, producing output like this:

```
...
✓ Browser application bundle generation complete.

Initial Chunk Files    | Names      |  Raw Size
vendor.js              | vendor     |   2.04 MB |
styles.css, styles.js  | styles     | 398.72 kB |
polyfills.js           | polyfills  | 314.27 kB |
main.js                | main       |  48.10 kB |
runtime.js             | runtime    |   6.52 kB |

                       | Initial Total |  2.79 MB

Build at: 2023-03-26T07:33:08.269Z - Hash: b52d7ae4c7e8d087 - Time: 3963ms


** Angular Live Development Server is listening on localhost:4200, open
your browser on http://localhost:4200/ **
...
```

Once the initial compilation has been completed, open a browser window and navigate to http://localhost:4200 to see the placeholder content created by the command in listing 18.2 and which is shown in figure 18.1.

Figure 18.1   Running the example application

18.2   *Understanding TypeScript in Angular development*

Angular depends on TypeScript decorators but has yet to be updated to use the standard decorators described in chapter 14. Instead, Angular relies on the previous TypeScript decorator implementation, which works largely the same way, but requires some additional compiler configuration settings.

Look at the contents of the `app.module.ts` file in the `src/app` folder, and you will see one of the decorators Angular relies on.

```
import { NgModule } from '@angular/core';
import { BrowserModule } from '@angular/platform-browser';

import { AppRoutingModule } from './app-routing.module';
import { AppComponent } from './app.component';

@NgModule({
  declarations: [AppComponent],
  imports: [BrowserModule, AppRoutingModule],
  providers: [],
  bootstrap: [AppComponent]
})

export class AppModule { }
```

Decorators are so important in Angular development that they are applied to classes that contain few or even no members, just to help define or configure the application. This is the `NgModule` decorator, and it is used to describe a group of related features in the Angular application (Angular modules exist alongside conventional JavaScript modules, which is why this file contains both `import` statements and the `NgModule` decorator). Another example can be seen in the `app.component.ts` file in the `src/app` folder.

```
import { Component } from '@angular/core';

@Component({
  selector: 'app-root',
  templateUrl: './app.component.html',
  styleUrls: ['./app.component.css']
})
export class AppComponent {
  title = 'angularapp';
}
```

This is the `Component` decorator, which describes a class that will generate HTML content, similar in purpose to the JSX classes I created in the stand-alone web app.

18.2.1 Understanding the TypeScript compiler configuration

The toolchain for Angular is similar to the one I used in chapters 15 and 16 and relies on webpack and the Webpack Development Server, with customizations specific to Angular. You can see traces of webpack in some of the messages that are emitted by the Angular development tools, but the details—and the configuration file—are not exposed directly. You can see and change the configuration used for the TypeScript compiler because the project is created with a `tsconfig.json` file, which is created with the following settings:

```
{
  "compileOnSave": false,
  "compilerOptions": {
    "baseUrl": "./",
    "outDir": "./dist/out-tsc",
```

```
        "forceConsistentCasingInFileNames": true,
        "strict": true,
        "noImplicitOverride": true,
        "noPropertyAccessFromIndexSignature": true,
        "noImplicitReturns": true,
        "noFallthroughCasesInSwitch": true,
        "sourceMap": true,
        "declaration": false,
        "downlevelIteration": true,
        "experimentalDecorators": true,
        "moduleResolution": "node",
        "importHelpers": true,
        "target": "ES2022",
        "module": "ES2022",
        "useDefineForClassFields": false,
        "lib": [
          "ES2022",
          "dom"
        ]
    },
    "angularCompilerOptions": {
        "enableI18nLegacyMessageIdFormat": false,
        "strictInjectionParameters": true,
        "strictInputAccessModifiers": true,
        "strictTemplates": true
    }
}
```

The configuration writes the compiled JavaScript files to the `dist/out-tsc` folder, although you won't see that folder in the project because webpack is used to create a bundle automatically.

The most important setting is `experimentalDecorators`, which enables the decorator implementation required by the Angular framework.

> **CAUTION**   Care is required when making changes to the `tsconfig.json` file because they can break the rest of the Angular toolchain. Most changes in an Angular project are applied through the `angular.json` File.

18.3   *Creating the data model*

To start the data model, create the `src/app/data` folder and add to it a file called `entities.ts`, with the code shown in listing 18.9.

> **Listing 18.9   The contents of the entities.ts file in the src/app/data folder**

```
export type Product = {
    id: number,
    name: string,
    description: string,
    category: string,
    price: number
};
```

```
export class OrderLine {
    constructor(public product: Product, public quantity: number) {
        // no statements required
    }

    get total(): number {
        return this.product.price * this.quantity;
    }
}

export class Order {
    private lines = new Map<number, OrderLine>();

    constructor(initialLines?: OrderLine[]) {
        if (initialLines) {
            initialLines.forEach(ol => this.lines.set(ol.product.id, ol));
        }
    }

    public addProduct(prod: Product, quantity: number) {
        if (this.lines.has(prod.id)) {
            if (quantity === 0) {
                this.removeProduct(prod.id);
            } else {
                this.lines.get(prod.id)!.quantity += quantity;
            }
        } else {
            this.lines.set(prod.id, new OrderLine(prod, quantity));
        }
    }

    public removeProduct(id: number) {
        this.lines.delete(id);
    }

    get orderLines(): OrderLine[] {
        return [...this.lines.values()];
    }

    get productCount(): number {
        return [...this.lines.values()]
            .reduce((total, ol) => total += ol.quantity, 0);
    }

    get total(): number {
        return [...this.lines.values()]
            .reduce((total, ol) => total += ol.total, 0);
    }
}
```

This is the same code used in chapter 15 and requires no changes because Angular uses regular TypeScript classes for its data model entities.

18.3.1 Creating the Data Source

To create the data source, add a file named `dataSource.ts` to the `src/app/data` folder with the code shown in listing 18.10.

Listing 18.10   The contents of the dataSource.ts file in the src/app/data folder

```
import { Observable } from "rxjs";
import { Injectable } from '@angular/core';
import { Product, Order } from "./entities";

export type ProductProp = keyof Product;

export abstract class DataSourceImpl {
    abstract loadProducts(): Observable<Product[]>;
    abstract storeOrder(order: Order): Observable<number>;
}

@Injectable()
export class DataSource {
    private _products: Product[];
    private _categories: Set<string>;
    public order: Order;

    constructor(private impl: DataSourceImpl) {
        this._products = [];
        this._categories = new Set<string>();
        this.order = new Order();
        this.getData();
    }

    getProducts(sortProp: ProductProp = "id", category? : string)
            : Product[] {
        return this.selectProducts(this._products, sortProp, category);
    }

    protected getData(): void {
        this._products = [];
        this._categories.clear();
        this.impl.loadProducts().subscribe(rawData => {
            rawData.forEach(p => {
                this._products.push(p);
                this._categories.add(p.category);
            });
        });
    }

    protected selectProducts(prods: Product[], sortProp: ProductProp,
            category?: string): Product[] {
        return prods
            .filter(p => category === undefined || p.category === category)
            .sort((p1, p2) => p1[sortProp] < p2[sortProp]
                ? -1 : p1[sortProp] > p2[sortProp] ? 1: 0);
    }
}
```

```
getCategories(): string[] {
    return [...this._categories.values()];
}

storeOrder(): Observable<number> {
    return this.impl.storeOrder(this.order);
}
}
```

Services are one of the key features in Angular development; they allow classes to declare dependencies in their constructors that are resolved at runtime, a technique known as *dependency injection*. The DataSource class declares a dependency on a DataSourceImpl object in its constructor, like this:

```
...
constructor(private impl: DataSourceImpl) {
...
```

When a new DataSource object is needed, Angular will inspect the constructor, create a DataSourceImpl object, and use it to invoke the constructor to create the new object, a process known as *injection*. The Injectable decorator tells Angular that other classes can declare dependencies on the DataSource class. The DataSourceImpl class is abstract, and the DataSource class has no idea which concrete implementation class will be used to resolve its constructor dependency. The selection of the implementation class is made in the application's configuration, as shown in listing 18.12.

One of the key advantages of using a framework for web application development is that updates are handled automatically. Angular uses the Reactive Extensions library, known as RxJS, to manage updates, allowing changes in data to be handled automatically. The RxJS Observable class is used to describe a sequence of values that will be generated over time, including asynchronous activities like requesting data from a web service. The loadProducts method defined by the DataSourceImpl class returns an Observable<Product[]> object, like this:

```
...
abstract loadProducts(): Observable<Product[]>;
...
```

A TypeScript generic type argument is used to specify that the result of the load-Products method is an Observable object that will generate a sequence of Product array objects. The values generated by an Observable object are received using the subscribe method, like this:

```
...
this.impl.loadProducts().subscribe(rawData => {
    rawData.forEach(p => {
        this._products.push(p);
        this._categories.add(p.category);
    });
});
...
```

In this situation, I am using the Observable class as a direct replacement for the standard JavaScript Promise. The Observable class provides sophisticated features for dealing with complex sequences, but the advantage here is that Angular will update the content presented to the user when the `Observable` produces a result, which means that the rest of the `DataSource` class can be written without needing to deal with asynchronous tasks.

18.3.2   *Creating the data source implementation class*

To extend the abstract `DataSourceImpl` class to work with the web service, I added a file named `remoteDataSource.ts` to the `src/app/data` folder and added the code shown in listing 18.11.

> **Listing 18.11   The contents of the remoteDataSource.ts file in the src/app/data folder**

```typescript
import { Injectable } from "@angular/core";
import { HttpClient } from "@angular/common/http";
import { Observable } from "rxjs";
import { map } from "rxjs/operators";
import { DataSourceImpl } from "./dataSource";
import { Product, Order } from "./entities";

const protocol = "http";
const hostname = "localhost";
const port = 4600;

const urls = {
    products: `${protocol}://${hostname}:${port}/products`,
    orders: `${protocol}://${hostname}:${port}/orders`
};

@Injectable()
export class RemoteDataSource extends DataSourceImpl {

    constructor(private http: HttpClient) {
        super();
    }

    loadProducts(): Observable<Product[]> {
        return this.http.get<Product[]>(urls.products);
    }

    storeOrder(order: Order): Observable<number> {
        let orderData = {
            lines: [...order.orderLines.values()].map(ol => ({
                productId: ol.product.id,
                productName: ol.product.name,
                quantity: ol.quantity
            }))
        }
        return this.http.post<{ id: number}>(urls.orders, orderData)
            .pipe<number>(map(val => val.id));
    }
}
```

The `RemoteDataSource` constructor declares a dependency on an instance of the `HttpClient` class, which is the built-in Angular class for making HTTP requests. The `HttpClient` class defines `get` and `post` methods that are used to send HTTP requests with the GET and POST verbs. The data type that is expected is specified as a type argument, like this:

```
...
loadProducts(): Observable<Product[]> {
    return this.http.get<Product[]>(urls.products);
}
...
```

The type argument is used for the result from the `get` method, which is an `Observable` that will generate a sequence of the specified type, which is `Product[]` in this case.

> **TIP** The generic type arguments for the `HttpClient` methods are standard TypeScript. There is no Angular magic happening behind the scenes, and the developer remains responsible for specifying a type that will correspond to the data received from the server.

The RxJS library contains features that can be used to manipulate the values generated by an `Observable` object, some of which are used in listing 18.11.

```
...
return this.http.post<{ id: number}>(urls.orders, orderData)
    .pipe<number>(map(val => val.id));
...
```

The `pipe` method is used with the `map` function to create an `Observable` that generates values based on those from another `Observable`. This allows me to receive the result from the HTTP POST request and extract just the `id` property from the result.

> **NOTE** In the stand-alone web application, I created an abstract data source class and created subclasses that provided local or web service data, which was loaded by a method called in the abstract class constructor. This is an approach that doesn't work well in Angular because the `HttpClient` is not assigned to an instance property until after the abstract class constructor is invoked with the `super` keyword, which means the subclass is asked to get data before it has been properly set up. To avoid this problem, I separated just the part of the data source that deals with the data into the abstract class.

18.3.3 Configuring the data source

The last step of creating the data source is to create an Angular module, which will make the data source available for use in the rest of the application and select the implementation of the abstract `DataSourceImpl` class that will be used. Add a file called `data.module.ts` to the `src/app/data` folder and add the code shown in listing 18.12.

```
import { NgModule } from "@angular/core";
import { HttpClientModule } from "@angular/common/http";
import { DataSource, DataSourceImpl } from './dataSource';
import { RemoteDataSource } from './remoteDataSource';

@NgModule({
  imports: [HttpClientModule],
  providers: [DataSource,
      { provide: DataSourceImpl, useClass: RemoteDataSource }]
})
export class DataModelModule { }
```

The DataModelModule class is defined just so that the NgModule decorator can be applied. The decorator's imports property defines the dependencies that the data model classes require, and the providers property defines the classes in the Angular module that can be injected into the constructors of other classes in the application. For this module, the imports property tells Angular that the module that contains the HttpClient class is required, and the providers property tells Angular that the DataSource class can be used for dependency injection and that dependencies on the DataSourceImpl class should be resolved using the RemoteDataSource class.

18.4   *Displaying a filtered list of products*

Angular splits the generation of HTML content into two files: a TypeScript class to which the Component decorator is applied and an HTML template that is annotated with directives that direct the generation of dynamic content. When the application is executed, the HTML template is compiled, and the directives are executed using the methods and properties provided by the TypeScript class.

Classes to which the Component decorator is applied are known, logically enough, as *components*. The convention in Angular development is to include the role of the class in the file name, so to create the component responsible for the details of a single product to the user, I added a file named productItem.component.ts in the src/app folder with the code shown in listing 18.13.

```
import { Component, Input, Output, EventEmitter } from "@angular/core";
import { Product } from './data/entities';

export type productSelection = {
    product: Product,
    quantity: number
}

@Component({
    selector: "product-item",
    templateUrl: "./productItem.component.html"
})
export class ProductItem {
```

```
    quantity: number = 1;

    @Input()
    product: Product = {
        id: 0, name: "", description: "", category: "", price: 0
    }

    @Output()
    addToCart = new EventEmitter<productSelection>();

    handleAddToCart() {
        this.addToCart.emit({ product: this.product,
            quantity: Number(this.quantity)});
    }
}
```

The `Component` decorator configures the component. The `selector` property speci-fies the CSS selector that Angular will use to apply the component to the application's HTML, and the `templateUrl` property specifies the component's HTML template. For the `ProductItem` class, the `selector` property tells Angular to apply this compo-nent when it encounters the product-item element and that the component's HTML template can be found in a file called `productItem.component.html` in the same directory as the TypeScript file.

Angular uses the `Input` decorator to denote the properties that allow components to receive data values through HTML element attributes. The `Output` decorator is used to denote the flow of data out from the component through a custom event. The `ProductItem` class receives a `Product` object, whose details it displays to the user, and triggers a custom event when the user clicks a button, accessible through the `addToCart` property.

To create the component's template, create a file called `productItem.component .html` in the `src/app` folder and add the elements shown in listing 18.14.

Listing 18.14 The contents of the productItem.component.html file in the src/app folder

```
<div class="card m-1 p-1 bg-light">
    <h4>
        {{ product.name }}
        <span class="badge rounded-pill bg-primary float-end">
            ${{ product.price.toFixed(2) }}
        </span>
    </h4>
    <div class="card-text bg-white p-1">
        {{ product.description }}
        <button class="btn btn-success btn-sm float-end"
                (click)="handleAddToCart()">
            Add To Cart
        </button>
        <select class="form-control-inline float-end m-1"
            [(ngModel)]="quantity">
            <option>1</option>
            <option>2</option>
```

```
            <option>3</option>
        </select>
    </div>
```
```
</div>
```

Angular templates use double curly braces to display the results of JavaScript expressions, such as this one:

```
...
<span class="badge rounded-pill bg-primary float-end">

    ${{ product.price.toFixed(2) }}
</span>
...
```

Expressions are evaluated in the context of the component, so this fragment reads the value of the `product.price` property, invokes the `toFixed` method, and inserts the result into the enclosing `span` element.

Event handling is done using parentheses around the event name, like this:

```
...
<button class="btn btn-success btn-sm float-end"
    (click)="handleAddToCart()">
...
```

This tells Angular that when the `button` element emits the `click` event, the component's `handleAddToCart` method should be invoked. Form elements have special support in Angular, which you can see on the `select` element.

```
...
<select class="form-control-inline float-end m-1" [(ngModel)]="quantity">
...
```

The `ngModel` directly is applied with square brackets and parentheses and creates a two-way binding between the `select` element and the component's `quantity` property. Changes to the `quantity` property will be reflected by the `select` element, and values picked using the `select` element are used to update the `quantity` property.

18.4.1 *Displaying the category buttons*

To create the component that will display the list of category buttons, add a file called `categoryList.component.ts` to the `src/app` folder and add the code shown in listing 18.15.

> **Listing 18.15 The contents of the categoryList.component.ts file in the src/app folder**

```
import { Component, Input, Output, EventEmitter } from "@angular/core";

@Component({
    selector: "category-list",
    templateUrl: "./categoryList.component.html"
})
export class CategegoryList {

    @Input()
```

```
    selected: string = ""

    @Input()
    categories: string[] = [];

    @Output()
    selectCategory = new EventEmitter<string>();

    getBtnClass(category: string): string {
        return  "btn btn-block " +
            (category === this.selected ? "btn-primary" : "btn-secondary");
    }

}
```

The `CategoryList` component has `Input` properties that receive the currently selected category and the list of categories to display. The `Output` decorator has been applied to the `selectCategory` property to define a custom event that will be triggered when the user makes a selection. The `getBtnClass` method is a helper that returns the list of Bootstrap classes that a `button` element should be assigned to and helps keep the component's template free of complex expressions. To create the template for the component, create a file named `categoryList.component.html` in the `src/app` folder with the content shown in listing 18.16.

> **Listing 18.16 The contents of the categoryList.component.html file in the src/app folder**

```
<div class="d-grid gap-2">
    <button *ngFor="let cat of categories" [class]="getBtnClass(cat)"
            (click)="selectCategory.emit(cat)">
        {{ cat }}
    </button>

</div>
```

This template uses the `ngFor` directive to generate a `button` element for each of the values returned by the `categories` property. The asterisk (the * character) that prefixes `ngFor` indicates a concise syntax that allows the `ngFor` directive to be applied directly to the element that will be generated.

Angular templates use square brackets to create a one-way binding between an attribute and a data value, like this:

```
...
<button *ngFor="let cat of categories" [class]="getBtnClass(cat)"
    (click)="selectCategory.emit(cat)">
...
```

The square brackets allow the value of the `class` attribute to be set using a JavaScript expression, which is the result of calling the component's `getBtnClass` method.

18.4.2 Creating the header display

To create the component that will display the summary of the user's product selections and provide the means to navigate to the order summary, add a file called `header.component.ts` in the `src/app` folder with the code shown in listing 18.17.

Listing 18.17 The contents of the header.component.ts file in the src/app folder

```
import { Component, Input, Output, EventEmitter } from "@angular/core";
import { Order } from './data/entities';

@Component({
    selector: "header",
    templateUrl: "./header.component.html"
})
export class Header {

    @Input()
    order = new Order();

    @Output()
    submit = new EventEmitter<void>();

    get headerText(): string {
        let count = this.order.productCount;
        return count === 0 ? "(No Selection)"
            : `${ count } product(s), $${ this.order.total.toFixed(2) }`
    }

}
```

To create the component's template, add a file named `header.component.html` to the `src/app` folder with the content shown in listing 18.18.

Listing 18.18 The contents of the header.component.html file in the src/app folder

```
<div class="p-1 bg-secondary text-white text-end">
    {{ headerText }}
    <button class="btn btn-sm btn-primary m-1" (click)="submit.emit()">
        Submit Order
    </button>
</div>
```

18.4.3 Combining the components

To define the component that presents the `ProductItem`, `CategoryList`, and `Header` components to the user, add a file named `productList.component.ts` to the `src/app` folder with the code shown in listing 18.19.

Listing 18.19 The contents of the productList.component.ts file in the src/app folder

```
import { Component } from "@angular/core";
import { DataSource } from './data/dataSource';
import { Product } from './data/entities';
```

```
@Component({
    selector: "product-list",
    templateUrl: "./productList.component.html"
})
export class ProductList {
    selectedCategory = "All";

    constructor(public dataSource: DataSource) {}

    get products(): Product[] {
        return this.dataSource.getProducts("id",
            this.selectedCategory === "All"
                ? undefined : this.selectedCategory);
    }

    get categories(): string[] {
        return ["All", ...this.dataSource.getCategories()];
    }

    handleCategorySelect(category: string) {
        this.selectedCategory = category;
    }

    handleAdd(data: {product: Product, quantity: number}) {
        this.dataSource.order.addProduct(data.product, data.quantity);
    }

    handleSubmit() {
        console.log("SUBMIT");
    }
}
```

The `ProductList` class declares a dependency on the `DataSource` class and defines `products` and `categories` methods that return data from the `DataSource`. Three methods respond to user interaction: `handleCategorySelect` will be invoked when the user clicks a category button, `handleAdd` will be invoked when the user adds a product to the order, and `handleSubmit` will be called when the user wants to move on to the order summary. The `handleSubmit` method writes out a message to the console and will be fully implemented in chapter 18.

To create the component's template, add a file named `productList.component` `.html` to the `src/app` folder with the content shown in listing 18.20.

> **Listing 18.20   The contents of the productList.component.html file in the src/app folder**

```
<header [order]="dataSource.order" (submit)="handleSubmit()"></header>
<div class="container-fluid">
    <div class="row">
        <div class="col-3 p-2">
            <category-list [selected]="selectedCategory"
                [categories]="categories"
                (selectCategory)="handleCategorySelect($event)">
            </category-list>
        </div>
```

```
        <div class="col-9 p-2">
            <product-item *ngFor="let p of products" [product]="p"
                (addToCart)="handleAdd($event)"></product-item>
        </div>
    </div>
</div>
```

This template shows how components are combined to present content to the user. Custom HTML elements whose tags correspond to the `selector` properties in the `Component` decorators are applied to the classes defined in earlier listings, like this:

```
...
<header [order]="dataSource.order" (submit)="handleSubmit()"></header>
...
```

The `header` tag corresponds to the `selector` setting for the `Component` decorator applied to the `Header` class in listing 18.17. The `order` attribute is used to provide a value for the `Input` property of the same name defined by the `Header` class and allows `ProductList` to provide `Header` with the data it requires. The `submit` attribute corresponds to the `Output` property defined by the `Header` class and allows `ProductList` to receive notifications. The `ProductList` template uses `header`, `category-list`, and `product-item` elements to display the `Header`, `CategoryList`, and `ProductItem` components.

18.5   *Configuring the application*

The application module is used to register the components the application uses as well as any additional modules that have been defined, such as the one I created for the data model earlier in the chapter. Listing 18.21 shows the changes to the application module, which is defined in the `app.module.ts` file.

> **Listing 18.21   Configuring the module in the app.module.ts file in the src/app folder**

```
import { NgModule } from '@angular/core';
import { BrowserModule } from '@angular/platform-browser';

import { AppRoutingModule } from './app-routing.module';
import { AppComponent } from './app.component';
import { FormsModule } from "@angular/forms";
import { DataModelModule } from "./data/data.module";
import { ProductItem } from './productItem.component';
import { CategegoryList } from "./categoryList.component";
import { Header } from "./header.component";
import { ProductList } from "./productList.component";


@NgModule({
  declarations: [AppComponent, ProductItem, CategegoryList,
      Header, ProductList],
  imports: [BrowserModule, AppRoutingModule, FormsModule, DataModelModule],
  providers: [],
  bootstrap: [AppComponent]
})
```

```
export class AppModule { }
```

The NgModule decorator's declarations property is used to declare the components that the application requires and is used to add the classes defined in the previous sections. The imports property is used to list the other modules the application requires and has been updated to include the data model module defined in listing 18.12.

To display the new components to the user, replace the content in the app.component .html file with the single element shown in listing 18.22.

```
<product-list></product-list>
```

When the application runs, Angular will encounter the product-list element and compare it to the selector properties of the Component decorators configured through the Angular module. The product-list tag corresponds to the selector property of the Component decorator applied to the ProductList class in listing 18.19. Angular creates a new ProductList object, renders its template content, and inserts it into the product-list element defined in listing 18.22. The HTML that the ProductList component generates is inspected, and the header, category-list, and product-item elements are discovered, leading to those components being instantiated and their content inserted into each element. The process is repeated until all the elements that correspond to components have been resolved and the content can be presented to the user, as shown in figure 18.2.

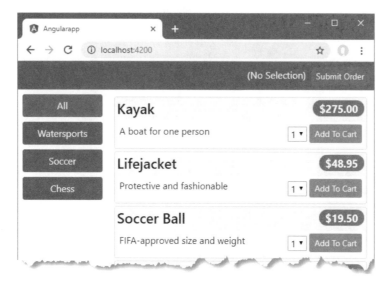

Figure 18.2   Displaying content to the user

The user can filter the list of products and add products to the order. Clicking Submit Order only writes a message to the browser's JavaScript console, but I'll add support for the rest of the application's workflow in the next chapter.

Summary

In this chapter, I explained the role that TypeScript has in Angular development. I explained that TypeScript decorators are used to describe the different building blocks that can be used in an Angular application. I also explained that Angular HTML templates are compiled when the browser executes the application, which means that TypeScript features have already been removed and cannot be used in templates.

- Angular provides tools for creating projects, including configuring the TypeScript compiler.
- The version of TypeScript used in Angular development is determined by the version of Angular used.
- Angular relies on decorators but has not yet been updated to use the latest decorator features described in chapter 14.
- Angular decorators are used to associate templates with code, allowing complex markup to be defined separately from the code that provides the data it requires.

In the next chapter, I complete the application and prepare it for deployment.

Creating an Angular app, part 2

19

This chapter covers

- Adding support for Angular URL routing
- Creating a deployment server and persistent data storage
- Deploying the application in a container

In this chapter, I continue the development of the Angular web application started in chapter 18 by adding the remaining features and preparing the application for deployment into a container. For quick reference, table 19.1 lists the TypeScript compiler options used in this chapter.

Table 19.1 The TypeScript compiler options used in this chapter

Name	Description
baseUrl	This option specifies the root location used to resolve module dependencies.
declaration	This option produces type declaration files when enabled, which describe the types for use in other projects.
downlevelIteration	This option enables support for iterators when targeting older versions of JavaScript.
experimentalDecorators	This option determines whether decorators are enabled.
forceConsistentCasing-InFileNames	This option requires files to be imported using correctly-cased names.

Table 19.1   The TypeScript compiler options used in this chapter *(continued)*

Name	Description
importHelpers	This option determines whether helper code is added to the JavaScript to reduce the amount of code that is produced overall.
lib	This option selects the type declaration files the compiler uses.
module	This option determines the style of module that is used.
moduleResolution	This option specifies how modules are resolved.
noFallthroughCasesInSwitch	This option enables errors when switch statements are allowed to fall through without a `break` statement.
noImplicitOverride	This option enables errors when a subclass redefines a member defined by the base class without using the `override` keyword.
noImplicitReturns	This option enables errors for functions and methods that return undeclared results.
noPropertyAccessFromIndex-Signature	This option enables errors when attempting to access existent properties on objects.
outDir	This option specifies the directory in which the JavaScript files will be placed.
sourceMap	This option determines whether the compiler generates source maps for debugging.
strict	This option enables stricter type checking, including preventing the implicit use of `any`.
target	This option specifies the version of the JavaScript language that the compiler will target in its output.
useDefineForClassFields	This option determines how class fields are defined in the output JavaScript.

19.1   *Preparing for this chapter*

For this chapter, I continue working with the `angularapp` project started in chapter 17. No changes are required to prepare for this chapter. Open a new command prompt, navigate to the `angularapp` folder, and run the command shown in listing 19.1 to start the web service and the Angular development tools.

> **TIP** You can download the example project for this chapter—and for all the other chapters in this book https://github.com/manningbooks/essential-typescript-5.

Listing 19.1   Starting the development tools

```
npm start
```

Once the initial build has completed, open a new browser window, and navigate to http://localhost:4200 to see the example application, as shown in figure 19.1.

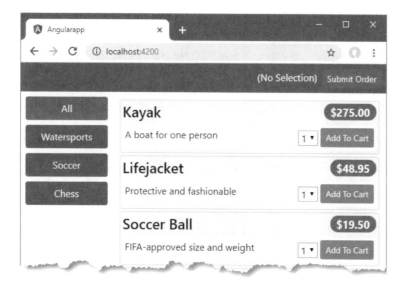

Figure 19.1   Running the example application

19.2   *Completing the example application features*

For the component that will display the details of an order, add a file named order-Details.component.ts to the src/app folder with the code shown in listing 19.2.

Listing 19.2   The contents of the orderDetails.component.ts file in the src/app folder

```
import { Component } from "@angular/core";
import { Router } from "@angular/router";
import { Order } from "./data/entities";
import { DataSource } from './data/dataSource';

@Component({
    selector: "order-details",
    templateUrl: "./orderDetails.component.html"
})
export class OrderDetails {

    constructor(private dataSource: DataSource, private router: Router) {}

    get order() : Order {
        return this.dataSource.order;
    }

    submit() {
        this.dataSource.storeOrder().subscribe(id =>
            this.router.navigateByUrl(`/summary/${id}`));
    }
}
```

The `OrderDetails` component receives a `DataSource` object through its constructor and provides an `order` property to its template. This component makes use of the Angular URL routing system, which selects the components displayed to the user based on the current URL. Table 19.2 shows the URLs that the example application will support and the purpose of each of them.

Table 19.2   The URLs supported by the application

Name	Description
/products	This URL will display the `ProductList` component defined in chapter 18.
/order	This URL will display the `OrderDetails` component, defined in listing 19.2.
/summary	This URL will display a summary of an order once it has been sent to the server. The URL will include the number assigned to the order so that an order whose ID is 5 will be displayed using the URL /summary/5.
/	The default URL will be redirected to /products so the `ProductList` component is shown.

The `Router` object received in the `OrderDetails` constructor allows the component to use the URL routing feature to navigate to a new URL and is used in the `submit` method.

```
...
submit() {
    this.dataSource.storeOrder().subscribe(id =>
        this.router.navigateByUrl(`/summary/${id}`));
}
...
```

This method uses the `DataSource` to send the user's order to the server, waits for the response, and then uses the `Router` object's `navigateByUrl` method to navigate to the URL that will display the summary to the user.

To create the template for the `OrderDetails` component, add a file named order-Details.component.html to the src/app folder with the content shown in listing 19.3.

Listing 19.3   The contents of the orderDetails.component.html file in the src/app folder

```
<h3 class="text-center bg-primary text-white p-2">Order Summary</h3>
<div class="p-3">
    <table class="table table-sm table-striped">
        <thead>
            <tr>
                <th>Quantity</th><th>Product</th>
                <th class="text-end">Price</th>
                <th class="text-end">Subtotal</th>
            </tr>
        </thead>
```

```
<tbody>
    <tr *ngFor="let line of order.orderLines">
            <td>{{ line.quantity }}</td>
            <td>{{ line.product.name }}</td>
            <td class="text-end">
              ${{ line.product.price.toFixed(2) }}
            </td>
            <td class="text-end">${{ line.total.toFixed(2) }}</td>
    </tr>
</tbody>
<tfoot>
    <tr>
        <th class="text-end" colSpan="3">Total:</th>
        <th class="text-end">
            ${{ order.total.toFixed(2) }}
        </th>
    </tr>
</tfoot>
    </table>
</div>
<div class="text-center">
    <button class="btn btn-secondary m-1" routerLink="/products">
      Back
    </button>
    <button class="btn btn-primary m-1" (click)="submit()">
      Submit Order
    </button>
</div>
```

```
</div>
```

The component displays details of the user's selected products and buttons that invoke the `submit` method or navigate to the `/products` list so the `ProductList` component will be displayed. Navigation is configured by applying the `routerLink` directive to the `button` element and specifying the URL that the browser will navigate to when the element is clicked.

```
...
<button class="btn btn-secondary m-1" routerLink="/products">Back</button>
...
```

The `routerLink` directive is part of the Angular routing feature and allows navigation without the need to use a `Router` object in the component class.

19.2.1 *Adding the summary component*

To create the component that will be displayed for the `/summary` URL, add a file named `summary.component.ts` to the `src/app` folder with the code shown in listing 19.4.

> **Listing 19.4 The contents of the summary.component.ts file in the src/app folder**

```
import { Component } from "@angular/core";
import { Router, ActivatedRoute } from "@angular/router";

@Component({
```

```
    selector: "summary",
    templateUrl: "./summary.component.html"
})
export class Summary {

    constructor(private activatedRoute: ActivatedRoute) {}

    get id(): string {
        return this.activatedRoute.snapshot.params["id"];
    }
}
```

The Summary component declares a dependency on an ActivatedRoute object, which Angular will resolve using its dependency injection feature. The ActivatedRoute class is responsible for describing the current route, which describes the currently active route through its snapshot property. The Summary component reads the value of a parameter named id, which will contain the identifier for the order. For a URL of /summary/5, for example, the value of the id parameter will be 5. To provide the template for the component, add a file named summary.component.html to the src/app folder with the content shown in listing 19.5.

> **Listing 19.5   The contents of the summary.component.html file in the src/app folder**

```
<div class="m-2 text-center">
    <h2>Thanks!</h2>
    <p>Thanks for placing your order.</p>
    <p>Your order is #{{ id }}</p>
    <p>We'll ship your goods as soon as possible.</p>
    <button class="btn btn-primary" routerLink="/products">OK</button>
</div>
```

The template displays the value of the id property, which is obtained from the active route, and presents a button element that will navigate to the /products URL when clicked.

19.2.2 *Creating the routing configuration*

To describe the URLs that the application will support and the components that each of them will display, make the changes shown in listing 19.6 to create the configuration for the Angular routing system.

> **Listing 19.6   Configuring the application in the app.module.ts file in the src/app folder**

```
import { BrowserModule } from '@angular/platform-browser';
import { NgModule } from '@angular/core';
import { AppRoutingModule } from './app-routing.module';
import { AppComponent } from './app.component';
import { FormsModule } from "@angular/forms";
import { DataModelModule } from "./data/data.module";
import { ProductItem } from './productItem.component';
import { CategegoryList } from "./categoryList.component";
import { Header } from "./header.component";
```

```
import { ProductList } from "./productList.component";
import { RouterModule } from "@angular/router"
import { OrderDetails } from "./orderDetails.component";
import { Summary } from "./summary.component";

const routes = RouterModule.forRoot([
    { path: "products", component: ProductList },
    { path: "order", component: OrderDetails},
    { path: "summary/:id", component: Summary},
    { path: "", redirectTo: "/products", pathMatch: "full"}
]);

@NgModule({
    declarations: [AppComponent,  ProductItem, CategegoryList,
                Header, ProductList, OrderDetails, Summary],
    imports: [BrowserModule, AppRoutingModule, FormsModule,
            DataModelModule, routes],
    providers: [],
    bootstrap: [AppComponent]
})
export class AppModule { }
```

The `RouterModule.forRoot` method is used to describe the URLs and the components that they will display, as well as the instruction to redirect the default URL to
/products. To tell Angular where to display the components specified by the routing
configuration, replace the contents of the `app.component.html` file with the element
shown in listing 19.7.

> **Listing 19.7 Replacing the contents of the app.component.html file in the src/app folder**

```
<router-outlet></router-outlet>
```

The final change is to change the `ProductList` component so that its `submit` method
uses the Angular routing feature to navigate to the `/order` URL, as shown in listing
19.8.

> **Listing 19.8 Navigating in the productList.component.ts file in the src/app folder**

```
import { Component } from "@angular/core";
import { DataSource } from './data/dataSource';
import { Product } from './data/entities';
import { Router } from "@angular/router";

@Component({
    selector: "product-list",
    templateUrl: "./productList.component.html"
})
export class ProductList {
    selectedCategory = "All";

    constructor(public dataSource: DataSource, private router: Router) {}

    get products(): Product[] {
        return this.dataSource.getProducts("id",
```

```
            this.selectedCategory === "All"
                ? undefined : this.selectedCategory);
    }

    get categories(): string[] {
        return ["All", ...this.dataSource.getCategories()];
    }

    handleCategorySelect(category: string) {
        this.selectedCategory = category;
    }

    handleAdd(data: {product: Product, quantity: number}) {
        this.dataSource.order.addProduct(data.product, data.quantity);
    }

    handleSubmit() {
      this.router.navigateByUrl("/order");
    }
}
```

Save the changes and wait while the development tools rebuild the application and reload the browser. The example application is complete, so you will be able to select products, see a summary of an order, and send it to the server, as shown in figure 19.2.

TIP If only the browser URL changes when you click the Submit Order button, the likely reason is that you did not replace the contents of the app.component .html file as shown in listing 19.7.

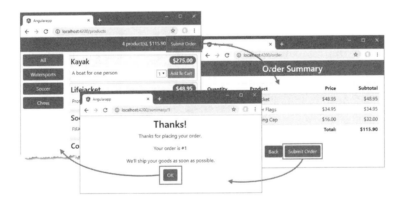

Figure 19.2   Adding components to the example application

19.3 Deploying the application

The Angular development tools rely on the Webpack Development Server, which is not suitable for hosting a production application because it adds features such as automatic reloading to the JavaScript bundles it generates. In this section, I work through the process of preparing the Angular application for deployment, which is a similar process for any web application.

19.3.1 Adding the production HTTP server package

For production, a regular HTTP server is required to deliver the HTML, CSS, and JavaScript files to the browser. For this example, I am going to use the Express server, which is the same package I use for all the examples in this part of the book and is a good choice for any web application. Use Control+C to stop the Angular development tools and use the command prompt to run the command shown in listing 19.9 in the `angularapp` folder to install the `express` package.

The second command installs the `connect-history-api-fallback` package, which is useful when deploying applications that use URL routing, and it maps requests for the URLs that the application supports to the `index.html` file, ensuring that reloading the browser doesn't present the user with a "not found" error.

> **Listing 19.9 Adding packages for deployment**

```
npm install --save-dev express@4.18.2
npm install --save-dev connect-history-api-fallback@2.0.0
```

19.3.2 Creating the persistent data file

To create the persistent data file for the web service, add a file called `data.json` to the `angularapp` folder and add the content shown in listing 19.10.

> **Listing 19.10 The contents of the data.json file in the angularapp folder**

```
{
  "products": [
      { "id": 1, "name": "Kayak", "category": "Watersports",
        "description": "A boat for one person", "price": 275 },
      { "id": 2, "name": "Lifejacket", "category": "Watersports",
        "description": "Protective and fashionable", "price": 48.95 },
      { "id": 3, "name": "Soccer Ball", "category": "Soccer",
        "description": "FIFA-approved size and weight", "price": 19.50 },
      { "id": 4, "name": "Corner Flags", "category": "Soccer",
        "description": "Give your playing field a professional touch",
        "price": 34.95 },
      { "id": 5, "name": "Stadium", "category": "Soccer",
        "description": "Flat-packed 35,000-seat stadium",
        "price": 79500 },
      { "id": 6, "name": "Thinking Cap", "category": "Chess",
        "description": "Improve brain efficiency by 75%", "price": 16 },
      { "id": 7, "name": "Unsteady Chair", "category": "Chess",
        "description": "Secretly give your opponent a disadvantage",
```

```
                    "price": 29.95 },
            { "id": 8, "name": "Human Chess Board", "category": "Chess",
                "description": "A fun game for the family", "price": 75 },
            { "id": 9, "name": "Bling Bling King", "category": "Chess",
                "description": "Gold-plated, diamond-studded King",
                "price": 1200 }
        ],
        "orders": []
}
```

19.3.3 Creating the server

To create the server that will deliver the application and its data to the browser, create a file called `server.js` in the `angularapp` folder and add the code shown in listing 19.11.

> **Listing 19.11   The contents of the server.js file in the angularapp folder**

```
const express = require("express");
const jsonServer = require("json-server");
const history = require("connect-history-api-fallback");

const app = express();
app.use(history());
app.use("/", express.static("dist/angularapp"));

const router = jsonServer.router("data.json");
app.use(jsonServer.bodyParser)
app.use("/api", (req, resp, next) => router(req, resp, next));

const port = process.argv[3] || 4001;
app.listen(port, () => console.log(`Running on port ${port}`));
```

The statements in the `server.js` file configure the `express` and `json-server` packages to serve the content of the `dist/angularapp` folder, which is where the Angular build process will put the application's JavaScript bundles and the HTML file that tells the browser to load them. URLs prefixed with `/api` will be handled by the web service.

19.3.4 Using relative URLs for data requests

The web service that provided the application with data has been running alongside the Angular development server. To prepare for sending requests to a single port, I changed the `RemoteDataSource` class, as shown in listing 19.12.

> **Listing 19.12   A relative URLs in the remoteDataSource.ts file in the src/app/data folder**

```
import { Injectable } from "@angular/core";
import { HttpClient } from "@angular/common/http";
import { Observable } from "rxjs";
import { map } from "rxjs/operators";
import { DataSourceImpl } from "./dataSource";
import { Product, Order } from "./entities";
```

```
// const protocol = "http";
// const hostname = "localhost";
// const port = 4600;

const urls = {
    // products: `${protocol}://${hostname}:${port}/products`,
    // orders: `${protocol}://${hostname}:${port}/orders`
    products: "/api/products",
    orders: "/api/orders"

};

@Injectable()
export class RemoteDataSource extends DataSourceImpl {

    constructor(private http: HttpClient) {
        super();
    }

    loadProducts(): Observable<Product[]> {
        return this.http.get<Product[]>(urls.products);
    }

    storeOrder(order: Order): Observable<number> {
        let orderData = {
            lines: [...order.orderLines.values()].map(ol => ({
                productId: ol.product.id,
                productName: ol.product.name,
                quantity: ol.quantity
            }))
        }
        return this.http.post<{ id: number}>(urls.orders, orderData)
            .pipe<number>(map(val => val.id));
    }

}
```

The URLs in listing 19.12 are specified relative to the one used to request the HTML document, following the common convention that data requests are prefixed with /api.

19.3.5 *Building the application*

To build the application for deployment, run the command shown in listing 19.13 in the angularapp folder to create the production build of the application.

Listing 19.13   Creating the production bundle

```
ng build --configuration "production"
```

The build process creates a set of optimized files in the dist folder. The build process can take a few moments to complete and will produce the following output, which shows which files have been created:

```
Browser application bundle generation complete.
Copying assets complete.
Generating index html...1 rules skipped due to selector errors:
  legend+* -> Cannot read properties of undefined (reading 'type')
Index html generation complete.

Initial Chunk Files          | Names     | Raw Size  | Size
main.16225861184cae00.js     | main      | 246.35 kB | 64.12 kB
styles.9c36b9530393e161.css  | styles    | 187.50 kB | 19.44 kB
polyfills.89ae3309894ba767.js| polyfills |  33.09 kB | 1.70 kB
runtime.2d99e508040b4ce1.js  | runtime   | 898 bytes | 518 bytes

                             | Total     | 467.82 kB | 94.77 kB


Build at: 2023-03-26T18:20:11.031Z - Hash: d8caebf2a4448e24 - Time: 20106ms
```

19.3.6 *Testing the production build*

To make sure that the build process has worked and the configuration changes have taken effect, run the command shown in listing 19.14 in the `angularapp` folder.

Listing 19.14   Starting the production server

```
node server.js
```

The code from listing 19.14 will be executed and will produce the following output:

```
Running on port 4001
```

Open a new web browser and navigate to http://localhost:4001, which will show the application, as illustrated in figure 19.3.

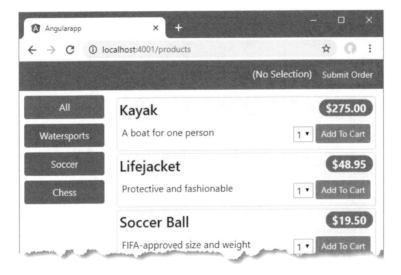

Figure 19.3   Running the production build

19.4 Containerizing the application

To complete this chapter, I am going to create a Docker container for the Angular application so that it can be deployed into production. If you did not install Docker in chapter 17, then you must do so now to follow the rest of the examples in this chapter.

19.4.1 Preparing the application

The first step is to create a configuration file for NPM that will be used to download the additional packages required by the application for use in the container. I created a file called `deploy-package.json` in the `angularapp` folder with the content shown in listing 19.15.

> **Listing 19.15 The contents of the deploy-package.json file in the angularapp folder**

```json
{
    "name": "angularapp",
    "description": "Angular Web App",
    "repository": "https://github.com/manningbooks/essential-typescript-5",
    "license": "BSD",
    "devDependencies": {
        "express": "4.18.2",
        "json-server": "0.17.3",
        "connect-history-api-fallback": "2.0.0"
    }
}
```

The `devDependencies` section specifies the packages required to run the application in the container. All of the packages for which there are `import` statements in the application's code files will have been incorporated into the bundle created by webpack and are listed. The other fields describe the application, and their main use is to prevent a warning when the container is created.

19.4.2 Creating the Docker container

To define the container, I added a file called `Dockerfile` (with no extension) to the `angularapp` folder and added the content shown in listing 19.16.

> **Listing 19.16 The contents of the Dockerfile file in the angularapp folder**

```
FROM node:18.14.0

RUN mkdir -p /usr/src/angularapp

COPY dist /usr/src/angularapp/dist/
COPY data.json /usr/src/angularapp/
COPY server.js /usr/src/angularapp/
COPY deploy-package.json /usr/src/angularapp/package.json

WORKDIR /usr/src/angularapp

RUN echo 'package-lock=false' >> .npmrc
```

```
RUN npm install

EXPOSE 4001

CMD ["node", "server.js"]
```

The contents of `Dockerfile` use a base image that has been configured with Node.js and that copies the files required to run the application into the container, along with the file that lists the packages required for deployment.

To speed up the containerization process, I created a file called `.dockerignore` in the `angularapp` folder with the content shown in listing 19.17. This tells Docker to ignore the `node_modules` folder, which is not required in the container and takes a long time to process.

> **Listing 19.17   The contents of the .dockerignore file in the angularapp folder**

```
node_modules
```

Run the command shown in listing 19.18 in the `angularapp` folder to create an image that will contain the example application, along with all of the packages it requires.

> **Listing 19.18   Building the Docker image**

```
docker build . -t angularapp -f Dockerfile
```

An image is a template for containers. As Docker processes the instructions in the Docker file, the NPM packages will be downloaded and installed, and the configuration and code files will be copied into the image.

19.4.3 *Running the application*

Once the image has been created, create and start a new container using the command shown in listing 19.19.

> **Listing 19.19   Starting the Docker container**

```
docker run -p 4001:4001 angularapp
```

You can test the application by opening http://localhost:4000 in the browser, which will display the response provided by the web server running in the container, as shown in figure 19.4.

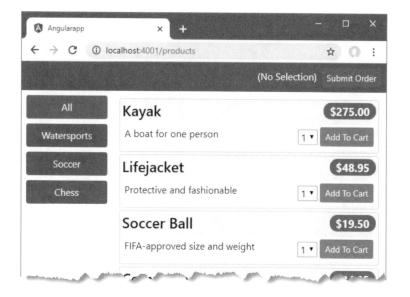

Figure 19.4   Running the containerized application

To stop the container, run the command shown in listing 19.20.

Listing 19.20   Listing the containers

```
docker ps
```

You will see a list of running containers, like this (I have omitted some fields for brevity):

```
CONTAINER ID        IMAGE               COMMAND             CREATED
48dbd2431700        angularapp          "docker-entry"      41 seconds ago
```

Using the value in the Container ID column, run the command shown in listing 19.21.

Listing 19.21   Stopping the container

```
docker stop 48dbd2431700
```

The Angular application is ready to deploy to any platform that supports Docker.

Summary

In this chapter, I completed the example Angular application by adding components and using the URL routing feature to specify when they will be shown to the user. I prepared the production build of the application and containerized it so that it can be easily deployed.

- Angular provides the development tools required to build a production version of an application and prepare it for deployment.
- Like any other TypeScript application, Angular projects are compiled to pure JavaScript and can be deployed using standard tools and containers.

In the next chapter, I create a web application using the React framework.

Creating a React app, part 1

This chapter covers

- Building a React project
- Setting up React components using the JSX format
- Creating class-based and function-based components
- Putting together a data store that stores local data and consumes an HTTP API

In this chapter, I start the process of creating a React application that has the same features as the standalone and Angular examples from earlier chapters. TypeScript is optional in React development, but there is good support available, and React development with TypeScript provides a good developer experience. For quick reference, table 20.1 lists the TypeScript compiler options used in this chapter.

Table 20.1   The TypeScript compiler options used in this chapter

Name	Description
allowJs	This option includes JavaScript files in the compilation process.
allowSyntheticDefault-Imports	This option allows imports from modules that do not declare a default export. This option is used to increase code compatibility.
esModuleInterop	This option adds helper code for importing from modules that do not declare a default export and is used in conjunction with the allowSyntheticDefault-Imports option.
forceConsistentCasing-InFileNames	This option ensures that names in import statements match the case used by the imported file.
include	This option specifies files and folders to include in the compilation process.
isolatedModules	This option treats each file as a separate module, which increases compatibility with the Babel tool.
jsx	This option specifies how HTML elements in TSX files are processed.
lib	This option selects the type declaration files the compiler uses.
module	This option determines the style of module that is used.
moduleResolution	This option specifies the style of module resolution that should be used to resolve dependencies.
noEmit	This option prevents the compiler from emitting JavaScript code, with the result that it checks code only for errors.
noFallthroughCasesInSwitch	This option enables errors when switch statements are allowed to fall through without a break statement.
resolveJsonModule	This option allows JSON files to be imported as though they were modules.
skipLibCheck	This option speeds up compilation by skipping the normal checking of declaration files.
strict	This option enables stricter checking of TypeScript code.
target	This option specifies the version of the JavaScript language that the compiler will target in its output.

20.1   Preparing for this chapter

React projects are most easily created using the create-react-app package. Open a new command prompt, navigate to a convenient location, and run the command shown in listing 20.1 to install the create-react-app package.

TIP You can download the example project for this chapter—and for all the other chapters in this book—from https://github.com/manningbooks/essential-typescript-5.

Listing 20.1 Installing the project creation package

```
npm install --global create-react-app@5.0.1
```

Once the package has been installed, run the command shown in listing 20.2 to create a project named `reactapp`.

Listing 20.2 Creating a React project

```
npx create-react-app reactapp --template typescript --use-npm
```

The `--template typescript` argument tells the `create-react-app` package to create a React project that is configured for use with TypeScript, which includes installing and configuring the TypeScript compiler and the declaration files that describe the React API and its related tools. The `--use-npm` command installs the packages using the NPM package manager, which I used throughout this book.

20.1.1 Configuring the web service

Once the creation process is complete, run the commands shown in listing 20.3 to navigate to the project folder, add the packages that will provide the web service, and allow multiple packages to be started with a single command.

Listing 20.3 Adding packages to the project

```
cd reactapp
npm install --save-dev json-server@0.17.3
npm install --save-dev npm-run-all@4.1.5
```

To provide the data for the web service, add a file called `data.js` to the reactapp folder with the content shown in listing 20.4.

Listing 20.4 The contents of the data.js file in the reactapp folder

```
module.exports = function () {
    return {
        products: [
            { id: 1, name: "Kayak", category: "Watersports",
                description: "A boat for one person", price: 275 },
            { id: 2, name: "Lifejacket", category: "Watersports",
                description: "Protective and fashionable", price: 48.95 },
            { id: 3, name: "Soccer Ball", category: "Soccer",
                description: "FIFA-approved size and weight",
                price: 19.50 },
            { id: 4, name: "Corner Flags", category: "Soccer",
                description:
                    "Give your playing field a professional touch",
                price: 34.95 },
```

```
        { id: 5, name: "Stadium", category: "Soccer",
            description: "Flat-packed 35,000-seat stadium",
            price: 79500 },
        { id: 6, name: "Thinking Cap", category: "Chess",
            description: "Improve brain efficiency by 75%",
            price: 16 },
        { id: 7, name: "Unsteady Chair", category: "Chess",
            description: "Secretly give your opponent a disadvantage",
            price: 29.95 },
        { id: 8, name: "Human Chess Board", category: "Chess",
            description: "A fun game for the family", price: 75 },
        { id: 9, name: "Bling Bling King", category: "Chess",
            description: "Gold-plated, diamond-studded King",
            price: 1200 }
    ],
    orders: []
}
}
```

Update the scripts section of the `package.json` file to configure the development tools so that the React toolchain and the web service are started at the same time, as shown in listing 20.5.

Listing 20.5   Configuring tools in the package.json file in the reactapp folder

```
...
"scripts": {
  "json": "json-server data.js -p 4600",
  "serve": "react-scripts start",
  "start": "npm-run-all -p serve json",
  "build": "react-scripts build",
  "test": "react-scripts test",
  "eject": "react-scripts eject"
},
...
```

20.1.2   *Installing the Bootstrap CSS package*

Use the command prompt to run the command shown in listing 20.6 in the `reactapp` folder to add the Bootstrap CSS framework to the project.

Listing 20.6   Adding the CSS package

```
npm install bootstrap@5.2.3
```

To ensure the Bootstrap CSS stylesheet is included in the application, add the `import` statement shown in listing 20.7 to the `index.tsx` file in the `src` folder.

Listing 20.7   Declaring a dependency in the index.tsx file in the src folder

```
import React from 'react';
import ReactDOM from 'react-dom/client';
import './index.css';
import App from './App';
```

```
import reportWebVitals from './reportWebVitals';
import 'bootstrap/dist/css/bootstrap.css';

const root = ReactDOM.createRoot(
  document.getElementById('root') as HTMLElement
);
root.render(
  <React.StrictMode>
    <App />
  </React.StrictMode>
);


reportWebVitals();
```

20.1.3 *Starting the example application*

Use the command prompt to run the command shown in listing 20.8 in the `reactapp` folder.

Listing 20.8 Starting the development tools

```
npm start
```

The web service and the React build tools will start, and you will see the following output:

```
Compiled successfully!
You can now view reactapp in the browser.
  Local:            http://localhost:3000
  On Your Network:  http://172.22.208.1:3000
Note that the development build is not optimized.
To create a production build, use npm run build.
```

A new browser window will open and navigate to http://localhost:3000, which shows the placeholder content provided during the project creation process, as shown in figure 20.1.

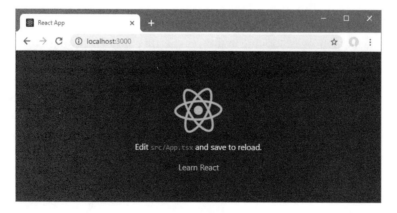

Figure 20.1 Running the example application

20.2   *Understanding TypeScript in React development*

TypeScript is optional when using React, and this is reflected in the way that the development tools and the TypeScript compiler are configured. Behind the scenes, the webpack and Webpack Development are used to create the JavaScript bundle and deliver it to the browser.

React development relies on the JSX format, which allows JavaScript and HTML to be mixed in a single file. The React development tools already have the ability to transform JSX files into pure JavaScript, which is done using the Babel package. Babel is a JavaScript compiler that allows code written using recent versions of JavaScript to be translated into code that works on older browsers, much like the version targeting feature provided by the TypeScript compiler. Babel is extensible through plugins, and support has grown to translate a wide range of other formats into JavaScript, including JSX files. Figure 20.2 shows the basic elements of the React development toolchain for a regular JavaScript project.

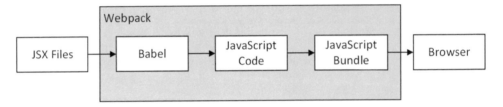

Figure 20.2   **The JavaScript React development toolchain**

The Babel plugin responsible for JSX plays the same role as the JSX factory class I created in chapter 16 and replaces HTML fragments with JavaScript statements, albeit using the more sophisticated and efficient React API. The transformation produces pure JavaScript, which is bundled into a file so that it can be received and executed by the browser. The bundle also includes JavaScript code to unpack any CSS or image resources that the application requires.

The way that the React toolchain deals with TypeScript is unusual, and you can get a sense of what is happening by looking at the TypeScript compiler configuration file that has been added to the project, shown here:

```
{
  "compilerOptions": {
    "target": "es5",
    "lib": [
      "dom",
      "dom.iterable",
      "esnext"
    ],
    "allowJs": true,
    "skipLibCheck": true,
    "esModuleInterop": true,
```

```
    "allowSyntheticDefaultImports": true,
    "strict": true,
    "forceConsistentCasingInFileNames": true,
    "noFallthroughCasesInSwitch": true,
    "module": "esnext",
    "moduleResolution": "node",
    "resolveJsonModule": true,
    "isolatedModules": true,
    "noEmit": true,
    "jsx": "react-jsx"
  },
  "include": [
    "src"
  ]

}
```

The setting worth noting is `noEmit`. When the `noEmit` setting is true, the TypeScript compiler won't generate JavaScript files. The reason for the unusual compiler setting is that it is the Babel package—and not the TypeScript compiler—that is responsible for transforming TypeScript code into JavaScript. The React toolchain includes a Babel plugin that transforms TypeScript into pure JavaScript.

Babel can transform TypeScript into JavaScript, but it doesn't understand the TypeScript features, and it doesn't know how to perform type checking. That task is left to the TypeScript compiler so that responsibility for dealing with TypeScript is split: the TypeScript compiler is responsible for detecting type errors, and Babel is responsible for creating the JavaScript code the browser will execute, as shown in figure 20.3.

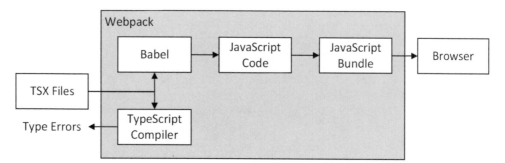

Figure 20.3　The TypeScript React development toolchain

The `noEmit` setting makes sense in this context since the TypeScript compiler doesn't need to create JavaScript files to perform its type checks.

The limitation of this approach is that Babel can't deal with every TypeScript feature, although there are surprisingly few limitations. At the time of writing, enums are not fully supported, and the namespace feature cannot be used (namespaces are a deprecated forerunner of JavaScript modules and are not covered in this book).

NOTE You may have received a warning when starting the development tools that warned you of a mismatch between TypeScript versions. This warning reflects the possible difference between the type-checking features implemented by the latest TypeScript compiler and the way the TypeScript code is translated into JavaScript by Babel. For a simple project like this one, there are unlikely to be serious issues, but you should consider using only the TypeScript versions that are explicitly supported by the `create-react-app` package.

You can change the TypeScript compiler configuration to suit the language features you require. For example, listing 20.9 selects the ES2022 version of JavaScript, which includes support for more recent language features, including the spread operator, which is one that I often use.

Listing 20.9   Changing the configuration in the tsconfig.json file in the reactapp folder

```
{
  "compilerOptions": {
    "target": "ES2022",
    "lib": [
      "dom",
      "dom.iterable",
      "esnext"
    ],
    "allowJs": true,
    "skipLibCheck": true,
    "esModuleInterop": true,
    "allowSyntheticDefaultImports": true,
    "strict": true,
    "forceConsistentCasingInFileNames": true,
    "noFallthroughCasesInSwitch": true,
    "module": "esnext",
    "moduleResolution": "node",
    "resolveJsonModule": true,
    "isolatedModules": true,
    "noEmit": true,
    "jsx": "react-jsx"
  },
  "include": [
    "src"
  ]
}
```

The Babel transformation can deal with the spread operator without needing a configuration change, and the effect of the `target` setting in listing 20.9 only prevents the TypeScript compiler from generating errors.

20.3   *Defining the entity types*

React focuses on presenting HTML content to the user and leaves other tasks, such as managing application data and making HTTP requests, to other packages. I'll add packages to the project later to complete the set of features required by the example application, but I am going to start by focusing on the features that React does provide and come back to deal with the ones it doesn't later. To get started, I need to define the entities that the application will use. Create the `src/data` folder and add to it a file named `entities.ts` with the code shown in listing 20.10.

```
export type Product = {
    id: number,
    name: string,
    description: string,
    category: string,
    price: number
};

export type ProductSelection = {
    product: Product, quantity: number;
}

export class ProductSelectionHelpers {

    public static total(selections : ProductSelection[]) {
        return selections.reduce((total, line) =>
            total + (line.product.price * line.quantity), 0);
    }

    public static productCount(selections: ProductSelection[]) {
        return selections.reduce((total, line) => total + line.quantity, 0)
    }
}

export class ProductSelectionMutations {

    public static addProduct(selections : ProductSelection[],
            product: Product, quantity: number)  {

        const index = selections
            .findIndex(line => line.product.id === product.id);
        if (index > -1) {
            selections[index].quantity += quantity;
        } else {
            selections.push({ product, quantity})
        }
    }

    public static remove(selections: ProductSelection[], id: number) {
        selections.forEach((line, index) => {
            if (line.product.id === id) {
                selections = selections.splice(index, 1);
            }
        });
    }

}
```

React and its main supporting packages work best with simple data structures, which are defined separately from the functions that alter them. In listing 20.10, I defined `Product` and `ProductSelection` types, along with a `ProductSelectionHelpers` class that defines static methods that will perform common calculations on those types, and a `ProductSelectionMutations` class, which defines static methods that alter them. These classes are not required by React, which places few restrictions on how code is structured, but I find it a useful way to define common operations consistently.

20.4   *Displaying a filtered list of products*

React uses the JSX format to allow HTML elements to be defined alongside JavaScript code, similar to the approach that I used when creating the standalone web application. During compilation, the HTML elements are transformed into JavaScript statements that use the React API to efficiently display content to the user, a much more elegant approach than the one I created in chapter 16.

The key building block in a React application is the component that is responsible for generating HTML content. Components are configured using props; they can respond to user interaction by handling events triggered by the HTML elements they render and can define local state data.

To display the details of a single product, add a file named `productItem.tsx` to the `src` folder and add the code shown in listing 20.11 to create a simple `React` component.

> **Listing 20.11   The contents of the productItem.tsx file in the src folder**

```
import React, { Component, ChangeEvent } from "react";
import { Product } from "./data/entities";

interface Props {
    product: Product,
    callback: (product: Product, quantity: number) => void
}

interface State {
    quantity: number
}

export class ProductItem extends Component<Props, State> {

    constructor(props: Props) {
        super(props);
        this.state = {
            quantity: 1
        }
    }

    render() {
        return <div className="card m-1 p-1 bg-light">
            <h4>
                { this.props.product.name }
```

```
                <span className="badge rounded-pill bg-primary float-end">
                    ${ this.props.product.price.toFixed(2) }
                </span>
            </h4>
            <div className="card-text bg-white p-1">
                { this.props.product.description }
                <button className="btn btn-success btn-sm float-end"
                        onClick={ this.handleAddToCart } >
                    Add To Cart
                </button>
                <select className="form-control-inline float-end m-1"
                        onChange={ this.handleQuantityChange }>
                    <option>1</option>
                    <option>2</option>
                    <option>3</option>
                </select>
            </div>
        </div>
    }

    handleQuantityChange = (ev: ChangeEvent<HTMLSelectElement>): void =>
        this.setState({ quantity: Number(ev.target.value) });

    handleAddToCart = (): void =>
        this.props.callback(this.props.product, this.state.quantity);
}
```

Using TypeScript requires data types that describe the props and state data are defined and used as generic type arguments to the `Component` class. The `ProductItem` component receives props that provide it with a `Product` object and a callback function to invoke when the user clicks the Add To Cart button. The `ProductItem` component has one state data property, named `quantity`, which is used to respond when the user picks a value through the `select` element. The props and state data are described by the `Props` and `State` interfaces, which are used as generic type parameters to configure the base class for components, like this:

```
...
export class ProductItem extends Component<Props, State> {
...
```

The generic type arguments allow the TypeScript compiler to check the component when it is applied so that only properties defined by the `Props` interface are used and to ensure that updates are applied only to properties defined by the `State` interface.

The declaration files for React include types for the events that HTML elements will produce through the `render` method. For the `change` event triggered by a `select` element, the handler function will receive a `ChangeEvent<HTMLSelectElement>` object. Changes to a component's properties must be performed through the `setState` method, which is how React knows that an update has been made.

```
...
handleQuantityChange = (ev: ChangeEvent<HTMLSelectElement>): void =>
    this.setState({ quantity: Number(ev.target.value) });
...
```

The TypeScript compiler will ensure that the right type of event is handled and that updates through the `setState` method are of the right type and update only the properties defined by the `State` type.

20.4.1 *Using a functional component and hooks*

The component in listing 20.11 is defined using a class but React also supports components defined using functions, which has become the most popular way to write React features and is the approach I followed for the rest of this chapter.

> **TIP** The choice between function and class components is a matter of personal preference, and both are fully supported by React. Hooks have become the most common choice, but they can be awkward to work with. Both approaches have their merits and can be freely mixed in a project.

When using TypeScript, functional components are annotated with the `Function-Component<T>` type, where the generic type `T` describes the props the component will receive. In listing 20.12, I redefined the `ProductItem` component so that it is expressed as a function instead of a class.

> **Listing 20.12   A functional component in the productItem.tsx file in the src folder**

```
import React, { FunctionComponent, useState } from "react";
import { Product } from "./data/entities";

interface Props {
    product: Product,
    callback: (product: Product, quantity: number) => void
}

// interface State {
//     quantity: number
// }

export const ProductItem: FunctionComponent<Props> = (props) => {

    const [quantity, setQuantity] = useState<number>(1);

    return <div className="card m-1 p-1 bg-light">
        <h4>
            { props.product.name }
            <span className="badge rounded-pill bg-primary float-end">
                ${ props.product.price.toFixed(2) }
            </span>
        </h4>
        <div className="card-text bg-white p-1">
            { props.product.description }
            <button className="btn btn-success btn-sm float-end"
                onClick={ () => props.callback(props.product, quantity) }>
                    Add To Cart
            </button>
```

```
        <select className="form-control-inline float-end m-1"
            onChange={ (ev) => setQuantity(Number(ev.target.value)) }>
                <option>1</option>
                <option>2</option>
                <option>3</option>
        </select>
    </div>
</div>
```
}

The result of the component's function is the HTML that should be displayed to the user and that is defined using the same combination of elements and expressions that class-based components produce from their `render` method.

Class-based components rely on properties and methods, accessed through `this`, to implement state data and participate in the lifecycle that React provides for applications. Functional components use a feature named *hooks* to achieve the same result, like this:

```
...
const [quantity, setQuantity] = useState<number>(1);
...
```

This is an example of a state hook, which provides a functional component with a state data property that will trigger a content update when it is modified. The `useState` function is provided with a generic type argument and an initial value, and it returns a property that can be read to get the current value and a function that can be invoked to change it. In this case, the property is assigned the name `quantity`, and the update function is assigned the name `setQuantity`, following a common naming convention. The result is that `quantity` can be used in expressions to get the state data value.

```
...
onClick={ () => props.callback(props.product, quantity) }>
...
```

The `quantity` property is constant, which means that it cannot be modified. Instead, changes must be applied through the `setQuantity` function, like this:

```
...
<select className="form-control-inline float-end m-1"
    onChange={ (ev) => setQuantity(Number(ev.target.value)) }>
...
```

The use of separate properties and functions ensures that all changes to state data trigger the React update process, and the TypeScript compiler checks the values passed to the function to ensure they correspond to the generic type argument provided to the `useState` function.

20.4.2 Displaying a list of categories and the header

To define the component that will display the list of categories, add a file named `categoryList.tsx` to the `src` folder with the contents shown in listing 20.13.

Listing 20.13   The contents of the categoryList.tsx file in the src folder

```
import React, { FunctionComponent } from "react";

interface Props {
    selected: string,
    categories: string[],
    selectCategory: (category: string) => void;
}

export const CategoryList: FunctionComponent<Props> = (props) => {
    return  <div className="d-grid gap-2">
                { ["All", ...props.categories].map(c => {
                    let btnClass = props.selected === c
                        ? "btn-primary": "btn-secondary";
                    return <button key={ c }
                            className={ `btn btn-block ${btnClass}` }
                            onClick={ () => props.selectCategory(c) }>
                        { c }
                    </button>
                }) }
            </div>

}
```

To create the header component, add a file named `header.tsx` to the `src` folder and add the code shown in listing 20.14.

Listing 20.14   The contents of the header.tsx file in the src folder

```
import React, { FunctionComponent } from "react";
import { ProductSelection, ProductSelectionHelpers } from "./data/entities";

interface Props {
    selections: ProductSelection[]
}

export const Header : FunctionComponent<Props> = (props) => {
    const count = ProductSelectionHelpers.productCount(props.selections);
    const total = ProductSelectionHelpers.total(props.selections);
    return <div className="p-1 bg-secondary text-white text-end">
        { count === 0 ? "(No Selection)"
            : `${ count } product(s), ` +
                `$${ total.toFixed(2)}` }
        <button className="btn btn-sm btn-primary m-1">
            Submit Order
        </button>
    </div>

}
```

20.4.3 *Composing and testing the components*

To create the component that will display the header, the list of products, and the category buttons, add a file named `productList.tsx` to the `src` folder and add the code shown in listing 20.15.

Listing 20.15   The contents of the productList.tsx file in the src folder

```tsx
import React, { FunctionComponent, useState } from "react";
import { Header } from "./header";
import { ProductItem } from "./productItem";
import { CategoryList} from "./categoryList";
import { Product, ProductSelection } from "./data/entities";

interface Props {
    products: Product[],
    categories: string[],
    selections: ProductSelection[],
    addToOrder: (product: Product, quantity: number) => void
}

export const ProductList: FunctionComponent<Props> = (props) => {
    const [selectedCategory, setSelectedCategory] = useState("All");

    const products = props.products.filter(p => selectedCategory === "All"
                        || p.category === selectedCategory);

    return <div>
        <Header selections={ props.selections } />
        <div className="container-fluid">
            <div className="row">
                <div className="col-3 p-2">
                    <CategoryList categories={ props.categories }
                        selected={ selectedCategory }
                        selectCategory={ setSelectedCategory } />
                </div>
                <div className="col-9 p-2">
                    {
                        products.map(p =>
                            <ProductItem key={ p.id } product={ p }
                                callback={ props.addToOrder } />)
                    }
                </div>
            </div>
        </div>
    </div>
}
```

Components are applied using custom HTML elements whose tag matches the component class name or function name. Components are configured using props, which can be used to provide data or callback functions, just as in chapter 17 when I created a custom JSX implementation. The `ProductList` component provides its functionality by composing the `Header`, `CategoryList`, and `ProductItem` components, each of which is configured using the props the `ProductList` component receives or its state data.

To make sure that the components can display content to the user, replace the contents of the `App.tsx` file with those shown in listing 20.16.

Listing 20.16   Replacing the contents of the App.tsx file in the src folder

```
import React, { FunctionComponent, useState } from 'react';
import { Product, ProductSelection, ProductSelectionMutations }
    from './data/entities';
import { ProductList } from './productList';

let testData: Product[] = [1, 2, 3, 4, 5].map(num =>
    ({ id: num, name: `Prod${num}`, category: `Cat${num % 2}`,
        description: `Product ${num}`, price: 100}))

export const App: FunctionComponent = () => {

    const [selections, setSelections] = useState(Array<ProductSelection>());

    const addToOrder = (product: Product, quantity: number) => {
        setSelections(curr => {
            ProductSelectionMutations.addProduct(curr, product, quantity);
            return [...curr];
        });
    };

    const categories = [...new Set(testData.map(p => p.category))];

    return  <div className="App">
                <ProductList products={ testData }
                    categories={categories }
                    selections={ selections }
                    addToOrder= { addToOrder } />
            </div>
}

export default App;
```

The `App` component has been updated to display a `ProductList`, which is configured using test data. I use the `setState` hook to ensure the component is only re-rendered when the product selections change. I'll add support for working with the web service later, but the changes in listing 20.16 are enough to show the list of products, as shown in figure 20.4. (You may have to reload the browser to see the changes because the auto-reload feature isn't always reliable.)

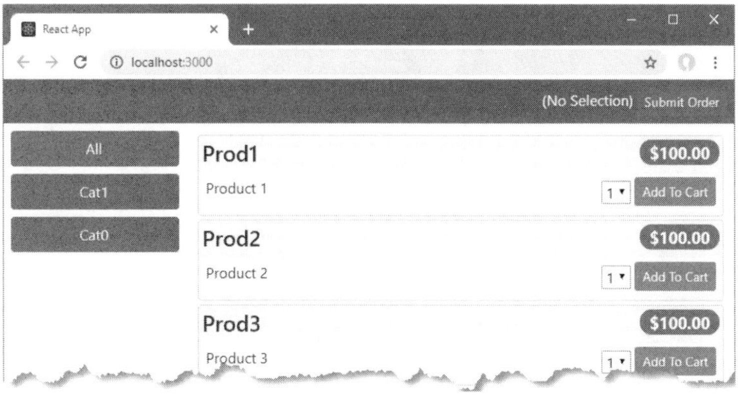

Figure 20.4 Testing the product list components

When you click an Add To Cart button, you may see more products displayed in the header than you expect. This is because the project is running in strict mode, in which the runtime repeatedly performs actions to detect problematic changes in components. You can ignore the effect of these additional operations, which will stop once the data store is added to the application in the next section. This feature is also disabled when any React project is compiled for production.

20.5 *Creating the data store*

In most React projects, the application data is managed by a data store. Several data store packages are available, but the most widely used is Redux. To add the Redux packages to the project, open a new command prompt, navigate to the `reactapp` folder, and run the commands shown in listing 20.17.

Listing 20.17   Adding packages to the example project

```
npm install redux@4.2.1
npm install react-redux@8.0.5
npm install @reduxjs/toolkit@1.9.3
npm install --save-dev @types/react-redux@7.1.25
```

The Redux package includes TypeScript declarations, but additional packages are required: the React-Redux package connects React components to a data store and the Redux Toolkit package, which is the standard way to use Redux.

The starting point is to create a slice, which is a combination of a name, some initial state data, and the functions that modify that state data—known as *reducers*. Slices are convenient ways to create all the features that are required to manage data in the store so that it can be accessed elsewhere in the application. To create a slice for the product selections, add a file named `selectionSlice.ts` to the `src/data` folder with the content shown in listing 20.18.

Listing 20.18   The contents of the selectionSlice.ts file in the src/data folder

```
import { createSlice, PayloadAction } from "@reduxjs/toolkit";
import { Product, ProductSelection, ProductSelectionMutations }
    from "./entities";

const productSelectionSlice = createSlice({
    name: "selections",
    initialState: Array<ProductSelection>(),
    reducers: {
        addToOrder(selections: ProductSelection[],
                action: PayloadAction<[Product, number]>) {
            ProductSelectionMutations.addProduct(selections,
                action.payload[0], action.payload[1])
        }
    }
});

export const reducer = productSelectionSlice.reducer;
export const { addToOrder } = productSelectionSlice.actions
```

The createSlice function is provided by the Redux Toolkit package and accepts an object with name, initialState, and reducers properties. (There are more configuration properties available, but these are the only ones I need). This slice is named selections, its initial state is an empty ProductSelection array, and there is one reducer function, named addToOrder, which adds a product selection to the array. The result produced by the createSlice function defines reducer and actions properties, which must be exported.

The next step is to use the slice to create a data store. Add a file named dataStore.ts in the src/data folder with the content shown in listing 20.19.

Listing 20.19   The contents of the dataStore.ts file in the src/data folder

```
import { configureStore } from "@reduxjs/toolkit";

import { reducer as selectionsReducer, addToOrder }
    from "./selectionSlice";
import { TypedUseSelectorHook, useDispatch, useSelector }
    from "react-redux";

export const dataStore = configureStore({
    reducer: {
        "selections": selectionsReducer
    }
});

export type AppDispatch = typeof dataStore.dispatch;
export type RootState = ReturnType<typeof dataStore.getState>;

export const useAppDispatch = () => useDispatch<AppDispatch>();
export const useAppSelector: TypedUseSelectorHook<RootState> = useSelector;

export const reducers = {

    addToOrder
}
```

This is a basic data store configuration that consumes the features created by the slice defined in listing 20.18 and exports features for use in the rest of the application.

> **NOTE** There are many different ways to create and configure a data store and connect it to React components. In this chapter, I have taken the simplest approach. What's important in this section is not how I use the datastore, but how I can use TypeScript annotations to describe the approach I have selected to the compiler, so that type checks can be performed.

Now that the data store has been created, I can use the features it provides to replace the local state defined by the `App` component, as shown in listing 20.20.

Listing 20.20 Using the data store in the App.tsx file in the src folder

```
import React, { FunctionComponent } from 'react';
import { Product } from './data/entities';
import { ProductList } from './productList';
import { useAppDispatch, useAppSelector, reducers }
    from "./data/dataStore";

let testData: Product[] = [1, 2, 3, 4, 5].map(num =>
    ({ id: num, name: `Prod${num}`, category: `Cat${num % 2}`,
        description: `Product ${num}`, price: 100}))

export const App: FunctionComponent = () => {

    const selections = useAppSelector(state => state.selections);
    const dispatch = useAppDispatch();

    const addToOrder = (p: Product, q: number) =>
        dispatch(reducers.addToOrder([p, q]));

    const categories = [...new Set(testData.map(p => p.category))];

    return  <div className="App">
                <ProductList products={ testData }
                    categories={categories }
                    selections={ selections }
                    addToOrder= { addToOrder } />
            </div>
}

export default App;
```

To read the selections data from the data store, I use the `useAppSelector` function that was exported in listing 20.19, which accepts a function that picks the data the component requires.

The process for making changes is a little awkward. First, I invoke the `useAppDispatch` function, which returns a function that can be used to call a reducer. In the first step, I assign the function returned by `useAppDispatch` to a constant named `dispatch`:

```
. . .
const dispatch = useAppDispatch();
. . .
```

To perform a change, I use the function assigned to `dispatch` to invoke the reducer:

```
. . .
const addToOrder = (p: Product, q: number) =>
        dispatch(reducers.addToOrder([p, q]));
. . .
```

Notice that the argument to the `addToOrder` reducer is a TypeScript tuple. Reducers only accept a single argument and, while there is a way to introduce preparatory functions that can marshal data values, the simplest approach is to bundle the required values into a tuple. The final step is to apply the data store, as shown in listing 20.21.

Listing 20.21   Applying the data store in the index.tsx file in the src folder

```
import React from 'react';
import ReactDOM from 'react-dom/client';
import './index.css';
import App from './App';
import reportWebVitals from './reportWebVitals';
import 'bootstrap/dist/css/bootstrap.css';
import { Provider } from 'react-redux';
import { dataStore } from './data/dataStore';

const root = ReactDOM.createRoot(
  document.getElementById('root') as HTMLElement
);
root.render(
    <React.StrictMode>
    <Provider store={dataStore}>
        <App />
    </Provider>
    </React.StrictMode>
);


reportWebVitals();
```

The introduction of the data store doesn't change the appearance of the application but does mean that the application has delegated the management of its data to the store.

20.5.1   *Implementing the HTTP API clients*

It may seem that setting up the data store is a lot of work for little benefit, but Redux offers some useful features once it has been integrated into a project. One of the most useful is the ability to quickly and easily create clients to consume RESTful web services so they can be used in React components.

To implement the API that produces the product data, add a file named `storeApis.ts` to the `src/data` folder with the content shown in listing 20.22.

Listing 20.22   The contents of the storeApis.ts file in the src/data folder

```
import { createApi, fetchBaseQuery } from '@reduxjs/toolkit/query/react'
import { Product } from './entities';

const protocol = "http";
const hostname = "localhost";
const port = 4600;

const baseUrl = `${protocol}://${hostname}:${port}`;

export const productsApi = createApi({
    reducerPath: "products",
    baseQuery: fetchBaseQuery({baseUrl}),
    endpoints: (builder) => ({
        getProducts: builder.query<Product[], void>({
            query: () => "products"
        })
    })
})

export const { useGetProductsQuery } = productsApi;
```

The `createApi` function provided by Redux Toolkit accepts a configuration object that describes the HTTP API and defines the features that will be presented to the rest of the React application. This configuration is simple and will expose a `useGetProducts-Query` hook to the rest of the application that will send an HTTP GET request to the HTTP service created at the start of the chapter and present the results as an array of `Product` objects.

Listing 20.23 updates the data store to include the features produced by the `createApi` function.

Listing 20.23   Adding the API in the dataStore.ts file in the src/data folder

```
import { configureStore } from "@reduxjs/toolkit";
import { reducer as selectionsReducer, addToOrder } from "./selectionSlice";
import { TypedUseSelectorHook, useDispatch, useSelector }
    from "react-redux";
import { productsApi, useGetProductsQuery } from "./storeApis";

export const dataStore = configureStore({
    reducer: {
        "selections": selectionsReducer,
        [productsApi.reducerPath]: productsApi.reducer,
    },
    middleware: (getDefaultMiddleware) =>
        getDefaultMiddleware()
            .concat(productsApi.middleware)
});

export type AppDispatch = typeof dataStore.dispatch;
export type RootState = ReturnType<typeof dataStore.getState>;

export const useAppDispatch = () => useDispatch<AppDispatch>();
```

```
export const useAppSelector: TypedUseSelectorHook<RootState> = useSelector;

export const reducers = {
    addToOrder
}

export const queries = {
    useGetProductsQuery

}
```

These changes add the API reducers to the data store and configure the store to use the API features, which are described in more detail at https://redux-toolkit.js.org/api/configureStore. This change also re-exports the `useGetProductsQuery` function from the API module so that application components don't have to import directly from other files.

Listing 20.24 replaces the test data used in earlier examples with data obtained through the data store.

Listing 20.24   Using the data store in the App.tsx file in the src folder

```
import React, { FunctionComponent, useMemo } from 'react';
import { Product } from './data/entities';
import { ProductList } from './productList';
import { useAppDispatch, useAppSelector, reducers, queries }
    from "./data/dataStore";

// let testData: Product[] = [1, 2, 3, 4, 5].map(num =>
//     ({ id: num, name: `Prod${num}`, category: `Cat${num % 2}`,
//         description: `Product ${num}`, price: 100}))

export const App: FunctionComponent = () => {

    const selections = useAppSelector(state => state.selections);
    const dispatch = useAppDispatch();

    const { data } = queries.useGetProductsQuery();

    const addToOrder = (p: Product, q: number) =>
        dispatch(reducers.addToOrder([p, q]));

    const categories = useMemo<string[]>(() => {
        return [...new Set(data?.map(p => p.category))]
    }, [data]);


    return   <div className="App">
                <ProductList products={ data ?? [] }
                    categories={categories }
                    selections={ selections }
                    addToOrder= { addToOrder } />
            </div>
}


export default App;
```

The test data is replaced with the results from the `useGetProductsQuery` function. This is the most basic way to get data from an API, but there are many useful features, such as loading notifications and good error handling.

Now that I am working with remote data, I have made some adjustments to this component. First, there will be a delay between the application starting and the data being obtained from the web service. I have taken the simplest approach and render an empty array when there is no data:

```
...
<ProductList products={ data ?? [] } categories={categories }

    selections={ selections } addToOrder= { addToOrder } />
...
```

Redux provides features for better managing this transition, but this approach is sufficient for a simple example application. The other change I made was to the way the list of categories was created:

```
...
const categories = useMemo<string[]>(() => {
    return [...new Set(data?.map(p => p.category))]
}, [data]);
...
```

The `useMemo` hook accepts a function that generates a value, along with a set of dependencies. The function is only invoked when one of the dependencies changes, which is a useful way of ensuring that operations are not performed every time the component is rendered.

The result is that the data is requested from the server and added to the data store, which triggers an update that leads the connected components to display new data, as shown in figure 20.5.

Figure 20.5 Using a data store

Summary

In this chapter, I started a React project that uses TypeScript. I explained the unusual developer tools configuration and the effect it has on the TypeScript compiler configuration. I created React components that are defined using TypeScript features and connected them to a simple Redux data store.

- React components use the JSX format and are responsible for rendering HTML.
- Components can be defined as classes or as functions with hooks.
- Redux is a popular choice for storing data and is configured using the Redux Toolkit package.
- Data stores can be configured to manage local data or consume HTTP APIs.

In the next chapter, I complete the development of the React project and prepare the application for deployment.

Creating a React app, part 2

21

This chapter covers

- Using the current URL to select components
- Consuming the orders web service
- Creating a deployment server and persistent data storage
- Deploying the application in a container

In this chapter, I complete the React web application by adding URL routing and the remaining components before preparing the application for deployment in a container. For quick reference, table 21.1 lists the TypeScript compiler options used in this chapter.

Table 21.1   The TypeScript compiler options used in this chapter

Name	Description
`allowJs`	This option includes JavaScript files in the compilation process.
`allowSynthetic-DefaultImports`	This option allows imports from modules that do not declare a default export. This option is used to increase code compatibility.
`esModuleInterop`	This option adds helper code for importing from modules that do not declare a default export and is used in conjunction with the `allowSyntheticDefault-Imports` option.

Table 21.1   The TypeScript compiler options used in this chapter *(continued)*

Name	Description
forceConsistent-CasingInFileNames	This option ensures that names in import statements match the case used by the imported file.
include	This option specifies files and folders to include in the compilation process.
isolatedModules	This option treats each file as a separate module, which increases compatibility with the Babel tool.
jsx	This option specifies how HTML elements in TSX files are processed.
lib	This option selects the type declaration files the compiler uses.
module	This option determines the style of module that is used.
moduleResolution	This option specifies the style of module resolution that should be used to resolve dependencies.
noEmit	This option prevents the compiler from emitting JavaScript code, with the result that it checks code only for errors.
noFallthroughCases-InSwitch	This option enables errors when switch statements are allowed to fall through without a break statement.
resolveJsonModule	This option allows JSON files to be imported as though they were modules.
skipLibCheck	This option speeds up compilation by skipping the normal checking of declaration files.
strict	This option enables stricter checking of TypeScript code.
target	This option specifies the version of the JavaScript language that the compiler will target in its output.

21.1   *Preparing for this chapter*

In this chapter, I continue to work with the reactapp project started in chapter 20. Open a command prompt, navigate to the reactapp folder, and run the command shown in listing 21.1 to start the web service and the React development tools.

> **TIP**   You can download the example project for this chapter—and for all the other chapters in this book—from https://github.com/manningbooks/essential-typescript-5.

Listing 21.1   Starting the development tools

```
npm start
```

After the initial build process, a new browser window will open and display the example application, as shown in figure 21.1.

Figure 21.1 **Running the example application**

21.2 *Configuring URL routing*

Most real React projects rely on URL routing, which uses the browser's current URL to select the components that are displayed to the user. React doesn't include built-in support for URL routing, but the most commonly used package is React Router. Open a new command prompt, navigate to the reactapp folder, and run the commands shown in listing 21.2 to install the React Router package.

Listing 21.2 Adding a package to the project

```
npm install react-router-dom@6.10.0
```

The React Router package supports different navigation systems, and the react-router -dom package contains the functionality required for web applications. Table 21.2 shows the URLs that the example application will support and the purpose of each of them.

Table 21.2 The URLs supported by the application

Name	Description
/	This URL will trigger a redirection to /products.
/products	This URL will display the ProductList component defined in chapter 20.
/order	This URL will display a component that displays details of the order.
/summary	This URL will display a summary of an order once it has been sent to the server. The URL will include the number assigned to the order so that an order whose ID is 5 will be displayed using the URL /summary/5.

The `BrowserRouter` component is used to enable routing for browser-based applications and is typically added at the top of the component hierarchy, as shown in listing 21.3.

Listing 21.3   Adding routing in the index.tsx file in the src folder

```
import React from 'react';
import ReactDOM from 'react-dom/client';
import './index.css';
import App from './App';
import reportWebVitals from './reportWebVitals';
import 'bootstrap/dist/css/bootstrap.css';
import { Provider } from 'react-redux';
import { dataStore } from './data/dataStore';
import { BrowserRouter } from 'react-router-dom';

const root = ReactDOM.createRoot(
  document.getElementById('root') as HTMLElement
);
root.render(
    <React.StrictMode>
        <Provider store={dataStore}>
            <BrowserRouter>
                <App />
            </BrowserRouter>
        </Provider>
    </React.StrictMode>
);


reportWebVitals();
```

The individual routes used by the application can be defined where they are required. Not all the components required by the application have been written, so listing 21.4 sets up the configuration for the /products and / URLs, with the others to be defined in the sections that follow.

Listing 21.4   Configuring URL routing in the App.tsx file in the src folder

```
import React, { FunctionComponent, useMemo } from 'react';
import { Product } from './data/entities';
import { ProductList } from './productList';
import { useAppDispatch, useAppSelector, reducers, queries }
    from "./data/dataStore";
import { Routes, Route, Navigate } from "react-router-dom";

export const App: FunctionComponent = () => {

    const selections = useAppSelector(state => state.selections);
    const dispatch = useAppDispatch();

    const { data } = queries.useGetProductsQuery();

    const addToOrder = (p: Product, q: number) =>
        dispatch(reducers.addToOrder([p, q]));
```

```
const categories = useMemo<string[]>(() => {
    return [...new Set(data?.map(p => p.category))]
}, [data]);

return (
    <div className="App">
        <Routes>
            <Route path="/products" element={
                <ProductList products={ data ?? [] }
                    categories={categories }
                    selections={ selections }
                    addToOrder= { addToOrder } />

            }/>
            <Route path="/" element={
                <Navigate replace to="/products" />
            } />
        </Routes>
    </div>
)
}
```

```
export default App;
```

The React Router package relies on components for configuration. The Routes component contains a series of Route components, each of which matches a URL path to content.

There are two routes in listing 21.4, each of which is described using a Route component. The first route matches the /product path and displays the ProductList component. The second route matches any path and uses the Navigate component to redirect to the /product path. The Navigate component is provided as part of the React Router package. When the changes are saved, the application will be rebuilt, and the browser will be redirected to the /products URL, as shown in figure 21.2.

Figure 21.2 Adding URL routing

21.3   *Completing the example application features*

Now that the application can display components based on the current URL, I can add the remaining components to the project. To enable URL navigation from the button displayed by the `Header` component, I added the statements shown in listing 21.5 to the `header.tsx` file.

Listing 21.5   Adding navigation in the header.tsx file in the src folder

```
import React, { FunctionComponent } from "react";
import { ProductSelection, ProductSelectionHelpers } from "./data/entities";
import { NavLink } from "react-router-dom";

interface Props {
    selections: ProductSelection[]
}

export const Header : FunctionComponent<Props> = (props) => {
    const count = ProductSelectionHelpers.productCount(props.selections);
    const total = ProductSelectionHelpers.total(props.selections);
    return <div className="p-1 bg-secondary text-white text-end">
        { count === 0 ? "(No Selection)"
            : `${ count } product(s), ` +
                `$${ total.toFixed(2)}` }
        { count > 0 ?
            <NavLink to="/order" className="btn btn-sm btn-primary m-1">
                Submit Order
            </NavLink>
            : <button disabled className="btn btn-sm btn-primary m-1">
                Submit Order
            </button>
        }
    </div>
}
```

The `NavLink` component produces an anchor element (an element whose tag is `a`) that navigates to a specified URL when it is clicked. The Bootstrap classes applied to the `NavLink` give the link the appearance of a button, which is replaced with a disabled `button` element when no products have been selected.

To display the details of the product selections order to the user, add a file called `orderDetails.tsx` to the `src` folder and add the code shown in listing 21.6.

Listing 21.6   The contents of the orderDetails.tsx file in the src folder

```
import React, { FunctionComponent } from "react";
import { ProductSelectionHelpers as Helpers }
    from "./data/entities";
import { NavLink } from "react-router-dom";
import { ProductSelection } from "./data/entities";

interface Props {
    selections: ProductSelection[],
```

```
        submitCallback: () => void
}


export const OrderDetails: FunctionComponent<Props> = (props) => {

    return <div>
        <h3 className="text-center bg-primary text-white p-2">
            Order Summary
        </h3>
        <div className="p-3">
            <table className="table table-sm table-striped">
                <thead>
                    <tr>
                        <th>Quantity</th><th>Product</th>
                        <th className="text-right">Price</th>
                        <th className="text-right">Subtotal</th>
                    </tr>
                </thead>
                <tbody>
                    { props.selections.map(selection =>
                        <tr key={ selection.product.id }>
                            <td>{ selection.quantity }</td>
                            <td>{ selection.product.name }</td>
                            <td className="text-right">
                                ${ selection.product.price.toFixed(2) }
                            </td>
                            <td className="text-right">
                                ${ Helpers.total([selection]).toFixed(2) }
                            </td>
                        </tr>
                    )}
                </tbody>
                <tfoot>
                    <tr>
                        <th className="text-right" colSpan={3}>Total:</th>
                        <th className="text-right">
                            ${ Helpers.total(props.selections).toFixed(2) }
                        </th>
                    </tr>
                </tfoot>
            </table>
        </div>
        <div className="text-center">
            <NavLink to="/products" className="btn btn-secondary m-1">
                Back
            </NavLink>
            <button className="btn btn-primary m-1"
                    onClick={ props.submitCallback }>
                Submit Order
            </button>
        </div>
    </div>
}
```

This component receives props that contain the product selections and a callback function that is invoked to submit the order.

21.3.1   *Adding the confirmation component*

Add a file named `summary.tsx` to the `src` folder and add the code shown in listing 21.7 to display a message to the user once the order has been stored by the web service.

Listing 21.7   The contents of the summary.tsx file in the src folder

```
import React, { FunctionComponent } from "react";
import { NavLink, useParams } from "react-router-dom";

export const Summary : FunctionComponent = () => {
    const { id } = useParams();

    return <div className="m-2 text-center">
        <h2>Thanks!</h2>
        <p>Thanks for placing your order.</p>
        <p>Your order is #{ id }</p>
        <p>We'll ship your goods as soon as possible.</p>
        <NavLink to="/products" className="btn btn-primary">OK</NavLink>
    </div>

}
```

This component uses the `useParams` hook, which provides access to the parameters matched by the route from the current URL path. This hook allows the component to get the ID of the order so it can be presented to the user. I define the route with an `id` parameter in listing 21.12.

21.3.2   *Consuming the orders web service*

Orders are created by sending the user's product selections to a web service, which was defined when the project was created in chapter 20. Listing 21.8 uses the features provided by the Redux Toolkit package to add support for the web service.

Listing 21.8   Implementing the web service in the storeApis.ts file in the src/data folder

```
import { createApi, fetchBaseQuery } from '@reduxjs/toolkit/query/react'
import { Product, ProductSelection } from './entities';

const protocol = "http";
const hostname = "localhost";
const port = 4600;

const baseUrl = `${protocol}://${hostname}:${port}`;

export const productsApi = createApi({
    reducerPath: "products",
    baseQuery: fetchBaseQuery({baseUrl}),
    endpoints: (builder) => ({
        getProducts: builder.query<Product[], void>({
```

```
                query: () => "products"
            })
        })
    })
})

export const ordersApi = createApi({
    reducerPath: "orders",
    baseQuery: fetchBaseQuery({baseUrl}),
    endpoints: (build) => ({
        storeOrder: build.mutation<number, ProductSelection[]>({
            query(selections) {
                let orderData = {
                    lines: selections.map(ol => ({
                        productId: ol.product.id,
                        productName: ol.product.name,
                        quantity: ol.quantity
                    }))
                }
                return {
                    url: "orders",
                    method: "POST",
                    body: {orderData}
                }
            },
            transformResponse: ((response: {id : number}) => response.id)
        })
    })
})

export const { useGetProductsQuery } = productsApi;

export const { useStoreOrderMutation } = ordersApi;
```

The `createApi` function is used to implement the API, with a mutation that sends the user's selections in an HTTP POST request. Listing 21.9 extends the data store to incorporate the new web service support.

Listing 21.9 Extending the data store in the dataStore.ts file in the src/data folder

```
import { configureStore } from "@reduxjs/toolkit";
import { reducer as selectionsReducer, addToOrder }
    from "./selectionSlice";
import { TypedUseSelectorHook, useDispatch, useSelector }
    from "react-redux";
import { ordersApi, productsApi, useGetProductsQuery,
    useStoreOrderMutation } from "./storeApis";

export const dataStore = configureStore({
    reducer: {
        "selections": selectionsReducer,
        [productsApi.reducerPath]: productsApi.reducer,
        [ordersApi.reducerPath]: ordersApi.reducer
    },
    middleware: (getDefaultMiddleware) =>
        getDefaultMiddleware()
```

```
            .concat(productsApi.middleware)
            .concat(ordersApi.middleware)
});

export type AppDispatch = typeof dataStore.dispatch;
export type RootState = ReturnType<typeof dataStore.getState>;

export const useAppDispatch = () => useDispatch<AppDispatch>();
export const useAppSelector: TypedUseSelectorHook<RootState> = useSelector;

export const reducers = {
    addToOrder, useStoreOrderMutation
}

export const queries = {
    useGetProductsQuery

}
```

21.3.3 Completing the application

There are a couple of changes required to complete the application. The first is to extend the data store so that I can reset the product selections once an order has been created, as shown in listing 21.10.

Listing 21.10   Adding a mutation in the selectionSlice.ts file in the src/data folder

```
import { createSlice, PayloadAction } from "@reduxjs/toolkit";
import { Product, ProductSelection, ProductSelectionMutations }
    from "./entities";

const productSelectionSlice = createSlice({
    name: "selections",
    initialState: Array<ProductSelection>(),
    reducers: {
        addToOrder(selections: ProductSelection[],
                action: PayloadAction<[Product, number]>) {
            ProductSelectionMutations.addProduct(selections,
                action.payload[0], action.payload[1])
        },
        resetSelections(selections: ProductSelection[]) {

            selections.length = 0;
        }
    }
});

export const reducer = productSelectionSlice.reducer;
export const { addToOrder, resetSelections }

    = productSelectionSlice.actions;
```

Listing 21.11 imports and exports the new reducer so that it can be imported consistently with the other data store feature.

```
import { configureStore } from "@reduxjs/toolkit";
import { reducer as selectionsReducer, addToOrder, resetSelections }
    from "./selectionSlice";
import { TypedUseSelectorHook, useDispatch, useSelector }
    from "react-redux";
import { ordersApi, productsApi, useGetProductsQuery,
    useStoreOrderMutation } from "./storeApis";

export const dataStore = configureStore({
    reducer: {
        "selections": selectionsReducer,
        [productsApi.reducerPath]: productsApi.reducer,
        [ordersApi.reducerPath]: ordersApi.reducer
    },
    middleware: (getDefaultMiddleware) =>
        getDefaultMiddleware()
            .concat(productsApi.middleware)
            .concat(ordersApi.middleware)
});

export type AppDispatch = typeof dataStore.dispatch;
export type RootState = ReturnType<typeof dataStore.getState>;

export const useAppDispatch = () => useDispatch<AppDispatch>();
export const useAppSelector: TypedUseSelectorHook<RootState> = useSelector;

export const reducers = {
    addToOrder, useStoreOrderMutation, resetSelections
}

export const queries = {
    useGetProductsQuery

}
```

In listing 21.12, I added new Route elements to display the OrderDetails and Summary components, completing the routing configuration for the example application.

```
import React, { FunctionComponent, useMemo } from 'react';
import { Product } from './data/entities';
import { ProductList } from './productList';
import { useAppDispatch, useAppSelector, reducers, queries }
    from "./data/dataStore";
import { Routes, Route, Navigate, useNavigate } from "react-router-dom";
import { Summary } from './summary';
import { OrderDetails } from './orderDetails';
import { resetSelections } from './data/selectionSlice';

export const App: FunctionComponent = () => {

    const selections = useAppSelector(state => state.selections);
```

```
const dispatch = useAppDispatch();

const { data } = queries.useGetProductsQuery();

const addToOrder = (p: Product, q: number) =>
    dispatch(reducers.addToOrder([p, q]));

const categories = useMemo<string[]>(() => {
    return [...new Set(data?.map(p => p.category))]
}, [data]);

const [ storeOrder ] = reducers.useStoreOrderMutation();
const navigate = useNavigate();
const submitCallback = () => {
    storeOrder(selections).unwrap().then(id => {
        dispatch(resetSelections());
        navigate(`/summary/${id}`);
    });
}

return (
    <div className="App">
            <Routes>
                <Route path="/products" element={
                    <ProductList products={ data ?? [] }
                        categories={categories }
                        selections={ selections }
                        addToOrder= { addToOrder } />
                }/>
                <Route path="/order" element= {
                    <OrderDetails
                        selections={ selections }
                        submitCallback={() => submitCallback()} />
                } />
                <Route path="/summary/:id" element={ <Summary /> } />
                <Route path="*" element={
                    <Navigate replace to="/products" />
                } />
            </Routes>
    </div>
)
}
```

```
export default App;
```

The `Route` component for the `OrderDetails` component provides it with the product selections and a callback function that sends the product selections to the server and extracts the ID assigned to the stored order. The selections are reset, and the browser is asked to navigate to the `/summary` path with a segment that contains the order number.

The other `Route` component displays the `Summary` component, and the route path defines an ID parameter that is read by the component so that it can be displayed to the user.

When the changes are saved, items can be added to the order, and the order can be sent to the web service, as shown in figure 21.3.

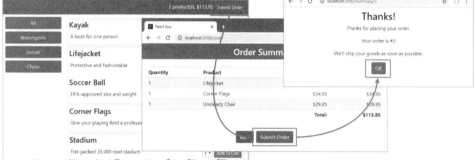

Figure 21.3   Completing the example application

21.4   *Deploying the application*

The React development tools rely on the Webpack Development Server, which is not suitable for hosting a production application because it adds features such as automatic reloading to the JavaScript bundles it generates. In this section, I work through the process of preparing the application for deployment, which is a similar process for any web application, including those developed using other frameworks.

21.4.1   *Adding the production HTTP server package*

For production, a regular HTTP server is required to deliver the HTML, CSS, and JavaScript files to the browser. For this example, I am going to use the Express server, which is the same package I use for the other examples in this part of the book and a good choice for any web application. Use Control+C to stop the development tools and use the command prompt to run the command shown in listing 21.13 in the `reactapp` folder to install the `express` package.

The second command installs the `connect-history-api-fallback` package, which is useful when deploying applications that use URL routing because it maps requests for the URLs that the application supports to the `index.html` file, ensuring that reloading the browser doesn't present the user with a "not found" error.

> **Listing 21.13   Adding packages for deployment**

```
npm install --save-dev express@4.18.2
npm install --save-dev connect-history-api-fallback@2.0.0
```

21.4.2 *Creating the persistent data file*

To create the persistent data file for the web service, add a file called `data.json` to the `reactapp` folder and add the content shown in listing 21.14.

Listing 21.14   The contents of the data.json file in the reactapp folder

```
{
    "products": [
        { "id": 1, "name": "Kayak", "category": "Watersports",
            "description": "A boat for one person", "price": 275 },
        { "id": 2, "name": "Lifejacket", "category": "Watersports",
            "description": "Protective and fashionable", "price": 48.95 },
        { "id": 3, "name": "Soccer Ball", "category": "Soccer",
            "description": "FIFA-approved size and weight",
            "price": 19.50 },
        { "id": 4, "name": "Corner Flags", "category": "Soccer",
            "description": "Give your playing field a professional touch",
            "price": 34.95 },
        { "id": 5, "name": "Stadium", "category": "Soccer",
            "description": "Flat-packed 35,000-seat stadium",
            "price": 79500 },
        { "id": 6, "name": "Thinking Cap", "category": "Chess",
            "description": "Improve brain efficiency by 75%",
            "price": 16 },
        { "id": 7, "name": "Unsteady Chair", "category": "Chess",
            "description": "Secretly give your opponent a disadvantage",
            "price": 29.95 },
        { "id": 8, "name": "Human Chess Board", "category": "Chess",
            "description": "A fun game for the family", "price": 75 },
        { "id": 9, "name": "Bling Bling King", "category": "Chess",
            "description": "Gold-plated, diamond-studded King",
            "price": 1200 }
    ],
    "orders": []
}
```

21.4.3 *Creating the server*

To create the server that will deliver the application and its data to the browser, create a file called `server.js` in the `reactapp` folder and add the code shown in listing 21.15.

Listing 21.15   The contents of the server.js file in the reactapp folder

```
const express = require("express");
const jsonServer = require("json-server");
const history = require("connect-history-api-fallback");

const app = express();

const router = jsonServer.router("data.json");
app.use(jsonServer.bodyParser)
app.use("/api", (req, resp, next) => router(req, resp, next));

app.use(history());
```

```
app.use("/", express.static("build"));

const port = process.argv[3] || 4002;
app.listen(port, () => console.log(`Running on port ${port}`));
```

The statements in the `server.js` file configure the `express` and `json-server` packages so they use the contents of the build folder, which is where the React build process will put the application's JavaScript bundles and the HTML file that tells the browser to load them. URLs prefixed with `/api` will be handled by the web service.

21.4.4 Using relative URLs for data requests

The web service that provided the application with data has been running alongside the React development server. To prepare for sending requests to a single port, I changed the `HttpHandler` class, as shown in listing 21.16.

Listing 21.16 Using relative URLs in the storeApis.ts file in the src/data folder

```
import { createApi, fetchBaseQuery } from '@reduxjs/toolkit/query/react'
import { Product, ProductSelection } from './entities';

//const protocol = "http";
//const hostname = "localhost";
//const port = 4600;

const baseUrl = "/api";

export const productsApi = createApi({
    reducerPath: "products",
    baseQuery: fetchBaseQuery({baseUrl}),
    endpoints: (builder) => ({
        getProducts: builder.query<Product[], void>({
            query: () => "products"
        })
    })
})

export const ordersApi = createApi({
    reducerPath: "orders",
    baseQuery: fetchBaseQuery({baseUrl}),
    endpoints: (build) => ({
        storeOrder: build.mutation<number, ProductSelection[]>({
            query(selections) {
                let orderData = {
                    lines: selections.map(ol => ({
                        productId: ol.product.id,
                        productName: ol.product.name,
                        quantity: ol.quantity
                    }))
                }
                return {
                    url: "orders",
                    method: "POST",
                    body: {orderData}
                }
            },
```

```
                transformResponse: ((response: {id : number}) => response.id)
        })
    })
})

export const { useGetProductsQuery } = productsApi;

export const { useStoreOrderMutation } = ordersApi;
```

21.4.5 *Building the application*

Run the command shown in listing 21.17 in the `reactapp` folder to create the production build of the application.

> **Listing 21.17   Creating the production bundle**

```
npm run build
```

The build process creates a set of optimized files in the `build` folder. The build process can take a few moments to complete and will produce the following output, which shows which files have been created:

```
Creating an optimized production build...
Compiled successfully.

File sizes after gzip:

  81.69 kB  build\static\js\main.61626b8e.js
  28.01 kB  build\static\css\main.ababef68.css
  1.78 kB   build\static\js\787.5480e000.chunk.js

The project was built assuming it is hosted at /.
You can control this with the homepage field in your package.json.

The build folder is ready to be deployed.
You may serve it with a static server:

  npm install -g serve
  serve -s build

Find out more about deployment here:
  https://cra.link/deployment
```

21.4.6 *Testing the production build*

To make sure that the build process has worked, and the configuration changes have taken effect, run the command shown in listing 21.18 in the reactapp folder.

> **Listing 21.18   Starting the production server**

```
node server.js
```

The code from listing 21.15 will be executed and produce the following output:

```
Running on port 4002
```

Open a new web browser and navigate to http://localhost:4002, which will show the application, as illustrated in figure 21.4.

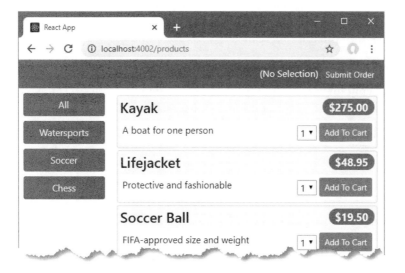

Figure 21.4   Running the production build

21.5   *Containerizing the application*

To complete this chapter, I am going to create a Docker container for the example application so that it can be deployed into production. If you did not install Docker in chapter 17, then you must do so now to follow the rest of the examples in this chapter.

21.5.1   *Preparing the application*

The first step is to create a configuration file for NPM that will be used to download the additional packages required by the application for use in the container. I created a file called `deploy-package.json` in the `reactapp` folder with the content shown in listing 21.19.

Listing 21.19   The contents of the deploy-package.json file in the reactapp folder

```
{
    "name": "reactapp",
    "description": "React Web App",
    "repository": "https://github.com/manningbooks/essential-typescript-5",
    "license": "BSD",
    "devDependencies": {
        "express": "4.18.2",
        "json-server": "0.17.3",
        "connect-history-api-fallback": "2.0.0"
    }
}
```

The devDependencies section specifies the packages required to run the application in the container. All the packages for which there are import statements in the application's code files will have been incorporated into the bundle created by webpack and are listed. The other fields describe the application, and their main use is to prevent warnings when the container is created.

21.5.2 *Creating the Docker container*

To define the container, I added a file called Dockerfile (with no extension) to the reactapp folder and added the content shown in listing 21.20.

Listing 21.20   The contents of the Dockerfile file in the reactapp folder

```
FROM node:18.14.0

RUN mkdir -p /usr/src/reactapp

COPY build /usr/src/reactapp/build/
COPY data.json /usr/src/reactapp/
COPY server.js /usr/src/reactapp/
COPY deploy-package.json /usr/src/reactapp/package.json

WORKDIR /usr/src/reactapp

RUN echo 'package-lock=false' >> .npmrc
RUN npm install

EXPOSE 4002

CMD ["node", "server.js"]
```

The contents of the Dockerfile use a base image that has been configured with Node.js and that copies the files required to run the application into the container, along with the file that lists the packages required for deployment.

To speed up the containerization process, I created a file called .dockerignore in the reactapp folder with the content shown in listing 21.21. This tells Docker to ignore the node_modules folder, which is not required in the container and takes a long time to process.

Listing 21.21   The contents of the .dockerignore file in the reactapp folder

```
node_modules
```

Run the command shown in listing 21.22 in the reactapp folder to create an image that will contain the example application, along with all the packages it requires.

Listing 21.22   Building the Docker image

```
docker build . -t reactapp -f  Dockerfile
```

An image is a template for containers. As Docker processes the instructions in the Docker file, the NPM packages will be downloaded and installed, and the configuration and code files will be copied into the image.

21.5.3 *Running the application*

Once the image has been created, create and start a new container using the command shown in listing 21.23.

Listing 21.23 Starting the Docker container

```
docker run -p 4002:4002 reactapp
```

You can test the application by opening http://localhost:4002 in the browser, which will display the response provided by the web server running in the container, as shown in figure 21.5.

Figure 21.5 Running the containerized application

To stop the container, run the command shown in listing 21.24.

Listing 21.24 Listing the containers

```
docker ps
```

You will see a list of running containers, like this (I have omitted some fields for brevity):

```
CONTAINER ID        IMAGE              COMMAND             CREATED
82352eba95a2        reactapp           "docker-entry"      51 seconds ago
```

Using the value in the Container ID column, run the command shown in listing 21.25.

Listing 21.25 Stopping the container

```
docker stop 82352eba95a2
```

The React application is ready to deploy to any platform that supports Docker.

Summary

In this chapter, I completed the React application by adding support for URL routing and by defining the remaining components. As with the other examples in this part of the book, I prepared the application for deployment and created a Docker image that can be readily deployed.

- Routing selects the components that are displayed based on the current URL.
- The routing package provides components that define routes and hooks that are used to access route data and perform navigation.
- Like any other TypeScript application, React projects are compiled into pure JavaScript and can be deployed using standard tools and containers.

And that is all I have to teach you about TypeScript. I started by creating a simple application and then took you on a comprehensive tour of the different features that TypeScript provides and how they are applied to the JavaScript type system. I wish you every success in your TypeScript projects, and I can only hope that you have enjoyed reading this book as much as I enjoyed writing it.

index